Lawmaking in Dutch Sri Lanka

LAWMAKING IN DUTCH SRI LANKA

Navigating Pluralities in a Colonial Society

Nadeera Rupesinghe

Leiden University Press

Cover design: Geert de Koning
Cover illustration: *Boom op Ceylon*, Jan Brandes, 1785–1786 (inv.no. NG-1985-7-2-16), Rijksmuseum, Amsterdam
Maps: Suranjan Fernando
Layout: Crius Group

ISBN 978 90 8728 375 9
e-ISBN 978 94 0060 424 7
https://doi.org/10.24415/9789087283759
NUR 680

This book is distributed in North America by the University of Chicago Press (www.press.uchicago.edu).

Printed and bound by CPI Group (UK) Ltd, Croydon, CR0 4YY

To H, who is testament that true love begins in the archives.

Contents

List of Maps, Figures and Tables

Acknowledgements

I started on this project in the autumn of 2010 in Leiden with a broad proposal including all of the voluminous Dutch legal records in the National Archives in Colombo, but I knew I would seek out a way to focus on disputes involving peasants or *hoi polloi.* Reading the testimony of eighteenth-century southern men and women, I developed an enduring interest in the law that led to my doctoral thesis, the basis for this book. I am immensely grateful for the sponsorship from the Dutch Scientific Organisation (NWO), first as a student and later as a teaching and research assistant at the Institute for History, Leiden University that enabled me to study in Leiden for six lovely years from 2007 to 2013.

Chapters three, four and five of the present work have previously appeared in a different version as the following: "Facing the Law in Eighteenth-century Galle," in *Uses of Justice and Legal Pluralism: A Global Perspective 1600–1900,* edited by Manon van den Heijden, Griet Vermeesch & Jaco Zuijderduin (Oxon: Routledge, 2019); "Defining Land Rights in Dutch Sri Lanka," *Portuguese Journal of Social Science* 16, no. 2, 2017; and "Do You Know the Ninth Commandment? Tensions of the Oath in Dutch Colonial Sri Lanka," *Comparative Legal History* 7, (2019). Furthermore, a part of chapter six appeared in 'Navigating Pluralities Reluctantly: The Marriage Contract in Dutch Galle,' *Itinerario* 42, no. 2, (2018). I thank the publishers for their permission to reuse these materials. This present work has been revised with assistance from the NWO funded postdoctoral fellowship I received through the Colonialism Inside Out: Everyday Experience and Plural Practice in Dutch Institutions in Sri Lanka (c. 1700–1800) research project at Leiden University.

This book has greatly benefitted from comments by Alicia Schrikker, Nira Wickramasinghe, Lodewijk Wagenaar, Albert van den Belt, Sujit Sivasundaram, Egbert Koops, Jos Gommans and the many anonymous reviewers of parts of this work that appeared as articles and the book as a whole. I thank Lodewijk for his assistance in translating numerous pages of Dutch sources and many conversations about this project, and Albert for his patient help and encouragement when I was pouring over legal archives in Colombo for the first time. Thank you for promising me that there will always be a system in the format of those documents that were initially overwhelming. I discovered, through perseverance, that the tiny remarks in the margin (*marginale opmerking*) transcribed with difficulty could contain little gems of stories about individuals. I embraced interdisciplinarity, in the belief that the complex web of norms that govern us can only be fully described through it.

There are many people whom I must thank for my life in The Netherlands, in particular Carla Risseeuw for hosting me so graciously in her home and for her erudite company. I also thank Carla's friend Marlein van Raalte for so generously adopting Carla's friend and being a pillar of support.

Back in Sri Lanka, my colleagues at the Open University of Sri Lanka were lovely to work with in the course of this journey from thesis to book, when I sojourned in their Faculty of Engineering to teach history courses on science and technology. To the staff at the Sri Lanka National Archives to whom I fear I became a necessary evil at a whole new level as Director General National Archives, I extend my grateful appreciation.

Finally, I thank my family. Most of all, I thank Harsha for appearing in the archives in Colombo when I haunted the place during the course of this study. Without his love, patience and unstinting support, this book, like the thesis before it, would have still been in process.

Notes on Usage

For ease of comprehension, proper names have been changed to their current spelling in Dutch and Sinhala where possible, but where there is doubt follow the eighteenth-century spelling in the original documents. Wherever possible, I have translated names from their Latinised forms such as Joan, Joanna and Joannes used in the sources to Johan, Johanna and Johannes. Place names are standardised to the current anglicised form.

For the text, Sri Lanka was preferred over Ceylon as that is the name by which the country is known today. I have also used the terms "Sinhalese" to refer to the people and "Sinhala" for the language. I use a modern Sinhala orthography except when quoting a source in which diacritical marks had not been used. Sinhala, Tamil and Dutch terms are italicised the first time they are used, where they are explained in the text or footnote or in the glossary that follows this note. Subsequent use is not italicised. For the plurals of non-English words, I mostly use the plural forms in those languages. Galle refers to the district, Galle town refers to the fort. Land register, land registration, cadastre, cadastral registration all refer to the thombo registration. Council in this text refers to the Landraad, a term more appropriate than the word "court" with its modern-day sense. Other councils will be referred to more specifically and are capitalised, such as the Governor in Council in Colombo, and the Political Council in Galle. I have also used the words councillor or member instead of judge of the Landraad. Dutch and VOC were used interchangeably, though of course the VOC consisted of more than one European group identity. I have not used the uppercase for caste and occupational identities, and official titles are not capitalised except when they are used with the name of the individual.

Abbreviations used in the book are SLNA (Sri Lanka National Archives), PLH (Principal Land Holder) and LHG (Land Holdings Group). Sources from the Department of National Archives in Sri Lanka are given as, for example, SLNA 1/2933 (which means lot 1 followed by the volume number), with a description of the volume, the folio number, a short title and date of the cited document. The dates of the reigns of kings follow K. M. de Silva's *A History of Sri Lanka.*

Translations from seventeenth- and eighteenth-century Dutch for this research are the author's own, with much-valued assistance from Lodewijk Wagenaar and Albert van den Belt. Naturally, the responsibility for errors remains mine.

Glossary

accommodessan	Maintenance grants.
ambalama	A resting place located by the road for the convenience of travellers.
*amuna (*pl. *amunu)*	A measurement of sowing capacity in paddy equalling 40 *kuruni* which is approximately two acres (this may vary from region to region). An *amuna* of areca nuts ranged from 24,000 to 26,000 nuts.
appuhamy (pl. *appuhamu*)	An honorific usually for an elite member of the *goygama* caste.
ārachchi	A minor village official.
atapattu	Guard of higher functionaries.
atapattu mudaliyār	*Mudaliyār* of the *dessave.*
bellale	Dutch for *vellālar*, also used to mean *goygama.*
binna	Marriage with uxorilocal residence.
bode	Messenger.
burger	Private citizens, or retired servants of the company.
burgerij	Community of urban citizens who formed a militia.
chando	Dutch for *durāva,* a caste group.
Chettiar	A merchant community of south Indian origin.
Civiele Raad	Civil Council.
contra-interrogatorieën	(List of) counter-questions used in a judicial forum.
diviya (pl. *divi*)	Trial by oath.
divi-dōsa	Evils of false oaths.
dessave	European governor of a district in Dutch-controlled territory.
dēvāla	Temple complex with shrines for deities.
dictum	Written request.

dīga	Marriage with virilocal residence.
disāva	Governor or minister at court in Kandy.
dessavony	A Sinhalese term for a province used by the VOC.
durāva	Dutch: *chando*; a caste associated with toddy-tapping.
Gamsabhāva	Village council.
gerechtigheid	That over which one exercises a right (tax).
guilder	Dutch currency equal to 20 stivers.
goygama	Highest caste in the traditional hierarchy among the Sinhalese, numerically the largest and associated with farming.
hakuru	An agricultural caste also associated with the production of jaggery.
hunu	Caste of lime burners.
Inlandse Boedelkamer	A board that managed the estate of deceased natives.
kangān	Overseer.
kaneelschiller	Cinnamon-peeler.
karāva	A caste primarily associated with fishing. Tamil: *karaiyar.*
kōrāla	Head of a *kōralē.*
kōralē	Subdivision of a commandment or a *dessavony.*
Landraad (*pl.* Landraden)	Land, country, or district council.
lascarin	Indigenous soldier who also served as guard and messenger.
Mahabadde	Cinnamon Department.
mahamudaliyār	An indigenous chief of the highest level; also referred to as gate *mudaliyār.*
Mahanaduva	Great Court of the Kandyan kingdom.
mahavidāne	Headman of an organised caste or trade, a rank above an *ārachchi* and below a *mohandiram.*
marallas	Death duties; also annual travelling assizes of Portuguese and local officials under Portuguese rule.
marelleiros	Portuguese legal officers who were assigned regions over which they held *marallas.*
mayorāl	A *gamarāla* (village head) who traditionally organised the compulsory service of *rājakāriya* due from the villagers. He reported to the Landraad on land matters and provided victuals for visiting VOC commissioners and headmen.

mohandiram	An indigenous chief below the rank of *mudaliyār.*
Moor	Muhammadans of south India and Sri Lanka.
mudaliyār	Highest rank of an indigenous chief in the low country.
muttettu	Land granted by the monarch which the grantee cultivated with the unpaid labour of other cultivators.
nanayakkāraya, (pl: nanayakkārayo)	Permanent native commissioners who inspected gardens and fields.
nainde	Husbandman who performed menial tasks as service.
ola	Palm leaf, used to write on.
onderkoopman	Junior merchant, the lowest "qualified" rank within the VOC.
ondertrouwd	Someone who has given notice of marriage.
onecht	Illegitimate.
opziender/opziener	Overseer (e.g. of a district; equivalent to *dessave* in Galle), also called superintendent.
otu	A tax of one-tenth of the produce.
padu	An agricultural caste.
paravar	A seafaring caste of south India that settled in coastal Sri Lanka.
paravēni	Ancestral land.
parra	A measure of grain equal to 40 Dutch pounds, thus 19.76 kilograms (1 pound being equal to 494 grams).
pattangatijn	A headman of the fishermen, similar to a *mohandiram.*
pattuwa	An administrative division within a *kōralē.*
pela	A quarter of an *amuna.*
plakkaat (pl. *plakkaten*)	Proclamation with legal force issued by the Dutch Government.
pottebakker	Potter.
procureur	Process representative/counsel/procurator.
Raad van Justitie	Council of Justice.
radā	Caste group traditionally associated with washing.
rājakāriya	Obligatory service.
Ratasabhāva	District-level tribunal in Kandyan kingdom.
ratmahara	Wasteland.
recollement	Confirmation (judicial).

rixdollar (rd)	About 48 stivers. Dutch: *rijksdaalder.*
rondvraag	Circulation of documents in the margin of which members of a council or college were asked to note their opinion, for the chairman to reach a decision.
sabandar	A native revenue official of a district.
Sākki Balanda	A coroner's court in the Kandyan kingdom.
salāgama	A caste traditionally associated with cinnamon peeling. Referred to as *sjalia* by the Dutch.
Scholarchale Vergadering	School Board.
schrijver	Writer.
sittuva (pl. *sittu*)	Written judicial decree.
soldijboekhouder	Bookkeeper of the personnel department.
stiver	A former Dutch coin; twenty stivers equaled a guilder.
tamblinjero	Drummer/tom-tom beater.
thombo	Land register of Dutch maritime Sri Lanka.
thombohouder	Thombo-keeper, the officer who maintained the thombo.
timmerman	Carpenter.
tolk	Interpreter
tombo	Land register of Portuguese maritime Sri Lanka.
uliyam	Unpaid public work by Muslims and Chettiars.
vaandrig	An ensign.
vāsagama	Lineage or ancestral name.
vellālar	Highest caste among Tamils. See also *bellale.*
vidāne	A minor indigenous chief with policing duties, also the administrative area under his jurisdiction.
vidānārachchi	A revenue collector in charge of one or more villages.
visser	Literally, fisherman, but also a coastal social group known as *karāva.*
vrijburger/vrijman	A European or Eurasian citizen no longer in company service.
wasser	Washerman; Dutch for the *radā* caste.
wibadde	A village-level official responsible for collecting paddy revenue from cultivators.

Maps

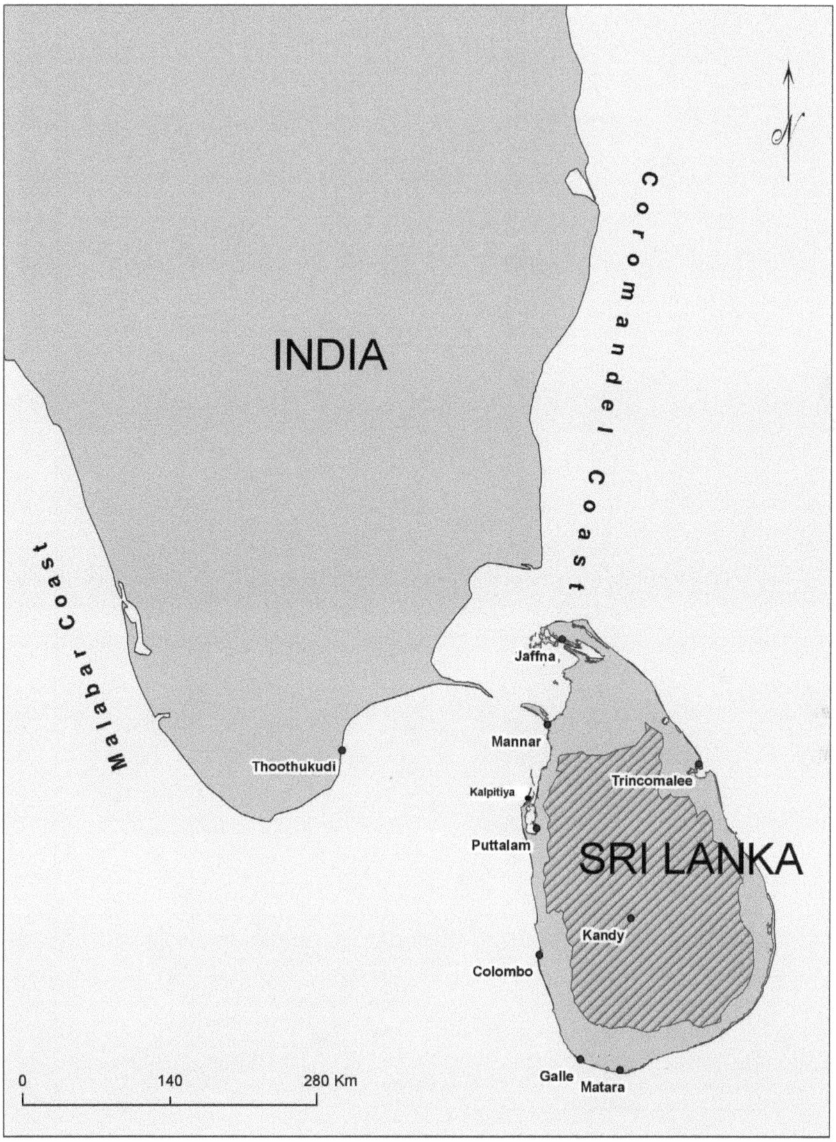

Map 1 India and Sri Lanka with the Kandyan kingdom in the middle and coastal Dutch territory in the late eighteenth century.

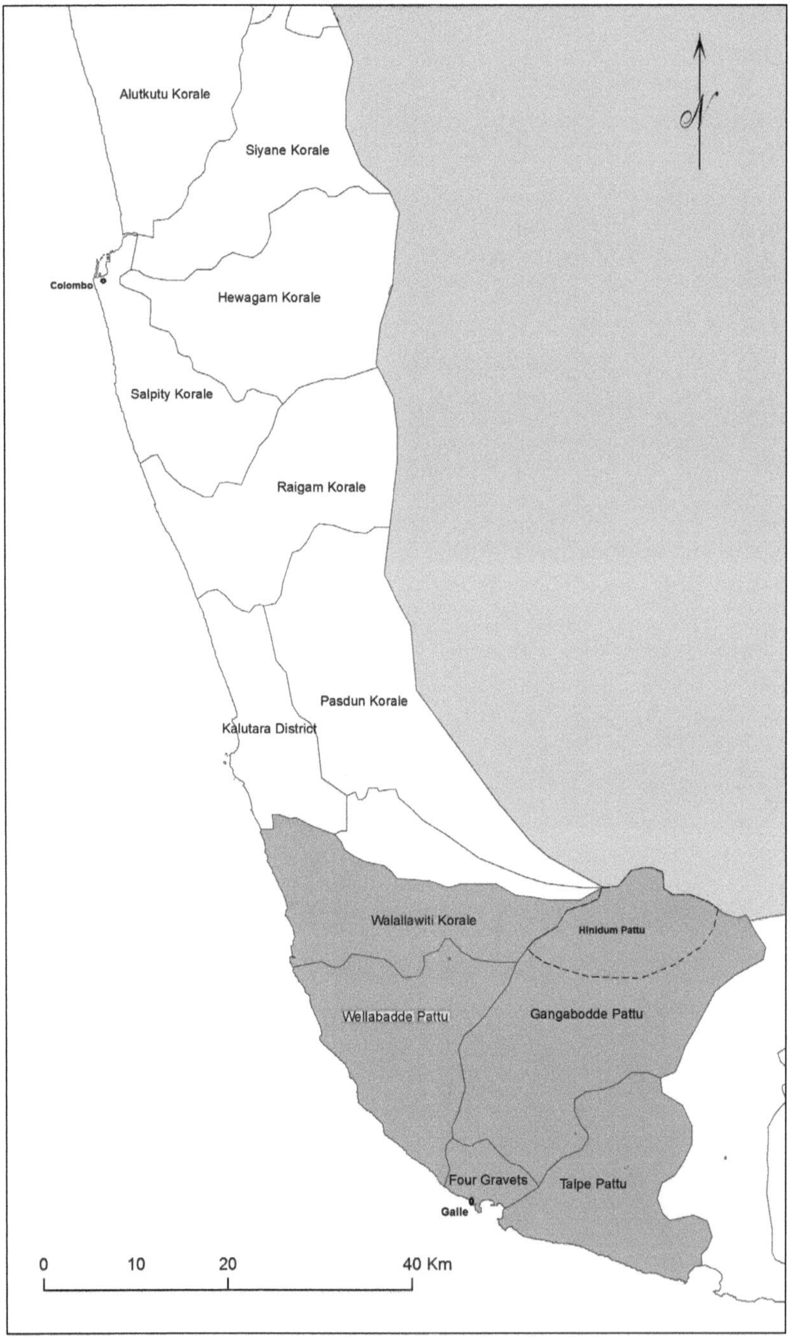

Map 2 Galle district under Dutch rule shown in dark grey. The Hinidum Pattuwa border is tentative.

INTRODUCTION

Conjecture and Deliberation

Abstract
In the popular imagination in Sri Lanka, Roman-Dutch law is given an almost hallowed status. Yet, the history of that law, first introduced by the Dutch East India Company, has followed an inconsistent path over the last two centuries. Despite an abundance of Dutch legal records, little is known of the use of Roman-Dutch law under Dutch rule. Did the Dutch apply the laws of the Sinhalese? The judicial forum of the Landraad set up by them had a majority of European officials and a subordinate minority of local headmen. Through an empirical approach and understandings of socio-legal studies of legal pluralism, this study of the Landraad provides insights into the lived experience of colonial law.

Keywords: Legal pluralism, pluralities, colonial law, colonialism, Sinhalese law, Roman-Dutch law.

In 1904, the case *Karonchihami v Angohami* raised the question of whether the Dutch power in Sri Lanka had enacted a regulation prohibiting couples engaged in adultery from marrying later. Through this case, numerous Sri Lankan law students learn that in the district-level courts in operation under Dutch rule, local officials tried disputes arising among the inhabitants.[1] The case concluded that local headmen could not be expected to have applied the principles of Roman-Dutch law. If not for *Karonchihami v Angohami*, it is likely that today we would know even less about the *Landraad* (variously translated as land, country, or district council; plural: *Landraden*). Judge A.J. De Sampayo, however, had not studied the Landraad and was misled into overestimating the influence of the local officials. The question of whose law the Dutch used was approached as an either/or dichotomy, far from the evidential reality of pluralities in practice that this monograph reveals. Yet, the 1904 reference is important, as it shows that a British court later recognised that indigenous laws were in use as far back as the eighteenth century. Negotiating with a pre-existing legal order was therefore seen as necessary.

In its administration of parts of Sri Lanka in the seventeenth and eighteenth centuries, the Verenigde Oost-Indische Compagnie (Dutch East India Company or

[1] *Karonchihami v Angohami*, 8 New Law Reports 1 (1904).

VOC) reluctantly acknowledged the necessity of being involved in judicial matters and variously adapted to the existing order and changing circumstances. Empires realised early on that "one law for all" would inevitably fail in practice. The lasting legacy of Dutch legal practices remains etched in Sri Lankan society.

In this book, I study people as objects, negotiators and consumers of the judicial system introduced by the Dutch through their everyday interactions with the Landraad of Galle. Whose law was used in the Landraad? In the practice of litigation under the VOC in eighteenth-century coastal Sri Lanka, local litigants, and the elite who served as their representatives, underlined distinctive characteristics of the local normative order that were unfamiliar to the Dutch. This book moves beyond the conventional top-down approach to legal history, which focuses primarily on legislation, official correspondence and governmental proceedings. By studying judicial proceedings, I analyse how ordinary people experienced colonial rule in practice through the language of the law. How did the Landraad function in its day-to-day operations? Who controlled it and who appeared before it? Did the Landraad draw on the dominant local normative order of southern Sri Lanka? Drawing on studies of legal pluralism, I have placed Sri Lanka's early colonial legal history in the growing body of work in this theoretical field.

Much of the work on eighteenth-century Sri Lanka has been on political, administrative and structural social change.[2] An emphasis on the nineteenth century in Sri Lanka's historiography of colonialism has often led to a neglect of the eighteenth century, rectified in recent times to some extent by Nirmal Dewasiri through his work on land tenure and caste relations; Alicia Schrikker on colonial policy-making and ideologies; and Sujit Sivasundaram on colonial knowledge production. All three scholars emphasise continuity from the eighteenth to the nineteenth

[2] For recent and older scholarship on Portuguese and Dutch rule on the island, see Zoltán Biedermann, *The Portuguese in Sri Lanka and South India: Studies in the History of Diplomacy, Empire and Trade, 1500–1650* (Wiesbaden: Harrassowitz Verlag, 2014); Alan Strathern, *Kingship and Conversion in Sixteenth-Century Sri Lanka: Portuguese Imperialism in a Buddhist Land* (New Delhi & Colombo: Cambridge University Press & Vijitha Yapa, 2010); Alicia Schrikker, *Dutch and British Colonial Intervention in Sri Lanka, 1780–1815: Expansion and Reform* (Leiden: Brill, 2007); Nirmal Ranjith Dewasiri, *The Adaptable Peasant: Agrarian Society in Western Sri Lanka under Dutch Rule, 1740–1800* (Leiden: Brill, 2008); Jorge Flores (ed), *Re-exploring the Links: History and Constructed Histories Between Portugal and Sri Lanka* (Wiesbaden: Harrassowitz Verlag, 2007); Chandra Richard de Silva, *The Portuguese in Ceylon 1617–1638* (Colombo: H.W. Cave, 1972); Kanapathipillai, Valli, "Dutch Rule in Maritime Ceylon 1766–1796" (PhD dissertation, University of London, 1969); Tikiri Abeyasinghe, *Portuguese Rule in Ceylon, 1594–1612* (Colombo: Lake House, 1966); Sinnappah Arasaratnam, *Dutch Power in Ceylon, 1658–1687* (Amsterdam: Djambatan, 1958); K.W. Goonewardena, *The Foundation of Dutch Power in Ceylon, 1638–1658* (Amsterdam: Djambatan, 1958). For an overview, see K.M. de Silva (ed), *University of Peradeniya, History of Sri Lanka (From c. 1500 to c. 1800)*, Vol. 2 (Peradeniya: University of Peradeniya, 1995).

century.[3] Among them, Dewasiri draws a picture of structural transformations in peasant life. However, Sri Lanka's rich legal history, which includes a mix of Dutch, English and customary normative systems, has received scant scholarly attention. The existing legal literature suffers from a lack of empirical research and inattention to the developing field of socio-legal studies of legal pluralism. Research into the unique legal sources of eighteenth-century Sri Lanka can enrich not only our understanding of the complex ways in which legal orders intersected, but can also provide reflection on how such studies further illustrate theories of European colonialism and its interaction with non-Western practices and ideas.

Sri Lanka's indigenous lowland polities since 1500 can be interpreted as being "unprotected" due to European territorial expansion.[4] Its prize possession, in European eyes, was cinnamon, which was shipped to Europe for international trading. In the sixteenth and seventeenth centuries, the Portuguese captured and consolidated power in parts of western Sri Lanka and the northern kingdom of Jaffna. Infighting within the ruling family weakened the western lowland kingdom of Kotte; this led to its division in the early sixteenth century. Of the indigenous powers, the Kandyan kingdom in the mountainous interior survived into Dutch times.[5] Relations between the Portuguese and the internal kingdom of Kandy were strained by repeated wars, and Rājasingha II of Kandy entered into an agreement with the VOC in 1638 to drive out the Portuguese and hand over the captured territory to Kandy. Events did not develop in that way: the Dutch drove the Portuguese out but also intended to stay.

I focus on the workings of the early colonial state at the district level of Galle in southern Sri Lanka, at a time when European rule seeped into the rhythms of everyday life. Although Galle was the VOC's first administrative base after they captured it from the Portuguese in 1640, it appears less culturally touched than Colombo, and thus is a more fitting site for the study of negotiations between local and external normative orders. The district is situated in the wet zone of the country; the lush terrain becomes hilly just a few miles from the coast. The monotonous, ritual nature of peasant life based on agriculture would have been more patent

[3] Dewasiri, *Adaptable Peasant*; Schrikker, *Dutch and British Colonial Intervention*; Sujit Sivasundaram, *Islanded: Britain, Sri Lanka, and the Bounds of an Indian Ocean Colony* (Chicago: University of Chicago Press, 2013).

[4] For an experiment in connecting Sri Lanka to Victor Lieberman's theory of "protected rimlands" of South East Asia, which he said shared "the same historical path from a milieu of warring little kingdoms to increasingly large, solid states," see Alan Strathern, "Sri Lanka in the Long Early Modern Period: Its Place in a Comparative Theory of Second Millennium Eurasian History," *Modern Asian Studies* 43, no. 4 (2009): 815–869.

[5] Despite its geographical isolation, Kandy was a cosmopolitan kingdom at least at the elite level, as Sujit Sivasundaram argues in *Islanded*, 41.

in eighteenth-century Galle.[6] Although Galle is not a natural harbour, it has long been used as one. The VOC administered its expanding territory on the island for sixteen years (1640–1656) from Galle, which remained the most important port for the company.[7] This study focuses on the eighteenth century, from the setting up of the Landraad in 1741 till the end of Dutch rule in 1796, when the maritime provinces came to be administered by the British East India Company. These provinces became a crown colony in 1802, and the rest of the island was annexed by a covenant with the Sinhalese chiefs, the Kandyan king having been deposed in 1815.

Conjecture and Deliberation

In the popular imagination in Sri Lanka, Roman-Dutch law is given an almost hallowed status. Most Sri Lankans with some general legal knowledge would say that the Dutch introduced their laws to Sri Lanka. At a higher educational level, judges of even recent times may be said to have followed its principles more than of other legal systems, and some appear to have been proud of their contributions to its preservation.[8] If Roman-Dutch law was the "state" law or the official law adopted by the colonial power, its dominant image is that of descending on customary, "non-state" laws in a linear way over many decades.

Yet, the history of Roman-Dutch law in Sri Lanka has its ambiguities and has followed an inconsistent path over the last two centuries. Despite robust claims about adopting Roman-Dutch law as state law in British times, jurisdictional confusion and complexity persisted into the twentieth century. The waxing and waning of its adoption in Sri Lanka has been remarked on.[9] Our understanding of its use in Sri Lanka by the Dutch among the majority Sinhalese population of the low country is sketchy at best due to a lack of research. Little is known of the use of Roman-Dutch law in the maritime provinces. But this is not due to a lack of sources. The reference

6 Dewasiri describes some aspects of the everyday life of the peasant in western Sri Lanka in *Adaptable Peasant*, 25–58.

7 See Lodewijk Wagenaar, *Galle, VOC-vestiging in Ceylon: Beschrijving van een koloniale samenleving aan de vooravond van de Singalese opstand tegen het Nederlandse gezag, 1760* (Amsterdam: De Bataafsche Leeuw, 1994), 7; Goonewardena, *Foundation of Dutch Power*, 37. Later, Colombo became the seat of government.

8 In a summary of a Japanese book, written in 1988 on the contemporary status of legal pluralism in Sri Lanka, Masaji Chiba says: "[s]ome high ranking legal agents today speak proudly of their contributions to the preservation of such an old law." "Legal Pluralism in Sri Lankan Society: Toward a General Theory of Non-Western Law," *Journal of Legal Pluralism and Unofficial Law* 25, no. 33 (1993): 204.

9 L.J.M. Cooray, *An Introduction to the Legal System of Sri Lanka* (Pannipitiya: Stamford Lake, 2003; repr. 2009), 94.

to the Landraad in the nineteenth-century case *Karonchihami v Angohami*, which I mentioned at the beginning of this introduction, is brought forward as evidence that the Dutch had applied the laws of the Sinhalese.[10] *Karonchihami v Angohami* shows that the exact extent of the application of customary law by the Dutch posed problems for later British jurists even in the early twentieth century. Incidentally, the judgement stated that there was no proof that the Dutch ordinance of 26 September 1658, which prohibited the marriage of persons who lived in adultery, was applied in Sri Lanka. Evidence on this question from the Dutch archives is still forthcoming.

Thambiah Nadaraja, a legal scholar, opines that the Dutch cases would be especially important in determining how Sinhalese customs were taken into account, if at all. Nadaraja says, "[w]ithout making a close study of what is still legible in the legal records of the Dutch period no conclusions can be reached regarding the order in which the different kinds of authorities would have been considered by a judge engaged in deciding a case."[11] He wrote this in the late 1960s, but such a study of the Dutch legal records has not been undertaken yet. This work is an attempt to fill that lacuna. As Nadaraja himself says, his ambitious history of the legal system of Sri Lanka, covering nearly 300 years in six chapters (often with endnotes that are longer than the chapters), was unable to draw upon preliminary studies that could be the foundation of such a sweeping history.[12] Through this study, I reveal for the first time the breadth of knowledge that can be made available to us through extensive research into the legal documents produced under Dutch rule.

The application, or non-application, of Sinhalese laws or customs in Dutch territory based on discussions surrounding a legal issue requires a full examination of enactments of the administration and judgements of the councils of law. Only a fraction of legal cases under Dutch rule has been studied to date. In her study of the law of compensation for improvements, Marleen van den Horst traces the evolution of that law into present times. She states that in the ninety-four volumes from the full range of Dutch legal records that she studied, she found no reference to the use of local, customary law.[13] She concludes that even a study of the cases, as Nadaraja recommends, would not answer the question of the application of Sinhalese law. The absence of stated reasoning for judgements is a key drawback.

[10] See, for example, Cooray, *Legal System*, 65.

[11] T. Nadaraja, *The Legal System of Ceylon in its Historical Setting* (Leiden: Brill, 1972), 14–16.

[12] Ibid., 1.

[13] Van den Horst says: "Though it is generally admitted that the Dutch respected and applied the local, customary laws, not a single reference to such laws could be discovered." However, in one of two volumes of the Galle Landraad that she had examined, she did find a reference to "general custom" in a decision. Marleen H.J. van den Horst, *Compensation for Improvements: The Roman Dutch Law in Sri Lanka* (Amsterdam: Free University Press, 1989), 121–22.

Van den Horst did not, however, study the Landraad extensively, and a more comprehensive study through case analyses makes it possible to provide insights into the design and operation of colonial law in eighteenth-century Sri Lanka.

Nineteenth- and twentieth-century chief justices and other judges have speculated on how far Dutch laws were used in the coastal areas of the island under the administration of the VOC. While many cases under British rule refer to Roman-Dutch law as the "common law" of the country, only a few judgements discuss its applicability.[14] Controversy arose because the British attempted to employ Roman-Dutch law for the low-country Sinhalese, in the belief that they were continuing the Dutch practice. Scholars present differing views on the question. Some even argue that Roman-Dutch law had always been subordinate to Sinhalese law along the coast.[15] The preamble to a report by Godfried Leonhard De Coste, a high-ranking official in late Dutch times, mentions that ancient Sinhalese laws and customs have been "completely obliterated" but "a few of them are still to be traced in their original form for information relative to the local laws and customs of the western and southern maritime provinces of Ceylon."[16] Gananath Obeyesekere argues that Roman-Dutch law probably applied only to Dutch residents of Sri Lanka and converted Sinhalese Protestants, while traditional laws governed the remaining majority.[17] R.W. Lee writes: "it has been doubted whether the Dutch ever applied their law to the native races of the low country."[18] Others contend that Sinhalese law had almost disappeared from the maritime provinces and was replaced by Roman-Dutch law.[19] Although Nadaraja pointed out that Dutch legal cases had to

[14] See *Karonchihami v Angohami*, 2 New Law Reports 276 (1896); *Karonchihami v Angohami*, 8 New Law Reports; *Daniel Silva v Johanis Appuhamy*, 67 New Law Reports 457 (1965).

[15] Among these are Adrian St. Valentine Jayewardene, *The Roman Dutch Law: As it Prevails in Ceylon, How Much of it is Applicable, and in What Localities?* (Colombo: Ceylon Examine Press, 1901); F.A. Hayley, *A Treatise on the Laws and Customs of the Sinhalese* (New Delhi: Navrang, 1923; repr. 1993), 20–27.

[16] CO 54/124, "Ceylon Native Laws and Customs, Part 2 Presented by Sir Alexander Johnston" (1770), 1, Schedule 8, National Archives, Kew. It is not clear who authored this preamble.

[17] Gananath Obeyesekere, *Land Tenure in Village Ceylon: A Sociological and Historical Study* (Cambridge: Cambridge University Press, 1967), 130.

[18] Robert Warden Lee, *An Introduction to Roman-Dutch Law*, fourth edition (Oxford: Clarendon Press, 1946), 11.

[19] See Ivor Jennings and H.W. Tambiah, *The Dominion of Ceylon: The Development of its Laws and Constitution* (London: Stevens, 1952), 195–96; A. Wood Renton, "The Roman-Dutch Law in Ceylon under the British Regime," *South African Law Journal* 49 (1932): 164. A.R.B. Amerasinghe says that the Sinhalese customs are likely to have disappeared, but also asks whether the Dutch would have risked sowing the seeds of discord by ignoring Sinhalese law. See A.R.B. Amerasinghe, "The Dutch Influence on the Legal System of Sri Lanka," in Saman Kelegama and Roshan Madawela (eds) *400 Years of Dutch-Sri Lanka Relations 1602–2002* (Colombo: Institute of Policy Studies of Sri Lanka, 2002), 293–94.

be studied, he believed that the "adulteration of the Sinhalese customary law may have been the reason for the Dutch authorities not having undertaken its codification, and the very absence of a code probably contributed further to the disuse of that law."[20] The question has thus not been satisfactorily answered.

By unravelling evidence of the use of various laws by the company, I propose that the answer to the question does not lie in a dichotomous either/or proposition. Rather, I argue for a broader understanding that focuses on jurisdictional pluralities that existed in practice. Such pluralities governed the day-to-day experiences of the early colonial subject. The conceptual framework for such a meticulous reconsideration, as I attempt here, is provided by the developing literature on legal pluralism, which connects with studies of colonialism in Dutch Sri Lanka. In that way, this research reveals the distinctiveness of this premodern period.

Conceptualising Colonial Lawmaking

This book argues for the study of everyday legal processes to unravel the complex workings of pluralities. Legal pluralism is the existence of two or more legal systems in varying degrees of synchronism.[21] Expanding the concept to include a pluralism of normative spheres, the Max Planck Institute for European Legal History extensively studied the use of the term "multinormativity."[22] My book is situated within the framework of institutional structures. This poses a methodological problem for legal pluralists who are being asked, as Lauren Benton and Richard Ross argue, "to uncover elusive subjective beliefs about the applicability and ordering of bodies of law." Yet we can only hope to investigate, in that way, the jurisdictional politics of colonial authorities. Benton and Ross advocate studying exactly where conflicts occur in this process and revealing jurisdictional divides, "rather than elusive and often inconsistently applied rules or norms." They call this a "methodological advantage" for historical research "because it becomes

[20] Nadaraja, *The Legal System of Ceylon*, 16.

[21] Classic studies on legal pluralism are John Griffiths, "What is Legal Pluralism?" *Journal of Legal Pluralism and Unofficial Law* 18, no. 24 (1986): 1–55; Sally Engle Merry, "Legal Pluralism," *Law and Society Review* 22, no. 5 (1988), 869–896; Brian Z. Tamanaha, "Understanding Legal Pluralism: Past to Present, Local to Global," *Sydney Law Review* 30 (2008): 375; Brian Z. Tamanaha, "The Folly of the Social Scientific Concept of Legal Pluralism," *Journal of Law and Society* 20, no. 2 (1993): 192–217.

[22] Thomas Duve, "Global Legal History: A Methodological Approach," Social Science Research Network (SSRN Scholarly Paper ID 2781104), 2016, http://papers.ssrn.com/abstract=2781104. Accessed 28 August 2016.

possible to analyse structural shifts propelled by the legal strategies of parties to jurisdictional conflicts."[23]

However, by focusing mostly on the mundane, everyday workings of the Landraad, this study aims to present the lived experience of colonial law in eighteenth-century Galle. It connects with Martha-Marie Kleinhans's and Roderick Macdonald's "critical legal pluralism," which focuses on individual agency in the use and interpretation of the law. This assigns more responsibility to individuals in creating their own legal subjectivity. It also takes the focus away from reifying law and essentialising cultures and communities.[24]

The VOC is believed to have applied at least some customary laws in the legal administration of its territory. Anthony Paviljoen, the Commander of Jaffna, said in 1665: "Justice is administered to the Dutch according to the laws in force in the Fatherland and the Statutes of Batavia. The natives are governed according to the customs of the country if these are clear and reasonable, otherwise according to our laws."[25] This may be true for the Jaffna that he wrote about, where a code of native laws applied. Over the course of the eighteenth century, some native laws were codified, such as the customs of the Tamils of Jaffna, the Muslims and Mukkuvars of Puttalam, and laws based on the Statutes of Batavia for other Muslims. This institutionalisation of customs gives the impression of the existence of a plural legal structure under a European power. A code was understood as a unified statement of law that could be consulted on its own.[26] The codification of customs of particular groups tends to reinforce their cultural differences. Indeed, this happened not only in Sri Lanka but was characteristic of the colonial world: "the colonial codes remain on the books on the subcontinent today."[27]

[23] Lauren Benton and Richard J. Ross, "Empires and Legal Pluralism: Jurisdiction, Sovereignty, and Political Imagination in the Early Modern World," in Lauren Benton and Richard J. Ross (eds), *Legal Pluralism and Empires, 1500–1850*, Kindle edition (New York: NYU Press 2013), 5–6. See also Lauren Benton, *Law and Colonial Cultures: Legal Regimes in World History, 1400–1900* (Cambridge: Cambridge University Press, 2001).

[24] Martha-Marie Kleinhans and Roderick A. Macdonald, "What is a Critical Legal Pluralism?" *Canadian Journal of Law and Society* 12, no. 2 (1997): 25–46.

[25] Sophia Pieters (trans), "Memoir by Anthony Paviljoen to His Successor, 1665," in *Instructions from the Governor-General and Council of India* (Colombo: H.C. Cottle, Govt. Printer, 1908), 117.

[26] James Gordley, "Comparative Law and Legal History," in Reinhard Zimmermann and Mathias Reimann (eds), *The Oxford Handbook of Comparative Law* (Oxford: Oxford University Press, 2006), 760. For the Dutch Sri Lankan context, see Alicia Schrikker, "Conflict Resolution, Social Control and Law-Making in Eighteenth Century Dutch Sri Lanka," in Catia Antunes and Jos Gommans (eds), *Exploring the Dutch Empire: Agents Networks and Institutions, 1600-2000* (London: Bloomsbury, 2015), 227–44.

[27] Elizabeth Kolsky, "A Note on the Study of Indian Legal History," *Law and History Review* 23, no. 3 (2005): 704.

In this work, I consider the Dutch and the dominant group in the south, the Sinhalese, without pitting them against the Tamils, Moors, Chettiars or other smaller groups, a perspective that falls beyond the scope of this study. This is not to assume that monolithic communities or cultures of "Dutch," "Sinhalese," "Tamil," etc. existed then; neither do they exist today. Their laws are similarly heterogeneous. This book does not attempt to achieve the impossible task of representing the entire experience of Dutch colonial law on the island; neither does it represent all Sinhalese areas, as it centres on Galle. But this focus on regional phenomena can still inform our understanding of inter-legality, or the recognition of two or more legal orders, in the eighteenth-century south. "Custom" in this context consists of the shared social rules of a "customary normative system," within which the term "indigenous law" was a label constructed for specific purposes under circumstances of colonisation.[28] In the words of Brian Tamanaha, "[o]nce created, these labels have been carried over and continue to the present in some form of coexistence with (or within) official legal systems."[29] The laws of the Kandyans, Jaffna Tamils and Muslims are now official customary law within Sri Lanka's state law.

The vastly developing literature on legal pluralism provides a framework for this inquiry. Paul Halliday describes it as "a device scholars use to impose interpretive order on otherwise chaotic worlds of both present and past."[30] The difficulty of defining law pervades the study of legal pluralism. Much has been written on that question alone. However, as Tamanaha writes after summarising the arguments on what can be regarded as law, "it is not necessary to construct a social scientific conception of law in order to frame and study legal pluralism." He shows that it is possible to analyse situations of legal pluralism without defining law. One way of avoiding conceptual problems is to accept "as 'legal' whatever was identified as legal by the social actors."[31] The seeming informality of local family laws can, for instance, be misleading. But the informality of a legal order is not in itself a disqualification from being a part of an institutionalised normative order. Sally Engle Merry also supported moving away from defining law.[32]

More recently, Benton and Ross have described legal pluralism as "encompassing all sources of law or rules of conduct in a given territory or social context." A "normative" legal pluralism could include "customs, habits, religious precepts and codes of etiquette." Such a non-essentialist view would help us better understand

[28] Tamanaha, "Understanding Legal Pluralism," 375.

[29] Ibid., 397.

[30] Paul Halliday, "Laws' Histories: Pluralisms, Pluralities, Diversity," in Lauren Benton and Richard J. Ross (eds), *Legal Pluralism and Empires, 1500-1850*, Kindle edition (New York: NYU Press, 2013), 262.

[31] Tamanaha, "Understanding Legal Pluralism," 396.

[32] Merry, "Legal Pluralism," 889.

the ways in which officials and colonial subjects dealt with the demands of everyday life. To this day, discussions on the legal history of Sri Lanka have drawn a veil over the flexibility of the various social formations and exaggerated the insularity of customary laws, especially in relation to the Sinhalese. As Benton and Ross say, opening up "a limitless horizon for the study of legal pluralism" by including "all ordered social behaviour" under its rubric is less dangerous than "the representation of imperial orders as comprising sets of neatly stacked and bounded legal spheres." The Sinhalese laws, where they were recognised in varying degrees by the Dutch, effectively became official law and thus retained their validity.[33]

Without using the term "legal pluralism," colonial officials studied it in early modern times as well.[34] Yet, we can observe this process only to a limited extent, because what remains with us today is what was recorded in code, proclamation, or, as I have studied in this work, judicial records. I omit the story of structural shifts and instead focus on restrained conflicts and perceptible continuities. I attempt "locally specific understandings of law and legal complexity as presented and debated by historical actors, including state agents"[35] to show subtle changes or divides in everyday judicial operations. Thus, my focus is on jurisdictional practices.

The presence of the individual peasant is felt throughout this story in both implicit and explicit ways. The jurisdictional conflicts are evident from their understated responses to the land registrar about tenurial rights that are duly recorded despite being in opposition to company predilections, in the recognition of Sinhalese practices of marriage, and in the adoption of local practices of the oath and Dutch laws of inheritance. In all this, we can see the constant thread of "elusive and often inconsistently applied rules or norms."[36] The conflicts in the story of Dutch legal intervention in Sri Lanka, as I present them here, may not always be obvious, but their complexity deepens our understanding of the everyday workings of jurisdictional politics. The strategies of the indigenous, who were seemingly subordinate to the coloniser, contributed to changes in jurisdictional practices and either maintained continuity with the past or upheld Dutch practices.

Research on legal practice in eighteenth-century Sri Lanka not only enriches our understanding of the complex ways in which legal orders intersected, but also reflects on how such studies further illustrate theories of European colonialism

[33] The quotations in this paragraph are from Lauren Benton and Richard J. Ross, "Empires and Legal Pluralism: Jurisdiction, Sovereignty, and Political Imagination in the Early Modern World," in Lauren Benton and Richard J. Ross (eds), *Legal Pluralism and Empires, 1500–1850*, Kindle edition (New York: NYU Press, 2013), 4.

[34] Ibid., 1.

[35] Ibid., 5.

[36] Ibid., 6.

and its interaction with non-Western normative structures. Some scholars of south India, a region close to Sri Lanka geographically and otherwise, argue for continuity with the past; others argue for transformation. David Ludden's work emphasises gradual rather than revolutionary change, with a primary role given to peasants, while Pamela Price's work on Indian kingship in Ramanad speaks to continuity rather than change. Nicholas B. Dirks and Arjun Appadurai, however, highlight a more radical change in south India under British rule.[37] My focus on indigenous engagement with colonial institutions provides, for the first time, a framework of legal studies that can enable a more detailed comparison with pre-colonial practices. This offers deep insights into the nature of early colonial rule.

In comparison with other imperial regimes, relatively less work has been done on the legal history of the Dutch empire. Almost the only exceptions are the publications on Indonesian law and Cape society. The adoption of *adat*, the customary law in Indonesia has linked the concept of pluralism to the legal structures of the VOC in many territories that it controlled. Without recognising the uniqueness of the Sri Lankan case in Dutch times, Benton, for instance, says that in South Asia, Dutch strategies "recognised VOC legal authority over mainly VOC employees, while local rulers continued to preside over their own legal forums."[38] The VOC was predominant in the forts (Colombo, Jaffna, Galle and Matara in Sri Lanka), which were enclaves that mostly housed officials.[39] But local rulers had less authority in Dutch Sri Lanka; the VOC's judicial authority spread beyond city walls into rural society, requiring intervention in the legal administration of territories under company control.

[37] David Ludden, *Peasant History in South India* (New Jersey: Princeton University Press, 1985); Pamela G. Price, *Kingship and Political Practice in Colonial India* (Cambridge: Cambridge University Press, 1996); Nicholas B. Dirks, *Castes of Mind: Colonialism and the Making of Modern India* (Princeton: Princeton University Press, 2001); *The Hollow Crown: Ethnohistory of an Indian Kingdom* (Michigan: University of Michigan Press, 1993); Arjun Appadurai, *Worship and Conflict under Colonial Rule* (Cambridge: Cambridge University Press, 1981). For continuity with a pre-colonial past, see also Susan Bayly, *Saints, Goddesses and Kings: Muslims and Christians in South Indian Society, 1700-1900* (Cambridge: Cambridge University Press, 1989).

[38] Benton, *Law and Colonial Cultures*, 131.

[39] Some writers have shown that administrations in Cochin and Batavia displayed a level of adaptability to local circumstances. See Anjana Singh, *Fort Cochin in Kerala, 1750–1830: The Social Condition of a Dutch Community in an Indian Milieu* (Leiden: Brill, 2010); Carla van Wamelen, *Family Life onder de VOC: Een Handelscompagnie in Huwelijks- en Gezinszaken* (Hilversum: Uitgeverij Verloren, 2014).

Sources and Research Design

The methodology of this study greatly facilitates the development of history from below. I have used an inductive approach by seeking narratives from the sources themselves, which tell stories of individuals, and of as many individuals as possible. Throughout the book, I present micro-histories of family life, which provide new horizons for recreating rural eighteenth-century Sri Lanka. Sanjay Subrahmanyam has aptly referred to "[t]he saliency of the micro-history (*microstoria*) approach, in particular given the nature of legal records as a privileged source that allows the historian to penetrate into the 'community' formations at the level of the family, or even the individual peasant."[40] Sri Lanka has a treasure trove of such sources.[41] Unique among them are the land registers referred to as *thombos* and the judicial records that I studied are some of the earliest extant for Sri Lanka. The Landraad of Galle, set up in the early 1740s to administer land matters, is the focus of the study, but I also study the thombos and other related documents.

Around sixty volumes from the Galle Landraad are deposited in the Sri Lanka National Archives today. The rolls (*rollen*), or minutes, form the bulk of the volumes. Other volumes include draft minutes, depositions, interrogations, transfer deeds, annexes and correspondence of the council. The annexes have valuable extra information about the cases that came up in the council, including requests, thombo extracts, *gift olas* (gift deeds) and other documents relating to land and debts. Unfortunately, the annexes are not bound together with references to the meetings in which they were brought up, making it time-consuming to connect them to the corresponding cases. Other documents I found among the volumes of the secretariat of Colombo are also part of the history of the Landraad. By extension, it can be argued that even the Galle thombos are a part of the archives of the Landraad, as they were drawn up and maintained by its members.

The thombos are unique for their historical value and socio-economic information on the eighteenth-century inhabitants and their property in Galle.[42] They are also unique in the world for their wealth of information on a pre-1800 Asian

40 Sanjay Subrahmanyam, "Peasants before the Law: Recent Historiography on Colonial India," *Etudes Rurales*, no. 149–150 (1999): 199–209.

41 Incidentally, this is very unlike the case in neighbouring India, where, "[u]ntil 1875, there was no official centralized system of law reporting and after 1875 the only courts of record were the High Courts." This is a serious methodological obstacle: "As the field of Indian legal history expands its scope of vision, we as scholars will have to be vigilant and imaginative in the ways we approach the critical issues of law, power and agency." Kolsky, "A Note," 706.

42 Mottau likened the records to the *Domesday Book*. There are indeed some similarities: in 1085 in England, the Norman conquest required that the new rulers had detailed knowledge of land ownership. S.A.W. Mottau, "Documents on Ceylon History (2): Documents Relating to the Tombo Registration

society. Primarily a basis for better taxation, the thombo is a dynamic document that reveals an early colonial example of how "the fiscal reformer needed a detailed inventory of land ownership to realize the maximum, sustainable revenue yield."[43] Over 200 villages in Galle have thombos that are kept in the archives in Colombo. They record personal details such as name, age, caste, service, residence, nonmarital birth, civil status and details of property held. We can also use them to study family ties in relation to property, the nature of property rights, partner choice, mortality, migration, marriage and birth patterns and diaspora. My use of the thombos focuses on the nature of the rights they describe and the assumptions behind them, and the legal disputes in connection with such rights. An analysis of the nature of rights listed in the thombos, together with the land disputes, reveals a number of legal concepts regarding what gave people rights to land. Importantly, the Landraad had to deal with issues arising from the registration process of the thombos. The thombos thus lie at the functional core of the Landraad, which was responsible for their creation and maintenance.

A source of inspiration for this study, due to the similarities in the form of the archives used, was Marie-Charlotte Le Bailly's work from 2001 for which she drew up a database of cases that came up in the Hof van Holland (Court of Holland) during 1457–1467. Her database was in turn partly based on a model for a legal history database developed by H. de Schepper and others in 1988.[44] The Landraad documents I examine for this work do not readily lend themselves to tabulation in a database. Naturally, these difficulties arise because the VOC did not draw up these records for the purposes for which I have used them. The information I required, therefore, was not always in the documents. While the documents were consistent in form, they were irregular in content such as the social background, residence, and gender of subjects. This makes tabulating their data difficult at times.

Despite this relative drawback, I obtained a wide range of data. I reconstructed around 100 consecutive cases that came up in the Landraad from May 1778 to

of the Dutch Administration in Ceylon: Instructions Issued to the Tombo Commissioners," *The Ceylon Historical Journal* 3, no. 2 (1953): 173.

43 James C. Scott, *Seeing Like a State: How Certain Schemes to Improve the Human Condition Have Failed* (New Haven: Yale University Press, 1999), 38.

44 Marie-Charlotte Le Bailly, *Recht voor de Raad* (Haarlem & Hilversum: Historische Vereniging Holland & Uitgeverij Verloren, 2001), 28; H. de Schepper et al., "Prolegomena voor onderzoek van rechtspraak en bestuur in de oude Nederlanden," in J. Koster van Dijk and A. Wijffels (eds) *Miscellanea forensia historica: Ter gelegenheid van het afscheid van Prof. Mr. J. Th de Smidt* (Amsterdam: Werkgroep Grote Raad van Mechelen, 1988), 263–94. In general, there is a lacuna in early modern studies of the courts of Holland. Schepper et al. had the intention of developing a common list of questions for the development of a juridical database, so that exchange and comparison of data would be possible. Naturally that is a difficult task even within the legal history of a single country, more so in the study of an attempted transplantation of a legal system on foreign land.

December 1779. These years represent a period of relative peace under Governor Iman Willem Falck (1765–1785), many years after the war with Kandy that ended in 1765 and before the greater emphasis on centralisation policies imposed by the next governor, Willem Jacob van de Graaff. In addition, I analysed cases from before and after this period, particularly those from after 1780. I have made every effort to trace the beginning and end of these cases in preceding and subsequent volumes of the council minutes. I identified individual cases by collating the case documents from the various volumes of minutes, depositions, interrogations and annexes into separate dossiers.[45] These cases can be identified by the parties involved, subject, and references to previous hearings. On closer reading of the sample cases, it turned out that while a few of them initially read as separate cases, they in fact referred to a single case. Thus, it was necessary to maintain a manageable number of cases for the study. In Sri Lanka, the practice of producing law reports began in the nineteenth century, and unlike in the courts of Holland, summaries (*regesten*) and indexes are not available for the eighteenth-century Dutch judicial records. Such summaries usually have the names of the litigants, descriptions of the dispute or offence and, at times, even the sentence.[46] Large-scale quantitative studies of legal history conducted elsewhere in the world have also benefited from summaries of cases and collaborative work, which this study lacked.[47]

The judicial and cadastral sources complement each other in building up our knowledge of litigants and reconstructing eighteenth-century rural families in southern Sri Lanka. When a case came up in the Landraad around the time of the thombo registration, the links were more definite. If the dispute involved a registration matter, notes on the council decision were often made on the thombo. For the cases analysed in this book, I established such links manually. A larger database of the Landraad and the thombos would naturally yield a better platform to automate, speed up and simplify such record linkage.[48] This study, however, has benefitted from manual record linkage; I hope to have minimised the space for unconscious biases and inconsistencies in this process. I have also used other sets of data on meetings, meeting attendance, litigants, witnesses and small-scale prosopographical

[45] Dossiers were made for the higher Dutch courts on the island and circulated among the councillors for their opinion. This was not a practice seen in The Netherlands according to B. Sirks and J. Hallebeek, "Uit het archief van de Raad van Justitie te Colombo: Rechtsbedeling in Ceylon in de 18de eeuw," *Libellus ad Thomasium: Essays in Roman Law, Roman-Dutch Law and Legal History in Honour of Philip J Thomas (Fundamina)* 16, no. 1 (2010): 390.

[46] Le Bailly, *Recht Voor de Raad*, 123–24.

[47] See Sally Engle Merry, *Colonizing Hawai'i: The Cultural Power of Law* (Princeton, NJ: Princeton University Press, 2000), 146.

[48] See Ian Winchester, "What Every Historian Needs to Know about Record Linkage for the Microcomputer Era," *Historical Methods* 25, no. 4 (1992): 149–65.

databases of the thombos of eight villages from Galle, and describe them in more detail in relevant chapters. The extant minutes quite easily yield a full breakdown of the members and the meetings at which they were present in the period of 1759–1796.[49] The Galle thombos that I selected for detailed study in this book were drawn up between 1760 and 1784. When compared to Landraad documents, the thombos present a somewhat easier form for transfer to the spreadsheets of a database, as they lend themselves more readily to tabulation. Page after page of the large folio volumes presents similar structures of information, as the Dutch Government required details on its subjects and resources. The thombos add quantitative data to the type of land rights that were recognised in practice.

As there is hardly any prior work on the Landraad, this case study is unprecedented. I carried out preliminary work on how the Landraad operated, who the councillors were and who came to the council, as such questions are inherently linked to that of whose laws were used in the council. I cover this area in the first three chapters of the book, and discuss the personal involvement in lawmaking of the various stakeholders within this new institutional framework in later chapters. The borders between description and analysis are, however, often blurred, and the questions that have informed the descriptive parts are likely to have been prompted by a particular worldview. The wealth of information that can be mined from the Landraad documents, together with sources such as discussions on property rights, proclamations, minutes of the Governor in Council in Colombo and Galle Political Council, contemporary descriptions of the land services and the much-mined memoirs of the governors provide a rich picture of eighteenth-century Sri Lanka.

The value of the sources I have used is apparent in Cornelia Vismann's work on the history of files in law and media technology. The documents of the Landraad and the thombos derive authority "from the fact that they came into being at the same time as the transactions they record." In that moment of transmission from the oral to the written, a translation from the vernacular to the Dutch also occurred, which "enables protocols to enter the sphere of officially recognized and communicated truth."[50] Through this process, the voices of social actors can be heard. However, legal sources in general contain problems of partiality. There may well be a gap between what was recorded and the actual events and proceedings of a case, as also between what a judge meant and what a litigant or witness understood. The lack of private sources such as letters and diaries is a further drawback. However,

[49] Records of an earlier period are available sporadically: SLNA 1/3215, "Copies of proceedings of Galle and Matara Landraden sent to Colombo" (1747 to 1748); SLNA 1/3216, "Copies of proceedings of Galle and Matara Landraden sent to Colombo" (1749 to 1752).

[50] Cornelia Vismann, *Files: Law and Media Technology* (Stanford, CA: Stanford University Press, 2008), 53–54.

although the council records are in a particular legal language and reflect only select information, they do offer a special lens into the everyday lives of the social players involved, if only because they are all that remain.

Transformations are inherent to an analysis of such everyday lives. I analyse changes in laws through what is known of the pre-colonial past, thus addressing the issue of the interplay of foreign and local laws in a colonial setting. This work reflects an intersection of legal, colonial and social histories, and the interdisciplinary practices that arise in the context of empirical studies.

Structure of the Book

To unravel the functioning of a small legal body in eighteenth-century Sri Lanka, I analysed the institutional development and functioning of the Landraad with aspects of procedural and substantive law that came up in the council. In chapter one I outline the available information on the judicial organisations that were in place before the Dutch arrived to understand the structure of the local legal order. I also detail the establishment of the Landraad, its operations, procedures and caseloads, as well as the related development of the thombo registration and sources of the law. In this way chapter one looks at the institutional development of the Landraad in the context of the local environment.

I discuss the members of the council and issues of efficiency in chapter two, examining the backgrounds of the European and indigenous members, the nature of their presence at meetings and the relative powers of the two groups. Occasional skirmishes for power raised tensions within the council from time to time. Chapter three offers a breakdown of the inhabitants who came before the councillors of the Landraad. I examine the gender, ethnicity and occupation of litigants and witnesses, along with the geographical location of the council, which may have influenced who appeared in the Landraad. Sources suggest that native women often flocked to colonial courts around the world, although a statistical survey of this phenomenon has not been done. Moreover, in reality, women's agency may have varied from empire to empire and over time. These questions in chapters two and three are important precursors to the larger question of which law was being used in the Landraad.

While the first three chapters thus discuss the logistics of the Landraad, the next three lean more heavily towards an analysis of the content of the law. First, I deal with a more procedural aspect through the specific practice of the oath in the Landraad in order to enter the discussion on navigating pluralities. In chapter one, I describe the Dutch procedure used in the Landraad, but this did not mean that adaptation to local conditions in procedural aspects did not occur. On the contrary, chapter four will show how as a result of the necessity to establish the "truth" in the council, the Landraad adapted local customs of oath-giving. The oath, including trial by oath in countries around the world, has been a traditional part of the law of evidence, and the Dutch incorporation of the local practices of the social actors on site is thus particularly significant.

It was mostly in connection with land matters that establishing the truth became particularly important in the Landraad. As attempted in chapter five, it is necessary to determine how the land rights of the people were defined. My concerns in this chapter lie mostly with definitions of the terms used in the thombo and their reinforcement in Landraad proceedings. The issue of importance to inhabitants, indigenous headmen and company officials was in determining who owned what and to what extent, as conflict was not conducive for a stable economy. Negotiating the question of land tenure took a more practical approach. The struggle to possess and control land as property in late eighteenth-century Dutch Sri Lanka is central to this work. By looking at the thombos in some detail, chapter five considers how the VOC and indigenous people defined the rights to land in the Galle district. It lists the types of land rights that were recognised in the Galle thombos and the regulatory role that the Landraad played in maintaining certain definitions of tenure. To what extent did company officials who came from different cultural, social, economic and legal environments adapt existing indigenous systems of land tenure? What motivated them in this process? Fiscal extraction, socio-economic control and legitimising colonial rule were often the primary motives.

I study inheritance law in the context of the family in chapter six, starting with a case in the Landraad that crosses two cultural systems, and through it, discuss the various laws of inheritance that may have been in operation at the time. As most societies have laws regulating how property should be divided after death, the inheritance laws of the Sinhalese could not have escaped observation by VOC officials. The British, for instance, mostly agreed on intestate laws in the Kandyan kingdom in the nineteenth century. I explore inheritance cases from the Landraad in order to seek patterns in the decisions made. As marriage, divorce, illegitimacy and the rights of widows impinge on issues of inheritance, I use documents of the Scholarchale Vergadering, or the School Board – which dealt with these issues – to understand changes in these areas. In this way, I attempt to draw a picture of family law in eighteenth-century Sri Lanka, with an emphasis on inheritance.

Finally, the conclusion addresses how this study contributes to legal and colonial history. I situate the issues inherent to the question of the application of Sinhalese law in the context of current discussions of legal pluralism, which could have a bearing on how we understand its history. In a pluralistic setting, it is difficult to predetermine which areas of the law are most likely to be borrowed. Pluralities are reflected in more than one conventional division of the laws of Sri Lanka at present

– this is a discussion that I will not engage in. Yet, this study helps us to understand how indigenous inhabitants experienced law in eighteenth-century Sri Lanka. The purpose, in essence, is to open up specific features of Sri Lanka's legal legacy during Dutch rule, through an exploration of its practice. I also touch upon British and postcolonial continuities of this legacy from time to time, but the focus remains on drawing a picture of an eighteenth-century colonial judicial forum. In that image, the Landraad is revealed as a site of legality that was in part constructed by the needs and actions of the colonialists, and in part by the indigenes.

CHAPTER 1

Building the Landraad

Abstract

The structure of the existing legal order that was in place before the Dutch arrived in Sri Lanka is an important backdrop to understand the establishment, procedures and operations of the Landraad. The registration of land and sources of the law had lasting effects on society. In this way the institutional development of the Landraad richly illustrates the dilemmas of an early colonial power. Sri Lankan peasants faced courts of record for the first time and the caseloads derived from a hundred cases reveal that the anxieties of the people seeking justice centred on rights to land. Such structural innovations within a new space retained certain family resemblances to local conditions, thereby confirming their plural character.

Keywords: Pre-colonial law, Roman-Dutch law, thombo, legal procedure, colonial law, VOC.

Throughout the Dutch Empire, including the area controlled by the West India Company (WIC) of The Netherlands, the Dutch made varied investments in territorial control and the establishment of commercial networks.[1] The VOC's mandate was a broad one: it was empowered to wage war, enter into treaties and alliances with Asian powers and maintain extensive fiscal and legal administrative regimes. Dutch jurist Hugo Grotius believed that the company was perfectly capable of waging war and signing treaties, which "led him to a theory of divisible sovereignty in which individuals and groups outside the state could possess rights to a public legal personality, particularly in the extra-European world."[2] Dutch intervention was far from uniform across its territories. The administrative apparatus set up by the Dutch company in Sri Lanka was more elaborate than what it established in contemporary Java, but the VOC was in conflict with the Kandyan kingdom, which disputed the legitimacy of Dutch territorial rule on parts of the island. Unlike in the seventeenth

[1] For a discussion of the importance of territorial conquest vis-a-vis the establishment of commercial networks, see Philip J. Stern, "'Bundles of Hyphens': Corporations as Legal Communities in the Early Modern British Empire," in Lauren Benton and Richard J. Ross (eds) *Legal Pluralism and Empires, 1500-1850* (New York: NYU Press, 2013).

[2] Ibid., 26–27.

century, when territorial conquest was central to the Dutch, by the eighteenth century they were less interested in territorial expansion despite the war with Kandy from 1760 to 1765. This was a trend seen in other Dutch territories as well.

Through property rights institutions, the Dutch East India Company developed the structures necessary for early colonial state formation in Sri Lanka. This chapter explores how and why the Galle Landraad was set up and how its history was intertwined with the development of land registration. In setting up such institutional arrangements, how responsive was the company to existing practices? Were the new practices invented or were they adapted from local practices? How did the Landraad, as an administrative encroachment in indigenous society, operate? Structurally, the council was a new institution. The thombo that was drawn up by the Landraad was a home-grown, yet considerably altered, production of cadastral knowledge.

The institutionalised, normative order of the territory that the VOC occupied could not be ignored. To understand that context, and the subsequent evolution of the Dutch legal system, this chapter first presents an overview of the existing literature on the judicial organisations that were in place in the Kandyan kingdom and under Portuguese rule in the low country. Characterising and setting the boundaries of the inherited normative order is no easy task. In other chapters of this book, this difficulty has been settled by examining potential or real conflicts between the two systems, i.e., the Dutch and the Sinhalese. These interactions, at least partly, reveal the contours of the local legal order and bring into sharp focus issues of inter-legality. To this, I have added a narrative of their operation in practice.

Next, this chapter will present an account of how the Landraad was set up and its operation and procedures. I have also dealt with the legal issues taken up in the Landraad. What types of cases could be heard? An analysis of the cases reveals the primary concerns of the local (mostly rural) society in Galle and the council's *ratione materiae*, or authority to decide a particular case. The council had exclusive jurisdiction on land matters. In this way, an analysis of the establishment and functioning of the institution that maintained the thombos and administered justice to eighteenth-century peasants will form the bulk of the chapter. A monumental exercise in documentation, the land registration of Galle will be described next. As a result of this exercise, land rights were compressed into large folio volumes that became an integral part of the administration of law.

The Inherited Order

The literature on pre-colonial law in Sri Lanka is strikingly sparse, but what is extant is adequate for drawing some ideas on the system. In the popular *A History of Sri Lanka* by K.M. de Silva, for instance, there are relatively brief references to the legal regime and the machinery of justice.[3] In the history of the country written in three volumes by the University of Ceylon and the University of Peradeniya over the latter half of the twentieth century, only the last volume has a separate chapter on the administration of justice (under British rule).[4] Work on the legal regime under Portuguese rule is rarer still. An exception is the fairly comprehensive account of the Kandyan legal system by the sociologist Ralph Pieris.[5] This concentration on the early modern and modern is due to the more ready availability of sources, chiefly European, for those periods and their continuing relevance to Sri Lanka's current legal system. In addition, in the "pre-colonial" period, there may have been a unification of custom and law that was an obstacle to research, given modern day prejudices on the matter. Setting aside such distinctions, former justice A.R.B. Amerasinghe provides an account of the Sri Lankan legal system from before European involvement in the island.[6] Understanding the role of normative practices in a society can facilitate research in legal history where primary sources such as legal texts are rare. Seeing the legal through a web of pluralities broadens our understanding of legal culture.

Our information on Sri Lanka's pre-colonial legal machinery and law is mostly based on nineteenth-century British sources on the Kandyan kingdom. The low country, however, had by then already been subjected to European influence for about three hundred years. This work is a first step towards comprehending Sinhalese law through Dutch sources. The English sources fail to provide a persuasive representation of the low country in pre-Dutch times. Some laws in the Kandyan kingdom were also applicable to the low country or, at the very least, inhabitants were not oblivious to the Kandyan system, given their tendency to flee to the king's lands in times of war and maintain kinships through marriage. In reality, the division between "low country" and "up country" was an artificial one, although some space must be allowed for the influence of many years of European rule by the coast. We have no native judicial records, as no tradition of recording judicial proceedings or precedents as is the practice in modern

[3] K.M. de Silva, *A History of Sri Lanka* (Delhi: Oxford University Press, 1981).

[4] Nicholas Attygalle (ed), *University of Ceylon, History of Ceylon: From the Earliest Times to 1505*, vol. 1 (Colombo: Ceylon University Press, 1959); K.M. de Silva (ed), *University of Peradeniya, History of Sri Lanka (From c. 1500 to c. 1800)*, vol. 2 (Peradeniya: University of Peradeniya, 1995); K.M. de Silva, (ed), *University of Ceylon, History of Ceylon: From the Beginning of the 19th Century to 1948*, vol. 3 (Peradeniya: University of Ceylon Press Board, 1973).

[5] Ralph Pieris, *Sinhalese Social Organization: The Kandyan Period* (Colombo: Ceylon University Press Board, 1956). He introduces early nineteenth-century case documents and other manuscript material in London to the discussion on Kandyan law.

[6] A.R.B. Amerasinghe, *The Legal Heritage of Sri Lanka* (Colombo: Royal Asiatic Society of Sri Lanka, 1999).

law existed in the Kandyan or pre-colonial legal system. The following account will necessarily rely on the few Portuguese, Dutch and British observations on Sinhalese law.

The earliest of such European accounts was by a Dutchman, Reverend Phillipus Baldaeus, but the section on Sri Lanka in his book, first published in 1672, is predominantly about the country's political, administrative and missionary history and life and customs in Jaffna, his missionary seat for many years. He spent a year in Galle when he arrived in the country in 1656, but his section on the Sinhalese is brief.[7] In contrast, Robert Knox's work, published in Europe in 1681, has been used extensively as a reference for the history of Kandy. He is (mis)quoted as saying that the Kandyan kingdom has had no laws in an account of his experiences living in the interior of the island for almost twenty years as a captive since 1660. He was probably making a comparison to laws as he knew them to exist in post-civil war England, his country of birth. Yet, he accepted that the local population had a system of recognised norms: "here are no Laws, but the Will of the King, and whatsoever proceeds out of his mouth is an immutable Law. Nevertheless, they have certain antient usages and Customes that do prevail and are observed as Laws; and Pleading them in their Courts and before their Governors will go a great way."[8] Knox may have been inclined to see a distinction between law and custom, but such a distinction, as is the case in many parts of the non-modern world, probably did not exist in the Kandyan kingdom. Compared to his English experience, it may have seemed that local customs did not have a clear formulation. By his own admission, however, he acknowledged that customs were "observed as laws," which indicates that Knox was an early witness of how social norms *were* law. The king was considered the "fountain of justice" in the local administration of justice. François Valentijn, a minister of the Dutch Reformed Church who used the VOC's administrative documents (and Knox's work, among other travel descriptions) to write an early eighteenth-century account of the island that he never visited, follows Knox in rejecting a view of the king's arbitrary power in a more explicit manner: "There are among them certain permanent land laws or old customs, according to which

[7] S.D. Saparamadu (ed), *A True and Exact Description of the Great Island of Ceylon by Phillipus Baldaeus*, trans. Pieter Brohier, vol. 42, The Ceylon Historical Journal Monograph Series (Dehiwala: Tisara Prakasakayo, 1960; repr. 2012), 380–86.

[8] Robert Knox, *An Historical Relation of Ceylon* (Dehiwala: Tisara Prakasakayo, 1681; repr. 1966), 190. Sarojini Jayawickrama cautions us to understand that the historical knowledge produced by his work had an ideological investment in the colonial and imperialist discourses of the time. See Sarojini Jayawickrama, *Writing that Conquers: Re-Reading Knox's an Historical Relation of the Island Ceylon* (Colombo: Social Scientists' Association, 2004), 2, 286. See also K.W. Goonewardena, "Some Comments on Robert Knox and His Writings on Ceylon," *University of Ceylon Review* 16, no. 1/2 (1958): 39–52.

most matters are directed, except where the Emperor makes any changes."[9] As does Knox, he follows this statement with a reference to inheritance law, which is a paraphrased version of Knox's observations. This indicates that Valentijn was most likely to have been influenced by Knox about the king's judicial powers.

Such norms appear to have had sources accepted by society. One problem in drawing a picture of the pre-colonial legal system is the paucity of written legislation for that period in forms that are readily recognisable today. No legal texts for Sri Lanka from before the nineteenth century exist, but references to local rulers adhering to laws are inscribed on stone slabs and are mentioned in ancient and modern historical accounts.[10] For example, one inscription of Parākramabāhu VI (1411–1466), who ruled the country from the littoral capital of Kotte, indicates that the king proclaimed edicts that functioned as laws.[11] The *Girā Sandēsaya,* a pastoral poem written during his reign, states that he strictly followed the *Manusmriti* or the laws of Manu,[12] a Sanskrit text originating in India that deals with matters of kingship and state and judicial administration. It was based in turn on the Indian *Vedas.* The *Mahāwamsa,* a fifth- or sixth-century historical text, states that King Tissa (209–31) abolished the practice of inflicting torture that had prevailed up to that period and was therefore known as Vohārika-tissa.[13] F.A. Hayley, however, states that "such ordinances seem to have been forgotten in course of time, or were disregarded by subsequent kings."[14] William Knighton, writing in 1845, is convinced that Dappula III (923-4) compiled a "distinct code of laws, which he had transmitted to posterity with the greatest care"[15] but the *Mahāwamsa* does not mention such a code. As L.J.M. Cooray points out, not everyone agreed. Charles Pridham said in 1849 that a code would go against the grain: "[I]n the absence of more conclusive reasoning and evidence, because it is clear that it was equally opposed to the genius of the king and the priesthood – the two fountains of law – to determine by a specific and definitive code, customs, which took their tone as much from the pressure

9 Francois Valentijn, *Francois Valentijn's Description of Ceylon,* trans. and ed. Sinnappah Arasaratnam, vol. 149, Hakluyt Society 2 (London: Hakluyt Society, 1978), 169.

10 See for these examples, M.B. Ariyapala, *Society in Mediaeval Ceylon: The State of Society in Ceylon as Depicted in the Saddharma-Ratnāvaliya and Other Literature of the Thirteenth Century* (Colombo: Dept. of Cultural Affairs, 1956; repr. 1997), 122–32; Amerasinghe, *Legal Heritage,* 11–14.

11 L.J.M. Cooray, *An Introduction to the Legal System of Sri Lanka* (Pannipitiya: Stamford Lake, 2003; repr. 2009), 103.

12 *Girā Sandēsaya* v. 127, quoted in Amerasinghe, *Legal Heritage,* 12.

13 Vohārika means judge or justice in Pali. Wilhelm Geiger, *The Mahāwamsa* (Colombo: Govt. Press, 1986), chap. 36, l 28.

14 F.A. Hayley, *A Treatise on the Laws and Customs of the Sinhalese* (New Delhi: Navrang, 1923; repr. 1993), 55.

15 William Knighton, *The History of Ceylon from the Earliest Period to the Present Time* (London: Longman, 1845), 191.

of circumstances and the contingencies of the moment, as from any prescriptive rights."[16] However, the accounts drawn up by Knighton and Pridham in the first half of the nineteenth century can hardly be considered authoritative works on the existence of a pre-colonial code. A more nuanced interpretation of the administration of justice in pre-colonial Sri Lanka is necessary. We may not be able to settle the issue of Dappula's "code" without new evidence but norms, even if they were subject to the whims of certain kings, are likely to have had known sources in both religious and secular texts and traditions. Seven sources of early Sinhalese customary law have been identified: (1) Hindu laws and customs, (2) Buddhist canonical writings, practices and rites, (3) Sakyan and Mauryan customs, (4) *Pera Sirit* (former or immemorial customs), (5) *Kula Sirit* (customs of clans and castes), (6) *Gam Sirit* (customs mainly connected with landholding in villages) and (7) south Indian customs. These sources of law have not, however, been comprehensively analysed.[17]

My focus here is not pre-colonial evidence, but the legal system of the Kandyan kingdom, which ran a parallel administration to the Dutch in the period under study. The following is based, among others, on the early nineteenth-century work of John D'Oyly, Britain's master spy and civil servant, Simon Sawers, another civil servant, John Davy an army doctor, and the early twentieth-century work of Hayley, a lawyer.[18] All products of British rule, some were commissioned by British powers. The Board of Commissioners of Kandyan Affairs (set up in 1816) was asked, for instance, to report on the customs of the Kandyan provinces when there was criticism that the setting up of the board would be a violation of the

16 Charles Pridham, *An Historical, Political, and Statistical Account of Ceylon and Its Dependencies* (London: T and W Boone, 1849), 1: 215.

17 Detailed accounts of these sources of law are hard to come by except in the case of Buddhist ecclesiastical law. See, among others, Steven Kemper, "The Buddhist Monkhood, the Law, and the State in Colonial Sri Lanka," *Comparative Studies in Society and History* 26, no. 3 (1984): 401–27; Andrew Huxley, "Studying Theravada Legal Literature," *Journal of the International Association of Buddhist Studies* 20, no. 1 (1997): 63–91; R.A.L.H. Gunawardana, "'Necessary Evil': The Growth of a System of Judicial Courts and the Responses it Evoked among the Buddhist Monastic Community in Ancient Sri Lanka," *Buffalo Law Review* 55 (2007): 685–90; Benjamin Schonthal, "The Legal Regulation of Buddhism in Contemporary Sri Lanka," in Rebecca Redwood French and Mark A. Nathan (eds), *Buddhism and Law* (Cambridge: Cambridge University Press, 2014), 150–66; W.S. Weerasooria, *Buddhist Ecclesiastical Law: A Treatise on Sri Lankan Statute Law and Judicial Decisions on Buddhist Temples and Temporalities* (Colombo: Postgraduate Institute of Management, 2011).

18 *The Niti-Nighanduva* was a publication from 1880 and said to be a translation of an earlier Sinhala work that is no longer extant, but as it refers more to the laws than to the judicial administrative setup which is the focus here, it will not be referred to here. C.J.R. Le Mesurier and T.B. Panabokke, trans., *Niti-Nighanduva or the Vocabulary of Law* (New Delhi: Navrang, 1880; repr. 1994). John Armour's grammar of Kandyan law has not been used in this chapter for the same reason. *Armour's Grammar of the Kandyan Law*, ed. Joseph Martinus Perera (Colombo: Examiner Press, 1861).

Kandyan Convention signed in 1815. D'Oyly and Sawers were the only two persons who as members of the board came forward to record the laws of the local population.[19] Through these sources, I will provide an overview of the infrastructure and organisation of the justice system in pre-colonial Sri Lanka for the purpose of comparison with the Dutch legal system, and more particularly, the operation of the Landraad. Cooray is of the opinion that there was an "elaborate judicial system" in ancient Sri Lanka. A certain hierarchy of legal officers connected to the king was maintained together with a system in which a village and district both had jurisdiction over a fixed territory. A direct line of appeal to the king from the lowest judicial body/official was believed to have existed. As civil and criminal law were not clearly demarcated, no explicit distinction in the jurisdictions of the courts or in their procedures used could be discerned. Cooray states that in the case of a robbery, a double penalty covering public and private justice was enforced. Both the wronged individual and the state had to be paid.[20]

The more important forums that administered justice were the Gamsabhāva, Ratasabhāva, Sākki Balanda and Mahanaduva. In addition, certain state officials wielded individual judicial authority.[21] The origin of the Gamsabhāva or village tribunal, which was composed of village elders, is said to date back to the origin of the village itself. D'Oyly said the Gamsabhāva met at an *ambalama* (a kind of resting place) or under a shady tree or other central place.[22] It dealt with minor offences such as boundary disputes, small debts, petty thefts and minor quarrels. The Gamsabhāva had a minor punitive jurisdiction to impose fines but only if the headmen were present.[23] The Gamsabhāva was not intended to mete out punishment, "their endeavours being directed to compromise," as D'Oyly writes.[24] Ralph Pieris shows with examples how the proceedings were "characterized by admonition, compromise and common sense, unsullied by legal technicality and rigid rules of procedure."[25] Dispute negotiation through compromise was more the order of the day.[26] Obeyesekere has also noted the situational nature of judging in

[19] Earle Modder, "Memoranda of the Laws of Inheritance &c., and Notes on Sir John D'Oyly's Exposition of the Kandyan Law by Simon Sawers" (n.d.), SLNA 25.98/4.

[20] Cooray, *Legal System*, 108–12.

[21] Pieris, *Sinhalese Social Organization*, 149–57; Ivor Jennings and H.W. Tambiah, *The Dominion of Ceylon: The Development of Its Laws and Constitution* (London: Stevens, 1952), 91–100.

[22] John D'Oyly, *A Sketch of the Constitution of the Kandyan Kingdom*, ed. Lewis James Barnetson Turner, vol. 24, *The Ceylon Historical Journal* (Dehiwala: Tisara Prakasakayo, 1929; repr. 1975), 42–43.

[23] Cooray, *Legal System*, 108.

[24] D'Oyly, *Constitution of the Kandyan Kingdom*, vol. 24:43.

[25] Pieris, *Sinhalese Social Organization*, 149.

[26] See, for an overview of the go-between, mediator, arbitration and the courts, Martin Shapiro, *Courts: A Comparative and Political Analysis* (Chicago: University of Chicago Press, 1986).

the Sinhalese legal order, where the concept of familial assistance was dominant (more on this follows in chapter six).[27] Such situational judging was not arbitrary; it drew upon a significant normative order that cannot be brushed aside as less than legal. Interestingly, we will see that the Dutch also recognised such an order.

Regional differences in institutional hierarchies must also be considered. These are likely in situations where power was not centralised, although scholars have expressed differing views on the matter. Hayley, Ivor Jennings and Henry Tambiah believe that it was possible to appeal to the district-level tribunal of the Ratasabhāva from the Gamsabhāva,[28] but Ralph Pieris believes this was limited to the dry zone of Nuvarakalāviya and Matale. Pieris points out that going by Hayley's own authorities of Pridham and Jonathan Forbes, the Ratasabhāva did not operate in other areas. He believes that in the Nuvarakalāviya villages, "law and order were maintained by institutions which were relatively independent of state control" and that distance from the capital had made the Ratasabhāva important in Matale and the Nuvarakalāviya which were north of Kandy.[29] Sujit Sivasundaram goes further to say that "[w]ithin Nuvarakalaviya, the region in which the ancient capital lay, there was a thriving sense of identity, fed by ancient ruins, the vegetation and legends from the past." He points out that the Nāyakkar kings of Kandy were keen to engage with that region in which the ancient capital of Anuradhapura lay in order to shore up support for their rule.[30] While Anuradhapura was important for its place in a spiritual topography, establishing judicial control in that region from the centre was more difficult. The Vanniyārs or chieftains of the Vanni, an imprecisely defined region above the Nuvarakalāviya, wielded judicial and police powers independent of the centre.[31]

The Ratasabhāva was composed of the delegates of each village in a particular district. It had original jurisdiction in matters relating to caste, marriage and social status. Its proceedings were attended with much ceremony: "The lengthy sessions of the Dry Zone *rata sabhās* were marked by etiquette, decorum, and punctilio, the *gamarāla* being responsible for providing meals for all those who assembled for these prolonged deliberations, while the meetings of the *uda rata* [up country]

[27] Gananath Obeyesekere, *Land Tenure in Village Ceylon: A Sociological and Historical Study* (Cambridge: Cambridge University Press, 1967), 49.

[28] Hayley, *A Treatise on the Laws and Customs*, 60; Jennings and Tambiah, *The Dominion of Ceylon*, 92.

[29] Pridham, *An Historical, Political, and Statistical Account*, vol. 1: 219; Jonathan Forbes, *Eleven Years in Ceylon* (R. Bentley, 1841), vol. 1: 71; Pieris, *Sinhalese Social Organization*, 150, 249.

[30] Sujit Sivasundaram, "Buddhist Kingship, British Archaeology and Historical Narratives in Sri Lanka c.1750–1850," *Past & Present* 197, no. 1 (2007): 114.

[31] See for an overview of the administration of the Vanni districts, Lorna S. Dewaraja, *The Kandyan Kingdom of Sri Lanka, 1707-1782*, Second Edition (Colombo: Lake House, 1988), 234–40.

village councils were brief and informal."[32] In most areas in the Kandyan kingdom, the next line of appeal after the Gamsabhāva was likely to have been state officials who had judicial powers, and not another board such as the Ratasabhāva. There was, however, another judicial forum, the Sākki Balanda,[33] which Davy believed operated under the Kandyan kings.[34] Much like a coroner's court, it was tasked with inquiring into sudden deaths. Davy claims that it was composed of the principal men of a district, including minor officials. He refers to the procedure adopted in the Sākki Balanda in a suicide case.

It seems, then, that after the Gamsabhāva and the Sākki Balanda, we must take into consideration the judicial powers of certain state officials. These state officials with powers of arbitration were *vidānes, liyanarālas, undirālas* and *korālas, mohottalas, ārachchis, lekams, ratēmahatayas, disāvas* and *adigārs* or *adhikāramas,* mostly in ascending order of their status in society. At the highest level were the adigārs, who were chief officers of state; at the other end of the spectrum were vidānes, who had much less authority in comparison. The jurisdiction of these officials, who acted virtually unaided and, in some cases, were possibly unchecked, has been dealt with in detail by early British writers and later scholars. I have confined myself to a description of the lowest and highest of such judicial officials.[35]

At the village level, the vidānes have been traditionally likened to police officers. D'Oyly believes they had civil and criminal judicial powers in dealing with small claims. They could levy fines that did not exceed two-and-a-half pieces of silver, keeping two pieces for themselves. Higher fines had to be reported and accounted for to the authority above them. They may have resembled the police officers of today to the extent that they had limited authority and could also impose fines, but they had more power with regards to physical punishment. D'Oyly says they occasionally punished lower caste people "by a few Blows with the open Hand

[32] Pieris, *Sinhalese Social Organization*, 150. See also Hayley, *A Treatise on the Laws and Customs*, 63.

[33] In literal terms, this means investigating evidence as *sākki* means evidence and *balanda* means to examine.

[34] John Davy, *An Account of the Interior of Ceylon, and of Its Inhabitants* (London: Longman, 1821), 180–81. Ralph Pieris and Amerasinghe agree that there is little information on the precise functions of this court except for that of Davy. Pieris, *Sinhalese Social Organization*, 151; Amerasinghe, *Legal Heritage*, 533 note 2. Pridham, for instance, writing in 1849, copied Davy's account of that court almost verbatim. Despite his denunciation of producing accounts of colonies by the month (though he also wrote an account of Mauritius) as "the most outrageous form of scissors and paste," Pridham also included "cut and paste" work that was not uncommon for his times. Pridham, *An Historical, Political, and Statistical Account*, vol. 1: vi-vii, 220.

[35] For a fuller account of these state officials, see D'Oyly, *Constitution of the Kandyan Kingdom*, vol. 24:34–42. Also Pieris, *Sinhalese Social Organization*, 152–56; Dewaraja, *Kandyan Kingdom*, 217–51.

inflicted standing."[36] Imprisonment also had to be reported to a higher authority except in some royal villages of Kandy. According to D'Oyly, the vidānes recovered fines by placing debtors in *veläkma*, a device of Kandyan procedural law. Veläkma, which means impeding or hindering, was simply a way of physically detaining a debtor in a confined space till payment was made.[37]

Almost at the pinnacle of the justice system, yet below the king, were the disāvas and adigārs, the latter being next in line to the king. The disāvas and adigārs had extensive jurisdiction over persons under their rule and could arbitrate over any civil or criminal case. The only exceptions were cases between members of the king's court. Paradoxically, despite their extensive powers, the adigārs and disāvas "were not well versed in the law, being persons drawn from the nobility and they had often to consult their inferior officers."[38] It was not new, in that case, that Dutch *dessaves,* European governors of a district in the low country, had to seek advice from headmen, as we will see. One forum through which the disāvas and adigārs could act was the Mahanaduva (Great Court), the next board of judges that the people could face after the Gamsabhāva, Sākki Balanda and, in some areas, the Ratasabhāva. It was perhaps originally a court that was called into action by the king when he did not want to handle a case that had been submitted to him. The disāvas and adigārs were required to report on the case to the king, who would then deliver the final verdict. D'Oyly states that there were cases that were originally instituted before the Mahanaduva as well, which, as Cooray argues, may have been a later development that was distinct from its earlier function of only advising the king.[39] The formal operation of the Mahanaduva is best described in the works of D'Oyly and Pieris.[40] The king was the final arbitrator who had extensive jurisdiction in

[36] D'Oyly, *Constitution of the Kandyan Kingdom*, vol. 24:42.

[37] Ralph Pieris gives a summary of D'Oyly's description of the process: "Confronted by his creditor, the latter stops him and draws a circle round him on the ground with a stick, or without even this ceremony, sits down beside him and forbids him by the King's command to move without discharging his debt. Neither can stir until another person either engages to be answerable for the debt, or undertakes in the presence of witnesses, to call both before the proper chief. This process was also employed by the principal headmen to recover fines. In such cases the culprit was required to sit down in the sun and sometimes obliged to hold with both hands a heavy stone laid on his shoulders, which weight he may shift from one side to another, but not cast off for fear of immediate corporal punishment." Knox also describes a similar procedure with an illustration of a man with a great stone on his back. Pieris, *Sinhalese Social Organization*, 158–59; D'Oyly, *Constitution of the Kandyan Kingdom*, vol. 24:40, 87; Knox, *An Historical Relation of Ceylon*, 196–97.

[38] Cooray, *Legal System*, 110.

[39] D'Oyly, *Constitution of the Kandyan Kingdom*, vol. 24:33; Cooray, *Legal System*, 110.

[40] D'Oyly, *Constitution of the Kandyan Kingdom*, vol. 24:32–34; Pieris, *Sinhalese Social Organization*, 157. Incidentally, the Board of Commissioners of Kandyan Affairs (of which D'Oyly and Sawers were members, as mentioned above), replaced the Mahanaduva. De Silva, *A History of Sri Lanka*, 260.

"suits arising between any principal servant or chief of his court, or where such a person was a defendant, and those relating to royal lands; suits between priests claiming rights to the incumbency of principal temples; serious crimes namely treason, rebellion and conspiracy against the king or his family and all homicides." The king could be approached by an official or a petitioner with regard to solving a case.[41] Further details on such an elaborate indigenous legal system can be found in the sources used here, but it must be kept in mind that any description must leave room for regional differences of which we know little or nothing.

The Portuguese were the first European power to enter this local legal "system" in the sixteenth and seventeenth centuries when they captured parts of the low country. They initially attempted to impose their laws but met with opposition. The Portuguese captain, João Ribeiro, whose first-hand account of the island was published a few years after that of Baldaeus and Knox, wrote that Sinhalese delegates who were faced with the prospect of being governed under Portuguese laws said,

> that they were Chingalas, brought up from the beginning in the laws which they possessed and observed: that it would be a very grave matter for them to abandon those laws and take in exchange what were now proposed; the result of so great a change would probably be that neither the one law nor the other would be properly observed....and as such they would serve him [the king of Portugal] with the laws in which they had been brought up; but those laws must be preserved by His Majesty and his Ministers without any alteration at any time.

Ribeiro says the agreement was certified by a document that both parties swore on.[42] For their administrative setup, the Portuguese drew up cadastres that will be discussed later. While some lower-level local legal institutions were likely to have been preserved, legal officers at higher levels came to be of Portuguese origin. By the 1620s and 1630s, the Portuguese adopted a policy of appointing Portuguese alone to the posts of disāva or district heads, who had considerable judicial powers including the right to impose capital punishment.[43] The Portuguese also created new posts such as that of captain general, the *vedor da fazenda* or controller of revenue, *ouvidor* or crown judge and a factor who had varying degrees of involvement with the judicial administration at a higher level. The captain general, for

[41] Cooray, *Legal System*, 110. See also answers given to Governor Falck in 1769 by Kandyan priests on the laws and customs of the country: Anthony Bertolacci, *A View of the Agricultural, Commercial, and Financial Interests of Ceylon* (London: Black, Parbury and Allen, 1817), 461.

[42] Joao Ribeiro, *The Historic Tragedy of the Island of Ceilao*, trans. P.E. Pieris (Colombo: The Ceylon Daily News, 1685; repr. 1948), 24–25.

[43] Chandra Richard De Silva, *The Portuguese in Ceylon 1617-1638* (Colombo: H W Cave, 1972), 158.

instance, revived the above-mentioned Mahanaduva, a part of the administration of the Kotte kingdom that the Portuguese controlled.[44] The powers of these judicial officials will not be discussed in detail here, but due to their particular relevance to this study, another Portuguese appointment, the *marelleiros,* will be examined.

Marelleiros were Portuguese legal officers who were assigned regions over which they held their own assizes called *marallas* once a year and decided cases according to the laws of the people. Ribeiro states that the four marelleiros were assisted by four natives each, including two interpreters who knew the laws of the people. A travelling court, they sent notice to the people of a province to be ready on an appointed day on which they would meet the inhabitants on the road, and be led by the people to their lodgings and receive their hospitality. Ribeiro says that "[a]ll the neighbouring inhabitants who had a complaint or a petition would come and remain there until their business was transacted and the same would be done in all the other provinces."[45] If documentation was generated in this process, it is not known to have survived. As they met only annually, the marallas could not have captured the imagination of the village, although they probably attempted to influence family life as a result of the conversion of many Sinhalese to Christianity.

If indigenous customs were transformed through this process, this suggests why the Dutch were silent on some aspects of local law that the British discussed. Hayley is convinced that the "laws of Portugal were never introduced to any material extent."[46] The people's engagement with the Catholic religion may not have been to the degree that was expected of them, but the Christian deity of the Portuguese faith had much in common with Buddhism, as Buddhism had been influenced by Hindu practice through the ceremonial making of vows and worship of relics and images.[47] The subtle manner in which family life was affected by Catholic conversions is under researched; yet, when they arrived, the Dutch appear to have drawn a blank on some laws such as inheritance law, as will be discussed in chapter six.

Pluralism was not introduced in Sri Lanka by the European powers alone; its origins can be traced further back in Sri Lanka's legal history. The Dutch, with their Roman-Dutch laws, textual traditions and elaborate court system in the republic, entered a legal environment in Sri Lanka that was already influenced by diverse sources. It is likely that the Gamsabhāva continued to function under Portuguese and Dutch rule despite being undermined, to some extent, by the repeated use of

44 See Chandra Richard de Silva for an overview of the functions of these officials. Ibid., 159–70.

45 Ribeiro, *Historic Tragedy*, 58.

46 Hayley, *A Treatise on the Laws and Customs*, 22.

47 See for Catholicism in Portuguese times, Alan Strathern, *Kingship and Conversion in Sixteenth-Century Sri Lanka: Portuguese Imperialism in a Buddhist Land* (New Delhi & Colombo: Cambridge University Press & Vijitha Yapa, 2010), 132–37.

the legal forums introduced by the colonial powers. They continued functioning into British times, although they had their ups and downs in the nineteenth century.[48] At the time of the consolidation of Dutch power, the island had its various sources of law and an elaborate legal system, at least in the Kandyan kingdom, which involved negotiating with indigenous headmen at an institutional level. The situational nature of local practices of adjudication further necessitated this.

Under Dutch rule, indigenous inhabitants were repeatedly ordered to first have their disputes heard at the village level by the headmen, failing which they could approach higher officials and, eventually, the Landraad. The gathering of elders under a tree to settle disputes was likely to have been the first means of arbitration. The Landraad could be approached if higher-level Dutch officials also failed to resolve the case. This process will be discussed in more detail below. On certain land matters, however, it became mandatory to approach the Landraad as a body of original jurisdiction – a change that was tied to the Landraad's acquired task of registering lands. Unavoidably, the Landraad had to include headmen; the Portuguese marallas had already familiarised the inhabitants with the concept of a mixed body of judicial officials. Legal authority was effectively divided, if unequally, between foreign and local powers. A further continuity (with modifications) to earlier times is seen in the practice of land registration under Portuguese and Dutch rule. How the cadastres were conceived of and created in the form that we find them in eighteenth-century Galle will be discussed in this chapter, after an introduction to the Landraad.

Setting up the Landraad

In the bureaucratic regime set up by the company in parts of the island, the company retained the local administrative arrangements of *dessavony, kōralē, pattuwa* and *vidāne.* The overall administration of the colony was carried out by the Dutch governor based in Colombo who answered to the High Government in Batavia and the Gentlemen Seventeen of the VOC in The Netherlands. The three main administrative units on the island were Colombo, Jaffna and Galle. Together with

[48] The Gamsabhāva was devalued after the cession of the kingdom to the British in 1815 and the appointment of the Board of Commissioners of Kandyan Affairs in 1816 brought in new machinery for the administration of justice. Although disregarded in that earlier reformist era, in a later time, communal machinery such as the Gamsabhāva was revived. It played a key role in the implementation of the Irrigation Ordinance of 1856 and the Village Communities Ordinance of 1871, which, among other things, also saw the trial of minor offences through the Gamsabhāva. De Silva, *A History of Sri Lanka*, 260, 300, 316, 322–23.

the Matara Dessavony, the Galle Kōralē made up the Galle Commandment.[49] The Galle Kōralē (referred to as Galle district in this book) consisted of six sub-districts: the Galle Four Gravets, the Gangaboda Pattuwa, Hinidum Pattuwa, Talpe Pattuwa, Walallawiti Kōralē and the Wellaboda Pattuwa (see map 2).[50] The district was roughly bordered by the sea to the south and the west, Kalutara district and the Sinharaja rainforest of the present-day Sabaragamuva Province to the north and the district of Matara to the east. The Matara Dessavony, the Galle district and the Galle Commandment were headed by Europeans. While a European governor of a district, the dessave, was appointed in Matara (and Colombo), the Galle district had an *opziender* or overseer/superintendent. At the head of the VOC administration in Galle in the eighteenth century was the commander, who was third in rank to the governor of Sri Lanka after the commander of Jaffna. The commander had both civil and military authority and was assisted by a Raad van Politie (Political Council), composed of the principal heads of departments in the town. The commander was also the head of the Raad van Justitie (Council of Justice or High Court), which was the highest appellate judicial body in the commandment. He reported to the Governor in Council in Colombo, which decided matters pertaining to Dutch territory on the island.

Three main legal bodies were set up with some minor variations at different times and in different parts of the coastal area under Dutch rule. These were the Raad van Justitie, the Civiele Raad (Civil Council) and the Landraad. At the pinnacle of the judicial system was the Raad van Justitie in Colombo, to which appeals could be forwarded from the Raden van Justitie in Jaffna and Galle for all civil cases involving sums exceeding certain specified limits and certain criminal cases.[51] The Raad van Justitie in Colombo was composed of the highest-ranking company officials and the *advocaat-fiscaal*, equivalent to a public prosecutor. All three Raden van Justitie in Colombo, Jaffna and Galle had original jurisdiction over company personnel in all criminal cases and over civil cases involving sums exceeding certain limits within their districts or commandments. They also acted as appeal courts for cases heard in the Civiele Raad and the Landraad under their jurisdiction. The Civiele Raad of the three main towns under Dutch control dealt with cases involving inhabitants of the towns (including natives), while the Landraad reached further inland and was the only judicial body that also had headmen as permanent members. The latter dealt mostly with cases related to land issues and

[49] A commandment was an administrative unit created by the VOC.

[50] The Four Gravets of Colombo, Jaffna, Galle and Matara were inland sub-districts immediately outside the forts of those towns.

[51] In addition, all concluded criminal cases from all over Sri Lanka had to be sent to Batavia every year. SLNA 1/6497, "Galle Landraad minutes" (1759), fols. 33r.

an appeal could be directed from a Landraad to the Raad van Justitie of that district. In the case of the Raden van Justitie of Galle and Jaffna, further appeal to the Raad van Justitie of Colombo was possible. In that sense, the Raden van Justitie in Galle, Colombo and Jaffna were not on the same level, as cases from Galle and Jaffna could be heard on appeal in Colombo. Thus, it appears that a civil case heard in the Raden van Justitie of Galle and Jaffna had a second chance in Colombo if the value of the action exceeded 300 rixdollars, but litigants of the same type of case heard first in the Raad van Justitie of Colombo had to go to Batavia for appeal.

This structure of command in eighteenth-century colonial law in Sri Lanka can be seen clearly in charts showing the hierarchy of courts drawn up in many conventional works on the subject.[52] That perspective of a streamlined legal administration obscures the fluidity of the institutional and normative practices in operation. For instance, it largely ignores the role played by the headmen as the first agents the people were required to approach. Headmen are likely to have resolved disputes through face-to-face consent, more or less mediating solutions through rituals or norms that were acceptable to both parties. At the same time, peasants could approach higher authorities such as the dessave, the commander or the Landraad directly in land matters. At the Landraad, they may have been promised access to justice according to customary law. But in the new institutional structure, disputes would ultimately have to be settled by Dutch judges if they were taken beyond the Landraad to the Raden van Justitie. Appealing to other councils did not hold the same possibility of an application of customary law, as an inheritance case highlighted in chapter six will show. The higher judicial councils adjudicated in the last resort by imposing rules rather than by producing a consensual decision. The multifaceted, perhaps even confused nature of such authority is combined with a plurality of forms and sources of law.

In 1661, the VOC believed that a favourable result of the havoc and depopulation of the Colombo district in recent years was that they were thereby not required to be bound to Sinhalese laws and customs.[53] At the end of the wars with Rājasingha II of Kandy in the late seventeenth century, considerable tracts of Dutch-held territory were depopulated. Governor Rijklof van Goens the senior (1664–1675) even imported slaves from south India and settled them around Colombo.[54] It was

[52] Marleen van den Horst, *The Roman Dutch Law in Sri Lanka* (Amsterdam: Free University Press, 1985), 39–47; Thambiah Nadaraja, *The Legal System of Ceylon in its Historical Setting* (Leiden: Brill, 1972), 5–9.

[53] L. Hovy, *Ceylonees plakkaatboek: Plakkaten en andere wetten uitgevaardigd door het Nederlands bestuur op Ceylon, 1638-1796* (Hilversum: Verloren, 1991), vol. 1; no. 62 (4), Instruction for the dessave of Colombo, 21 Jun 1661.

[54] Sinnappah Arasaratnam, *Dutch Power in Ceylon, 1658-1687* (Amsterdam: Djambatan, 1958), 130–31.

thought, as Lodewijk Hovy points out, that it was easier to impose a new law in an empty land than in a populated land, but such a blank slate was a fallacy as the company later had to reverse its neglect of Sinhalese law.[55] This may have been due to emigrants to the Kandyan territories returning from the late seventeenth century onwards.[56]

Hovy discovered that Governor Cornelis Jan Simons (1703–1707) took steps to grant the local law and headmen a more important place in the judicial system. The first *plakkaat* (proclamation issued by the Dutch government; pl. *plakkaten*) in this connection came out in 1706, indicating that the native population had to bring their complaints in the first instance to their headmen and then in the second instance to the Dutch administrators.[57] Further developments can be seen in the 1740s, following the recommendations of the "enlightened" Governor Gustaaf Willem Baron Van Imhoff (1736–1739), as we will see below.

For the most part, the company understood that it had to inquire into existing laws. In the early years in Galle (when it was the company's administrative capital), *commissarissen der dagelijkse zaken* (commissioners of daily affairs) were required to handle minor civil and criminal disputes among both Europeans and Sinhalese in the first instance. In an ordinance made in 1648, the company resigned itself to the fate of having to adjudicate because, as it said, many quarrels arose in Galle town and its surroundings to which the Governor in Council could not attend. At least one or two prominent Sinhalese were also commissioners in this body who could vote, because most matters that arose would concern the Sinhalese. All such members were to be chosen by the Governor in Council. In Sinhalese matters, they had "in principle to rule according to the old laws and customs of the land, in so far as they could be adopted and were not contrary to any specific plakkaten."[58] The appointment of native commissioners is significant in that it was an early recognition of the necessity to settle disputes in an acceptable way and establish continuity with the past. This body of *commissarissen der dagelijkse zaken* that was in operation for ten years is likely to have later evolved into the Civiele Raad, which may have initially also included local members. Hovy believes it is also likely that

[55] Hovy, *Plakkaatboek*, vol. 1; cxxiii.

[56] Arasaratnam, *Dutch Power in Ceylon*, 132. D.A. Kotelawele surmises that the population shift from north and north-central Sri Lanka to the south-west, which had begun after the so-called collapse of the Rajarata civilisation, was still continuing; these migrations were a perpetuation of that shift. D.A. Kotelawele, "Agrarian Policies of the Dutch in South-West Ceylon, 1743-1767," *A.A.G. Bijdragen* 14, no. 8 (1967): 21.

[57] Hovy, *Plakkaatboek*, vol. 1; cxxiii–cxxiv.

[58] Ibid., vol. 1; nr. 16, Ordinance for the commissioners of daily affairs as lawcourt in the first instance in the Galle district, with regulations concerning the registration of the alienation of immovable goods and the prescription law, 16 Jul 1648.

with the establishment of the Landraden after 1740, headmen had stopped being members of the Civiele Raad, which became a judicial forum attending exclusively to civil disputes among Europeans.[59] Landraden came to be established in Jaffna and Matara by the late seventeenth century. Some indications that they were also established in Colombo and Galle at that time can be seen in plakkaten, but they do not seem to have operated efficiently.[60] At times, the Civiele Raad adjudicated disputes among the natives, but there is evidence that in Colombo and Galle, the task mostly fell to the European dessave, referred to as an opziender in the Galle district. Before the reintroduction of the Landraad, the dessave and opziender tried petty cases that came up outside the town limits in consultation with the headmen. Local laws could not be brushed aside easily.

Yet, this state of affairs was unsatisfactory for the company. Governor Van Imhoff believed that the dessave had too much work and was unable to navigate all the legal discussions. The German Johann Wolffgang Heydt, who served the Dutch company in Sri Lanka in the 1730s, commented that "[f]or a small matter or a thing of no consequence [the people] begin a quarrel, so that our Desauwa has always enough to do in settling their disputes."[61] Heydt said that often, twenty to thirty litigants appeared in one day. Van Imhoff believed that at times the dessave was so busy that he was forced to leave disputes to be settled by the native officers, who engaged in "underhand dealings." In recommending the re-establishment of the Landraden in Colombo and Galle in 1740, Van Imhoff wished to release that officer from some of the hundreds of small disputes that were presented to him daily and to commission the new Landraden with the verification and registration of the ownership and possession of land. He envisaged that the dessave would thereby be less influenced by his native entourage as the Landraad was more difficult to mislead than a single person and because the council would include natives knowledgeable in traditional law. This was to maintain the peace, which he believed was crucial to safeguard the interests of both the company and the people.[62] The Landraad and land registration were ways of containing headmen, which the governor wished to do.

59 Hovy, *Plakkaatboek*, vol. 1; c.

60 Ibid., vol. 1; civ, n. 186.

61 Johann Wolffgang Heydt, *Heydt's Ceylon*, trans. R. Raven-Hart (Colombo: Ceylon Govt. Information Dept, 1952), 115. Heydt's book was first published in 1744.

62 Baron van Imhoff, *Memoir Left by Baron van Imhoff to His Successor, 1740*, trans. Sophia Pieters (Colombo: H.C. Cottle, Govt. Printer, 1911), 19–23; Hovy, *Plakkaatboek*, vol. 1; cv. See also Van Imhoff's "considerations" on management. SLNA 1/78, "Governor in Council minutes" (1740), 22-26 Feb 1740; SLNA 1/2784 & SLNA 1/2785, "Considerations by Governor Van Imhoff on the Management of the Island" (1740).

Van Imhoff served as governor-general in Batavia from 1743 to 1750 and was referred to even in the eighteenth century as an "enlightened" senior employee of the VOC.[63] Jonathan Israel writes that Van Imhoff thought it necessary "to extend control, rationalize administration, law, and health measures as well as trade."[64] In his memoir, in which he spells out his proposals for the thombo and the Landraad, Van Imhoff says the subject of his treatise is the interests of the company, which to him lies "in the right of exclusive occupation and in the peaceful possession of such territory as is necessary for obtaining the profits which the country yields, and under suitable administration; so that there may be a surplus and no deficit in these profits."[65] The expansion of trade was high on his agenda, but he still had wide intellectual interests, and administrative and legal matters were important to him.

Van Imhoff's recommendations were passed on till the end of company rule. His ideas for the Landraad were given at the start of volumes of instructions for the Galle Landraad, and were referred to in discussions during proceedings of the council, and in reference to the thombo registration in as late as 1791.[66] Alicia Schrikker refers to the later use of Van Imhoff's writings in her comments on the philosopher Abbé Raynal's advice to the VOC in the 1770s to restore harmony in the colonies by promoting agriculture and redistributing land to the poor: "Van de Graaff's predecessors like Van Goens and Van Imhoff had also expressed their intention to contain the native headmen and to encourage agricultural development of the island. Although they never succeeded in this, their writings may have served as much as examples for the officials on Ceylon as that of Raynal." Further reflecting Van Imhoff's wide influence, Raynal himself relied on his comments on the company.[67] More research is necessary to determine if Van Imhoff was influenced by contemporary European intellectual thought, but it is possible that his extended experience of local considerations led to the promulgation and implementation of his reforms.

[63] Jonathan I. Israel, *Democratic Enlightenment: Philosophy, Revolution, and Human Rights 1750-1790* (Oxford: Oxford University Press, 2011), 543.

[64] Ibid., 544.

[65] Van Imhoff, *Memoir Left by Van Imhoff*, 6.

[66] See an early discussion in SLNA 1/2805, "Galle Landraad minutes (20 Dec 1745) and Governor's comments (5 Feb 1746)" (1745–1746). Summaries of his recommendations for the Landraad and thombo are given in SLNA 1/5658, "Extracts of resolutions, orders, etc. regarding the Landraad and the thombo compilation" (1740 to 1745), fols. 4r–6v; SLNA 1/6204, "Digest of orders & extracts from council minutes etc. received by the Galle Landraad" (1745 to 1779), fols. 1r–6v. In 1791 as well, the Governor in Council cited Governor Van Imhoff's memoir of 12 March 1740. SLNA 1/214, "Governor in Council minutes" (1791), 9 Apr 1791.

[67] Alicia Schrikker, *Dutch and British Colonial Intervention in Sri Lanka, 1780-1815: Expansion and Reform* (Leiden: Brill, 2007), 101. Abbe Raynal's work is the multivolume *Histoire Philosophique et Politique des Établissements et du Commerce des Européens dans les Deux Indes*, first published in 1770.

Although most consider it Van Imhoff's idea to start a new registration and set up more Landraden on a solid footing, these measures gained momentum under Governor Julius Valentijn Stein van Gollonesse in the 1740s. Van Gollonesse, a company official of some merit, was the commander of Malabar before he took up the governorship of Dutch Sri Lanka in 1743. He served there till 1751, when he was appointed director-general in Batavia.[68] He had had some experience with the administration of justice in Malabar, where he had called for diligent work by the members of the court.[69] After Van Imhoff's departure in 1739, Willem Maurits Bruyninck and Daniel Overbeek held office till 1743.[70] Some work towards the establishment of the Landraad and thombos began in their terms, but it was Van Gollonesse who issued the first set of instructions on thombo registration, and S.A.W. Mottau remarks that he seemed to adhere strictly to Van Imhoff's recommendations.[71] Van Gollonesse, as we will see in his intervention in a discussion in the mid-1740s, played a key role in the company's attempt to set up a standardised social and economic regime through the Landraad and thombo registration.

Landraden came to be established throughout coastal Sri Lanka following further territorial expansion and administrative encroachment after 1766. By 1789, ten Landraden were in operation in Sri Lanka. The Landraden in Matara and Jaffna were the oldest – they were in operation as far back as at least 1661.[72]

[68] A. Galletti, *The Dutch in Malabar: Being a Translation of Selections Nos. 1 and 2* (Madras: Govt. Press, 1911), 37. Van Gollonesse is associated in Sri Lanka mostly with the building of the Wolvendaal Church in Colombo. R.L. Brohier, *De Wolvendaalsche Kerk* (Colombo: Consistory of Wolvendaal Church, 1957), 3.

[69] On leaving Malabar, Van Gollonesse states in his memoir: "Justice was pretty irregularly administered when I arrived here. The Court of Justice has now been provided with good books, among others the Ceylon Blaffert kindly sent to us from that island by the Right Worshipful van Imhoff. Moreover all extracts from political Council Resolutions and Home and Batavia letters are now communicated to the Court of Justice, and are bound together and properly indexed. By this the work of the members of this court is not a little lightened, if they will only take the trouble to go through the papers diligently." Galletti provides a note on "blaffert," calling it a list or register and stating that it was probably a collection of ordinances from Batavia. Galletti, *The Dutch in Malabar*, 80.

[70] Overbeek admits that nothing was done since van Imhoff first gave orders for the registration. Daniel Overbeek, *Memoir of Daniel Overbeek, Governor of Ceylon*, trans. K.D. Paranavitana (Colombo: Dept of National Archives, 2009), 62.

[71] S.A.W. Mottau, "Documents on Ceylon History (2): Documents Relating to the Tombo Registration of the Dutch Administration in Ceylon: Instructions Issued to the Tombo Commissioners," *Ceylon Historical Journal* 3, no. 2 (1953): 175. See also Van Gollonesse's memoir: Julius Stein van Gollenesse, *Memoir of Julius Stein van Gollenesse*, 1751, trans. Sinnappah Arasaratnam (Colombo: Dept of National Archives, 1974), 53–55.

[72] Instructions issued in 1661 refer to the re-establishment of the Landraad in Matara, so its inception was at an even earlier date. Sophia Pieters, trans., *Instructions from the Governor-General and Council of India to the Governor of Ceylon, 1656 to 1665* (Colombo: H.C. Cottle, Govt. Printer,

The Colombo and Galle Landraden began operating on a stable footing from 1741. Other locations with Landraden from time to time were Chilaw, Puttalam, Mannar, Mullaitivu, Trincomalee, and Batticaloa. They did not all operate in the same manner; Governor Van Imhoff highlighted the lack of efficiency in the Matara Landraad in his memoir. He wrote that former dessaves were negligent in their duties.[73] While the smooth functioning of the indigenous administration was vital for the profits of the VOC, aims akin to governmentality behind establishing the Landraden are not absent. Van Imhoff stressed that the purpose of the Landraden was "to help the people."[74] In the next section, I shall address the procedure for the new platform of the Landraad as faced by its inhabitants.

The Landraad in Operation

The Landraden had exclusive authority in disputes between natives who lived outside towns, but also heard cases involving Europeans.[75] It was said that they took on only cases involving sums between ten to eighty rixdollars, but it is possible that they also exercised authority in cases of higher value.[76] Disputes related to higher values could be submitted to the Civiele Raad or the Raad van Justitie. In general, the Landraad was a sort of court of first instance, after the chiefs immediately above the prospective litigants and the overseer (or dessave) had been approached. While the village headmen came first, people were permitted to reject their verdict and approach the Landraad under some circumstances. It is possible that headmen resolved most petty crimes and disputes, but in disputes over large amounts of property, indigenous litigants could seek out the Landraad if the verdict from the lower-ranking headmen, overseer, or commander proved unsatisfactory. Furthermore, if European officials believed that they could not handle a case, it could be heard in the Landraad. Governor Jan Schreuder, however, stipulated that

1908), 55, Instructions for the Guidance of the Dessave of Matura, having authority over the lands of Galle between the rivers Alican and Walawe, 21 Jun 1661. Nadaraja shows that the Matara and Jaffna Landraden may have existed since at least 1661. Marleen van den Horst states that the Matara Landraad was constituted in 1699, but did not function well. Nadaraja, *The Legal System of Ceylon*, 7; Van den Horst, *The Roman Dutch Law in Sri Lanka*, 41.

[73] Van Imhoff, *Memoir Left by Van Imhoff*, 19.

[74] Ibid.

[75] Most cases involving Europeans were heard in the judicial councils situated in the forts. In 1791, the Governor in Council quoted Governor Van Imhoff's memoir to note that the Landraad was really meant to settle disputes between the natives. SLNA 1/214, "Governor in Council minutes," 9 Apr 1791.

[76] Hovy, *Plakkaatboek*, vol. 1; cvii.

land matters must go to the Landraad.[77] It thus acquired an original jurisdiction over land disputes and in administering the sale of lands.

If regarded as a theatre, the Landraad was potentially dramatic. Specific rules and regulations strengthened its establishment as a new judicial forum for litigation. The Landraad of Galle was in Kumbalwella, about two kilometres north of an enclave of VOC officials in Galle Fort. The village was the seat of the overseer of Galle, who was also the president of the Landraad. The doors of the council were usually closed. Only the councillors, litigants and their *procureurs* (procurators or process representatives) or special representatives could be present in the room at any given moment. An exception was made when a sentence was pronounced; this was done with open doors (*met opene deuren*).

Members of the Landraad were assigned distinct tasks and had to follow protocol. The councillors took an oath of allegiance on their first appointment to the Landraad and on a yearly basis thereafter.[78] The registrars of the thombo were also members of the Landraad. The importance accorded to ceremony is evident from a perceived offence committed when introducing two new local members, an incident that I will discuss in chapter two. When the president's duties in the countryside prevented him from attending Landraad meetings, the vice-president – chosen from among the members of the Galle Political Council – would preside in his absence.[79] Meetings at which both the president and vice-president were absent were rare.[80] In the Landraad, the secretary was a pivotal figure responsible for the council's administration. He maintained the archives and drew up documents such as declarations and copies of orders for litigants. Record-keeping was well regulated, if not always followed through properly. The secretary's duties were articulated clearly in the instructions of 1789.[81] The *bode* (messenger) of

[77] Jan Schreuder, *Memoir of Jan Schreuder Governor of Ceylon Delivered to His Successor Lubbert Jan Baron van Eck on March 17, 1762*, trans. E. Reimers (Colombo: Ceylon Govt. Press, 1946), 50.

[78] Hovy, *Plakkaatboek*, vol. 2; nr. 628, (I, 12; IV, 15), Instructions for the Landraden, including extracts from resolutions, 25 Jun 1789. See for translation S.A.W. Mottau, trans., "Instructions for the Respective 'Landraden' of this Government (Extract from the Dutch Political Council Minutes of 25th June 1789)," *Journal of the Dutch Burger Union of Ceylon* 55, no. 1–4 (1965): 14. The formulas of these oaths are given in SLNA 1/5666, "Miscellaneous Documents of the Galle Landraad Including Instructions" (1761 to 1789), fols. 20v–22v.

[79] Hovy, *Plakkaatboek*, vol. 2; nr. 488 (21), Instructions for the Overseer of the Galle Kōralē, 28 Jul 1766.

[80] The 1789 instructions state that if the president and the vice president were both unavailable, the oldest member in rank should preside over a meeting. Hovy, *Plakkaatboek*, vol. 2; nr. 628, (I, 2), 25 Jun 1789.

[81] Other duties included maintaining the council's accounts on fines and taxes on immovable property and the payment of salaries to the councillors. Ibid., IV, 6-7

the Landraad held the responsibility of informing members about meetings and circulating documents.

Table 1.1 Galle Landraad meetings 1760–1795

Type	*1760–65*	*1766–71*	*1772–77**	*1778–83*	*1784–89*	*1790–95*	*Total*
Full sittings	41	114	88	159	105	93	600
Commissioners	-	-	3	61	38	10	112
Rondvraag	8	-	-	-	10	1	19
Unknown	-	-	3	-	-	-	3
Total	49	114	94	220	153	104	734

**Note: Records for the years 1773 and 1777 are not available.*
Sources: SLNA 1/6498-6525, Galle Landraad minutes from 26 April 1760 to 12 December 1795.

Records show three types of Landraad consultations apart from the registration meetings of the thombo commissioners. They are full sittings, commissioners' meetings, and decision-making through *rondvraag* (by circulation of documents). Table 1.1 shows the types of over seven hundred meetings held from 1760 to 1795 at six-year intervals.[82] This data must be considered keeping in mind that there are some gaps in the available minutes. Full sittings were mostly referred to as ordinary meetings, and a majority of the members were expected to be present for these; they only took up matters that could be decided by the full council. Seven meetings were called extraordinary meetings, and two had the words "express" and "extraordinary express." As all members had full-time jobs in the company, some duties were delegated to the *beurthebbende leden* (rotated members) of the council, who decided on matters or deferred decisions to the full board. Such commissioners' meetings had two members, usually European, and on one rare occasion, four. The Landraad minutes reveal that they were mostly responsible for hearing interrogations in connection with the oath – I will discuss this further in chapter four. Commissioners also presided over the execution of land transfers.[83] Minutes that carry the word rondvraag contain decisions that the members arrived at by circulating papers among themselves without a physical meeting. The Landraad usually met on Saturdays (576 times out of 734), and sometimes also on weekdays that seem to have been reserved for commissioners' meetings. No meetings were recorded to have been held on Sundays.

82 In general, I use the word "meetings," but it must be kept in mind that the few consultations by *rondvraag* were not strictly speaking physical meetings.

83 These were recorded in separate volumes.

Issues of efficiency did affect the Landraad. Governor Van Imhoff had wished for the council to meet once a week, and the 1789 instructions state that the president could summon the council for both ordinary and extraordinary sessions as often as necessary.[84] Based on the available minutes, the first six years saw less than half the number of meetings of the following six-year periods. This was an expected result of the instability caused by the war with Kandy in 1760–1765. The available records throughout the period 1760–1778 contain gaps, with no records at all for 1773 and 1777. If there had been records for these years, the 1772–1777 period would have had a higher number of meetings.[85] From around May 1778, the available meeting data appears continuous, and we see a significant increase in the volume of meeting records thereafter. Despite Van Imhoff's recommendation, in practice, the council did not hold meetings every week and a clear decline in the number of meetings is seen in the last few years. This may be due to the inefficiency that I discuss below. Meetings of both the full council and the commissioners show a sudden increase from 1781 to 1785 and a decline thereafter.[86] The increase in the first half of the 1780s may have been due to better administration – which came into effect when, for over four years, Anoldus de Lij and Willem Jacob Van de Graaff were commanders and the junior Abraham Samlant was the overseer. It may have been because more thombos were registered in those years, which could have led to increased litigation and resultant pressure on the council to settle disputes.

Colonial courts were often poorly staffed.[87] The Galle Landraad and its thombo registration work inevitably ran into difficulties due to lack of commitment, knowledge and time on the part of the members. I detail concerns regarding the thombo commissioners below and address the issue of non-attendance, especially of "white" members, in the next chapter. A case taken up in December 1779 was delayed till the litigants reappeared in July 1784 and complained that the commissioners'

[84] Van Imhoff, *Memoir Left by Van Imhoff*, 21; SLNA 1/5658, "Galle Landraad, extracts of resolutions," fols. 5r–5v, Extracts from Van Imhoff's memoir; Hovy, *Plakkaatboek*, vol. 2; nr. 628, (I, 3), 25 Jun 1789. Cleghorn's minute states that it met five times a week under the Dutch. Ralph Pieris, "Administration of Justice and Revenue on the Island of Ceylon under the Dutch Government ('The Cleghorn Minute')," *Journal of the Ceylon Branch of the Royal Asiatic Society*, n.s., 3 pt. 2 (1953): 138. That was only required for a certain period for those members who were in charge of the thombo registration. SLNA 1/5658, "Galle Landraad, extracts of resolutions" fols. 2v, Index of principle orders regarding the Landraad and thombo registration.

[85] References to decisions made in the gap years can be found, so the records would have existed at some point.

[86] In the years for which there is continuous meeting data, the figures are: 1779: *26*; 1780: *26*; 1781: *41*; 1782: *44*; 1783: *54*; 1784: *35*; 1785: *37*; 1786: *19*; 1787: *29*; 1788: *17*; 1789: *16*; 1790: *14*; 1791: *14*; 1792: *17*; 1793: *21*; 1794: *19*; 1795: *19*.

[87] Sally Engle Merry, "Colonial Law and its Uncertainties," *Law and History Review* 28, no. 4 (2010): 1067.

investigation had not been completed.[88] In 1793, the then secretary of the council, Jan Pieter Simon Cadenski, who had served for almost seven years since October 1786, was demoted and replaced by Pieter Arend de Moor. In subsequent meetings, Cadenski was berated for not maintaining proper records and delaying cases unnecessarily. Many litigants came forward in 1793 with complaints regarding his inefficiency. Cadenski's superiors were, of course, also to blame. He was probably made the scapegoat for their lack of efficiency, as the records show that other members of the Landraad were at fault as well. Councillors, not excluding the president, were often absent on *springtochten* (trips) to Colombo and other places, and the office of the president saw changes in 1787, 1788 and 1790. Furthermore, eight members died while serving on the Landraad during Cadenski's tenure. In 1792, a year when just seventeen meetings were held, two consecutive full meetings were cancelled, as only two councillors apart from the president and the secretary were present.[89] Collaboration with headmen also declined that year; compared to other years they were absent from the most number (six) of full meetings. I address their absence in more detail in the next chapter. Cadenski's term as secretary hit a low that was not seen before or after (except during war), but this exception reveals how the Landraad's administration could go unchecked for many years.

The quality of records maintained during Secretary Cadenski's term was low.[90] The Landraden were among the first "courts" of record, where oral proceedings were also recorded, unlike in the indigenous legal system. In the local system, proceedings were oral and did not have written pleas. At times, official responses in the Landraad were noted in some detail in the margins of the council minutes and – despite being laborious to transcribe – provided valuable information on the stand of a given litigant on a suit's narrative. Written replies submitted by parties have either not survived in the archives or are difficult to trace among the annexes that remain. In their absence, marginal comments (*marginale opmerkingen*) could provide a record of each party's version of events. For the first time, peasants were faced with considerable requirements for potentially costly paperwork at the Landraad.

[88] Augustinus Ferdinandus Wiresinghe, Christian Hendrik Haartel and Harmanus Engelbregt had been appointed to investigate the matter, but in 1784 only Wiresinghe remained on the council. He said that although the investigation had been conducted, the report had not been written as the other members had left the council. The Landraad ordered a new investigation. SLNA 1/6512, "Galle Landraad minutes" (1779), fols. 98r, 11 Dec 1779; SLNA 1/6521, "Galle Landraad draft minutes" (1779 to 1780), fols. 38v, 24 Dec 1779; SLNA 1/6525, "Galle Landraad draft minutes" (1784 to 1786), fols. 45r, 10 Jul 1784.

[89] SLNA 1/6515, "Galle Landraad minutes" (1787 to 1793), fols. 357v–358r, 22 Sept 1792; 358v, 13 Oct 1792.

[90] SLNA 1/6515 is a meeting volume that covers more than five years, and the haphazard and careless manner in which it was maintained appears to have been his particular style.

The council primarily operated in Dutch, with interpreters translating from the vernaculars at sessions involving natives. The introduction of the Dutch language in Sri Lanka was not a success.[91] Yet, evidence of some borrowing from administrative (and other) forms of Dutch can be seen in Sinhala. The Landraad was likely referred to as the *lānthrāduva* up to the early nineteenth century and *citātie* (summons) still exists as *sithāsi* in the Sinhala lexicon.[92] The original *olas* of deeds submitted in Sinhala and Tamil were kept among the annexes of the Landraad, and are thus visibly present in the archives – testimony to the wide reach of the council. The language in use at the time – including all the connotations that a single word could arouse in the minds of a speaker, hearer, writer or reader – would constitute a separate study by itself; in this work, I have only made an attempt to analyse terminology where relevant. Historians face an uphill task when attempting to understand how eighteenth-century officials grasped local customs and land tenure. At least some, if not all, native councillors were conversant in Dutch and could follow proceedings without interpreters.

Thus, the indigenous inhabitants faced a new language of proceedings in the Landraad. The interpreter (*tolk*), who had to be present at sessions of both commissioners and the full council,[93] played an important role. Most cases, it can be imagined, were heard in at least two languages, except where litigants also spoke Dutch and the full proceedings could be carried out in that language (assuming that all headmen present understood Dutch). Depositions were written out in reported speech in Dutch, and interrogations had to be prepared in advance; their answers were also recorded in reported speech. Other documents produced in the Landraad were also in Dutch, including the thombos and their extracts, which were given out to peasants – who did not understand the language.[94] But this did not mean that they underestimated the importance of the thombo, as chapter five shows. An interpreter always signed depositions and interrogations. In such a setting, the interpreter could have been amenable to bribes.[95] It is likely that they played a key

[91] J. van Goor, *Jan Kompenie as Schoolmaster: Dutch Education in Ceylon 1690-1795* (Groningen: Wolters-Noordhoff, 1978), 41–43.

[92] The word *lānthrāduva* was found among early nineteenth-century documents in the private collection of Siran Deraniyagala. Carter traces the origin of *sithāsi* to Portuguese, but it is more likely to have spread among the inhabitants in Dutch times. Charles Carter, "Sithāsi," in *A Sinhalese-English Dictionary* (Colombo: M.D. Gunasena & Co. Ltd, 1924; repr. 1965), 679.

[93] Hovy, *Plakkaatboek*, vol. 2; nr. 628, (V, 2), 25 Jun 1789.

[94] In Jaffna, the thombos were maintained in both Tamil and Dutch. Alicia Schrikker, "'Op de dijk gezet': Schuld, onrust en bestuurlijk onzekerheid in Jaffna in de achttiende eeuw," in Lodewijk Wagenaar (ed), *Aan de overkant: Ontmoetingen in dienst van de VOC en WIC (1600-1800)* (Leiden: Sidestone Press, 2015), 161.

[95] The case of the tolk Don Bastiaan is found in SLNA 1/2893, "Diary kept by the Commissioner Abraham Samlant during an Investigation into the Revolts in the Matara Dessavony" (1757 to 1758),

role in helping the natives understand the new legal space of the Landraad, while councillors were forbidden from counselling or advising litigants or prospective litigants.[96]

The local system had not included lawyers, but in the Landraad, procureurs of European origin or *burgers* (private citizens, or retired servants of the company) were active to a limited extent. At the least, petitioners needed assistance drawing up legal documents. Litigants were not required to engage a procurator unless they wished to.[97] They could be represented by procurators at their own cost; most cases were not argued by procurators. In contrast, procurators were common in other councils of law. In 1794, however, VOC decided not to allow procurators in the Colombo Landraad.[98] Justinus Rutgard Visser was one such procurator who appeared on behalf of litigants in the Galle Landraad. Born in Colombo, his first appointment was in 1755 as a *hooploper* (untrained sailor); he was appointed as an assistant in 1763 and a bookkeeper in 1771.[99] This indicates that a procurator was likely to have been self-made. In one case, we also see a pretender to the position: in 1778, the Landraad instructed the messenger to warn a *vrijman* (a European/Eurasian who had left company service) not to prepare any more documents as they were incomprehensible.[100] Procurators had the power to speak in a litigant's absence.

Dissemination of information is an important aspect of the operation of a judicial body. In the pre-colonial or Kandyan system as well, knowing exactly how to approach the king, an official or judicial body in order to receive justice was part of its efficient operation. Such knowledge of procedure was an essential part of the power structure that enabled the central state to enforce authority. Before sessions dedicated to thombo registration, villagers were summoned by *tamblinjeros* (drummers), a tool of authority for the company. Plakkaten or proclamations by the Governor in Council, translated into Sinhala and Tamil, were set up in ambalam, churches or on prominent trees and read out aloud. A printing press set up in 1737 was important in this regard. The means of transmitting information about the contents of laws and legal administrative structures became critical for the

fols. 10r–14r, 23-26 Sept 1757. I thank Dr Lodewijk Wagenaar for providing me access to a transcription of this document.

96 Hovy, *Plakkaatboek*, vol. 2; nr. 628, (I, 8), 25 Jun 1789.

97 Ibid., II, 33. See also Marie-Charlotte Le Bailly, *Recht voor de Raad* (Haarlem & Hilversum: Historische Vereniging Holland & Uitgeverij Verloren, 2001), 140.

98 SLNA 1/226, "Governor in Council minutes" (1794), 8 Apr 1794.

99 S.A.W. Mottau, "Alphabetical Index to the Registers of the Acts of Appointments of Company's Servants of the Dutch East India Company Issued at the Galle Secretariat (1645-1796)" (n.d.), Research Room, Sri Lanka National Archives.

100 SLNA 1/6520, "Galle Landraad draft minutes" (1778 to 1779), fols. 44v, 31 Oct 1778.

circulation of law. Headmen were responsible for serving written summons, for which they used *lascarins* (soldiers). Such written traditions thus intermixed with oral traditions within new institutional structures.

Legal Procedure

In today's world, we take for granted that any legal system requires rules to ensure that a judicial body deals with all cases in an equitable manner. English lawyer Sir Jack Jacob argues that the function of civil procedural law is "to infuse life into all other areas of the law, to bring into actual being and to give reality and effect to all the legal rights and duties of every person and body in society."[101] Procedural and substantive law tends to be studied individually, but the study of law *in* society requires a combination of the two. The Landraad would have been "new" in so far as its laws *and* methods were new. Knowledge of the procedure to sue someone could have been vital for a litigant. For an ordinary peasant, what were the hurdles to having a complaint heard in the Landraad, building up a case with evidence and ensuring the enforcement of a sentence? We may never know the answer in full and from all angles, but we can attempt to reconstruct the legal procedure that the peasant was willingly or unwillingly subject to. The local legal order used various devices in the pursuit of justice, including the veläkma mentioned previously, oaths and ordeals linked to a divine power, and witnesses on trial. I will describe the overlaps between the two legal orders here and in still more detail in chapter four on the matter of the oath. The norms of different groups in adjudication practices could collide or coexist.

By the company's own admission, lawsuits were long drawn out and litigants faced financial difficulties. It was the company's stated intention to expedite and simplify legal procedures for the convenience of poorer indigenous litigants. The VOC recognised that the primary reason for delays were the procedures followed in the Landraad. The more complicated procedures would have been alien to the natives. The Landraad adopted two options for proceeding with a case: a summary or non-summary method. These methods resemble the *eigenlijke rechtspraak* and *oneigenlijke rechtspraak* described in Dutch legal literature. In the first, a *cas van oppositie* (case of opposition) followed, and in the second, the supplicant requests the authorities to reach a decision without such a case.[102] In 1745, they decided that disputes heard at the Landraad would adopt the summary (*de plano* or *summier*)

[101] Sir Jack I.H. Jacob, *The Fabric of English Civil Justice* (London: Stevens & Sons, 1987), 63.

[102] H. de Schepper et al., "Prolegomena voor onderzoek van rechtspraak en bestuur in de oude Nederlanden," in J. Koster van Dijk and A. Wijffels (eds), *Miscellanea forensia historica: Ter gelegenheid van het afscheid van Prof. Mr. J. Th de Smidt* (Amsterdam: Werkgroep Grote Raad van Mechelen, 1988), 279.

method and not produce pleas and counter-pleas.[103] In the summary method, which was a short oral procedure, decisions were quickly delivered. Still, many cases did go through the more complicated non-summary procedure, for which the litigants required assistance. In that process, what the litigants had to say needed to be given in writing.

The summary method, according to the 1789 instructions, had "already been generally observed by some Landraads with good results" and dispensed with the need for "filing of plaints, answers, counter-pleas and rejoinders, of questions and counter-questions or *reprochen* [objections] and *salvatiën* [salvations], of deductions, memoranda or inventories, etc." But it was applicable only in so far as both parties were natives; if native chiefs and other prominent persons were involved in an important case, they could request the non-summary method (with due regard by the Landraad for possible exploitation by influential natives). If a company servant or burger was a defendant in a case, he or she could choose the non-summary method. If both parties were company servants or burgers, either party could opt for the summary method, otherwise the usual, full procedure would follow.[104]

Concluding the matter as fast as possible and at low cost meant that cases were dealt with economically. The summary method was assigned early on in 1745, but the 1789 instructions for the Landraad state that the influence of the procureurs led to the procedure gradually resembling that of the Raad van Justitie, where the non-summary method was in use.[105] This, the Governor in Council believed, would disadvantage the peasants, for whom the case itself often cost more than the value of the dispute. Litigants would plea for a swift conclusion due to poverty or for consideration for *pro deo*.[106] While in the Landraad costs increased due to the procedure, in the pre-colonial system the absence of a fixed fee led to corruption.[107] The fixed charges of the Landraad pre-empted this. Landraad procedures and the loss of cultivation rights resulted in pecuniary difficulties. Next I will detail the procedures followed when a case was referred to the Landraad, presumably by the dessave or commander or on the initiative of a litigant.

103 SLNA 1/94, "Governor in Council minutes" (1745), fols. 111r, 11 Feb 1745; SLNA 1/5658, "Galle Landraad, extracts of resolutions," fols. 18r, Extract from the resolution dated 11 Feb 1745.

104 Hovy, *Plakkaatboek*, vol. 2; nr. 628, (II, 29-37), 25 Jun 1789.

105 Ibid., 903.

106 SLNA 1/6513, "Galle Landraad minutes" (1780), fols. 19v, 1 Apr 1780. *Pro deo* was awarded to one woman: SLNA 1/6511, "Galle Landraad minutes" (1778), fols. 89v, 28 Nov 1778. Two other requests for *pro deo* were made, but decisions on them were delayed: SLNA 1/6514, "Galle Landraad minutes" (1781), fols. 94v–95r, 21 Jul 1781.

107 Cooray, *Legal System*, 111.

From rekest to sententie

The procedure followed in courts in the Dutch Republic is, in essence, likely to have been the template for the non-summary procedure practised in Dutch judicial councils in Sri Lanka as well. However, the exact variations in practice can only be understood through extensive case analysis.[108] Prospective litigants first sent in written requests or petitions or presented their cases orally. The full council would hear the initial petition in Kumbalwella. Usually, a stamped petition called a *rekest* or *rekwest* (request) from the supplicant or his procureur was first addressed to the Landraad's president and other members of the council. The request did not have to be in writing – it could also be delivered orally. Some requests are in the annexes of the Landraad.[109] The precise date on which the petition was brought forward is not always possible to determine. The petition itself may no longer be available, and if it is, it may have been undated; but as Schepper et al. decided, when working with process bundles, the date on the *appoinctement* (decision) or *apostil* (minute) on the petition is considered the first known date of a case.[110] The Landraad often recorded in the minutes the day that a request was made; they summarised it, but did not include its text. If a request involved a complaint against another party, the council was required to issue summons to both parties and their witnesses and fix a returnable day.[111] The procedure for issuing summons, however, was different if the defendant was a burger.[112] Non-appearance by plaintiffs and defendants was punished with fines of half or one rixdollar.[113] The instructions state that the fines

[108] An example of an image from the minutes from the Staatse Raad of Vlaanderen in Middelburg in 1784 closely resembles documentation found in the Landraad. Marie-Charlotte Le Bailly, *Staatse Raad van Vlaanderen te Middelburg (1599-1795): De hoofdlijnen van het procederen in civiele zaken voor de Staatse Raad van Vlaanderen, zowel in eerste instantie als in hoger beroep*, Procesgids 6 (Hilversum: Verloren, 2007), 47.

[109] See SLNA 1/6526, "Annexes to Galle Landraad minutes" (1780 to 1782), fols. 56r. Claas Fontijn's request before the Landraad can be illustrative to some degree of how an individual made a request before the council. His case is explored in greater detail in chapter six.

[110] Schepper et al., "Prolegomena," 278.

[111] An example of summons signed by a Landraad clerk can be found in SLNA 7/2353, "Inward Letters, Galle Landraad" (1778 to 1801), Citatie dated 15 Nov 1782. The parties concerned, the day of the next hearing and the issue at hand are mentioned in this. The 1789 instructions refer to a specimen and state that the Sinhalese and Tamils who had lawsuits before the Landraad were not required to use stamped paper in order to ease the financial burden on them. Hovy, *Plakkaatboek*, vol. 2; nr. 628, (II, 7-11; IV, 12), 25 Jun 1789. In any case, no money was given to a scribe for writing summons for the thombo compilation as that may have hindered the registration process. SLNA 1/5658, "Galle Landraad, extracts of resolutions," fols. 13r-v, Extract resolution from 14 Sept 1744; SLNA 1/92, "Governor in Council minutes" (1744), 222v–24, 14 Sept 1744.

[112] Hovy, *Plakkaatboek*, vol. 2; nr. 628, (II, 11), 25 Jun 1789.

[113] Ibid., II, 13-14

went into a Landraad "box," but the minutes refer to the diocese poor being the beneficiary.[114]

According to the summary procedure described in the 1789 instructions, the plaintiff, defendant and witnesses were summoned before the commissioners of the council for a first hearing, during which the commissioners would attempt to settle the case to the satisfaction of both parties. If such mediation was not possible, the commissioners had to examine both parties and their witnesses, and inquire into all the facts of the case as far as possible. A maximum of four hearings could be held before the commissioners for each case, after which a report had to be submitted to the full council, which would then decide on a judgement. The commissioners could provide their opinions on the case and make necessary observations.[115] However, there is no evidence that the commissioners carried out this procedure in practice; most of their meetings in Galle that I found only heard counter-interrogations. The full council of the Galle Landraad, however, did apply the summary method, possibly applying its own variations of the practice.

The summary method was meant as a primarily oral process, but was essentially a mix of oral and written practices. In the non-summary method, pleas and counter-pleas provided the mechanisms through which evidence and statements could be presented. Yet, provision was made for native inhabitants to also file papers, including written plaints and depositions of witnesses.[116] As evidence, they produced supporting documents such as thombo extracts, olas in Sinhala and Tamil and their translations, oral statements or depositions by witnesses. If witnesses were necessary, depositions could be made as required, usually before the secretary of the Landraad at his residence, or they could provide oral evidence in the council. The witnesses, the secretary, two other witnesses and the interpreter signed the depositions. They were always made on the promise of an oath, but another procedure had to be followed in order for them to be allowed to swear on a statement: a deposition had to be brought in *forma probanti*, a process that I will explain in more detail in chapter four. In that process, the opposing parties challenged each other's witnesses by producing *contra-interrogatorieën* (counter-interrogations) that procureurs drew up beforehand. The aim was to dissuade the council from allowing the oath to be admitted to the witnesses. The list of questions can be quite illuminating of the particulars of the case at hand; the carefully thought-out arguments of both sides aimed to sway the Dutch and indigenous councillors in the Landraad in a particular direction. In the non-summary procedure, witnesses may

114 See SLNA 1/6512, "Galle Landraad minutes," fols. 43r, 19 Jun 1779.

115 Hovy, *Plakkaatboek*, vol. 2; nr. 628, (II, 17-20, 39), 25 Jun 1789.

116 Ibid., II, 31

also be summoned along with the parties concerned for the first hearing and their oral statements recorded in the minutes.[117]

The summary procedure required that a decision be arrived at as soon as possible. It was not as formal as when the Landraad produced a *sententie* or sentence, which was heard in public. Before a more formal sentence, the decision to deliver judgement would be announced at the previous meeting, and the relevant documents would be circulated among the members of the council. The sentence identified the plaintiff and defendant clearly. Figure 1.1 illustrates its format. They took decisions based on a majority of votes.[118] The council was ordered to deliver the sentence even if the defendants did not appear.[119] All judgements had to be made in the name of the "Hoogmogende," or members of the States General in The Netherlands.[120] The 1789 instructions state that they also had to provide reasons for their judgements.[121] However, the council minutes hardly ever gave justifications for judgements, as Marleen van den Horst has discussed. A subsequent order from 1791 allowed the Landraad to keep decisions short and simple.[122] In the pre-colonial legal order, a decree was communicated to the parties orally or, occasionally, in writing.[123] In land cases decided by the king, after referring such cases to the Mahanaduva, "Decrees written on Ola called Sittu are signed and given by the Senior Adikar present, or sometimes by the 2nd Adikar, for Lands situated within his general local Jurisdiction."[124] The Mahanaduva did not give a copy of the decree to the losing party or retain one itself, but the Landraad was required to maintain accurate records of all cases brought before it.[125]

The Landraad was encouraged to deal with cases in a summary manner with as little expense as possible to the litigants, but some did go to appeal. In the pre-colonial legal order, an appeal on a judgement could be made at any point, and the procedure was quite simple – the party who wished to appeal presented the matter

117 Hovy, *Plakkaatboek*, vol. 2; nr. 628, (II, 16-18).

118 When the vote was equally divided between members, the 1789 instructions said the dispute should be decided in favour of the defendant. Hovy, *Plakkaatboek*, vol. 2; nr. 628, (I, 5), 25 Jun 1789.

119 SLNA 1/5658, "Galle Landraad, extracts of resolutions," fols. 9r, Extract resolution of 7 Mar 1744.

120 SLNA 1/6497, "Galle Landraad minutes," fols. 41v.

121 Hovy, *Plakkaatboek*, vol. 2; nr. 628, (I, 11), 25 Jun 1789.

122 Marleen H.J. van den Horst, *Compensation for Improvements: The Roman Dutch Law in Sri Lanka* (Amsterdam: Free University Press, 1989), 121–22.

123 Cooray, *Legal System*, 111.

124 The *sittu* mentioned the names of the parties concerned, the name of the land in question, the decision and the date, and the authority of either the king or the Mahanaduva. D'Oyly, *Constitution of the Kandyan Kingdom*, vol. 24:34.

125 Hovy, *Plakkaatboek*, vol. 2; nr. 628, (IV, 1), 25 Jun 1789.

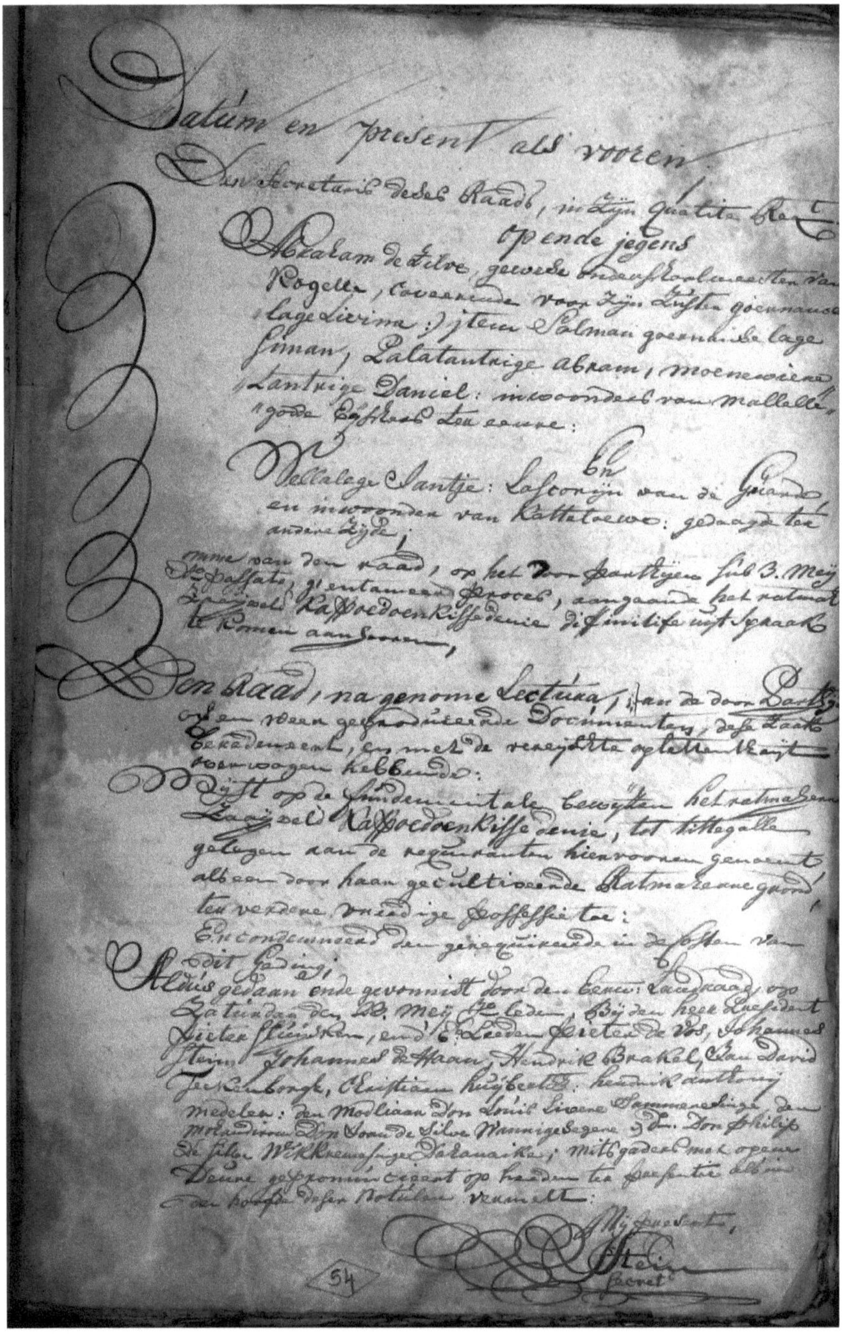

Figure 1.1 A sentence from the Galle Landraad minutes. SLNA 1/6502, fols. 54r, 13 June 1767.

to a higher court either in person or through a headman.[126] In the Dutch system, a defeated party had to give notice of the intention to appeal to the secretary of the Landraad within ten days of the judgement. First, the sentence was stayed, and a petition from the defeated party had to be transferred with a report from the Landraad to the commander of Galle, who would in turn seek the consideration of the Galle Political Council as to whether the appeal should be granted. The decision was to be minuted on the petition and its notice given to the president of the Landraad, who had to then inform the parties concerned. If the appeal was allowed, the minuted petition and all the documents of the case were sent to the Raad van Justitie before whom the case would be taken up in appeal. If that council found that the papers submitted were comprehensive, it could provide a judgement based on them, but if they were found to be lacking in some way, or if the parties concerned had further evidence to provide, the council gave an interlocutory order to produce that evidence. The party against whom such evidence was led could produce counter-questions or other evidence.[127]

Caseloads and Jurisdiction

What kinds of legal matters did litigants raise? To understand the nature of the issues heard in the Galle Landraad, I mapped out the administration of justice in that council through almost a hundred cases from the minutes of 1778–1779.[128] A larger sample that can show change over time was beyond the scope of this study, as the documents relating to each case were not filed in separate dossiers and had to be compiled from many registers of minutes, depositions, interrogations, annexes and correspondence. The Landraad minutes are indiscriminate collections of all the business transacted by the council. I did not follow a strict chronology, tracing as far as possible the start and end of each case, thereby in some instances effectively extending the period covered by the sample cases to both before and after 1778–1779. They include simple requests that the council settled immediately,

[126] Cooray, *Legal System*, 111.

[127] Hovy, *Plakkaatboek*, vol. 2; nr. 628, (III, 1-18), 25 Jun 1789. See also a resolution of the Governor in Council on 8 June 1773 in SLNA 1/5666, "Galle Landraad miscellaneous documents" fols. 26r.

[128] SLNA 1/6511, "Galle Landraad minutes"; SLNA 1/6512, "Galle Landraad minutes." Some entries, for unknown reasons, were found only in the draft minutes. SLNA 1/6520, "Galle Landraad draft minutes"; SLNA 1/6521, "Galle Landraad draft minutes." A larger sample or samples from before and after the period already studied could reveal either an increase or decrease in cases or include new issues. It would be especially interesting to see what happened during the time of Secretary Cadenski, who was recalled for inefficiency. However, further expansion of the historical reconstruction attempted on a small scale here depends on the accessibility of high-quality archival material in digital form.

ones where it appointed commissioners from the council to travel to a village to write a report, others where the supplicants had to provide more evidence, and cases that became civil suits with a plaintiff and defendant. The definition of a case used here is thus any matter involving a litigant brought before the Landraad. Strictly speaking, they are not all cases of litigation, but the incidence of any issue involving a supplicant in the council is taken as a historical event in this analysis.

The Landraad took up a small number of administrative matters; among them were notes on various orders that originated from the commander of Galle or the Governor in Council in Colombo and matters such as changes in appointments of councillors. The council addressed matters concerning incoming and outgoing members throughout its operation, as well as issues concerning the attendance, composition and competency of members. Outside the sample period, this included the discharge of inefficient members, as in the case of Johan Pieter Simon Cadenski mentioned earlier in this chapter. In addition, administrative matters pertaining to the thombos and other land concerns were also noted in the minutes of the Landraad. Thus, no sharp differentiation was made in the minutes between the spheres of the administration of justice and administrative matters of the council.[129]

Classifying cases under separate categories of law is not easy, and therefore I only attempt an overview of their nature here. The causes of litigation are too complex and ambiguous, and thus defy categorisation. Litigants, procurators and councillors made no reference to laws that were recorded in the sources. In some cases, we only know the names of the parties who appeared. This difficulty in grouping cases by subject was the result of different factors: the style of the council records; the fact that not all cases resulted in a sentence as high procedural costs and settlements may have led to their withdrawal; and patchy records (particularly in the minutes from 19 October 1776 to 16 May 1778, just before the sample taken here, and the available annexes). Although we do not know the outcome of some of the cases, we can assume that they were either settled or abandoned.[130]

Civil issues relating to immovable property form the bulk of the cases under private law. To a certain extent, this is a trivial conclusion, given that dealing with land issues was the principal task assigned to the council, though it also heard

[129] Cornelis van Bynkershoek, as a judge of the Hoge Raad (Supreme Court) of Holland, Zeeland and Westfriesland made notes in Latin and Dutch of cases that came before that court in the eighteenth century. Lee says many cases "turn upon intricate questions of procedure." Although it was further back in time, this was the case in the Hof van Holland in the fifteenth century as well. Robert Warden Lee, "Bynkershoek's Observationes Tumultuariae," *Journal of Comparative Legislation and International Law*, Third Series, 17, no. 1 (1935): 41; Le Bailly, *Recht voor de Raad*, 248. I thank Egbert Koops for drawing my attention to Bynkershoek's work.

[130] I have closely followed Le Bailly's solutions for the same problems that she faced in analysing the fifteenth-century Hof van Holland cases. Le Bailly, *Recht Voor de Raad*, 28–29.

other civil matters. Many cases involved land in some way (86 per cent); the rest were mostly debt issues, some of which were not related to land. Almost half the land matters concerned the transfer of property rights. Disputes about inheritance and possessory actions to recover lands feature prominently, as do disputes about the provision of labour services. From pre-Dutch times, different social formations performed obligatory services for the state (known as *rājakāriya*) that survived into Dutch and British times. The new colonial power assumed the administrative duties of such obligations. In return for performing various services in the roles of high- and low-level headmen, soldiers, artisans and coolies, among others, the sovereign awarded fixed amounts of land.[131] In the final analysis, as disputes over the service recorded in company documents had to do with access to property, such cases were also connected to land.

The occurrence of service issues is especially important in understanding that inhabitants regarded the thombo record as critical. In 1778, the heirs of a family by the name of Kandege in the Galle district asked to be recognised as *mayorāls* instead of *naindes*, a request that the Landraad granted. Among other duties, the mayorāl traditionally organised the compulsory service due from a village to the ruling power. He also reported to the Landraad on land matters and provided victuals for visiting commissioners and headmen. He was entitled to approximately four acres of land in return for his services. A nainde, in contrast, received an acre of land in return for performing menial tasks in the village. Four local councillors supported the Kandege family's claim, asserting that it was an old custom that when there were no mayorāls in a village the naindes took over the task. Accordingly, Kandege Jantje, his two sons Apponsu and Johannes, and his five nephews were entered in the new registration system of the thombo as mayorāls.[132] In another case heard that same year, a mayorāl of Naranowita successfully requested that the Landraad register his son by his first wife as a mayorāl as well because such titles were hereditary. Witānachchige Bastiaan said he had married his son Jantje's mother in the customary way. Jantje's mother's brother[133] claimed to be ignorant of his sister's marriage, although stating that Jantje was indeed her son and that he had brought up the boy when he was young till Bastiaan had taken him away. Another mayorāl and *schrijver* (writer) of a village nearby, said that they were not aware of the circumstances of his birth, but that Jantje had always been known as Bastiaan's son and had performed the mayorāl service for many years. Despite doubts about

131 See appendix III for this list.

132 SLNA 1/6511, "Galle Landraad minutes," fols. 37r, 11 Jul 1778.

133 He was also Bastiaan's cross cousin, and was married to Bastiaan's sister, so Jantje was both his and his wife's biological nephew.

a recognised marriage the council conceded to Bastiaan's request.[134] Also in my sample, the Landraad settled another service issue by allowing the litigants to perform the mayorāl service on a yearly rotating basis.[135] Much earlier, in 1760, Laurens Dias, who was a vidāne (a minor local headman), took mayorāls to task for registering his mother as a coolie.[136] Such negotiations on service identification through requests for changes in registration were important in gaining affluence, as service titles were connected to land holdings.

Movable property cases were also brought before the Landraad. One case concerned the ownership of a cow resulting from a dispute about its purchase.[137] Yet another case primarily concerned debt, but included a dispute about the ownership of a distillery kettle (and garden) used for the preparation of arrack, and which Cornelis Hendeling claimed back from Pellekettie Christina, who had had a son by his late son Matthijs Hendeling. Matthijs had left debts that Cornelis claimed to have settled. Christina, against whom Cornelis initiated the possessory action, argued that she had nothing to live on and wanted the case to be defended *pro deo* on her behalf, a request that was granted. Yet, she lost the case, and was required to pay Cornelis all that he had paid as settlement for his son's debts in a sentence that referred to the case as a debt matter.[138]

The Landraad frequently acted in an official capacity. It was involved in disposing of property belonging to a deceased person; in one case, an official of the Inlandse Boedelkamer (native estate board) appeared in the council for that purpose.[139] Another case involved an investigation into land belonging to a revenue

134 SLNA 1/6511, "Galle Landraad minutes," fols. 41r, 25 Jul 1778; SLNA 1/7512, "Naranowita (Walallawiti) Thombo" (1778), 13 (Group nr 5).

135 SLNA 1/6511, "Galle Landraad minutes," fols. 77r, 31 Oct 1778; 84r, 28 Nov 1778.

136 SLNA 1/6498, "Galle Landraad minutes," fols. 14r, 3 May 1760.

137 Like many others, this case has interesting interrogations that focus on trying to prove that the opposing parties' witnesses were not true Christians, in order to disprove their testimonies. See for the documentation of this case SLNA 1/6511, "Galle Landraad minutes," fols. 30r, 31r, 9 Jul 1778; 43r, 8 Aug 1778; 49r, 15 Aug 1778; 53r, 12 Sept 1778; 65r, 10 Oct 1778; SLNA 1/6512, "Galle Landraad minutes," fols. 14v, 6 Mar 1779; 20r, 27 Mar 1779; SLNA 1/6534, "Galle Landraad Interrogations" (1778 to 1784), fols. 2r–10v, 11r–15v, 9 Jul 1778.

138 Such cases of women coming forward were not rare as is further explained in chapter three. See SLNA 1/6494, "Galle Landraad depositions" (1778 to 1781), fols 4r, 17 Jul 1778; 43r–44r, 14 Apr 1779; SLNA 1/6511, "Galle Landraad minutes" (1778), fols 8r, 6 Jun 1778; 89v, 28 Nov 1778; SLNA 1/6512, "Galle Landraad minutes" (1779), fols 18r, 27 Mar 1779; 23r, 24 Apr 1779; 84r, 20 Nov 1779; 87r-v, 27 Nov 1779; SLNA 1/6514, "Galle Landraad minutes" (1781), fols 33r, 24 Feb 1781.

139 These cases were usually uneventful. See SLNA 1/6511, "Galle Landraad minutes," fols. 71r, 10 Oct 1778; SLNA 1/6512, "Galle Landraad minutes," fols. 11r, 20 Feb 1779; 66v, 11 Sept 1779; 80v, 20 Nov 1779; 91r, 27 Nov 1779; SLNA 1/6521, "Galle Landraad draft minutes," fols. 35v, 11 Dec 1779.

farmer and its subsequent sale to recover arrears in rent payments.[140] However, no cases of revenue farming involving rent payers and farmers were recorded in the sample registers, although such disputes fell under the jurisdiction of the Landraad.[141] In another case, Coenraad Hendeling, a sergeant in the *burgerij,* a community of urban citizens who formed a militia, was instructed to pay the mayorāl of Unawatuna twelve stivers as garden tax that remained in arrears for the accounting year of 1778–1779 and the costs of the case. Hendeling did not appear for the first summons nor a second served in September 1779, but he appeared in November. Together with the procurator Albertus Hissink, he handed over a request that was read out in the council; unfortunately, this is not available in the records.[142] Inhabitants often defaulted on tax payments.[143] This case indicates that the taxes recorded in the thombo were taken seriously and that the council could summon transgressors. Yet, such cases involving taxes or rents were rare, with only one example of each in the sample.

The emergence of a land market can already be seen at this time. In 1748, the Galle Political Council expressed concern that too many Sinhalese were transferring their lands to Moors, which they feared would lead to the Sinhalese "losing everything."[144] Permission for the sale of lands was frequently sought. The Landraad instructions of 1789 detail the regulations governing the sale of land.[145] The council appeared to be engaging in very ordinary business such as handling simple requests to sell land, but its approval was necessary to establish that the seller's title was alienable. This, as we will see in more detail in chapter five, was

[140] SLNA 1/6511, "Galle Landraad minutes," fols. 4r, 23 May 1778; 11r, 6 Jun 1778; 29v, 27 Jun 1778; 40v, 25 Jul 1778; 47r, 8 Aug 1778.

[141] Nadeera Rupesinghe (writing as Seneviratne), "Strange Cooperation: Revenue Farmers in Eighteenth-century Sri Lanka" (MPhil Dissertation, Leiden, Leiden University, 2010).

[142] It possibly held something that was unacceptable to the council, because when Hendeling is ordered to pay the garden tax according to the thombo, Hissink is also advised to abstain from "such thoughtless expressions." SLNA 1/6512, "Galle Landraad minutes," 64r, 11 Sept 1779; 68r, 25 Sept 1779; 76v, 20 Nov 1779.

[143] See Joan Gideon Loten, *Memoir of Joan Gideon Loten, Governor of Ceylon, Delivered to His Successor Jan Schreuder 1757*, trans. E. Reimers (Colombo: Ceylon Govt. Press, 1935), 23–24.

[144] SLNA 1/104, "Governor in Council minutes" (1748), 19 Apr 1748. The Governor in Council decided that Moors and "heathens" would only be allowed to possess those lands that they had planted, cultivated or legally inherited but not purchased, unless with special consent. It is not clear if this order was enforced. In one case, a Moorman was accused of raising the land price unreasonably. SLNA 1/6517, "Galle Landraad minutes" (1794), fols. 131v, 13 Dec 1794.

[145] Hovy, *Plakkaatboek*, vol. 2; nr. 628, (II, 43), 25 Jun 1789. For prohibition of sale of lands without the permission of the Landraad, see SLNA 1/98, "Governor in Council minutes" (1746), fols. 271v–272r, 11 Jul 1746. A new law was passed in 1784 stating that all transfers of land, whether by last will or otherwise, must be submitted to the Landraad. SLNA 1/188, "Governor in Council minutes" (1784), 9 Feb 1784.

the result of a perceived feudal nature of owning land. If entered as a *paravēni* (ancestral) plot in the thombo, a share could be easily sold. But before the Landraad permitted the sale of gardens, native commissioners had to investigate whether the land had cinnamon.[146] The perceived need to preserve existing cinnamon reflects the constant concern of the company regarding its supply. The investigations appear to have taken place in the presence of village headmen and the owners. The prospective seller had to pay the costs of the native commissioners in such an operation.[147] Outside my sample, in 1783, they found that twelve cinnamon trees were growing on a piece of land, and the council permitted the sale on the condition that the buyer lets the trees grow.[148] It was also necessary for the *thombohouder* (thombo-keeper) to confirm ownership.[149] In one case, drummers issued summons for claimants to come forward before the sale.[150] At times, disputes centred on whether a transaction was a sale or mortgage (*verpanding*),[151] although such instances did not occur in my sample. For example, Maria Bouman, who reappears in chapter six, claimed that she and Jacob Floorman had not sold, but mortgaged the land that the opposing party was claiming as their own.[152] In another case, a previous "sale" of land by Kallehe Paandige Johan to his cousin Francina's husband and cousin Matthijs was challenged by Johan's daughters Edirihami and Punchihami. They said that they did not know whether their father had sold the half-acre in question or mortgaged it.[153] The Landraad had to approve land sale olas and gift olas. Once a sale was completed, the thombo had to be updated and many such entries were made.[154]

Land sale matters are also linked to inheritance law, which leads to a further overlap of issues. Warnesuriepattebendige Dona Maka appeared three times

146 SLNA 1/6512, "Galle Landraad minutes," fols. 76v, 20 Nov 1779. It was said to be the practice in Colombo as well; two commissioned local officers submitted a report after a visit in 1783. SLNA 1/6527, "Annexes to Galle Landraad minutes" (1782 to 1785), fols. 9r, 7 Feb 1783.

147 SLNA 1/6511, "Galle Landraad minutes," fols. 83v, 31 Oct 1778; SLNA 1/6521, "Galle Landraad draft minutes," fols. 35v, 11 Dec 1779.

148 SLNA 1/6524, "Galle Landraad draft minutes" (1783), fols. 64v, 30 Aug 1783.

149 SLNA 1/6523, "Galle Landraad draft minutes" (1781 to 1782), fols. 64r, 27 Apr 1782.

150 SLNA 7/2354, "Miscellaneous documents of the Galle Landraad with conditions of auction sales, notices etc." (1776 to 1779), 29, 25 Jul 1778.

151 The translation of the Dutch word "*verpanding*" is "mortgage," which does not represent the more informal agreements made by southern villagers in which they offered their lands as collateral in order to borrow money. At times, the words *huur* (rent/lease) and *verpand* were used interchangeably. SLNA 1/6504, "Galle Landraad minutes" (1769), fols. 18r, 18 Feb 1796; 29r, 18 Mar 1769.

152 SLNA 1/6513, "Galle Landraad minutes," 47r, 20 May 1780.

153 Ibid., fols. 60r, 24 Jun 1780.

154 One thombo was updated regarding a sale of land years later on 22 April 1785, although the Landraad proof was dated 23 February 1752. SLNA 1/7557A, "Unawatuna (Talpe) Thombo" (1748), 13.

before the council during the years 1778 and 1779 (and many times afterwards) in connection with the sale of land.[155] In September 1778, she had to prove exactly how many people laid claim to the gardens she wanted to sell by appearing before the council with other family members who would corroborate her story. The Landraad gave a decision on the matter, but later that year, it decided that as the land had been a wedding gift, she was entitled to sell a greater share of the estate. On both occasions, the council said that her children had to agree to the sale. When Don Johan de Silva Wijesiriwardena Dissanayake, a former *mudaliyār* (native headman of high rank), wished to sell a piece of land, he was also asked to secure the approval of all prospective heirs.[156] These and other cases indicate the enforcement of the principle of bilateral inheritance, where property is divided equally among both male and female children.

The sample cases demonstrate that the primary preoccupation of the people who came before the Landraad was land litigation. The kind of cases that did not come up can also be telling. For instance, public concerns were not raised in the council. This is not surprising, considering that the Landraad held the whip hand. It could impose corporal punishments on those who breached justice by withholding information or were guilty of contempt, thereby demonstrating its policing powers.[157] I found no cases against the procedures or policies of the Landraad, or any disputes over its competency. Such resistance could be observed in a more understated manner, such as through villagers who claimed errors in the registration, which resulted in the punishment of the thombohouder. Other subtle means of resistance are also described later in this book. Petitions were likely to have been the avenue through which people complained directly about governing issues.[158]

Over time, the jurisdiction of the Landraad was expanded. In 1743, the VOC ordered that all civil cases involving natives outside the Four Gravets of Colombo could be brought before the Raad van Justitie of Colombo only after the Landraad had given a decision and leave to appeal had been granted by the governor. After 1789, this was extended to other Landraden as well. Batavia disputed this extension of jurisdiction, but it was in reality a confirmation of the status quo.[159] All sorts of

155 SLNA 1/6511, "Galle Landraad minutes," fols. 52v, 29 Aug 1778; 62r, 26 Sept 1778; SLNA 1/6512, "Galle Landraad minutes," fols. 88r, 27 Nov 1779; SLNA 1/6520, "Galle Landraad draft minutes," fols. 45r, Nov 1778.

156 SLNA 1/6511, "Galle Landraad minutes," fols. 57r-v, 12 Sept 1778.

157 See chapter three for occasions on which the Landraad resorted to judicial corporal punishment.

158 I thank Lodewijk Wagenaar for providing me with access to a transcription of some registers (SLNA 1/2897 and SLNA 1/2898) of petitions, which, however, do not reveal issues about the Landraad.

159 Nadaraja, *The Legal System of Ceylon*, 30n.

cases were to be brought before the Landraad.[160] Later, the civilian and criminal judicial forums were merged; the Landraden in places that were far from Raden van Justitie such as Trincomalee and Batticaloa were authorised to carry out the preliminary hearings of criminal cases.[161] This was also extended to Galle; two volumes of inquiries by Landraad commissioners in cases of theft and other offences dated between 1784 and 1795 remain to be studied in the archives.[162]

In our attempt to measure litigiousness through the relative frequency of lawsuits, we have no parameters by which to assess a hundred cases. Many factors, including social standing, distance and costs, would have contributed to whether litigants engaged with a colonial judicial forum. Further complications were introduced when the company drew up the thombo of a village, and several disputes arose from that process. Dodampe (Wellaboda), profiled in chapter five, has six cases that all came up around 1780, the year in which the thombo of the village was drawn up. It is thus likely that there is a correlation between the cadastral registration of a village and land-related cases heard in the council. Some thombos, however, including all six Hinidum Pattuwa thombos drawn up in 1760, have no references at all to disputes heard in the Landraad. Proximity to the centre, which Hinidum lacked, would have led to a greater predisposition towards seeking legal redress. Nonetheless, the significance of the thombos and the process of creating them is likely to have reached even such remote areas.

The Thombos

The word thombo is Portuguese in origin, meaning register.[163] The Sinhala form of the word is *thombuva,* and it entered popular parlance in a way that retained its use and significance in Dutch times while also extending its meaning.[164] The Portuguese started their land and revenue registration work at the end of the

160 SLNA 1/214, "Governor in Council minutes," 9 Apr 1791.

161 Nadaraja, *The Legal System of Ceylon*, 8, 30n.

162 SLNA 1/6532, "Notes of inquiries by Galle Landraad commissioners in cases of theft and other offences" (1784 to 1793); SLNA 1/6533, "Notes of inquiries by Galle Landraad commissioners in cases of theft and other offences" (1795).

163 The plural form used by the VOC was thombo's; I will use thombos in this book.

164 In Sinhala, bragging about one's ancestry is referred to as turning the pages of the thombo. Or on making a passionate claim, you could be asked if you have a thombo for it: *"Umbata ekata thombuvak thiyanavada?"* ("Do you have a thombo for that?"). Here the word "thombuva" has acquired the meaning of a "right." It may also refer to inherent faults: *"Ube thombuva mama dannava"* ("I know your thombo"); *"Ube thombuva man lava ahaganna epa"* ("Don't let me recite your thombo"); *"Anunge thombo hoyanne epa"* ("Don't look for the thombo of others").

sixteenth century. The first Portuguese *tombo* (spelled differently), completed in 1599, was a *foral* or revenue register listing some ports, coastal settlements and royal villages in Kotte. A later venture that was completed in 1615 was more ambitious and reportedly involved translating Sinhala records and consulting Sinhalese officials. For each village, including those of the Galle district, the land extent, crop type, average yield per acre, number of craftsmen and dues owed to the king were included. Other areas were added to this later, but the earlier tombo was not updated. The Portuguese, like the Dutch after them, wished to reduce their dependence on native officials through the land registration.[165] José Vicente Serrão writes of how institutional and legal changes to property rights under Portuguese rule were necessarily conservative. Pragmatism was key, and the least possible changes were imposed.[166] For this, it would have been necessary to tap into the expertise of headmen and existing records such as the *lēkam miti*, which were land rolls written on palm leaves maintained by the local kings.[167] If, as popularly believed, the Dutch thombos drew from Sinhala and Portuguese land registers, investigating their evolution would be a noteworthy study.

Whatever its antecedents, the registration of land that took place in seventeenth-century Galle was ridden with problems.[168] These older Galle thombos are referred to as the *oude thombo* or old thombo in the newer eighteenth-century thombos. The old thombos from the years 1693–1696, which could not be located at the Sri Lanka National Archives for many years till they were found again in 2018, have not yet been reconstructed or studied.[169] A discussion in the Galle Landraad

165 De Silva, *Portuguese in Ceylon*, 171–74. See also S.G. Perera (ed), *The Tombo of the Two Korales* (Colombo: Ceylon Govt. Press, 1938); Chandra Richard de Silva, "The First Portuguese Revenue Register of the Kingdom of Kotte, 1599," *The Ceylon Journal of Historical and Social Studies* 5 (1975): 69–153.

166 José Vicente Serrão, "The Portuguese Land Policies in Ceylon: On the Possibilities and Limits of a Process of Territorial Occupation," in Bárbara Direito et al. (ed), *Property Rights, Land and Territory in the European Overseas Empires* (Lisbon: CEHC-IUL, 2014), 193.

167 For an introduction to the *lēkam miti*, see H.A.P. Abhayawardena, *Lekam Miti Vimarshanaya (A Critical Study of Lekam Miti)* (Colombo: Dept. of National Archives, 2009).

168 Some discussion on the thombo compilation took place in the Galle Political Council in 1663. Maria Wilhelmina Jurriaanse, *Catalogue of the Archives of the Dutch Central Government of Coastal Ceylon, 1640-1796* (Colombo: Ceylon Govt. Press, 1943), 243. For early developments with regard to the thombo in Jaffna, see also Hendrick Becker, *Memoir of Hendrick Becker, Governor and Director of Ceylon for His Successor Isaac Augustyn Rumpf, 1716*, trans. Sophia Anthonisz (Colombo: H.C. Cottle, Govt. Printer, 1914), 6–8.

169 H.W. Codrington refers to them in his bibliography in *Ancient Land Tenure and Revenue in Ceylon* (Colombo: Ceylon Govt. Press, 1938). Archivists from the National Archives in The Hague who visited the Sri Lanka National Archives in May 2018 located the old thombos listed in appendix 1 of Mottau's inventory. Till then, staff at the Sri Lanka National Archives had not been able to locate them despite attempts made from (at least) 2012. The archivists from The Hague assigned archival numbers (SLNA 1/7571–7598) to these volumes, which previously had only bundle numbers.

from 1745/46, with the governor's marginal comments, indicates that there were many drawbacks in the old thombos, which were never approved by the authorities.[170] The old thombos may have included fraudulent claims on abandoned lands subsequent to migration from the coastal lands to the king's territory during the wars between the Dutch and Rājasinghe II,[171] but we do not have sufficient proof of this. They are said to have been incomplete, as evidence of ownership was not recorded: the Landraad lamented that in many places only the single word paravēni was written down. During the new registrations in the eighteenth century, it was inconvenient for the company that, for the most part, the people fell back on the old thombos for proof. Thus, in 1745, extracts from the old thombos were banned but those that had already been issued were honoured. However, the governor said they could not let it be known that everything registered in the old thombos was false. He conceded that legally they merited no credit, but if used with discretion, they could occasionally shed some light. He did concede that "till now, they have contributed more towards confusion, than extracting any value or advantage."[172] Yet, for the registrars, the old thombos were a convenience, as they were for some property owners.[173] In practice, many eighteenth-century thombos of Galle referred to the descriptions in the old thombos as authoritative, and references to the lack of an old thombo for a particular village have also been found.[174] Decades later, the people appealed to a colonial creation of a document that may have been initially rejected.

The Galle thombos from the eighteenth century were recorded and added to over a period of about fifty years.[175] The slow progress is attributed to rebellions

170 SLNA 1/2805, "Galle Landraad minutes (20 Dec 1745)" f. 36r. This document, which is a discussion of land rights with marginal comments by the governor, is considered in more detail in chapter five.

171 Cleghorn suggests this in his minute. Pieris, "The Cleghorn Minute," 138.

172 SLNA 1/2805, "Galle Landraad minutes (20 Dec 1745)" fols. 30v–31v, 33v, 34v. See also SLNA 1/5660, "Extracts of resolutions, orders, etc. regarding the Landraad and the thombo compilation" (1740 to 1770), fols. 7r, Extract of letter dated 20 July 1745 from Colombo to Galle. Even as late as in 1757, the registrars had to be reminded not to refer to the old thombos. Ibid., fols. 31v–32r, Letter dated 2 Jun 1757 from Colombo to Galle.

173 This happened with the Matara registration as well. It turned out that the Matara dessave had not stopped giving extracts from the old thombos. The registrars asked that Colombo allow them to use the old thombos, which was permitted if done with the "utmost secrecy and also for the advantage of the company and not of the inhabitants." The inhabitants were not to be allowed to appeal using the old thombos, which Colombo said deserved no merit at all because they had been drawn up inaccurately by "unsworn" persons who had not signed them. This proves that Matara also had old thombos that are no longer extant. SLNA 1/5660, "Galle Landraad, extracts of resolutions," fols. 29r, Letter from Colombo to Galle in July 1757; 32r-v, Letter dated 2 Jun 1757 from Colombo to Galle.

174 See SLNA 1/7419A, "Dadalla (Four Gravets) Thombo" (1782 to 1784).

175 There are around 175 volumes of the Galle thombos at the Colombo archives (SLNA 1/7395 to 1/7570). Note that the numbers given in Mottau's inventory have been replaced since. S.A.W. Mottau,

and the war of 1760–65 with the Kandyan kingdom.[176] The thombos of Colombo are different in that the company revised them on three specific occasions in the eighteenth century, thereby facilitating some degree of comparison.[177] The Galle thombo compilation followed an altogether different chronology. It is possible that as the Galle registration fell behind schedule, they could not keep up with the Colombo registrations. They were drawn up in various years over the course of the eighteenth century.[178]

While it is difficult to determine the registration procedure used for each of the Galle thombos, officials either called people to the Landraad or sent thombo commissioners to the villages. Three instructions were used for the Colombo registrations.[179] The first set of instructions were issued in November 1745, for the compilation in Colombo, Galle and Matara. Two other instructions that refer specifically to the updating of the Colombo registration were issued in December 1759 and September 1766. The first set of 1745, issued by Governor Van Gollonesse, required summoning the inhabitants to the Landraad with their deeds of evidence and witnesses, as recommended by Van Imhoff.[180] Van Imhoff believed that sending commissioners with native chiefs to villages would not be successful, as it was

Inventory of the Archives of the Dutch Government in the Divisions of Galle (Matara) and Jaffnapatnam 1640-1796 (The Hague: General State Archives, 1975).

176 D.A. Kotelawele, "The VOC in Sri Lanka, 1658–1796: Social and Economic Change in the Maritime Regions," in K.M. de Silva (ed), *University of Peradeniya, History of Sri Lanka (From c. 1500 to c. 1800)*, vol. 2 (Peradeniya: University of Peradeniya, 1995), 420–21.

177 The volumes of the first registration, which spanned the terms of office of five successive governors over a period of seventeen years from 5 June 1742 to 6 August 1759 are no longer extant, as its files were used for the next revision. The volumes of the next two revisions from 9 June 1760 to 13 November 1761 and from 5 September 1766 to 9 September 1771 span a shorter period than the first and are available in the archives.

178 An overview of the years in which the Galle thombos were drawn up can be seen in Mottau's catalogue of the Galle records. Colombo asked Galle in 1757 to prepare an account of when or in which year the thombos of Galle and Matara were begun, which villages were completed and were being registered at that moment, and which other villages had to be registered. SLNA 1/5660, "Galle Landraad, extracts of resolutions," fols. 30v, Letter dated 1 Feb 1757 from Colombo to Galle. It appears that a list of registered thombos came to be included in the compendiums.

179 Hovy, *Plakkaatboek*, vol. 2; nr. 355, Instructions for the commissioners of the Landraad who are responsible for drawing up the new land- and headthombo of the Colombo and Matara dessavonys and of the Galle kōralē, 15 Nov 1745; 446, Instructions for the thombo-keeper: Guidelines for the renewal of the head- and landthombo in the Colombo dessavony, 20 Dec 1759; 491, Instructions for the commissioned members of the Landraad and the thombohouder by the renewal of the head- and landthombo of the Colombo dessavony, 5 Sept 1766. See for translation S.A.W. Mottau, "Documents on Ceylon History (2): Documents Relating to the Tombo Registration of the Dutch Administration in Ceylon: Instructions Issued to the Tombo Commissioners," *The Ceylon Historical Journal* 3, no. 2 (1953): 173–89.

180 Van Imhoff, *Memoir Left by Van Imhoff*, 21–23.

troublesome to the commissioners and the final decision thereby depended on the honesty of a few headmen and not a whole assembly like the Landraad. Prior notification of the process was published in the plakkaten.[181] During the second revision of the Colombo thombos under Governor Schreuder, thombo commissioners, their assistants and native officers were sent out to villages. For the third revision under Governor Falck, from 5 September 1766 to 9 September 1771, it was clear to the company that they should choose the better of the two methods used previously. The council debated as to whether the first or the second method would be best,[182] and the first method (recommended by Van Imhoff) was implemented.

How far these changes in procedure affected the registration in Galle is unknown. The first and third instructions mentioned above, which called for the inhabitants' presence in the Landraad for the registration, together with other instructions and decisions regarding the thombos and the Landraad are found in registers that were diligently maintained in Galle. Colombo ordered that they be properly foliated, numbered and provided with indexes, and that they always be available for reference on the table during a registration.[183] These volumes show that at least the Galle and Matara registrations were closely connected, and an order on 18 May 1743 from Colombo said that the Galle registration should follow the form in Matara.

Whether they operated from the Landraad or were sent out to the villages, we know that permanent thombo commissioners or registrars were assigned the task of carrying out the registration. They were attached to the Galle Landraad and appear to have functioned in that capacity throughout its operation.[184] Jurriaanse says this officer is first mentioned on 16 August 1759.[185] Thombo-keepers were required to take the oath. A surveyor was also involved in the process from time to time, although not consistently. In the words of R.G. Anthonisz: "The only instances, and these are comparatively few, where measurements are stated are of those lands sold by the Company, and therefore previously surveyed by qualified officers of the

181 Printed by the VOC press in Colombo. Jurriaanse, *Catalogue*, 245.

182 SLNA 1/149, "Governor in Council minutes" (1766), 5 Sept 1766.

183 SLNA 1/5658, "Galle Landraad, extracts of resolutions," fols. 19r, Letter from Colombo dated 20 Aug 1745; 20v, Extract from resolution dated 14 Aug 1745. The 1789 instructions for the Landraad also refer to the maintenance of a digest of extracts from resolutions and letters including local laws. This was to be maintained by the secretary. Hovy, *Plakkaatboek*, vol. 2; nr. 628, (I, 10; IV, 3), 25 Jun 1789.

184 In the early years of the new registration, a resolution of 18 May 1743 said the registration should be carried out by commissioned members on five days of the week, and after they had submitted their reports to the full Landraad, the council would order the formal registration. On 11 April 1744, another resolution said the registration should be carried out twice a week from 8 to 12 am and 3 to 6 pm. SLNA 1/5658, "Galle Landraad, extracts of resolutions," fols. 7r, 10r. See also Mottau, *Inventory of the Archives*, 56.

185 Jurriaanse, *Catalogue*, 245.

Government; and it is in these cases only that the boundaries are mentioned."[186] The thombo of the Colombo Four Gravets, for instance, includes boundaries, but similar thombos were not found for the Galle district. At times, there was also a surveyor on the board of the Landraad.[187] His involvement does not seem to have been consistent. Yet, the company intended to employ more surveyors in 1743 and instructions for them were issued in 1745 and 1758.[188] Incidentally, Governor Van Gollonesse was disappointed that surveying was not done according to European methods of measurement but with seed as the unit of measurement.[189] Since this was essentially how inhabitants understood production, following indigenous practice in this regard was unavoidable.

The registration undoubtedly suffered from a lack of commitment and effectiveness on the part of record-keepers, headmen and inhabitants. On 4 July 1744, Colombo expressed the desire that the thombo work in Galle be carried out with "more zeal and deliberation," as up to then it had been unsatisfactory.[190] Expertise on "land and legal affairs" was considered to be low among the thombo commissioners.[191] Thombo commissioners were frequently upbraided, as seen in the Governor in Council resolutions and letters to Galle.[192] At the meeting held in December 1745 referred to above, the Landraad in Galle was also rather sceptical about the enthusiasm of the locals regarding the registration process:

> ...the inhabitants were rather good at appearing for the registration, but when they appeared they left behind a part of their family, whose names they could not report, and

[186] R.G. Anthonisz, *Report on the Dutch Records in the Government Archives at Colombo* (Colombo: H.C. Cottle, Govt. Printer, 1907), 113.

[187] In 1781, a surveyor was said to be too busy and was relieved from his duties at the Landraad. SLNA 7/2353, "Galle Landraad inward letters," Letter dated 12 Jun 1781 from Commander Anoldus de Lij to Landraad.

[188] SLNA 1/5658, "Galle Landraad, extracts of resolutions," fols. 7v, Extract resolution of 4 Jun 1743; Hovy, *Plakkaatboek*, vol. 2; nr. 345, 10 Apr 1745 & 432, 3 Oct 1758, Instructions for surveyors.

[189] SLNA 1/5659, "Extracts of resolutions, orders, etc. regarding the Landraad and the thombo compilation" (1743 to 1744), fols. 21r, Extract of resolution in Council of Ceylon, 23 Oct 1743.

[190] SLNA 1/5658, "Galle Landraad, extracts of resolutions," fols. 10v–11r, Extract from letter from Colombo dated 4 Jul 1744. The shortcomings of the thombos of the Morrua Kōralē (Matara Dessavony) are listed under seven points in that letter, with a promise to send a model of how the registration was done in Colombo so that it could be followed in Galle and Matara. Similar criticisms followed. Ibid., 11v–12v, Extract from letter dated 28 Aug 1744 from Colombo to Galle.

[191] Governor Van Gollonesse said that the commissioners could not be regarded as "men having the required experience in land and legal affairs". SLNA 1/2805, "Galle Landraad minutes (20 Dec 1745)," fols. 48v–49r.

[192] See for example, among other orders, an extract from a resolution taken in the council on 1 December 1746. SLNA 1/5660, "Galle Landraad, extracts of resolutions," fols. 22r-v.

> sometimes they couldn't produce the necessary evidence of purchase or gift. The case was then left as inconclusive, and they went away and sometimes did not come back for days. Moreover, the inhabitants were, as a rule, so secretive, it was said that the authorities had to force the words out of their mouths so to speak with continuous questioning and re-questioning. When the registration of a new village was started, they quite wanted to come forward and make declarations, but towards the end of a registration they showed themselves to be very lazy about it. Even the village headmen keep away under the pretense of being occupied in the service of the company, as a result of which the commissioners sometimes found themselves having to perform the embarrassing task of dispatching the necessary summons to those [headmen] who were absent. The documents that were handed over by the headmen were found to be so deficient, that even the interpreter could hardly make them out. He would confess that many a time such old, foolish and decrepit people would be found among those who came forward that the commissioners could not obtain the least amount of explanation from them.[193]

Resistance to the registration came from both peasants and headmen. Regulations ordering the inhabitants to cooperate with the registration or face serious consequences were published so that no one could claim ignorance.[194] On 3 October 1744, all headmen from the lowest to the highest grade were ordered to ensure that their subjects appeared for the registration at the correct time, failing which they would face a moderate fine or punishment (evidently corporal) as an example to others.[195] However, this was not successful. Van Gollonesse says that complaints of inefficiency were not heard of in Colombo:

> It is surprising that we have not heard such complaints here, but only in Galle, and we cannot even imagine what the presumed foolishness and infirmity of the village headmen signifies that there should be such simple people who would not know what they own. We perceive this rather as a subtle trick to exempt themselves, under the pretext of an appearance of a simple countenance, from providing an accurate declaration of their properties to the afore-mentioned commissioners.[196]

The governor was clearly aware of the possibility that the people were deceiving the company. In Galle, the headmen were also perceived as being reluctant to

[193] SLNA 1/2805, "Galle Landraad minutes (20 Dec 1745)," fols. 40r–41v.

[194] SLNA 1/5660, "Galle Landraad, extracts of resolutions," fols. 20v–21r, Extract letter [from Colombo] dated 24 Sept 1746.

[195] SLNA 1/5658, "Galle Landraad, extracts of resolutions," fols. 13v, Extract resolution of 3 Oct 1744.

[196] SLNA 1/2805, "Galle Landraad minutes (20 Dec 1745)," fols. 40r-v.

participate in the registration process. Van Imhoff wrote in 1740 that in Matara, the registration was obstructed as "the native chiefs do not like it and would rather keep matters in the confusion in which they are at present, in order that they may make as much of it themselves as they can."[197] This was echoed in other areas of the country as well, where the thombo registration even caused violent resistance.[198] The instructions to the thombo commissioners of 1745 state that the "influential" actively opposed the registration.[199]

Still, men and women came to the Landraad with extracts of the thombo to prove their rights. Despite opposition and issues of efficiency, the thombos were considered a permanent record and were used as such. In 1784, Pieter Sluijsken, a high-level official of the company, said that the thombo was the "essential law book"[200] and the ultimate reference for property disputes: "the settlement of complaints regarding lands, injustice or caste disputes over lands and inheritance law absolutely requires consulting the land and head thombo which is deposited with the overseer, and is never given away than with the foreknowledge of the whole Landraad, as being a law book according to which the cases are decided."[201] The thombo was the law, he argued. The extent to which it was used in conflict resolution can be seen in the pages of the Landraad minutes. For example, in a sample case used in this study, Totagoda Gamage Kattona et al. v Mandenayake, a thombo extract was taken as the law.[202] Litigants recognised the purpose of the thombos and their value and obtained extracts to prove their case.

This legal use of the thombos continues today, as extracts are still issued by the Sri Lanka National Archives for production in court. By being functional in this way, the thombo is a kind of evergreen document. In 1766, the thombohouder was paid twenty-four stivers for an extract from the thombo (without the stamp); today it costs 1200 rupees per translated page.[203] Till the end of Dutch rule when it was still being updated, it was a living document, and to some extent continued to

[197] Van Imhoff, *Memoir Left by Van Imhoff*, 20.

[198] Governor Van Gollonesse attempted to introduce systematic surveys in the Hina Kōralē (Colombo Dessavony) which were opposed by the people. Sinnappah Arasaratnam, "Introduction," in Julius Stein van Gollenesse, *Memoir of Julius Stein van Gollenesse* 1751 (Colombo: Dept. of National Archives, 1974).

[199] Hovy, *Plakkaatboek*, vol. 2; nr. 355, 15 Nov 1745 (13).

[200] Pieter Sluijsken, "Eene beschryving van de landdienst op Ceylon: Zo uyt ondervinding als uyt oude papieren tezaemen gebragt (A Description of the Land Services of Ceylon: Compiled from both investigations and old papers)" (Colombo, 1784), vol. 1: 307, RP-31/32 Colonial Collection (KIT), Leiden University.

[201] Ibid., vol. 1, 367-368.

[202] SLNA 1/6511, "Galle Landraad minutes," fols. 29r, 27 Jun 1778; 44r, 8 Aug 1778.

[203] SLNA 1/5660, "Galle Landraad, extracts of resolutions," fols. 38r, "Advertisement" dated 25 Oct 1766.

be so in early British times when marginal notes indicated changes in ownership through land sales. Notes on thombo extracts that were passed on to applicants were also made on the thombo itself in the nineteenth century.[204] The legal value of these extracts, despite being prized by inhabitants, especially in earlier times, has undoubtedly reduced. R.G. Anthonisz, the first Government Archivist of Sri Lanka had this to say about their use in the early twentieth century: "it is but an inferior title after all which the Thombu Extract, so much prized by the villager even now, enables him to establish. It was a common practice formerly for those in possession of so-called ancestral property, imagining that the thombo was bound to support their title, to apply for extracts whenever they entered into litigation with the Crown or with their neighbours."[205] A proper review of their use in court today is timely.[206] The thombo was considered a source of law in a non-technical

[204] A thombo clerk in charge of the records, who was earlier the thombohouder, was employed by the British government till at least the mid-nineteenth century. Anthonisz, *Report on the Dutch Records*, 10.

[205] Ibid., 114. Anthonisz further states that the small fee that was affixed to the time-consuming task of searching for "supposed entries" considerably reduced the number of applications for extracts. He writes that the average number of applications for three years in the early 1900s was as little as seventeen. The Government Archivist in 1951, J.H.O. Paulusz, reported that there were 519 applications for "information centred around entries in the Land Registers and in deeds and instruments affecting property." J.H.O. Paulusz, *Administration Report of the Government Archivist for 1951* (Colombo: Ceylon Govt. Press, 1952). This higher figure could be due to applications from documents other than the thombos being counted together. Mottau, who was Assistant Government Archivist, seems to believe at one point that they are all thombo extracts, adding that they were a small source of revenue for the government. Mottau, "Documents on Ceylon History," 174. In 2002 and 2003, the number of requests was 134 in each year, with 101 and 47 completed applications in the respective years. Saroja Wettasinghe, "Digitisation of Land Records for Access and Preservation," in *Public Requirements and National Archives: Archives Week Souvenir* (Colombo: Sri Lanka National Archives, 2004), 5.

[206] After assuming office as Director General National Archives at the Department of National Archives in 2017, I produced two thombos to courts in Homagama and Mathugama in 2018. From among the existing staff, only one officer had produced a thombo in court on one occasion previously. In the first case, I provided evidence in Homagama and the opposing lawyer questioned me at length about the fact that a certain piece of land was described as company's land, due to the lack of proof of ownership. It was, however, chiefly described as the service land of the family. It was common for many lands to be described in the thombos as company lands due to the lack of proof of ownership, but that did not mean that the property rights of the family were rescinded in practice. The lawyer in question, however, was adamant that I should not use my specialised knowledge but base my answers on the meaning of the words in the translation. Fortunately, the judge did not support him on that and asked me to answer with my specialised knowledge. Much interest in the thombos and their history was shown by the judge and the other presiding lawyers. In the second case in Mathugama, it was the number of children of a sub-family in a thombo that was under question – the lawyer wished to confirm that the said family had only two children, as the opposing party claimed that there had been another child. Obviously, it was only possible to confirm that at the time the thombo had been

sense in its heyday, but has suffered some loss in value since then. The following section will introduce a preliminary discussion on the other sources of the law used in Landraad decisions.

Sources of the Law

Three sources of law were said to have been employed in the Dutch colonial system: the laws in force in The Netherlands, the Statutes of Batavia, and the enactments of the Governor in Council of the VOC in Sri Lanka.[207] The last of these were possibly the more important for the inhabitants as they governed local affairs. Such enactments covered matters related to slaves, religion, marriage, concubinage and adultery, theft, Moors and Hindus, burgers or city dwellers, and land. However, criminal law is believed to have been based on Roman-Dutch law, as was the civil law employed in the Civiele Raden of the towns.[208] As argued in this book, the Landraad was at least one legal body in Dutch times where it was difficult to permanently fix the laws that were in use. The 1789 instructions ordered councillors

written, only two children were registered. I was also questioned on whether the land in dispute may be mentioned under other thombo groups, a possibility that could be confirmed by studying the entire thombo for that village. The legal interest in such details contained in documents from 250 years ago in a modern-day court of law is intriguing to say the least. In both cases, as also in many extracts given out daily to the public, I have observed that extracts from the same entries were given out over the course of the nineteenth century as well. The litigants almost always say that the cases had been inherited by them from their grandparents and they are unable to trace who had begun the disputes.

[207] I will deal with the relevant details of Roman-Dutch law as they arise in the book. The Statutes of Batavia were a set of rules and regulations based largely on Dutch practices and laws to be employed by the VOC in the east, first issued in 1642 and updated in 1766. J. van Kan, "Bataviasche statuten en de buitencomptoiren," *Bijdragen tot de Taal-, Land- en Volkenkunde van Nederlandsch-Indië* 100 (1940): 255–82.

[208] It remains to be seen through an examination of the cases in the higher courts whether "discursive bridges with the religious and social norms of the subject population" were built. Radhika Singha states that this was the case in connection with Thomas Macaulay's draft penal code of 1837 in British India. Even "[t]he criminal law, its machinery and procedure, was therefore tied up with earlier institutions, personnel and legal-sacred texts." Radhika Singha, *A Despotism of Law: Crime and Justice in Early Colonial India* (Delhi: Oxford University Press, 1998), viii-x. Certain groups, such as the Brahmans, for instance, were exempted from capital punishment in British India. Although death sentences were meted out in Dutch courts, they could not be executed without confirmation by the Dutch governor. For a preliminary survey of how Dutch governors in Sri Lanka overturned decisions in criminal cases in consideration of local circumstances, see Alicia Schrikker, "Conflict Resolution, Social Control and Law-Making in Eighteenth Century Dutch Sri Lanka," in Catia Antunes and Jos Gommans (eds), *Exploring the Dutch Empire: Agents Networks and Institutions, 1600-2000* (London: Bloomsbury, 2015), 227–44.

to be guided by Dutch laws and statutes.[209] But in practice, it was not as simple. The presence of headmen in an advisory role (more on this will follow in chapter two) complicated the picture, and speculation on their role in official documents and in academic literature over the nineteenth and twentieth centuries is common. This section will offer some preliminary observations on the sources of the law in the Landraad; this aligns with the central question of this book on whose law was used by the Dutch. The issue will be examined further in later chapters.

Efforts to use the argument of legal tradition in ethnographic writing and official documents prevailed. Sluijsken writes how "[t]his tax dates from the king's times and is levied till today in the kingdom of Kandy"[210] and "[t]his is all customary according to the old ways."[211] The few references to custom in Landraad judgements give some idea of how decisions were made. For custom to have been mentioned at all, it must have been a decisive factor in at least those cases, if not others. Indigenous norms are referred to in the counter-interrogations about "tradition" that the council engaged in. Questions on indigenous customs were posed to witnesses in counter-interrogations that were carried out on behalf of the opposing party by the councillors. Litigants and their procureurs perhaps believed that if they asked the correct questions about the customary laws, they could influence the councillors in their final decision. For instance, in 1778, it was to Puswellage Johan's advantage to ask the witnesses of the opposing party "whether it was not a constant custom among the Sinhalese that the owner of animals, which they hand over to someone for raising, gets two-thirds [of the earnings], and the person who looks after the animals gets one-third from them." It was followed up with the question of "whether it is also a custom, that the person who looks after the animals can hand over such animals to a third person, and what then the last-mentioned person can profit from them."[212] The answers to the first question were in the affirmative and to the second that no such custom existed. This would have been the desired outcome of the party asking the question and its significance would not have been lost on the councillors.[213]

Such inquiries into customs indicate their relevance to the council. Despite the lack of a formal codification of the laws of the Sinhalese, they do not seem to have been eliminated from the Landraad. However, further study of the decisions made by the council as attempted in this book is necessary to establish the extent to which

209 Hovy, *Plakkaatboek*, vol. 2; nr. 628, (I, 10), 25 Jun 1789.

210 Sluijsken, "A Description of the Land Services," vol. 1: 264.

211 Ibid., 1: 338.

212 SLNA 1/6534, "Galle Landraad interrogations," fols. 15r, 9 Jul 1778.

213 The purpose of questioning witnesses in this example was to dissuade the councillors from admitting them to the oath. The matter of the oath was referred to the full council in order to decide if the said witnesses could take the oath. More on this practice will follow in chapter four.

they were adopted. Van den Horst argues that the references to custom by the counsel alone are not conclusive evidence that the law was applied by the courts.[214] Yet, litigants and/or their procureurs clearly wished to direct the councillors in a certain direction, and procureurs would not have taken the trouble to include such leading questions if they did not have a considerable impact on the final decision. What is important to establish here is that a mixed legal system, wherein both local and foreign principles were at work, was in operation.

Evidently, it was a complex situation. Colonial courts often suffered from a lack of understanding of the local customs. For instance, in 1793, Landraad Secretary Pieter Arend de Moor pleaded for help in explaining to the Raad van Justitie of Galle the basis on which a judgement was made in a case that was to be taken up in appeal – he said he himself had feelings contrary to the judgement and therefore did not know how to justify the judgement.[215] It was officially recognised that there was a need to understand local customs. If there was an old custom that was contrary to the orders from the government, this had to be communicated to the Governor in Council for further orders. Inherent in this was the understanding that government orders should not be contravened. If there were cases not covered by existing orders, the issuing of a final decision had to be suspended and the approval of the Governor in Council had to be sought in order to prevent any mistreatment.[216] The Landraad did not always do this, but a comprehensive case-by-case analysis of its decision-making is beyond the scope of this study. The next three chapters of this book will attempt to shed light on at least three aspects of the law in practice: evidence, land rights and inheritance law.

Conclusion

The development of the Landraad richly illustrates the dilemmas of an early colonial power advancing legal institutions that are suited to local circumstances. The inheritance of an existing normative order, however alien, could not be brushed aside. Initially, the VOC believed that they had a free hand to impose foreign laws as a result of seventeenth-century migration (later reversed) of the indigenous inhabitants to the Kandyan kingdom. Inherent in the company's implied recognition that a territory had to be empty of original inhabitants to introduce new laws was the acceptance that a once sovereign people would have their own way

[214] Van den Horst, *Compensation for Improvements*, 121.

[215] SLNA 1/6516, "Galle Landraad minutes" (1793), fols. 69v–70v, 26 Nov 1793.

[216] SLNA 1/5658, "Galle Landraad, extracts of resolutions," fols. 19v–20r, Extract letters [from Colombo] 8 Oct 1745; 26r–v, 20 Nov 1745.

of life that could not be ignored. Dutch law could not be introduced into a vacuum; it inevitably had to interact with pre-existing norms. This connected with a sense of natural justice, which in the new legal regime was chiefly achieved through the presence of native headmen in the Landraad. They gave the new judicial forum an aura of appropriateness. The company had the success of conquest and powers of coercion behind them, but their economic, political and social powers were consolidated through collaborations with the indigenous elite. However, the fact that the headmen participated in the Landraad alone is inconclusive; the full impact of their role requires the further study that has been attempted in this book. The degree of representation afforded to indigenous headmen would have contributed to a long-term commitment from the peasants to the new and adapted institutional structures of the Landraad. Institution building was both handed down from the top and arrived at through a negotiation of received and evolving practice.

For the first time, Sri Lankan peasants faced courts of record through the Dutch legal system. Bhavani Raman made a compelling analysis of the role played in establishing the protocols of law by scribes and their micropractices of writing in south India under the British East India Company, an argument that may well be extended to the textual bureaucracy established by the Dutch in Sri Lanka.[217] Despite efforts to retain oral procedures, the textual nature of proceedings in the Landraad would have become increasingly apparent to local inhabitants over the eighteenth century in particular. The image of justice in the Landraad was of an enclosed area into which they were sent in and out and wherein sat foreign figures of authority, with a few of their own kind among them. They spoke, for the most part, a foreign language.

The Landraad frequently referred to accompanying documents as evidence and witnesses were often required to provide signed depositions that had to be read out in the council, thus deviating from legal practices under the local normative order. While a written tradition was not wholly absent from that order, as *sannas* (royal grants) for large land deeds and decrees by the king were in writing, judicial proceedings were usually oral. Yet, the summary nature of proceedings in the Landraad, which was facilitated by the Dutch system, almost mirrored the oral nature of local legal practices. Resemblances in procedural aspects were thus a potential advantage in successfully introducing an otherwise new institutional development.

An analysis of the caseloads reveals the anxieties of the people seeking adjudication at the Landraad in relation to the ownership of land, their most precious asset. The agricultural and rural character of the Landraad cases can be seen – people

[217] Bhavani Raman, *Document Raj: Writing and Scribes in Early Colonial South India* (Chicago: University of Chicago Press, 2012).

used the council to reconfirm what they thought was theirs. This is reflected in the extensive use of the thombos, which are among primary supporting documents used in the Landraad. They were a crucial part of the Landraad proceedings. Land registration was a necessary technology of colonial rule. The thombos were a process of establishing a social and economic regime that was clearly defined. That clarity was not limited to the textual; more on that will follow in chapter five. The thombo in its Dutch form may have been an innovation to the people, but eventually its wide acceptance is testimony to its success. Texts can serve different purposes at different moments for both ruler and the ruled, as we saw in the controversy over the old thombo that top level company officials deemed inaccurate but which both the registrars and the people referred to in practice. The new thombo served as an authoritative record over the nineteenth and twentieth centuries and into the twenty-first century as well. The files of the thombo, as those of the Landraad, thus acquired a claim to truth capable of providing proofs but changing in value over time.

In all this, the daily, inefficient workings of judicial forums in almost any context should also be kept in mind. The Landraad was an institutional development that introduced structural innovations within a new space, while retaining certain family resemblances to local conditions and thereby confirming its plural character.

CHAPTER 2

Divided Authority

Abstract

The social backgrounds of the European and indigenous members of the Landraad and the nature of their presence in the council highlight the relative powers of the two groups and issues of efficiency. The colonial enterprise of identifying cultural differences through representations of inhabitants was seen to be necessary for realising economic advantages. The relationship of law to the dominant classes is evident, as a result of a small, closely-knit group with cross-cultural connections controlling the Landraad. Yet, despite a professed intention to favour the local normative order, the powers of the local members were secondary to that of the European members. Subtle skirmishes for the consolidation of power that raised tensions were articulations of difference that played out in the council room.

Keywords: Judges, legal elites, protocol, cultural difference, VOC, early-colonial rule.

When a new member was appointed to the Landraad, the standard practice was to formally introduce them to the older members at their first meeting. In 1786, the newly appointed Don Balthasar Dias Abeysinghe Siriwardene, son of the influential *mahamudaliyār* Nicolaas Dias Abeysinghe, was affronted that the Landraad had failed to follow protocol when council members did not introduce him formally along with another newly appointed local member. The European members had felt uncomfortable escorting local members from the antechamber into the council hall, and there were no local members present to perform the duty. Usually, two of the youngest members of the council performed the task; however, that day, the council chose to avoid the practice altogether and allowed the new members to walk in on their own, much to the consternation of the younger Abeysinghe. However, the Landraad was quick to make amends at a subsequent meeting. This dispute over protocol highlights the subtle tug of war between the local and European members of the judicial forum. Don Adriaan Goonewardene Ponnamperuma, another local member on the Landraad, claimed on a separate occasion that the "white" members took little notice of the opinions of the local members who were regarded as foolish, inexperienced and ignorant. The votes of the headmen were not formally counted; they could only participate in an advisory capacity. Navigating the duty of judging was clearly not an easy task.

In mirror theories that link law to society, "law mirrors society or some aspect of it in a consistent, theoretically specifiable way." However, for Alan Watson the mechanisms of legal change "are largely controlled 'internally' within legal systems by legal professional elites such as makers of codes or drafters of legislation, judges or jurists."[1] Watson's view suggests that the legal elites of eighteenth-century Dutch Sri Lanka, professional or not, played a potentially significant role in defining colonial law. With little or no separation of powers between the legislature, executive and judiciary, this would have been especially true of early modern times. In the 1920s and 1930s, the realists challenged legal formalism, which emphasises the independence of the law from externalities and the idea that judging was an objective process, by emphasising the inadequacies of the law and the role of the personal biases, beliefs and politics of judges.[2] This requires studying the legal elites to understand their role in shaping the law. With this is mind, in this chapter, I identify the councillors of the Landraad and their backgrounds, controlling power and worldview. Their capacity to decide on questions of law was greater than what is projected in formalist ideas of the capacity of the law to be mechanically applied to any case.[3]

Who became members of the Landraad? What were their backgrounds? How influential were headmen in the decision-making process, which was effectively also the rule-making process? Decision-making involved representatives from seemingly different social fields, the European and the Sinhalese. Was it a mutual interaction among equals? Was the decision-making capacity of both parties nearly equal or prearranged to favour one social field? At the same time, both social fields were subject to influences from each other and other social fields. They were a mixed lot, even by blood and I explain later in this chapter that the term European is used in reference to people of mixed descent as well. In this case, we may expect a reality of pluralities.

To understand the role of personal beliefs in judicial decision-making, we must first understand the identity of the councillors and their outlook on local society. Landraad councillors had the authority to decide on cases, so they were in a position of power vis-a-vis society when they were appointed to serve in the Galle Landraad. We may not be able to determine to what degree a judge or a group of judges was

[1] For an overview of this debate, see Roger Cotterrell, *Law, Culture and Society: Legal Ideas in the Mirror of Society Theory* (Hampshire: Ashgate Publishing, 2006), 109–10.

[2] See Brian Z. Tamanaha, *Beyond the Formalist-Realist Divide: The Role of Politics in Judging* (Princeton: Princeton University Press, 2010), 1–7.

[3] New studies evaluating approaches to judging have emerged in recent times. See part three of Tamanaha's book on studies of judging in *Beyond the Formalist-Realist Divide.*

able to directly affect a case, but it is important that headmen were physically present in a colonial body that has been much appraised for including them. I shall first consider the backgrounds and participation of the all-male European and local councillors who served from 1759 to 1796. Thereafter, I will examine the varying levels of influence of and dynamics between the two groups through a discussion of their authority in the council and Dutch representations of the locals, as evident in the work of Pieter Sluijsken, one-time president of the Galle Landraad.

European Councillors and Their Social Context

Most councillors were European, affluent, and worked closely with the Dutch government. At the beginning of their careers, those who had entered VOC service as soldiers or sailors had to serve a period of apprenticeship.[4] A few moved into administration and trade as bookkeepers and merchants. Some councillors were already prominent company officials who went on to reach high positions in the administration in Colombo; they came from families that represented the old guard of VOC servants. The Governor in Council in Colombo made European and local appointments to the Landraad; there is evidence that the Political Council of Galle made some recommendations as well.

In general, the European members controlled the Landraad. Presidents, vice-presidents and secretaries were Europeans (see Table 2.1). As I mentioned in chapter one, the opziender (overseer) of Galle was also the president of the Landraad. Pieter Sluijsken, who had served in the company since 1758, was president of the Landraad for one and a half years, from 1766 to 1767. Sluijsken was a diligent president, attending twenty-seven of twenty-nine meetings held during his term of office and missing just two on the grounds of indisposition. He later claimed that he learned much about the country and its people and customs through his experience in the VOC (more on this below), and it is likely that his term in the Galle Landraad would have contributed towards that. Abraham Samlant Jr. was president of the Landraad from December 1779 to June 1785, and at the time of capitulation to the British in 1796, Samlant was a merchant and *negotie boekhouder* (trade bookkeeper) in Colombo.[5] His father, Abraham Samlant Sr.,

[4] For careers of VOC personnel, see Albert van den Belt, *Het VOC-bedrijf op Ceylon: Een voorname vestiging van de Oost-Indische Compagnie in de 18de eeuw* (Zutphen: Walburg Pers, 2008), 236–39.

[5] R.G. Anthonisz, *Report on the Dutch Records in the Government Archives at Colombo* (Colombo: H.C. Cottle, Govt. Printer, 1907), 63; Lodewijk Wagenaar, *Galle, VOC-vestiging in Ceylon: Beschrijving van een koloniale samenleving aan de vooravond van de Singalese opstand tegen het Nederlandse gezag, 1760* (Amsterdam: De Bataafsche Leeuw, 1994), 30.

son of Barent Samlant and grandson of Barent Barentsz Samlant of Haarlem, a *vrijburger* in Colombo, was the commander of Galle.[6] Adriaan Sebastiaan van de Graaff, who was appointed president of the Galle Landraad in May 1785 as he was the overseer of the Galle district, was the brother of Governor Willem Jacob van de Graaff.[7] Other Landraad top brass (presidents and vice-presidents in particular) were also from influential families. Diederick Thomas Fretz was president for almost nine years from 1770 to 1779, the longest term on record. He was also present at most meetings (160 of 175). At times, the same officials ran the council for many years. Petrus Jacobus Rosemale Cocq was a bookkeeper when the Dutch government appointed him secretary of the Landraad in 1778.[8] He served till 1785, when he was transferred to serve as the secretary of the Colombo Landraad, but returned as president of the Galle Landraad in December 1790. Vice-President Andreas Everhardus de Lij was a *meester in de rechten* (Master of Laws), and was perhaps the most educated of the councillors in the field of law.

At times, it was difficult to find a secretary. Wilhelmus Gijsbert van Zitter took the oath as secretary on 8 July 1786 and served in that capacity at that particular meeting, but did not appear again. Some weeks later, in October 1786, Johan Pieter Simon Cadenski assumed duties as secretary at a special meeting held only for his appointment, but his seven-year-long term of office was highly unsatisfactory, as discussed earlier in chapter one.

The Galle Landraad was headed by European officials who served in high-level judicial, executive and legislative capacities. While in Galle, Cornelis de Cock was a junior merchant and overseer of the district.[9] He served in the Galle Landraad from September 1767 to December 1769, and was later a dessave of Colombo. Later in his life, he also served as chairman of the Colombo Landraad. He was born in Emden, northern Germany, but as he had spent much of his thirty years in Sri Lanka, he may have had some understanding of the vernaculars.[10] He served in

[6] Wagenaar, *Galle, VOC-vestiging in Ceylon*, 30. He had his first appointment in 1731, as a soldier, and was made junior merchant in 1742. He was appointed commander in 1758 and served in that post till 1766.

[7] For his first day in the Landraad, see SLNA 1/6525, "Galle Landraad draft minutes" (1784 to 1786), fols. 100v, 14 May 1785. For an account of the family see F.H. de Vos, "The Dutch Governors of Ceylon," *Journal of the Dutch Burger Union of Ceylon* 2, no. 3 (1909): 142.

[8] SLNA 7/2353, "Inward Letters, Galle Landraad" 1778 to 1801, Letter dated 7 May 1778 from Commander Anoldus de Lij to the Galle Landraad.

[9] SLNA 1/6503, "Galle Landraad minutes" (1768), fols. 53r, 16 Jul 1768.

[10] Remco Raben and Max De Bruijn, (eds), *The World of Jan Brandes, 1743-1808: Drawings of a Dutch Traveller in Batavia, Ceylon and Southern Africa* (Zwolle, Amsterdam: Waanders Publishers, Rijkmuseum, 2004), 258, 260. For extensive details of his career, see Frits van Dulm, *"Zonder eigen gewinne en glorie": Mr. Iman Wilhelm Falck (1736-1785), gouverneur en directeur van Ceylon en onderhorigheden* (Hilversum: Verloren, 2012), 73–74, 21n.

various capacities, such as a private secretary to the governor and chief warehouse keeper during the embassy from Kandy in 1772; he is depicted in an illustration of the audience at that event by Carel Frederik Reimer.[11] He is also featured in an illustration by the minister Jan Brandes, a Lutheran like himself, who appears to have struck up a friendship with him soon after his arrival in 1785. De Cock is shown conversing with his Sinhalese officers in a relaxed fashion in the verandah of his office in Hulftsdorp, Colombo, just two months before his departure from Sri Lanka.[12] The German Diederick Thomas Fretz, who served as president of the Galle Landraad, also became dessave in Colombo later on.[13] He was captain of the Mahabadde or the Cinnamon Department, dessave of Matara in 1785, and then dessave in Colombo in 1787, but he returned to Galle as commander in 1792.[14] Fretz was one of the first VOC servants to pledge alliance to the British in 1799 and serve in the civil court of Galle. At the same time, he had hopes that the Dutch would regain control of Sri Lanka and wished to be installed as governor.[15] Fretz died in 1815, shortly after the takeover of the Kandyan kingdom by the British. Sluijsken, who was *hoofd administrateur* (chief administrator) towards the end of his career, may have also had ambitions of being appointed governor in the event that the British returned Sri Lanka to the Dutch,[16] and he did not encourage alliance to the British administration.[17]

[11] R.G. Anthonisz, "Governor Falck's Audience with the Kandyan Ambassadors," *Journal of the Dutch Burger Union of Ceylon* 2, no. 4 (1909); Carel Frederik Reimer, *Ontvangst van de Gezanten van de Koning van Kandy Door Gouverneur Imam Falck*, 1772, h 280 mm × b 430 mm, 1772, Rijksmuseum, Amsterdam, https://www.rijksmuseum.nl/nl/collectie/RP-T-1904-18.

[12] Although the Rijksmuseum website identifies the image as a scene from the Landraad, probably following Wilhelmus Hermanus Vroom's analysis, Remco Raben and Jan Veenendaal have pointed out that if it were a gathering of that council, other European officers would have been present. Nevertheless, the dessave's residency in Colombo was also the seat of the Landraad. Jan Brandes, *Cornelis de Cock with Sinhalese Officers in Hulftsdorp, Colombo, Seated in His Verandah to Settle the Affairs and Disputes of the Natives*, November 29, 1785, Watercolour over sketch in pencil, 19.5 x 15.5, November 29, 1785, Rijksmuseum, Amsterdam, https://www.rijksmuseum.nl//en/collection/NG-1985-7-1-9; Wilhelmus Hermanus Vroom, "Jan Brandes, de Landraad Te Colombo in 1785," *Bulletin van Het Rijksmuseum* 37 (1989): 253–55; Raben and De Bruijn, *The World of Jan Brandes*, 259.

[13] Raben and De Bruijn, *The World of Jan Brandes*, 309.

[14] van den Belt, *Het VOC-bedrijf op Ceylon*, 199; J.P. Lewis, "Dutch Extracts and the Dutch Company in the Matara District," *Journal of the Dutch Burger Union of Ceylon* 1, no. 4 (1908): 197.

[15] Alicia Schrikker, *Dutch and British Colonial Intervention in Sri Lanka, 1780-1815: Expansion and Reform* (Leiden: Brill, 2007), 144, 243n.

[16] Personal communication from Alicia Schrikker.

[17] Schrikker, *Dutch and British Colonial Intervention*, 144–45.

Table 2.1 Some presidents, vice-presidents and secretaries 1759–1795

Function and Name	Recorded in Minutes	
	First	Last
Presidents		
Toussaint, Johannes	29 Sept 1759	6 Dec 1760
Marci, Adolph Fredrik	17 Sept 1762	6 Aug 1764
Balthazar Hendrik Stroebbe	14 Jul 1764	15 Jan 1766
Sluijsken, Peter	15 Jan 1766	27 Jun 1767
Cock, Cornelis de	5 Sept 1767	30 Dec 1769
Fretz, Diederick Thomas	24 Feb 1770	24 Dec 1779
Samlant, Abraham	24 Dec 1779	11 Jun 1785
Graaff, Adriaan Sebastian van den	14 May 1785	24 Mar 1787
Johannes Franciscus Gratiaan	14 Apr 1787	5 Apr 1788
Pieter William Ferdinand Adriaan van Schuler	12 Nov 1788	23 Oct 1790
Roosmale Cocq, Petrus Jacobus	11 Dec 1790	12 Dec 1795
Vice-Presidents		
Velde, Egbert van de	29 Sept 1759	6 Dec 1760
Cramer, Hendrik	20 Jul 1763	16 Aug 1766
Velzen, Adriaan van	21 Feb 1767	26 Nov 1768
Bergh, Adrianus van den	15 Jul 1769	7 Jan 1775
Martheze, Nicolaas Bernardus	7 Jan 1775	21 Sept 1776
Conradie, Johan Fredrik	16 May 1778	9 May 1779
Lij, Andreas Everhardus de	31 Mar 1781	12 Oct 1782
Vos, Pieter de	8 Jun 1765 16 Nov 1782	21 Mar 1772 2 Feb 1793
Hendrik Anthon Johnson	10 May 1793	12 Dec 1795
Secretaries		
Johannes Stein	26 Apr 1760	15 Jul 1775
Roosmale Cocq, Petrus Jacobus	16 May 1778	19 Aug 1785
Cadenski, Johan Pieter Simon	25 Oct 1786	28 Jun 1793
Pieter Arend de Moor	19 Jul 1793	12 Dec 1795

Sources: SLNA 1/6497 to 6525, Minutes of the Galle Landraad.

European councillors were Christian (Dutch Reformed or Lutheran) and were likely to have been privileged inhabitants of the Galle Fort with close political, economic and social ties to each other. The company frequently depended on foreigners to satisfy its requirements for personnel.[18] More than 60 per cent of civil servants in Galle were of mixed parentage, so it is not surprising that some councillors were Eurasian – Abraham Samlant, Egbert van de Velde, Johannes Toussaint, Johannes de Leeuw, Nicolaas Lasge, Hendrik Brakel, Harmanus Engelbregt and Pieter de Vos, to name a few.[19] For convenience, I have used "European" as an umbrella term that includes persons of European birth and mixed descent.[20] Many VOC officials were born in the towns of Sri Lanka or in other VOC settlements in south India. Of the various birthplaces of a majority (seventy out of seventy-five) of the European councillors in the Galle Landraad, 30 per cent were born in Galle, 17 per cent in Colombo and 43 per cent in Europe. Many company servants who served the Landraad were second- and later-generation Europeans. Abraham Samlant and his father, also named Abraham Samlant (1713–1766), were born in Colombo, and the senior Samlant is described in the records as mixed. They were well established in the company and community.[21] We see such extensive cultural mixing, both through intermarriage and day to day interactions, that it appears there was a spectrum of social power spanning an array of social formations including ethnic categories.[22] However, when disputes arose in official matters, divisions focused on "white" and native categories, as we will see later.

A majority of the councillors were thus rooted in Sri Lanka and served in the island for many years before they were appointed to the Landraad. Records show

[18] Femme Gaastra says that around 1770, 80 per cent of soldiers and 50 per cent of all seamen in company service were born outside The Netherlands. The total number of VOC personnel in Sri Lanka was 4,652 in 1753 and 3,784 in 1780, the second highest in Asia after Batavia. He further says: "Around 1786, no less than a quarter of the European Personnel on Ceylon, where there was a considerable European community, had been born in Asia." Femme S. Gaastra, *The Dutch East India Company: Expansion and Decline* (Zutphen: Walburg Pers, 2003), 81–82, 87. For 1760, Wagenaar gives a figure of three-quarters of the administrative personnel. Wagenaar, *Galle, VOC-vestiging in Ceylon*, 134. Jan van Goor says that under Governor Falck (1765–1785), who was himself born in Sri Lanka, "more than two-thirds of the civil servants had come from the East Indies and Ceylon." J. van Goor, *Jan Kompenie as Schoolmaster: Dutch Education in Ceylon 1690–1795* (Groningen: Wolters-Noordhoff, 1978), 17.

[19] Raben and De Bruijn, *The World of Jan Brandes*, 342; Wagenaar, *Galle, VOC-vestiging in Ceylon*, 48–49, 133, 137.

[20] The class of "Europeans" in the general muster rolls included a considerable number of company servants born in Asia and people of Eurasian descent. Gaastra, *The Dutch East India Company*, 87.

[21] The senior Samlant was described as "poesties." NL-HaNA, VOC 12,424. Generale Monsterrollen van Ceylon. As reproduced in Wagenaar, *Galle, VOC-vestiging in Ceylon*, 137. Wagenaar explains "poesties" as the offspring of *casties* (half-European) parents. Ibid., 48.

[22] I thank the anonymous reviewer of this book who pointed this out.

movement between Colombo, Galle and other areas in Sri Lanka, with some movement from south India as well. Robert Ross and Alicia Schrikker have shown that the VOC families in the Cape, for instance, displayed similar mobility and rootedness.[23] Some started as soldiers and sailors; Hendrik Brakel was a ship's boy when he took up service with the company. At the time of their appointment to the Landraad, many held the rank of bookkeeper; among them were Steven Anthonisz, Bernhard Hendrik van Bergheim, Roelof Frits, Dirk François van Gijsel, Hendrik Johannes Hingert, Nicolaas Lasge, Petrus Jacobus Roosmale Cocq and Lourens Jolles. The Landraad councillor, Coenraad Otto, for instance, was born in the Fort of Mannar and began service in the company as a soldier in 1751. In 1785, he was employed at the *negotiekantoor* (trade office) as a bookkeeper and earned 30 guilders per month.[24] We know from a painting by Jan Brandes that his residence was in Galle Fort.[25] It is obvious that not many of them had much experience dealing with the law.

The councillors were propertied people who likely lived in houses that matched their status and had access to the best goods and services due to their proximity to Galle Fort. Lodewijk Wagenaar describes life in Galle Fort as combining European and Asian features.[26] Pomp and circumstance, displayed through carriages and slaves and servants, were important aspects of life in fortified towns such as Batavia and the settlement of Cape Town.[27] Galle was probably no exception to the development of this colonial society. Despite the distance, the top brass among the company servants also kept in touch with developments in Europe. An inventory of books at the secretariat at Galle lists a number of legal texts.[28] Intellectually, Europe and the Netherlands were not so far from Asia.[29]

Councillors were not remunerated for serving in the Landraad beyond a small *mantel geld* or cloak fee.[30] Their salaries as bookkeepers and merchants were low,

[23] Robert Ross and Alicia Schrikker, "The VOC Official Elite" in Nigel Worden (ed), *Cape Town between East and West* (Johannesburg: Jacana, 2012), 26–44.

[24] Raben and De Bruijn, *The World of Jan Brandes*, 342.

[25] Ibid., 340–43.

[26] Wagenaar, *Galle, VOC-vestiging in Ceylon*, 67–105. See also Lodewijk Wagenaar, "The Cultural Dimension of the Dutch East India Company," in Thomas Da Costa Kaufmann and Michael North (eds) *Mediating Netherlandish Art and Material Culture in Asia* (Amsterdam: Amsterdam University Press, 2014).

[27] Gaastra, *The Dutch East India Company*, 104; Nigel Worden, "Introduction," in Nigel Worden (ed), *Cape Town: Between East and West, Social Identities in a Dutch Colonial Town* (Auckland Park & Hilversum: Jacana Media, 2012).

[28] Wagenaar, *Galle, VOC-vestiging in Ceylon*, 139, 214n.

[29] Schrikker, *Dutch and British Colonial Intervention*, 100.

[30] Nadaraja quotes Jacob Burnand, a VOC official who stayed on till British times, who believed that it was 30 or 40 rixdollars a year. T. Nadaraja, *The Legal System of Ceylon in its Historical Setting* (Leiden: Brill, 1972), 33n.

but private trading and corruption allowed company servants to amass wealth.[31] They were also compensated for their costs when inquiries had to be held at some distance from where the council usually sat.[32] Councillors were commissioned to go to villages to investigate matters of ownership or to examine whether lands that were to be sold had cinnamon trees. At times European members of the Landraad complained that they were not receiving enough remuneration.[33] It was forbidden for Dutch officials and headmen in the Landraad to accept presents from persons who had or seemed likely to have a case before the council, "upon the penalty of loss of office and arbitrary disciplinary action." In the oath of office taken by members, they swore to abstain from any corruption.[34] The Landraad was not the only body they served in: the secretary served in other bodies in that capacity,[35] the president served primarily as the overseer of the Galle district, and some councillors also served in the Galle Political Council, the Raad van Justitie or the Inlandse Boedelkamer, to name a few. Some councillors appeared for long periods in the Landraad, while a few died on the job.[36]

The Europeans in the Landraad had close economic connections with the headmen. Sluijsken invested in a project started by a high-ranking local headman, Nicolaas Dias Abeysinghe Amarasekera, and his son Balthasar to develop a large fertile land, called Diviture,[37] northwest of the Galle district, and his business in

31 Much has been written on this topic. See for an overview Gaastra, *The Dutch East India Company*, 95–101. For a more detailed study, see Chris Nierstrasz, *In the Shadow of the Company: The Dutch East India Company and its Servants in the Period of its Decline (1740-1796)* (Leiden: Brill, 2012).

32 This appears to have been one or two rixdollars per half a day. For the costs of various documents drawn up by the secretary, see also SLNA 1/6502, "Galle Landraad minutes" (1767), fols. 50r, 1 Jun 1767. An earlier listing of this is given in SLNA 1/94, "Governor in Council minutes" (1745), fols. 111r, 11 Feb 1745.

33 Johan Casper German, Steven Anthonisz and Laurens Jolles said that when two officials from Galle had served on the Matara Landraad, they had been paid a fee of a quarter rixdollar for each sitting, either for the *recoleeren* (reading aloud) of a declaration or for hearing an interrogation. SLNA 1/6526, "Annexes," fols 197r–198r, Letter (n.d.) to the Landraad President from German, Anthonisz & Jolles.

34 Hovy, *Plakkaatboek*, vol. 2; nr. 628, (I, 12), Instructions for the Landraden, including extracts from resolutions, 25 Jun 1789. See for translation S.A.W. Mottau, trans., "Instructions for the Respective 'Landraden' of this Government (Extract from the Dutch Political Council Minutes of 25th June 1789)," *Journal of the Dutch Burger Union of Ceylon* 55, no. 1–4 (1965). See the formula of this oath in SLNA 1/5666, "Miscellaneous documents of the Galle Landraad including instructions" (1761 to 1789), fols. 22v, n.d.

35 SLNA 1/6525, "Galle Landraad draft minutes," fols. 191r, 8 July 1786. The secretary of the Landraad was also the secretary of the Scholarchale Vergadering.

36 For example, Floris van Swieten's last participation in the Landraad was by *rondvraag*, dated 15 October 1762, and his employment with the VOC ended shortly afterwards, with his death on 25 November 1762. SLNA 1/6499, "Galle Landraad minutes" (1760 to 1763), fols. 63r, 15 Oct 1762; Nationaal Archief at The Hague, "VOC Opvarenden (VOC Sea-Voyagers)," accessed December 5, 2014, https://www.nationaalarchief.nl/onderzoeken/index/nt00444.

37 Schrikker, *Dutch and British Colonial Intervention*, 44.

Galle was headed by a *mohandiram* (a headman below the rank of mudaliyār) by the name of Simon de Silva.[38] Sluijsken was also involved in revenue farming and signed as guarantor to the renter of the chank fishery in 1786.[39] When he became dessave of Colombo, Fretz was among those company officials who attempted to amass some wealth through plantations, justifying it as necessary due to his small income as a dessave. The plantations were cultivated by cheap labour supposedly provided by headmen with whom he is likely to have collaborated.[40] Company servants and local headmen maintained private patronage relationships with each other, but at times VOC officials felt that the local headmen threatened their power, as illustrated by Schrikker.[41]

Councillors in close family relationships were not allowed to serve together in the Landraden.[42] But marriages between influential families in Galle and Colombo meant that the community of VOC servants was closely knit. The councillor August Christian Anthon Graaf van Ranzow[43] was married to Petronella Anthonica, the daughter of Jacobus de Bordes, a trade commissioner also featured in Reimer's illustration of the Kandyan embassy of 1772. Another figure who featured in Reimer's illustration, Political Secretary Martinus Mekern, had a daughter who married Johan Frederik Conradi, another councillor of the Galle Landraad.[44] The councillor Abraham Samlant's sister, Agnita Clara, married Willem Jacob van de Graaff, the later governor.[45] A list of such connections would be endless.[46] Many wives of company servants were of mixed origins (*mestiças*),[47] including those who spoke Portuguese instead of Dutch. We see that their male offspring also took up service with the company; some were sent to the Netherlands to be educated.[48]

38 Schrikker, Dutch and British Colonial Intervention, 72, 229n.

39 Nadeera Rupesinghe (writing as Seneviratne), "Strange Cooperation: Revenue Farmers in Eighteenth-century Sri Lanka" (MPhil Dissertation, Leiden, Leiden University, 2010).

40 Schrikker, *Dutch and British Colonial Intervention*, 71–73.

41 Ibid., 68–69.

42 No judicial body could have a father and son, brothers or a father-in-law and son-in-law serving together. Hovy, *Plakkaatboek*, vol. 2; nr. 628, (I, 6).

43 He was from the elite Ranzow family, which included Daniel Ditloff Count van Ranzow, who was a junior merchant and member of the Landraad in Colombo in 1785. Jan Brandes drew Daniel's manor. Raben and De Bruijn, *The World of Jan Brandes*, 239–41.

44 Anthonisz, "Governor Falck's Audience with the Kandyan Ambassadors," 150–51.

45 Anthonisz, *Report on the Dutch Records*, 63; Wagenaar, *Galle, VOC-vestiging in Ceylon*, 30.

46 For family networks and social mobility in the VOC world at large, see Ulbe Bosma and Remco Raben, *Being "Dutch" in the Indies: A History of Creolisation and Empire, 1500-1920*, trans. Wendie Shaffer (Singapore: NUS Press, 2008); Jean Gelman Taylor, *The Social World of Batavia: European and Eurasian in Dutch Asia* (Wisconsin & London: University of Wisconsin Press, 1983).

47 Wagenaar, *Galle, VOC-vestiging in Ceylon*, 142–45.

48 van den Belt, *Het VOC-bedrijf op Ceylon*, 260, 266; Gaastra, *The Dutch East India Company*, 104.

Some couples adopted Sinhalese children: Councillor Johannes Stein and his wife Assertia Christoffels adopted Johanna Sophia, a Sinhalese girl.[49] In this and other ways, such as through common religious practices and lifestyles, distinctions between so-called Europeans and headmen were potentially eroded.

Local Councillors and Their Social Context

The local members of the Landraad were expected to be intermediaries between the peasant population and the European members. They were all high officials in the native department of the colonial government (see Table 2.2). Members of a multicultural elite, they had autonomous power over most of the Sinhalese peasant population. Their elite status was dependant on office holding, and the highest ranking among them were members of the Landraad.[50] The headmen had patron-client relations with the peasants, which also sometimes included debt bondage.[51] Such relations meant that the company was dependent on the headmen. Access to labour was a key factor in this relationship. The local councillors were also large landowners and belonged to families that continued to be influential in British times. The vast estates that they possessed, some of which extended to thirty land holdings, can be seen in their last wills.[52] D.A. Kotelawele and Schrikker agree that their power increased considerably over the eighteenth century.[53] For the purpose of office bearing, they adopted the Dutch Reformed religion at least nominally; some may have been practising Calvinists.

Nicolaas Dias Abeysinghe Amarasekera, who served in the Galle Landraad for more than twenty years, from 1764 to 1785, rose high in the native department of government. He was born on 8 May 1719, and it was in his forties, during the war with Kandy (1760–1765), that he truly began to rise in eminence. At the time, other Sinhalese officials were defecting to the king of Kandy, and those who remained were rewarded for their loyalty to the company. Abeysinghe was probably an educated man, as he was keeper of the school thombos when he was promoted to the

[49] Wagenaar, *Galle, VOC-vestiging in Ceylon*, 93.

[50] D.A. Kotelawele, "Nineteenth-Century Elites and Their Antecedents," *Ceylon Historical Journal* 25, no. 1–4 (1978): 211.

[51] Schrikker, *Dutch and British Colonial Intervention*, 68.

[52] D.A. Kotelawele, "Agrarian Policies of the Dutch in South-West Ceylon, 1743–1767," *A.A.G. Bijdragen* 14, no. 8 (1967): 16. For numerous references to large estates, see P. E. Pieris, *Notes on Some Sinhalese Families: Ilangakon*, vol. 4 (Colombo: Times of Ceylon, n.d.).

[53] D.A. Kotelawele, "Some Aspects of Social Change in the South West of Sri Lanka c. 1700-1833," *Social Science Review* no. 4 (1988): 96–97; Schrikker, *Dutch and British Colonial Intervention*, 67.

Table 2.2 Local members at the Landraad 1759–1796

Name	*Title*	*Recorded in minutes*	
		First	*Last*
Adriaan de Silva Jayetilleke Seresinghe	Kōralē mudaliyār	8 Apr 1775	28 May 1785
Augustinus Ferdinandus Wiresinghe	Titular mudaliyār	29 Jan 1774	2 Dec 1786
Don Balthasar Dias Abeysinghe Siriwardene	Mahamudaliyār & Native Sabandar	27 May 1786	12 Dec 1795
Don Bastiaan Wijenaike	Mohandiram	29 Sept 1759	6 Dec 1760
Don Bastiaan Jayatilleke Gooneratne	Atapattu mudaliyār	18 Jun 1791	12 Dec 1795
Don Constantine de Saram Wijesinghe	Mohandiram	29 Jan 1774	11 Mar 1780
Don Johan Anthony Alvis Abeyesiriwickreme Jayawardene	Kōralē mudaliyār	27 May 1786	12 Dec 1795
Don Johan de Silva Wanigasekere	Mohandiram	29 Sept 1759	11 Dec 1779
Don Louis Livere Wickremenaike Samarasinghe	Mohandiram	29 Sept 1759	25 Mar 1775
Don Matthijs de Silva Abeyewardene Wijeyesekere	Kōralē Mohandiram	1 Apr 1780	4 Jun 1791
Don Philip de Silva Wickremesinghe Dahanayake	Mohandiram	14 Jul 1764	26 Jul 1788
Nicolaas Dias Abeysinghe Amarasekera	Mahamudaliyār	14 Jul 1764	12 Nov 1788

Sources: SLNA 1/6497–6525, Minutes of the Galle Landraad.

high rank of mahamudaliyār to the commander of Galle. Hereditary appointments to the native department were otherwise the norm (Abeysinghe's father was a mohandiram). His allegiance to the VOC was rewarded with two gold medals that he received from governors Schreuder and Van de Graaff in 1762 and 1785. In 1764, he began to appear in the Galle Landraad minutes. His involvement with the council stopped in 1785 when Governor Van de Graaff appointed him mahamudaliyār of the governor's gate in Colombo, in which capacity he served for more than nine years till his death. As was apparently the practice for a mahamudaliyār and other headmen, Abeysinghe was perhaps not allowed to wear shoes or sit in

Figure 2.1 Mahamudaliyār Nicolaas Dias Abeysinghe Amarasekera. Watercolour over sketch in pencil, 41.4 x 32.6 cm. Rijksmuseum Amsterdam, inv.nr. NG-1985-7-3-124 (detail). Jan Brandes, the artist, appears to have written the following: "Mudaliyār or interpreter of the governor of Ceylon wearing a green velvet coat and golden bandoleer with a golden sword, and a golden chain." Translation from Raben and De Bruijn, The World of Jan Brandes, *309.*

the presence of the governor,[54] but that did not undermine his position as Van de Graaff's confidante.[55]

Most recently, Schrikker has analysed Abeysinghe's power with an in-depth account of his influence over the governor.[56] Van de Graaff undermined the Galle commander by extending his own authority over the native department through Abeysinghe. One commander who was affected by this was Pieter Sluijsken. In earlier work, the historian Valli Kanapathipillai left Sluijsken's staunch criticism of Abeysinghe's growing power in Colombo unquestioned.[57] Sluijsken went so far as to suggest that Van de Graaff and Abeysinghe had committed treason. The mahamudaliyār was in charge of correspondence between Kandy and the governor, and Sluijsken said that there was a great deal of secrecy around this communication. He said Abeysinghe and his accomplices in Kandy had maintained a façade of cordiality between the VOC and the Kandyans, and that he had instigated war and unrest in the country for fear of being exposed. Anthony Bertolacci, a civil servant under the first British governor Frederick North, also gives a disparaging account of the mahamudaliyār. He says Abeysinghe fabricated letters addressed to the governor from the adigār, and that he retained the governor's expensive presents to him.[58] Schrikker points out that Sluijsken's accusations must be seen in the context of his troubled relationship with Van de Graaff. She suggests that Sluijsken's status was adversely affected by the governor's policy of sidelining his authority as commander of Galle, that Sluijsken failed to assign credible motives for treason on the part of the governor and his trusted mahamudaliyār, and that he was badly informed. Van de Graaff appears to have been aware that Abeysinghe was corresponding secretly with the first adigār of Kandy. We may never know what happened, but the speculation around Abeysinghe's power shows that high-ranking headmen and company servants engaged in a tug of war for power.

54 The first British Governor of Sri Lanka, Frederick North, refers to this practice. Quoted in Rajpal Kumar de Silva and Willemina G.M. Beumer, *Illustrations and Views of Dutch Ceylon 1602–1796: A Comprehensive Work of Pictorial Reference with Selected Eye-Witness Accounts* (Leiden: Brill, 1988), 477, n. 6. Depictions of embassies from Kandy by C.F. Reimer and Jan Brandes show the headmen going barefoot. Reimer, *Ontvangst van de Gezanten*; Raben and De Bruijn, *The World of Jan Brandes*, 308.

55 I obtained biographical details for this account from P.E. Pieris, *Notes on Some Sinhalese Families: Being the Diary of Adirian de Alwis Goonetilleke Samaranaike*, vol. 3 (Colombo: The Colombo Apothecaries Co., 1911); Raben and De Bruijn, *The World of Jan Brandes*, 311.

56 Schrikker, *Dutch and British Colonial Intervention*, 68–71, 118–21.

57 Kanapathipillai, Valli, "Dutch Rule in Maritime Ceylon 1766–1796" (PhD dissertation, University of London, 1969), 161–62.

58 Anthony Bertolacci, *A View of the Agricultural, Commercial, and Financial Interests of Ceylon* (London: Black, Parbury and Allen, 1817), 53.

Caste headmen, such as Augustinus Ferdinandus Wiresinghe,[59] were also prominent figures in Galle society. Wiresinghe was a titular mudaliyār of the *karāva* (fisher) caste and the Tamil interpreter at the Political and Judicial Secretariat. He obtained his promotion from mohandiram to mudaliyār on the strength of his loyalty to Governor Lubbert Jan Baron van Eck (1762–1765) in the war with Kandy.[60] He was from Negombo and a widower when in January 1774 he gave notice of marriage to Elizabeth Maria van Houten of Galle, a burger going by her name.[61] He appears in the Landraad records from 1774 till his death in 1786.[62]

A few months before he died, Wiresinghe was in trouble. He was accused of instigating a riot among the karāva and *durāva* (toddy-tapping) castes against the company, and in December 1785 the Raad van Justitie in Galle convicted him along with three others, while nine other accused were released. Wiresinghe's punishment was demotion from his post of Tamil interpreter. Yet, Colombo softened its stance on all four who were sentenced, stating that the case involved "more carelessness than bad intention." Wiresinghe was only to be suspended for six months. He was absent from Landraad meetings during the crisis and suspension, but reappeared in five meetings towards the end of 1786, from September to November, till his death. It is possible that his services were necessary to the company, perhaps resulting in the changed sentence. Wiresinghe's influence over his caste is seen in the riot case. The dispute concerned the instructions issued to the headmen of Galle and Matara. Galle Commander Cornelius Dionisius Kraijenhoff informed Colombo that the karāva and durāva castes in the Galle district were troubled that the instructions had ranked them among the lower castes.[63] Kraijenhoff and Fretz, dessave of Colombo, were appointed to examine the instruction and recommend necessary changes; their proposal to remove some phrases from the instruction was approved.[64] Wiresinghe worked for his caste, but at least caste divisions did not seem to have been so acute that he could not preside over sessions that heard evidence by members of the *goygama* farmer caste, who had a higher ritual status.[65]

[59] Another source mentions his name as Augustinus Ferdinandus Kurukula Surawiresinghe. SLNA 1/193, "Governor in Council minutes" (1786), 18 Feb 1786.

[60] SLNA 1/5713, "Register of Acts of Appointment of Native Officials" (1767 to 1775), fols. 66r-v, 1 Feb 1772.

[61] New No. 5/2, "Marriage Register, Dutch Reformed Church, Galle" (1774 to 1789), Christian Reformed Church.

[62] The secretary of the Inlandse Boedelkamer came before the Landraad in connection with Wiresinghe's estate in 1793. SLNA 1/6516, "Galle Landraad minutes" (1793), f. 4v-5r, 28 Jun 1793.

[63] SLNA 1/191, "Governor in Council minutes" (1785), 1 Aug 1785.

[64] Ibid., 9 Aug 1785; SLNA 1/192, "Governor in Council minutes" (1785), 13 Sept 1785.

[65] For just one example, see SLNA 1/6525, "Galle Landraad draft minutes," f. 50v, 16 Aug 1784; 58v, 23 Sept 1784.

The headmen networked closely with different groups on the island. Abeysinghe himself was willing to associate closely with karāvas and Europeans alike. To execute his will, he appointed, among others, a free merchant called Philip Solomon de Waas, mahamudaliyār Johannes de Saram, mohandiram of the guard Louis de Saram, and the mudaliyār of the karāvas, Renaldus de Andrado.[66] Matara mahamudaliyār Don Johan Abeysiriwardena Ilangakoon was also known to collaborate closely with Chettiars and Moors, and appointed members of these communities as executors to his will.[67] Pieter Arend de Moor, most probably the councillor of the Landraad with that name and presumably close to the family, attested his joint will with his second wife.[68] Economic cooperation between diverse groups of office holders was not unknown, but it did not extend to marriage alliances and sharing of places of worship beyond those who had adopted Calvinism.[69] High-ranking goygamas, Europeans, Chettiars, Moors and a few non-goygama caste headmen were closely connected on various fronts. This elite group shared a common lifestyle.

It is not surprising that the mudaliyārs were closely linked through marriage. Nicolaas Dias Abeysinghe Amarasekera's second marriage was to Ilangakoon's daughter by his first wife, Dona Adriana Gertruyda. Nicolaas was also an executor to Ilangakoon's joint will with his first wife.[70] In a cross-cousin union, Abeysinghe's daughter, Anne Gertruyda, married Don Bastiaan Jayatilleke Gooneratne (1758–1812), another Landraad councillor and member of a prominent southern family, whose mother was Abeysinghe's sister.[71] Abeysinghe's first wife was Gooneratne's aunt. A British official in the early nineteenth century referred to such closely knit family connections[72] among Sinhalese headmen as "an imperium in imperio,"

66 Nicolaas also named his sons, Don Balthazar Dias and Johannes Wilhelmus Dias, his son-in-law the *atapattu mudaliyār* Don Bastiaan Gooneratne, and *mudaliyār* of the Belligam Kōralē, Johannes Wijeywardene, as executors. Pieris, *Notes on Some Sinhalese Families*, 3:24. Sluijsken also mentioned Nicolaas's executors. See Schrikker, *Dutch and British Colonial Intervention*, 73, 229n.

67 See Pieris, *Notes on Some Sinhalese Families: Ilangakon*, 4:90–91. Recently published private correspondence also shows close connections between Chettiars and some Sinhalese. Herman Tieken, *Between Colombo and the Cape: Letters in Tamil, Dutch and Sinhala Sent to Nicolaas Ondaatje from Ceylon*, vol. 6, Dutch Sources of South Asia (New Delhi: Manohar, 2015).

68 Pieris, *Notes on Some Sinhalese Families: Ilangakon*, 4:110.

69 Rupesinghe, "Strange Cooperation."

70 Pieris, *Notes on Some Sinhalese Families: Ilangakon*, 4:91, 114.

71 More details about the family can be found in a coffee-table book about the house in which they lived, half a mile from the Galle Fort. Janaka Goonetilleke (ed), *Atapattu Walawwa: Residence of the Gooneratne & Dias Abeyesinghe Families of Galle* (Galle: Atapattu Walawwa, 2012). Don Bastiaan Jayatilleke Gooneratne is said to have had the house constructed towards the end of the eighteenth century; it is, for the most part, still intact.

72 These involved cross-cousin marriages and siblings marrying other pairs of siblings.

and the durāva caste objected to the formation of a subordinate government of goygamas consisting of the likes of the Abeysinghes and Ilangakoons.[73]

The high-level Sinhalese headmen were wealthy and their lifestyle resembled that of the Europeans. It is uncertain if this increased their prestige among eighteenth-century peasants in Sri Lanka, whose understanding of foreign material culture has not been researched. This tendency of the local elites to emulate the Europeans is seen in a statement made by an early nineteenth-century observer. Jacob Burnand, a Swiss official of the VOC who served in the 1780s and 1790s and remained on the island in British times, remarked that the higher ranks of the Sinhalese headmen "fit up their houses in the European style and burn wax candles in silver candlesticks, instead of the lamp which served them before."[74] A 1797 inventory of the property of Nicolaas Dias Abeysinghe lists among other items more than nine thousand rixdollars worth of jewellery, and eleven slaves "valued" at more than a thousand rixdollars.[75] Lists of movable property belonging to high-ranking headmen show that silver spoons, Japanese crockery, teapots, cups and saucers, other porcelain items, and wine glasses and the like were common possessions.[76] Many also owned Dutch-style homes and furniture. In further imitation of company servants, the higher ranks of the native department also had slaves. They seem to have had considerable sums of money at their disposal. In one list, a single set of gold ornaments with Sri Lankan rubies was valued at over four thousand rixdollars, but the cash allowance of the mahamudaliyār was just eight rixdollars.[77] A cash surplus appears to have been within their reach as the company paid in cash for plantation produce.[78] Dutch rule brought in new wealth and the new institutional space of the Landraad, within which local elites could exert their power over the rural population and potentially consolidate their influence over company officials.

Divided Authority

The headmen were intermediaries who could provide Europeans access to the laws and customs of local society. The Landraad purportedly provided a space where the peasants, through the intermediary, could be heard by the dominant European power. The intermediary, in turn, was supposedly checked by the peasant farmers.

[73] Kotelawele, "Nineteenth-Century Elites," 207–8.

[74] Jacob Burnand, "Fragments on Ceylon," *Asiatic Journal* 12 (June 1821): 560.

[75] "Inventory of Nicolaas Dias Abeysinghe" (1797), Private collection of Siran Deraniyagala.

[76] Pieris, *Notes on Some Sinhalese Families: Ilangakon*, 4:67–69, 92–107. For a mid nineteenth-century list of movable and immovable property, see Ibid., 4:150–75.

[77] Pieris, *Notes on Some Sinhalese Families: Ilangakon*, 4:91.

[78] Schrikker, *Dutch and British Colonial Intervention*, 67; Kotelawele, "Agrarian Policies," 15–16.

Yet, it was the Europeans who exercised control over the council. As explained above, the majority of councillors and the president, vice-president and secretary of the Landraad were always European. From 1759 to 1796, 86 per cent (or seventy-five) of the members were European. Thus, the influence of the intermediary in the case of the Landraad was likely to be limited.

The company attached great value to the local councillors in theory, but whose voice was heard most? Existing literature suggests that a sitting had to include local members if it were to decide on land matters.[79] Despite espousing lofty principles such as engaging local headmen in the early days of its inception, in 1747 the Landraad of Colombo asked for permission from the governor to pronounce judgements in the absence of local members in order to expedite the resolution of cases. This was expressly forbidden, as the local chiefs were "well versed in the language and often gave explanations of the cases and usually knew the litigating parties."[80] Van Imhoff also intended the headmen to be present in the Landraden, recommending that they be partly, if not half, composed of locals.[81] It was Nadaraja who first asked the question: "Did the Asian members of the Landraad have the same powers as the European?" Nadaraja quotes Jacob Burnand, who said that the local members in the Landraad of Colombo could advise but not take part in decision-making.[82] The Landraad records confirm that they worked in an advisory capacity but did not have the power of the vote.

The company favoured the presence of more European members in the council. Emphasis was not laid exclusively on "Europeanness," but included "whiteness." For example, "whites" were contrasted with "blacks" in a letter from Colombo to Galle in 1745. All too often, it was written, there were only a few "white" members at the thombo registration for all kinds of reasons, which had made their numbers weaker than that of the "blacks."[83] The letter said that at least three Europeans ought to be present with two locals, and because they absolutely did not desire it to happen again, the absence of permanent members of the registration had to be filled by other assigned members. The land registration, the Dutch believed, had to be supervised closely by their own kind, given the opposition of the headmen

[79] Maria Wilhelmina Jurriaanse, *Catalogue of the Archives of the Dutch Central Government of Coastal Ceylon, 1640–1796* (Colombo: Ceylon Govt. Press, 1943), 245.

[80] SLNA 1/273, "Governor in Council Draft Ordinary Minutes" (1747), fols. 236r-v, 31 Oct 1747.

[81] Baron van Imhoff, *Memoir Left by Baron van Imhoff to His Successor, 1740*, trans. Sophia Pieters (Colombo: H.C. Cottle, Govt. Printer, 1911), 21.

[82] Nadaraja, *The Legal System of Ceylon*, 33.

[83] "En zulx blijkt ook maar al te dikmaals aan de wijnige blanke leden die zig laten vinden bij den beschrijving indiervoegen dat op allerhande voorwendzelen meer dan eens haar getal zwakker is dan der swarten." SLNA 1/5660, "Extracts of resolutions, orders, etc. regarding the Landraad and the thombo compilation" (1740 to 1770), fols. 9v, Extract of letter dated 24 Dec 1745 from Colombo to Galle.

to the process. The same preference is seen in the Landraad meetings. President Fretz, councillors Roosmale Cocq and Daniel Gerrardus Kersse and the locals Abeysinghe, Wiresinghe, Wanigasekere and Dahanayake attended a meeting held on 30 May 1778. The local councillors outnumbered the European members present that day. After the customary prayer, the first matter to be decided, on the president's proposal, was urging the commander of Galle to

> equip the body with some European or white members because many members generally excuse themselves as sick, by which the gathering becomes so weak, that there is a danger that sometimes matters must stay unfinished, and thus the natives are unnecessarily held back, as it happened in this meeting when only the hon. president and two European members were present, so that there was just the correct number to be able to give a judgement. But it is very necessary and advantageous that the disputes be settled by more members.[84]

It is thus confirmed that the headmen did not have the power to vote in the Landraad, and that a quorum of three European members was sufficient to give a judgement. The presence of more European members was considered so important that a decision on a case was delayed till the next meeting due to the scarcity (*geringeheijd*) of members.[85] Members took a vote regarding the case at the next meeting, which was attended by five European members and three headmen.[86] They took up the issue of the absence of European members again the following year, in July 1779. Four European members – President Fretz, Huijbertsz, Engelbregt and Kersse – along with the headmen Seresinghe, Wanigasekere and Dahanayake, were present. They did not pronounce judgement on two cases due to the scarcity of members and expressed a hope that more members would attend the next meeting.[87] But the next meeting also saw just four European members and three headmen, which was again referred to as a minority of members. It was decided that the members should hand in their votes in writing and, in case of absence, send in their votes.[88] Members must have been admonished for their absence, because at the next meeting, the Europeans in attendance were double the number of locals.[89] Much earlier, in 1760, a meeting was cancelled because

[84] SLNA 1/6511, "Galle Landraad minutes" (1778), fols. 5r-v, 30 May 1778.
[85] Ibid., fols. 7v, 30 May 1778.
[86] Ibid., fols. 12v, 6 Jun 1778.
[87] SLNA 1/6512, "Galle Landraad minutes" (1779), fols. 52r, 56v, 24 Jul 1779.
[88] Ibid., fols. 63r, 21 Aug 1779.
[89] Ibid., fols. 64r, 11 Sept 1779.

all the European members were absent. The local members were not mentioned.[90] Obviously, they could not assemble by themselves.

Europeans were thus crucial in the operation of the Landraad. The headmen, we may assume, played a significant role in advising them. However, for that purpose, their presence would have been necessary. From 1759 to 1795, the full bench of the Landraad or, less often, sessions with just two commissioners, met at erratic intervals with longer gaps during periods of conflict, as in the 1760s during the war with Kandy.[91] The council had thirteen to seventeen members at times, including the president and vice-president. Three to six members were headmen. On some occasions, as few as six members were present; often the headmen were absent from such meetings. From 1759 to 1795, no headmen were present at thirty-seven (5 per cent) of 737 consultations, seven of which were by *rondvraag*, or circulation of documents. In 1792 and 1793, local councillors did not attend as many as six and five meetings, respectively. A common reason for their absence was engagement elsewhere, referred to as being in service, in the company's service, or in his "actual" service as headman. Indisposition was also an oft-cited excuse. Incidentally, European councillors made the same excuses for their absence, so much so that the council decided they should not entertain such frivolous explanations.[92] Hendrik Koene once told the council's messenger that he had no time to attend.[93] Hendrik Aldons was fined ten rixdollars for staying away without excusing himself from the council.[94] Apart from full sittings of the council, the Landraad also had sessions usually led by two councillors, as seen in chapter one. From 1781 to 1788, only ten such meetings included a local councillor, and none were appointed to such meetings in other years.[95] The influence of the headmen as decision-makers in the judicial body is therefore questionable.

At least one local Landraad councillor questioned the judicial powers of the headmen. Don Adriaan Goonewardene Ponnamperuma, a mudaliyār in Galle and member of the Landraad,[96] clashed with the Landraad president Robbert Cornelis

90 SLNA 1/6498, "Galle Landraad minutes" (1760), fols. 45r, 9 Aug 1760.

91 See Table 1.1 in chapter one.

92 SLNA 1/6513, "Galle Landraad minutes" (1780), fols. 15r, 19 Feb 1780.

93 SLNA 1/6507, "Galle Landraad minutes" (1772), fols. 107v, 26 Sept 1772.

94 SLNA 1/6524, "Galle Landraad draft minutes" (1783), fols. 45v, 12 Jul 1783.

95 Don Matthijs de Silva Abeyewardene Wijeyesekere, Don Johan Anthony Alvis and Augustinus Ferdinandus Wiresinghe were assigned to such sessions.

96 A list of members of various Galle institutions mentions Ponnamperuma as a replacement for the deceased *mudaliyār* Denijs Alvis. SLNA 1/5046, "Galle Political Council minutes" (1743 to 1746), fols. 24r, 3 Mar 1744.

Bagilet on 19 September 1744.[97] Talgahenege Panikige Francisco appeared for his mother, the widow of Panikige Bastiaan, and his heirs, against Panikige Philippu (alias Wattuwa) who was also present at the Landraad that day. Francisco claimed that his father had bought the land named Dikowitte through a purchase deed dated 29 January 1729, and that despite that, Wattuwa had cultivated the land illegally. He stated that he had no more evidence to bring forward and asked that justice be meted out on the basis of the purchase deed. Four members were in favour of dismissing Wattuwa's claim, but the local members present, Ponnamperuma and Don Bastiaan, were in favour of granting the land to Wattuwa on the condition that he paid half of the purchase price paid by Francisco's father. The president, Bagilet, did not agree with either group of councillors, and attempted to influence them to allow the litigants to reach an agreement because, as he claimed, a minority of members were present that day. He also said that the litigants appeared to be willing to come to an agreement if Wattuwa were asked to pay the purchase price, perhaps with interest, assuming Francisco's mother and brothers agreed. He said that as the members were not in agreement, it would be best to allow the litigants to come to a settlement. Ponnamperuma reacted angrily to that by standing up, speaking out of turn in a raised voice and slamming his hand on the table. The president intimated that Ponnamperuma was biased, and claimed that he had not believed the stories to that effect that had reached him earlier. The mudaliyār became angrier, this time kicking his chair back and demanding that the Landraad removes him immediately. He said that he was not being adequately respected as a mudaliyār and that he spoke according to his conscience. He added that the assembly had affronted him and that it appeared that his vote did not count any more. It was recorded that he made such a noise that those outside the Landraad came rushing to the open door to watch. Francisco and Wattuwa were still inside.

The spectacle would no doubt have made a lasting impression on those who witnessed it. Bagilet proceeded to severely criticise Ponnamperuma's behaviour. Other members claimed that when they went out with him as commissioners, they often sensed that Ponnamperuma was biased, taking the side of a litigant without hearing the other side. They said that he had gravely insulted the Landraad that day with his unacceptable behaviour. Ponnamperuma reiterated his request to be removed from the council, and when asked for his reasons, he said he was a sick, weak man with little knowledge who did his best when he came to Landraad meetings but was not respected. The council decided to recommend his dismissal

[97] SLNA 1/93, "Governor in Council minutes" (1744), fols. 73r–78v, 3 Nov 1744; SLNA 1/5658, "Extracts of resolutions, orders, etc. regarding the Landraad and the thombo compilation" (1740 to 1745), fols. 16v, Extract resolution of 3 Nov 1744. No Landraad meetings for this period are available, but extracts from the relevant minutes are included in the Governor in Council minutes.

to the commander and said that it did not want to settle the disputes of the inhabitants while also dealing with their internal quarrels, much to the detriment of the reputation of the Landraad.

The dispute eventually reached the Governor in Council, who believed that Bagilet should not have delayed the case by pushing for a settlement. Moreover, the Governor in Council believed that when Bagilet realised that the case would not be settled to his liking, he should not have attempted to stop the proceedings by claiming that there were only a few members present, when there were actually eight that day. The Governor in Council said that it was understandable that Ponnamperuma was provoked and warned Bagilet to exercise caution. In his complaint following the altercation, Ponnamperuma claimed that Wattuwa, as the planter of the garden, had a claim to half of it. His complaint included, among other things, a condemnation of the inefficiency of the thombo registration, which he said must be investigated. He claimed that it was to the advantage of some to delay the registration as much as possible, and that the commissioners arrived at meetings whenever they felt like, without showing the least fear. The thombo registration in Galle was indeed delayed and did not proceed as smoothly as the registration in Colombo. It appears that the Governor had already questioned the Landraad on this, as Ponnamperuma referred to correspondence on the matter.

Around the beginning of the year 1745, Ponnamperuma made another complaint to Governor Van Gollonesse against Bagilet. He said the thombo registration could have easily been completed in two or three years if not for self-interest. He also made a searing attack on the local members of the Landraad:

> The white members of the Galle Landraad, seeing that the native headmen who have seats in that body are foolish, inexperienced and ignorant in the cases that are heard in that body, take little notice of the latter's opinions, which are also not recorded. But they use their names in the written decisions, just as if they had also voted. A Sinhalese who has knowledge of the gospel is not seen as a good person by the aforementioned Landraad. When the sun comes up in the morning she overrides by the power of her glow all that had given some light during the night, but the aforementioned body, without knowing this, has excluded me from it, saying afterwards whatever pleases them. And despite the infinite laws and ordinances that the God the Lord has given the people in order to maintain law and order, that gathering commits much injustice.[98]

[98] SLNA 1/94, "Governor in Council minutes," fols. 95r-v, 5 Feb 1745.

Ponnamperuma had an axe to grind with Bagilet, and appears to have believed that he would provide much illumination to the council.[99] His complaint contained twenty-four points replete with self-promotion. He was right in saying that the headmen's names were misleadingly inserted in the list of those who pronounced judgement as if they had also voted (see an image of a sentence in Figure 1.1). His statement, which may have some truth to it, is damning of the headmen's influence in the Landraad.

On the other hand, the evidence supports the possibility that the local councillors had some power, however limited. In some cases, the final judgement includes references to local custom as an explanation for the sentence. At one point a direct reference to their advice was made: "the fellow native members of this body being the mudaliyār of the gate Nicolaas Dias Abeysinghe Amarasekera the korale mudaliyār Seresinge, the titular mudaliyār Augustinus Ferdinandus Wiresinghe and the Mohandiram Wanigasekere affirmed that it is an old practice and a custom of the country, that when there are no mayorāls in the villages, naindes are allowed to perform that service."[100] Questions regarding local customs posed to witnesses also point to the local influence on the judgement. Moving into the village, mayorāls were important in investigating cases and could be called to the council. We also know that at least on a few occasions, the local councillors were also appointed to perform such duties on a weekly basis. The question of the power of the headmen hinges on to what degree local customs were accepted in the council, an issue that is central to this study.

The seemingly minor dispute over protocol that was touched on at the beginning of this chapter reveals the tensions between the European and local councillors in the Landraad. No local councillors were present at the meeting held on 27 May 1786. Two new local members had been chosen; they appeared in the antechamber to the council hall. Don Balthasar Dias Abeysinghe Siriwardene and Don Johan Anthony Alvis Abeyesiriwickreme Jayawardene should have been led in as new members. Since the president was absent, vice-president Pieter de Vos

[99] In December 1744, a list of ten local headmen was drawn up with comments that three of them, including Ponnamperuma, were often out in the countryside and that six of them had a blood relationship to at least one other headman on the list. Ponnamperuma's "full" brother, Salomon Ponnamperuma, was also a mohandiram on the list. As a solution, one mahamudaliyār on the list (Jan Alwis Wickremesinghe) was appointed a permanent member of the Landraad while the others were rotated between the Landraad and thombo registration on a monthly basis in a way that ensured that blood relations did not work together. SLNA 1/5046, "Galle Political Council minutes," fols. 60r–61r, 4 Dec 1744. This may have been a stopgap measure to limit Adriaan Ponnamperuma's presence in the Landraad.

[100] SLNA 1/6511, "Galle Landraad minutes," fols. 37r, 11 Jul 1778. This case involving the Kandege family is described in chapter one.

led a decision to call them in on the basis that the session had no local members who could escort them in and that European members were not authorised to accompany them into the hall. Balthasar questioned the manner in which they were introduced. After the two new members took the oath and were shown their seats by the vice-president, Balthasar asked why they had not been introduced by two members "as it is always customary on the election of new members here." The vice president's recorded answer is a perfunctory "it happened thus because it was determined and decided by the gathering." Balthasar would have been displeased.[101]

Balthasar and Alvis did not appear at the next full sitting on 10 June 1786; it is possible that they were affronted and had decided to boycott the meeting.[102] The introduction of new members was the first matter that President Adriaan Sebastian van de Graaff took up. He asked the members why they had not followed the custom by which two younger members accompany new members inside before introducing them. He asked if they were ready to address that omission at the next meeting in order to prevent all unpleasantness and introduce the two new members who had been "scorned so badly" by being denied "the honour that they are entitled to." The members said that they had meant no contempt at all to the new members, but that they had presumed that local members must be introduced by their own kind, and that no local members had been present that day. They said they would be pleased to rectify the "unwittingly committed mistake" by following the president's proposal.[103] At the following meeting, Balthasar appeared in the antechamber for the second time. The other headmen were absent (as was Alvis), and he was led inside by two European members, Pieter Simonsz de Silva and Dirk François van Gijsel. He was congratulated by the president on behalf of the others as well and shown his seat. The president announced that the new introduction was to pay Balthasar the honour that he had been previously denied.[104] There was no mention of formally introducing Alvis when he finally attended a meeting on 25 October 1786, after the first ignominious day on 27 May 1786.[105] It is possible that for the most part, only Balthasar wished to rake up the issue. He used a foreign protocol to effectively demand equality.

We must also factor in Balthasar's personal influence over the president. Adriaan Sebastiaan van de Graaff was the brother of Governor Van de Graaff, who in turn held Balthasar's father Nicolaas Dias Abeysinghe Amarasekera in great trust. The senior Abeysinghe had just been appointed to Colombo as mahamudaliyār the

101 SLNA 1/6525, "Galle Landraad draft minutes," fols. 172r-v, 27 May 1786.

102 No excuses were recorded at the meeting.

103 SLNA 1/6525, "Galle Landraad draft minutes," fols. 182r, 10 Jun 1786.

104 Ibid., fols. 191v, 8 Jul 1786.

105 Ibid., fols. 205r, 25 Oct 1786.

year before the incident in the Galle Landraad. The European members were quick to realise the significance of the president's insistence on rectifying a perceived dishonour. Yet, their assumption that two local members would introduce a new local member was not without precedent.[106] Later on, Balthasar and Alvis also introduced another headman.[107] It is likely Balthasar's assertiveness arose from the familiarity his father, a high-ranking local headman, had with a high-ranking European family.

Thus, there were teething problems and more serious issues concerning the value attached to local opinion. The story that emerges is that the headmen were not inconsequential to the operation of the Landraad, yet they were considered easily dispensable. From time to time the company realised the political value of their presence, while also ignoring their absence. However, headmen could also assert themselves and be heard on legal matters. In this way, the cross-cultural space of the Landraad saw subtle struggles for power among its councillors.

Dutch Representations of Inhabitants

Company servants and European clergy attempted to create ethnographic descriptions of the locals on VOC territory. Femme Gaastra writes of a "cultural awakening" among company servants in the late seventeenth century.[108] The Dutch Reverend Phillipus Baldaeus, the English Captain Robert Knox, Portuguese Captain Joao Ribeiro, the Dutch clergyman Francois Valentijn and the German Johann Wolffgang Heydt, who served in the VOC, wrote some early descriptions of the inhabitants of Sri Lanka. In memoirs addressed to their successors, governors also engaged in such knowledge production. Pieter Sluijsken attempted this as well. Some of these texts played a significant role in informing company servants of local society. It was necessary that they understood the intricate social formations within the local society in order to exploit the services it offered and govern it well.

VOC servants generally had a low opinion of the locals, whom they perceived as unreliable, indolent, unenterprising and unchristian. The Galle Landraad in 1745, commenting on those who came forward for thombo registration, said the

106 Two "native" members introduced Don Matthijs de Silva Abeyewardene Wijeyesekere, who was appointed to replace the late Mohandiram Wanigasekere. SLNA 1/6513, "Galle Landraad minutes," fols. 19r, 1 Apr 1780. The local members' names were not mentioned. But the members present at Balthasar's and Anthony's first meeting on 27 May 1786 were not part of that meeting in 1780. There were so few local members in the Landraad that their appointments were few and far between, and Matthijs's introduction was the last before Balthasar and Alvis were appointed.

107 SLNA 1/6515, "Galle Landraad minutes" (1787 to 1793), fols. 313r, 18 Jun 1791.

108 Gaastra, *The Dutch East India Company*, 106.

inhabitants were secretive and very lazy, and that many times "old, foolish, infirm and decrepit people" came forward.[109] Governor Van Imhoff referred to the "capricious nature and deceitful character" of the locals.[110] Sluijsken was not the first to say that the Sinhalese have a "lazy character."[111] As his work is little known, the following is an account of his description of the Dutch encounter with the various social fields of eighteenth-century Sri Lanka.

Sluijsken argued that to govern the subjects well and profitably, it was necessary to rule them according to their own laws. His work was an attempt to sensitise European officials to cultural norms, for which purpose he knew that ethnographic descriptions were necessary. Ethnography is simply defined here as an interest in other cultures. It was also seen as a useful tool for colonialism in other parts of the world.[112] Sluijsken considered his descriptions of the land services important for judges operating on the island. Without using the term pluralism, he recognised pluralities in the legal sphere as a central organising concept when dealing with regional difference. In his two-volume description of the customs of the people under VOC control in Sri Lanka, he says, "[i]t is well known that every country has special privileges, laws and customs and is inhabited by special kinds of people who are divided into classes by which one can differentiate the lower from the higher" and that "[t]here is no greater advantage for the landowner than peace and order among his subjects but what is peace and order after all than that the lower judges are very well-versed in the prerogatives and customs of the subjects."[113] The VOC's experience in Sri Lanka in connection with Sinhalese law was to rely on their local informants to define practices. In Sluijsken's case, it is possible that he spoke and understood Sinhala or Tamil or both. He wrote that he had learned what he knew as much from experience as from (unspecified) old documents handed over to the land regents as law. He had a wide knowledge of the island at the time he wrote his account in 1784. When he was president of the Landraad from 1766–1767, he had already been in the country for around eight years, and our knowledge of his diligence suggests that his quest for knowledge remained active in that period.

109 SLNA 1/2805, "Galle Landraad minutes (20 Dec 1745) and Governor's comments (5 Feb 1746)" (1745 to 1746), 40r–41v. The full quotation is given in chapter one.

110 Van Imhoff, *Memoir Left by Van Imhoff*, 12.

111 Pieter Sluijsken, "Eene beschryving van de landdienst op Ceylon: Zo uyt ondervinding als uyt oude papieren tezaemen gebragt (A Description of the Land Services of Ceylon: Compiled from both investigations and old papers)" (Colombo, 1784), vol. 1: 20, RP-31/32 Colonial Collection (KIT), Leiden University.

112 See comments on this by Jeremy Ravi Mumford, "Litigation as Ethnography in Sixteenth-Century Peru: Polo De Ondegardo and the Mitimaes," *Hispanic American Historical Review* 88, no. 1 (2008).

113 Sluijsken, "A Description of the Land Services," vol. 1: 3-5.

Litigation, through the access it provided to a discussion of local customs, was an effective forum for investigating local practices.

The bulk of Sluijsken's 1784 account of land services details the customs of the various caste groups among the Sinhalese and provides an elaborate description of the local administrative system. It is followed by an account of the customs of the inhabitants of Chilaw, Puttalam and Jaffna (including the codification of laws known as the Thesavalamai), special laws concerning the Moors and other non-Christians, including the "jentiven," and the Muslim code. The Thesavalamai or the laws of the Jaffna Tamils were commissioned in 1706 and approved by Governor Cornelis Jan Simons and the Governor in Council in 1707, while the Muslim code is from the New Statutes of Batavia of 1766, which Governor Falck is said to have received from Batavia in 1770, since, according to him, Muslims in Sri Lanka at the time were ignorant of their laws.[114] The section on "jentiven," by which Sluijsken likely meant Hindu tradesmen,[115] is a manual cut and paste from the Batavian plakkaten.[116] This appears to have been sloppy work, but on the other hand, he may have seen that the Batavian description bore similarities to the customs of some Hindus in Sri Lanka, which is not impossible to imagine. Sluijsken gives the most comprehensive account of the coastal inhabitants in Dutch times and the only compilation of what he believed to be the laws of certain groups on the coast. His aim was to facilitate governance as effectively as possible for the VOC. Thus, practical reasons drove the ethnographic description that he attempted. We do not know if the VOC used his work, but it is significant as an attempt (if that is all it was) to (mis)understand "other" cultures. Sluijsken embodies the colonial enterprise of identifying cultural differences, a task that was seen to be necessary for realising economic advantages and one that he performed in the Landraad in the course of his duties.

114 Nadaraja, *The Legal System of Ceylon*, 13–14.

115 Jentiven is a variant spelling of the Portuguese adjective *gentio* or "heathen." The Portuguese in India used the word *gentio* or "heathen" for the non-Muslim local people, that is, the Hindus. The VOC generally used the term to imply Hindu tradesmen and non-Christian Chettiars; they also used it in opposition to Moors in India. See also Hans Martin Kramer, Jenny Rahel Oesterle, and Ulrike Vordermark, *Labeling the Religious Self and Others: Reciprocal Perceptions of Christians, Muslims, Hindus, Buddhists, and Confucians in Medieval and Early Modern Times* (Leipzig: Leipziger Universitatsverlag, 2010).

116 Jacobus Anne van der Chijs, *Nederlandsch-Indisch plakaatboek, 1602-1811*, vol. 6 (1750–1754) (Batavia: Landsdrukkerij, 1885), 164, http://archive.org/details/nederlandschind12chijgoog.

Conclusion

It is no easy task to determine the role of councillors in the lawmaking and decision-making process in a period and place in history like eighteenth-century Sri Lanka, which lacks private accounts. The role of the legal elites cannot be fully explored in this scenario. I have attempted a brief introduction here and a more comprehensive analysis may be possible if we study a wide range of decisions. For, "[a]s judges and attorneys give life to the law, their backgrounds, training, and social location shape the way they impose meaning on the stream of litigants they encounter."[117] This is applicable to both civil and criminal cases. Did the councillors show concern for careful evidentiary assessments? Justifying the refusal of an appeal from the Galle Landraad to the Raad van Justitie of Colombo, the Governor in Council said that the Landraden consisted of "people instructed on the country's laws, practices and customs."[118] We cannot underestimate their role in creating the practices by which the Landraad functioned. Yet, their involvement appears to have been curtailed.

The relationship of law to the dominant classes is evident. A small, closely-knit group with cross-cultural connections controlled the Landraad. Marriage ties, affluence and ethnicity separated a majority of the members from most litigants and witnesses. The Europeans on the council who could determine judicial decision-making represented the old guard in the region. As Wagenaar says, politics and the judiciary were mixed up. The same people who exploited the countryside attended Landraad sittings. In fact, it was difficult to achieve a balance between trade and government.[119] There was an overlap between those serving in the political level of the company and those performing the public duties of the Landraad. In both the local system and The Netherlands, there was no division in law and politics. As explained above, the headmen on the council worked in an advisory capacity without the power to vote. Councillors carried out their tasks in the Landraad with a keen awareness of their social categories of identity and those of the litigants and witnesses – this will be the subject of the next chapter.

If the Landraad was authorised to favour the Sinhalese normative order, we do not observe a relationship marked by the domination of headmen. It is not, as the early twentieth-century case *Karonchihami v Angohami*[120] suggests, that

[117] Sally Engle Merry, *Colonizing Hawai'i: The Cultural Power of Law* (Princeton: Princeton University Press, 2000), 118.

[118] SLNA 1/165, "Governor in Council minutes" (1772), 24 Nov 1772. I discuss this case of Godage Mienga further in the next chapter.

[119] Wagenaar, *Galle, VOC-vestiging in Ceylon*, 147.

[120] *Karonchihami v Angohami*, 8 New Law Reports 1 (1904).

the Landraad was composed of mostly local officials. On the contrary, a majority of VOC officials and a smaller number of headmen presided. The power of the headmen was secondary to that of the European members, although there were subtle skirmishes for the consolidation of power. These were articulations of difference that played out in the council room. The mudaliyār Ponnamperuma, himself a Landraad member, vehemently condemned local participation as a farce and alluded to the need for headmen to rule by Christian laws. European members, he said, took no notice of the headmen even though they were well versed in the gospel. Local participation was stressed in the early days of the Landraad's operation, but at a number of later meetings, no headmen were present. This may indicate the dominance of the official Dutch laws that were espoused by European members of the council – but that is a question we will explore later in this book. Let us first examine who appeared before the motley collection of councillors I have described here.

CHAPTER 3

Facing the Law

Abstract

As a result of the Dutch administration of land tenure, men and women entered extensively into the colonial legal system if distance was not a heavy deterrent. This chapter examines the identities and processes of identification among those who made representations to the Landraad. Higher status groups who held service titles appeared in the Landraad, but the lack of status was not an eliminating factor in facing the law. Women and lower-ranking persons also appealed to the Landraad. Inhabitants became acquainted with the Landraad and its land registration and began to understand procedures and best practices of strategy as they were keen to rectify inaccuracies. For litigants with plural identities, the Landraad was a location of identification and a site for navigating a plural legal landscape.

Keywords: Plural identities, litigants, witnesses, gender, status, Galle.

When served with a summons in 1780, Kalegana Bastian Naidelage Maria of Dutch-controlled Galle in southern Sri Lanka was displeased. She was reported to have brazenly responded that even her dog would not appear before the judicial forum that had summoned her. The council decided that Maria would be flogged for this perceived affront.[1] While her brashness reveals how locals subverted the authority of their early colonial rulers, this was more often the exception than the rule. From the sixteenth century, successive European occupations influenced Sri Lanka's legal culture to varying degrees. From at least the late seventeenth century onwards, indigenous litigants in Sri Lanka had been bringing their lawsuits before panels of Dutch and local judges.

The rise of a colonial power and its implications for the structure of power in society is reflected in the way the authorities execute the law. Given Maria's example, to what extent did the locals perceive the Landraad as intruding on local affairs? Legal practices may be inherently inclusive or exclusive, or may be deliberately made so by those in power. Colonial judicial bodies are known to have stimulated

1 SLNA 1/6513, "Galle Landraad minutes" (1780), fols. 29r, 1 Apr 1780.

relatively marginalised groups in society to come forward.[2] Similarly, in Sri Lanka, supplicants, in the form of litigants, sought justice by applying to the Landraad. By extension, witnesses who bolstered case narratives were involved in this pursuit and I will consider them as individuals who were required to engage with the law.

Did ordinary men and women make representations to the plural legal order of the Landraad? This chapter considers questions relating to the reception of the Landraad and its role in civil litigation. Which social groups came to the Landraad? We can understand how social hierarchies were represented in judicial matters by examining the identification processes practised by local participants and officials in the Landraad. Status could potentially influence the resolution of a case, and recording status was therefore necessary. Examining issues such as female agency, occupation and social background provide insights into the operations of the Landraad. The samples of litigants and witnesses analysed here paint a picture of the everyday workings of the Landraad and the legal consciousness of colonial subjects.

Personal jurisdiction, i.e. the authority of the Landraad over litigants, extended chiefly to those who lived outside the Galle town but within the Galle district. This was, to some extent, overridden by the location of the dispute in connection with lands registered in the thombos, in which case inhabitants of the town who had claims to land outside the town also approached the Landraad. Naturally, witnesses would not have felt the same exigencies as litigants; but the knowledge of legal processes that they acquired through their participation, and that they were selected as witnesses, are important aspects in a full understanding of societal participation in the Landraad. Both litigants and witnesses faced the law in this new legal institution. The distance from the individual's residence to the council either hampered or facilitated such involvement with the council. The residence of litigants is difficult to determine, but this chapter will deal with the geographical reach of the council through an analysis of *ratione loci*, which refers to jurisdiction over a dispute location, and the residence of witnesses.

We cannot overestimate the importance of the law in the everyday lives of the elite and peasant subjects of colonial Galle. It was the responsibility of the Landraad to settle disputes regarding lands registered in the thombo, which shareholders could not disregard. The thombo was a vehicle for the company to extend its rule in the countryside. The VOC would not have been able to envisage how the locals would perceive the Landraad. However, from records that reveal its prominent role in land litigation and the participation of women and low-caste groups, we may glean that it was effectively accepted by the late eighteenth century. First, I will outline the various groups on the island at the time – people whose identities were essentially in flux.

[2] Sally Engle Merry, "Colonial Law and its Uncertainties," *Law and History Review* 28, no. 4 (2010): 1068.

Social Formations in Galle

Coastal inhabitants survived by engaging in fishing, construction work, boatbuilding and agriculture. The inhabitants of the more rural hinterland survived through peasant agriculture alone. Many villages seem to have been self-sufficient in terms of rice cultivation and interdependent in the provision of essential services. Most inhabitants of Galle were Sinhalese, but in the larger villages, which seem to have been economic centres, there were diverse groups of people, including Moors and Chettiars, traditionally associated with trade. Being a coastal region, it was naturally diverse and attracted migrants from southern India. Europeans mostly lived in or around the Fort and were either part of the VOC or interacted with it closely. Ethnic and caste-based divisions are clearly defined in Sri Lanka today, but it would be anachronistic to assume such clarity existed in eighteenth-century Galle. Based on thombo data, the total population of the district was roughly 95,000 individuals.[3]

Among the Sinhalese, the goygama (farmer) caste, consisting primarily of agriculturalists, was the largest. In the absence of reliable census data from the eighteenth century, some of the earliest figures emerge from later British rule in the country. An 1824 census of the caste composition of the Sinhalese of the low country reveals that 54.3 per cent were of the goygama caste. Three non-farmer castes, which were controversially believed to be of low status, karāva (15.7 per cent), *salāgama* (7.5 per cent) and durāva (5.6 per cent), together constituted almost 30 per cent of the low-country population.[4] The goygama were also situated above the *hakuru* and *padu* – both agricultural castes – in the social hierarchy. Dewasiri argues that they had easier access to the better paddy lands in a village.[5] Members of the goygama caste, who were mostly Buddhists who had converted to Christianity under Portuguese and Dutch rule – at least nominally, for legal and administrative purposes – remained the most influential on the island. They are likely to have been the group that appealed most frequently to the Landraad. Their influence did not, however, go unchallenged. The salāgama group gained political power and the right to govern their affairs in Dutch times through their headmen. Meanwhile, the karāva headmen, as we saw in chapter two, served as councillors of the Landraad. Yet, real power was vested with male goygama chiefs, and proximity to the Galle town gave them greater leverage.

[3] Albert van den Belt, Jan Kok, and Kees Mandemakers, "Digital Thombos: A New Source for 18th Century Sri Lankan Family History," *The History of the Family* 16, no. 4 (2011): 484.

[4] Kumari Jayawardena, *Nobodies to Somebodies: The Rise of the Colonial Bourgeoisie in Sri Lanka* (London: Zed Books, 2000), 164; Bryce F. Ryan, *Caste in Modern Ceylon: The Sinhalese System in Transition* (New Brunswick: Rutgers University Press, 1953), 264.

[5] Nirmal Ranjith Dewasiri, *The Adaptable Peasant: Agrarian Society in Western Sri Lanka under Dutch Rule, 1740-1800* (Leiden: Brill, 2008), 143, 167.

The company understood the nuances within such identities to some degree, as we can see in official classifications. The Dutch knew that the karāvas (whom they mostly referred to as *vissers* or fishermen) engaged in a variety of activities apart from fishing, such as carpentry, construction and transportation, which were important to the colonial power. They knew that the salāgama (whom they called *sjalia*) not only engaged in cinnamon peeling as their traditional occupation but also went to sea. At that time, cinnamon peeling was not their exclusive occupation; and fishing and carpentry were not exclusive to the karāvas, as is the popular belief today. The company recognised various grades of fishermen, divided by birth on what fishing equipment they were permitted to use. Pieter Sluijsken, who described the land services in areas under VOC control, identified nine "classes" of vissers according to the fishing equipment that they were permitted to use: *orru karāva, madel karāva, dandu karāva, kespa karāva, baddudel karāva, porrewekarean, godekeula, tokkeula,* and *indimalkeula.*[6] Sluijsken also observed that the first five divisions despised the lower four groups. The last group of *indimalkeulas,* who fished with casting nets and baskets, were allowed to decorate their wedding huts with only certain wildflowers in contrast to the highest groups that were permitted to decorate their huts more elaborately. These were inherent divisions within the caste that helped maintain a particular status quo – a kind of intra-caste hierarchy.

Social identities were in flux at this time. The visser identity of the eighteenth century is associated with the karāva caste group of present-day Sri Lanka. Said to have been of Dravidian origin from southern India,[7] their assimilation into coastal society in the western, south-western and southern seaboards of Sri Lanka was quite significant. They may have had to master south Indian languages including Tamil for their commercial activities on the coast. This indicates linguistic diversity *within* a so-called group. Sluijsken's work also shows a merging of seemingly caste-based identities and linguistic and ethnic identities. In such a situation, it is problematic to use the Sinhalised term "karāva" to refer to all those whom the company calls "visser," or even "Sinhalese." Though I acknowledge that a more nuanced understanding of the classification is required, I have used the terms "visser" and "karāva" interchangeably.

Other identities that were in flux at the time were those of the burgers and Chettiars. In Dutch times, the burgers were, generally speaking, European settlers, but

[6] Pieter Sluijsken, "Eene beschryving van de landdienst op Ceylon: Zo uyt ondervinding als uyt oude papieren tezaemen gebragt (A Description of the Land Services of Ceylon: Compiled from both investigations and old papers)" (Colombo, 1784), vol. 1: 39-41, RP-31/32 Colonial Collection (KIT), Leiden University.

[7] Michael Roberts, *Caste Conflict and Elite Formation: The Rise of a Karāva Elite in Sri Lanka, 1500-1931* (Cambridge: Cambridge University Press, 1982), 21ff.

also "respectable" families of Portuguese descent who had entered the *Hollandsche* (Dutch) clan. Company officials who left the service became *vrijburgers* (free citizens). The British, who mixed with these burgers later, referred to them as "Burghers." They now form a separate ethnic group in the country. To avoid confusion, I will use the spelling "burger," which is also the form that appears in Landraad documents and in the thombos. Many burgers of Dutch times became tavern keepers, butchers, tailors, bakers and shopkeepers, and some even became overseas merchants.[8] Remco Raben writes of how manumitted slaves and *karāvas* were granted burger status based on petitions that they made.[9] The Chettiars formed yet another group whose identity was ambiguous. Traditionally, they were traders of southern Indian origin. Chettiar or Chetty is written as *setthi* in Pali, *hetti* or *situ* in Sinhala and *etti* in Tamil. Dewasiri has examined the integration of the Chettiar community with the goygama agricultural caste and the karāvas.[10] He examined thombo records to show how the term "*sitty*," used by the Dutch, may have been integrated into present-day goygama (and some karāva) names. Intermarriages of Europeans and Chettiars with locals made such identities malleable and vague during early colonial rule, a feature that in fact continued well into the nineteenth century, as reflected in the diverse categorisations that the British employed. Influenced by the Portuguese presence on the island, the Chettiars also acquired Portuguese surnames that they added to their own – such as Rodrigo Candappa, Silva Pulle, Tissera Pulle, Nonis Candappa, Fernandopulle and Perera Pulle. In revenue farming contracts, they signed almost exclusively in the Tamil script and occasionally in Roman characters.[11] Unlike the Chettiars in the north, most Chettiars in Colombo and Chilaw were Christians.[12] To those who were not, the company attached the word *heidense* or "heathen". Letters exchanged between a Chettiar whom the VOC exiled to South Africa in 1727, and

[8] Michael Roberts, Ismeth Raheem, and Percy Colin-Thomé, *People Inbetween: The Burghers and the Middle Class in the Transformations within Sri Lanka, 1790s-1960s* (Ratmalana: Sarvodaya Book Pub. Services, 1989), 38. Most signed revenue farming contracts in roman characters, while some used Sinhala. Adriaan Perera, a burger in Negombo, signed in Sinhala. Nadeera Rupesinghe (writing as Seneviratne), "Strange Cooperation: Revenue Farmers in Eighteenth-century Sri Lanka" (MPhil Dissertation, Leiden University, 2010), 36.

[9] Remco Raben, "Batavia and Colombo: The Ethnic and Spatial Order of Two Colonial Cities 1600-1800" (PhD Thesis, Leiden University, 1996), 270.

[10] Dewasiri, *Adaptable Peasant*, 201–2. He presented a more extensive work in progress on it at a conference: "Chetties in Early-Modern Sri Lanka: Some Aspects of the Social History of Sri Lanka" Monsoon Asia in the Age of Revolutions: Changes of Regime and their Aftermath,' 12-14 Jan 2010, Mumbai, January 13, 2010.

[11] Rupesinghe, "Strange Cooperation," 37.

[12] Sinnappah Arasaratnam, "Social History of a Dominant Caste Society," in *Ceylon and the Dutch, 1600-1800: External Influences and Internal Change in Early Modern Sri Lanka* (Brookfield, Vt.: Variorum, 1996), 390.

Chettiars and others on the island, provide rare insights into the social life of the group.[13] Titles and company positions were clearly considered lucrative.

The legal status of the Moors and Chettiars on Dutch territory was ambiguous. Raben writes of how they migrated to Colombo from the Coromandel, encouraged by the "gradual and partial liberalization of trade."[14] Temporary settlers among them, at the very least, had to perform *uliyam* service, or unpaid public work every three months – for example, maintaining public infrastructure or carrying palanquins – as a kind of payment for residence. A poll tax on the *absente uliaamers* was imposed on all those who absconded from the service. Lists of all Moors and Chettiars living in coastal areas were drawn up. A more settled community of Moors and Chettiars also lived on the island and often appear in the thombos. VOC regulations that were not always enforced prohibited Moor ownership of immovable property from the seventeenth century onwards, but these restrictions were lifted in the mid-eighteenth century.[15]

By the late seventeenth century, the Dutch appointed Muslim headmen to facilitate dealings with the Muslim community.[16] Such Moor headmen would settle disputes, but debt and land matters involving Moors did occasionally come up in the Landraad. Many land sales were also made to Moors. It is possible to conduct more research into the Moor presence on the island with the use of Dutch sources, which will contribute greatly to an understanding of their history. In phases from the nineteenth century onwards, Muslim leaders represented their community as either a religious or racial group. In the popular imagination, they are regarded as having been persecuted by not just the Portuguese but by the Dutch as well, although this was not always the case. It is believed that a Muslim elite and the consciousness of a Muslim identity arose with the expansion of merchant capital in the nineteenth century.[17] However, from pre-colonial times, Muslim men settled on the island, married local women and engaged in trade and agriculture. Lorna Dewaraja writes of how Kandyan Muslims cultivated Buddhist temple lands and provided services to temples as part of their rent.[18] Others were temporary trad-

[13] Herman Tieken, *Between Colombo and the Cape: Letters in Tamil, Dutch and Sinhala Sent to Nicolaas Ondaatje from Ceylon*, vol. 6, Dutch Sources of South Asia (New Delhi: Manohar, 2015), 14–20.

[14] Raben, "Batavia and Colombo," 106.

[15] See K.W. Goonewardena, "Muslims under Dutch Rule up to the Mid-Eighteenth Century," in M.A.M. Shukri (ed), *Muslims of Sri Lanka: Avenues to Antiquity* (Beruwala: Jamiah Naleemia Inst., 1986), 189–210.

[16] D.A. Kotelawele, "Muslims under Dutch Rule in Sri Lanka," in M.A.M. Shukri (ed), *Muslims of Sri Lanka: Avenues to Antiquity* (Beruwala: Jamiah Naleemia Inst., 1986), 176.

[17] Jayawardena, *Nobodies to Somebodies*, 220–26.

[18] Lorna S. Dewaraja, "The Muslims in the Kandyan Kingdom (c. 1600–1815): A Study of Ethnic Integration," in M.A.M. Shukri (ed), *Muslims of Sri Lanka: Avenues to Antiquity* (Beruwala: Jamiah Naleemia Institute, 1986), 218–22.

ers, such as Indian merchants from Golconda, Bengal and Coromandel. By at least the late eighteenth century, the Dutch fully recognised the need to cooperate with the Moors, some of whom were also involved in the collection of paddy rents in the hinterland.[19]

In addition to the dominant peasant agriculture, Galle was a centre for "sizeable seaborne trade and concentrations of non-farmer social elements."[20] Since the Moors and Chettiars were essentially Tamil-speaking groups, it is likely that other groups from southern India who also resided in Galle retained their language and Hindu religion. The varied populace in Galle included groups such as the Malays who served in the Eastern militia, slaves from further across the Indian Ocean, from Madagascar to South East Asia and manumitted slaves who appeared in the Landraad in defence of their rights to property. Galle was part of a wide political and economic network that was linked to the Cape, Colombo and Batavia.

That group identities were vague is without doubt. Classifications more closely associated with caste today (for example, *bellale,* visser, sjalia, *chando, wasser*) were at times used in conjunction with terms signifying occupational specialisations and title-holding (*kaneelschiller, timmerman*, schrijver, mudaliyār, mohandiram, lascarin, mayorāl, etc). There was little mutual exclusivity among castes where occupations were concerned, as occupational diversity was high. While the ethnic identities of groups such as the Jaffna Tamils, Moors, Chettiars and Malays received official recognition to the point where some of their laws were codified, John D. Rogers points out that the social identities that the Dutch used in their day-to-day administration were the "caste-like groups" that the Portuguese had also used.[21] More specifically, inhabitants were primarily identified with regards to their occupation and service to the company in Landraad documents. As the historian Robert J. Morris argues, "[t]he purpose of the document is the likeliest guide to the risks being taken in making an inference about occupation from occupational title."[22] We must keep in mind that there was little agreement in the company bureaucracy on the criteria for determining the boundaries of a social group or a group's name. VOC officials in Sri Lanka often used the Dutch term *geslacht* to mean caste, ethnicity, nation or lineage, and the term could refer to a present-day ethnic or caste group alike. Later in this chapter, I shall explore how such identifications panned out in the Landraad.

[19] Rupesinghe, "Strange Cooperation," 76.

[20] Dewasiri, *Adaptable Peasant*, 85.

[21] John D. Rogers, "Early British Rule and Social Classification in Lanka," *Modern Asian Studies* 38, no. 3 (2004): 630.

[22] Robert J. Morris, "Occupational Coding: Principles and Examples," *Historical Social Research* 15, no. 1 (1990): 9.

Litigants and Witnesses

While it is a popular stereotype that the natives in Sri Lanka were particularly litigious,[23] such assumptions must be questioned as there are many factors that affect involvement in a judicial forum. The ninety-nine cases in my sample involved a total of 243 litigants. They all appeared in registers from the years 1778 and 1779, but may have also appeared before and after those years in connection with their cases. The examples of dispute locations used in this chapter are also from the same registers. At times the same persons reappeared in the council (occasionally on the same day) in connection with different cases, and in such instances I counted them only once. Following Le Bailly's practice, I have taken a case and not a legal issue as the point of departure, as a person involved in a process that involved two or more legal issues would otherwise be enumerated more than once.[24] A small number (eighteen) appeared in two cases, and a smaller number (eight) in more than two.

Defining a litigant is not an easy task. *Ratione personae* refers to the particular jurisdiction of a judicial body over plaintiffs or defendants living in a territory. A litigant may have appeared many times in connection with a case or perhaps just once. Not all defendants, plaintiffs or supplicants appeared in the council at every hearing, especially in cases with collectives as parties.[25] They were, however, required to be present when the sentence was pronounced. I have not attempted to remove from the enumeration those who were not physically present despite having their names mentioned as litigants; their numbers are small. Principal litigants from a collective, or husbands, procurators or other authorised persons, appeared on behalf of these absent litigants. I have assumed that such litigants were at least tangentially aware of the proceedings and included them in the count, along with their special representatives. I have left out only the procurators, who were professional process representatives officially delegated to plead a case in the name of a principal party. Occasionally, officials appeared as part of the VOC government or the native department – such as the clerk of the Inlandse Boedelkamer – and in particular mayorāls, who gave oral evidence. I did not include them in the count of those who appeared before the council as litigants or participants outside their official duties. Where the minutes mention their names, I counted everyone in collectives of litigants separately. This differs from the practice applied by Schepper

[23] James Emerson Tennent, *Ceylon: An Account of the Island*, vol. 2, fourth edition (London: Longman, Green, 1860), 543.

[24] Marie-Charlotte Le Bailly, *Recht voor de Raad* (Haarlem & Hilversum: Historische Vereniging Holland & Uitgeverij Verloren, 2001), 219.

[25] I have not separated the litigants into plaintiffs and defendants, as it is not always possible to do this correctly.

et al.,[26] but it was important to build an image of those involved with the Landraad in a certain period. I counted litigants who were referred to collectively (for example, as the heirs of a certain person) but with no further details, as one, but they obviously involved more than a single litigant.[27]

For this analysis of the reach of the Landraad, I have included a sample of 264 witnesses from a register of depositions[28] for the years 1778–1781. A deposition, which in most cases involved more than one witness, almost always recorded the individual's age, occupation, village of residence and religion, thereby providing information on witness participation and the use of evidence. As I explain further in chapter four, the recording of the (official) religious identity of the witnesses was consistent, since it was practically important for the judicial oath, which took different forms. Other information recorded on the witnesses included their occupation, which had a direct bearing on their credibility. Most witnesses were adults (some as old as ninety years old), while the youngest I found was fifteen years old. In some instances, they would appear in more than one case. I eliminated recurring witnesses as far as possible from the sample, although name variations and possible changes in residence made this process problematic. Not surprisingly for a society that displayed pronounced age heaping[29] – in brief, the rounding off of ages to the nearest five or ten – the recorded ages from deposition to deposition of a seemingly single person often did not match. When name, occupation and village are matched, as many as twenty-one witnesses (8 per cent) seem to have appeared twice. Haputantrige Johan appeared four times and Haputantrige Michiel three times. VOC officials were not blind to the possibility that some individuals were serving as professional witnesses, as I discuss further in chapter four.

The Landraad minutes show no consistency in the recording of personal information. Where available, I have used the data on litigants and witnesses to explore issues of gender and social status. Age, religion, title and village of residence are more readily available in witness depositions. The mix of information included in the Landraad minutes and depositions reveals to us the preoccupations of an early colonial judicial council with social categories.

[26] In a collective of litigants, only the first-mentioned person's details were recorded. H. de Schepper et al., "Prolegomena voor onderzoek van rechtspraak en bestuur in de oude Nederlanden," in J. Koster van Dijk and A. Wijffels (eds), *Miscellanea forensia historica: Ter gelegenheid van het afscheid van Prof. Mr. J. Th de Smidt* (Amsterdam: Werkgroep Grote Raad van Mechelen, 1988), 272–74.

[27] In The Netherlands as well, parties were sometimes referred to as the children, heirs or wives, widows, etc. of certain persons; they were not named. Ibid., 271.

[28] SLNA 1/6494, "Galle Landraad depositions" (1778 to 1781). The Landraad recorded some witnesses in the minutes, but I did not include them in the sample.

[29] See Fabian F. Drixler and Jan Kok, "A Lost Family-Planning Regime in Eighteenth-century Ceylon," *Population Studies: A Journal of Demography* 70, no. 1 (2016): 93–114.

Gender: Women and Law

The Dutch colonial regime intersected with the lives of urban and rural women in civil matters such as marriage, legitimacy of children and property through ordinances and judicial practice. The justice system was male-dominated, but this did not deter female litigants from approaching the Landraad. Land disputes were as important to women as they were to men. In the sample of men and women who made representations at the Landraad, 174 (73 per cent) were men and 64 (27 per cent) women.[30] The women, who were mostly Sinhalese, were connected with fifty-one cases (52 per cent of the sample cases), either singly or in groups.[31]

In Sri Lanka, there was no femme couvert. I have not found direct evidence of such an attempt, but it was not possible to make the legal position of a woman in Galle subordinate to that of her husband, as in seventeenth- and eighteenth-century Holland, where a married woman could not appear before the judiciary without her husband's support.[32] Women "except a mother and grandmother, and they only so long as they have not contracted a second marriage" were also prohibited from being guardians in Holland.[33] Some women relied on representatives to plead on their behalf in the Landraad, perhaps due to an imposition of a rule, a reluctance to appear before it, or for reasons of convenience. In the sample, six men represented the interests of their wives. The widow Jemoniga Jebel was represented by a former *kangān* (overseer), and another indisposed woman by her son.[34] Yet others participated actively in the Galle Landraad, including married women who went to the Landraad alone. Maria, who insulted the Landraad when she was served her summons, illustrates the agency of women in eighteenth-century Sri Lanka. Outside my sample, Kosmulage Lisa, whose case I describe in more detail in chapter six, appeared without her husband, the vidāne of Hinatigala Willalege Janis, although she does appear to have had his active support. She was defending a gift of land from her mother against her sisters. In another case, the widow Godage Mienga appealed her case against Don Pedru Bastiaan de Silva over a property dispute,

30 I have not included five groups of litigants, referred to as heirs, children and/or grandchildren without any indication of their gender, in these figures.

31 Forty-nine of the sixty-four women were Sinhalese, three were Moors and one European. The ethnicity of eleven women could not be identified: six had the name de Silva, which is ambiguous; two were recorded as the wives of their husbands, who represented them in the Landraad.

32 Donald Haks, *Huwelijk en gezin in Holland in de 17de en 18de eeuw (Marriage and Family in Holland in the 17th and 18th Centuries)*, second edition (Utrecht: HES, 1985), 153; Robert Warden Lee, *An Introduction to Roman-Dutch Law*, fourth edition (Oxford: At the Clarendon Press, 1946), 65.

33 Lee, *An Introduction to Roman-Dutch Law*, 106.

34 SLNA 1/6512, "Galle Landraad minutes" (1779), fols. 89r, 27 Nov 1779; SLNA 1/6514, "Galle Landraad minutes" (1781), fols. 2r, 6 Jan 1781.

escalating it from the Landraad to the Raad van Justitie of Galle, which refused her appeal. Displaying remarkable perseverance, she then appealed to the Raad van Justitie in Colombo, which also rejected her request.[35] In all this, the relative independence of women at the Landraad shows an inability to limit women under the authority of males in their role as paterfamilias. A transfer of control over women's bodies if attempted, could not be fully achieved in Sri Lanka.

Femaleness was at times coupled with widowhood and social inferiority in the Landraad. In fact, twenty of the female litigants (almost one-third) were widows. By the seventeenth century, widows were majors (legal personae) according to the law of Holland.[36] Widows often came to the council in connection with property that belonged to their late husbands. In a case outside my sample but which was taken up shortly afterwards, Gamage Livina of Dodampe made claims in the Landraad to property that she believed had been unlawfully appropriated by a relative. She was the widow of a kangān, but had not come to the Landraad in connection with her husband's property. She claimed what she believed was her legacy from her father, which a cousin had had registered in the thombo under his name alone. The case is discussed further in chapters five and six. Low-caste women also made representations to the Landraad. Sepala Hakuruge Dominga of Kumbalwella was a Sinhalese woman from the ritually low status hakuru caste. She wished to appeal the Landraad's decision in a case against a fellow caste member to the Raad van Justitie in Galle.[37] A former female slave also had a lawsuit heard in the Landraad on a matter concerning two gardens in Galupiadde (Four Gravets): Rachel, a freed slave who lived in Kumbalwella, appeared against Constantino De Costa, a Chettiar who lived in the same village.[38] In another case, the emancipated slaves Roselijn and Benjamin proceeded against a Sinhalese man whom they accused of forcibly appropriating their land.[39] Sramata, a freed slave woman, claimed a revenue farmer's property that was to be sold to recover his arrears.[40] Rikittu Naatja, a coolie woman, came to the Landraad with thombo extracts and requested that a garden and paddy-field be registered under her name.[41] The

35 SLNA 1/165, "Governor in Council minutes" (1772), 24 Nov 1772.

36 J.W. Wessels, *History of the Roman-Dutch Law* (Grahamstown, Cape Colony: African Book Co., 1908), 428.

37 SLNA 1/6516, "Galle Landraad minutes" (1793), fols. 4r-v, 28 Jun 1793. A case from 1793 also involved hakuru caste persons including a female. SLNA 1/6515, "Galle Landraad minutes" (1787 to 1793), fols. 371r, 10 May 1793.

38 SLNA 1/6501, "Galle Landraad minutes" (1765 to 1766), fols. 117r-v, 4 Oct 1766; 119r, 20 Dec 1766; SLNA 1/6502, "Galle Landraad minutes" (1767), fols. 4v, 7 Feb 1767. Other documents in this case could not be traced.

39 SLNA 1/6525, "Galle Landraad draft minutes" (1784 to 1786), fols. 201r-v, 30 Sept 1786.

40 SLNA 1/6511, "Galle Landraad minutes" (1778), fols. 40v, 25 Jul 1778.

41 SLNA 1/6515, "Galle Landraad minutes," fols. 290, 17 Apr 1790.

proximity of their villages to the Landraad seat in Kumbalwella gave these groups greater agency in their lives.[42] Warnesuriepattebendige Dona Maka, a karāva woman from Galupiadde, whom we met in chapter one in connection with the sale of land, was unusually active in the Landraad, appearing in connection with land sale matters as both a litigant and a witness on several occasions. In 1781, a deposition recorded her as being 62 years old (to the best of her memory), a Christian, and a widow, appearing as a witness for the thombo copyist Josua Hopman in a debt case.[43] Female identity was differentiated by socio-economic status, social formation and residence in coastal urban areas or rural settings.

In stark contrast to their frequency as litigants, very few women appeared as witnesses, although there was no legal impediment to their testimony. Only ten from the sample, about four per cent, were female. They all provided depositions from 13 July 1778 to 14 August 1781. A rare occasion when a deposition had mostly female witnesses was a case where it was necessary to prove that a woman had died in childbirth a few hours before her newborn son had died.[44] In that case, women were obviously in a better position than men to attest to the facts. Women were not considered as the best choice to verify evidence in other matters, which were mostly related to confirming ownership of land. Very few females were assigned credibility; the striking male dominance indicates the control service holders such as lascarins held over judicial truth by frequently appearing as witnesses.

The general belief, supported by ancient and medieval sources, is that the teachings of Buddhism were instrumental in promoting the relative independence of women.[45] Early European observers such as Knox recorded female participation in agricultural work and in harvest rituals that were ingrained in Kandyan society.[46] The relationship between husband and wife is presented in the literature as that of equals, the protection of the wife by her husband was assumed but did not act as a restriction on the wife.[47] Female heirs were of special importance in inheritance law. If there had been an attempt to introduce ideas of female subordination

[42] Dewasiri points out that the hakuru caste showed a tendency to concentrate around the colonial centre. Dewasiri, *Adaptable Peasant*, 210.

[43] SLNA 1/6494, "Galle Landraad depositions," fols. 95r, 16 Feb 1781.

[44] This case is described in detail in chapter six.

[45] Barbara Watson Andaya, *The Flaming Womb: Repositioning Women in Early Modern Southeast Asia* (Honolulu: University of Hawai'i Press, 2006), 32–33; Indrani Munasinghe, *Sri Lankan Woman in Antiquity (Sixth Century B.C. to Fifteenth Century A.C.)*, trans. S.B. Herath (Colombo: Author Publication, 2004), 179.

[46] Robert Knox, *An Historical Relation of Ceylon* (Dehiwala: Tisara Prakasakayo, 1681; repr. 1966), 19–22.

[47] Munasinghe, *Woman in Antiquity*, 147–49. Knox says: "the Woman reckons her self as much obliged to the Man for his Company, as he does to her for hers." Knox, *An Historical Relation of Ceylon*, 173.

through Roman-Dutch law, they did not take hold of the female imagination in Sri Lanka in Dutch times.

Social Status and Local Actors

To what social and socio-economic groups did those who came to the council belong? It is necessary to categorise identity data into recognisable groups to facilitate referencing, but this can be fraught with pitfalls in practice. The process encounters some semantic problems, as our understanding of caste, occupational and ethnic differences today is not the same as in eighteenth-century Sri Lanka. As Morris has pointed out on the topic of occupational coding, variations in judgement, the purpose of the document or the economic context could also lead to considerable variation in classification practices.[48] Any analysis of the data has to be approached with these considerations in mind.

Table 3.1 Social formation of litigants and witnesses

Social Formation	*Litigants 1778–79*	%	*Witnesses 1778–81*	%
Sinhalese	191	79.0	246	93.0
Moor	19	7.8	5	2.0
European	14	5.8	8	3.2
Chettiar	1	0.4	1	0.4
Paravar	-	-	1	0.4
Unknown	18	7.0	3	1.0
Total	243	100	264	100

Sources: SLNA 1/6494, Depositions; SLNA 1/6511, 1/6512, 1/6520, 1/6521, Minutes.

The various documents produced by the Landraad use different categories of information. The thombos carry information on both caste and service in separate columns, with service being considered important in identifying the land parcels due to individuals. At times, the company also identified persons as "Sinhalese" in the Landraad, curiously without mentioning their caste-like identity.[49] The minutes mention the current and former service holdings such as mayorāl, lascarin and

[48] Morris, "Occupational Coding: Principles and Examples," 9–12.

[49] Dewasiri has also noticed this phenomenon in some thombos. See Dewasiri, *Adaptable Peasant*, 200.

vidāne and other titles of about one-fifth of litigants in the sample. Title demonstrated credibility and rank in society, an important factor with regard to both litigants and witnesses. The legal production of such socio-economic identities through the land holdings attached to them made it non-essential to articulate a Sinhalese identity in the daily workings of the Landraad.

Most litigants and witnesses were Sinhalese, 79 and 93 per cent, respectively. Ethnicity was mentioned infrequently in Landraad documents, and the data in Table 3.1 were mostly deduced from names. If the litigants were Sinhalese, it is likely that the witnesses they produced would also be Sinhalese. Collectives of litigants rarely came from different ethnic backgrounds. There was also little diversity among witnesses, with only around ten per cent of sixty-seven depositions evidently including a cross-section of ethnic formations. Moors were often mentioned as such, but in general, hardly any mention was made of other ethnic categories in the records. Those present at a hearing may have easily differentiated Europeans and natives by their appearance and dress. Malabars, the Dutch term for Tamils, was not mentioned in the sample period.

The more privileged category of burger, those of European or Eurasian descent (all indicated here as European), was insignificant in number: they comprised 5.8 per cent of litigants and 3.2 per cent of witnesses. Names such as De Silva and Perera under the "unknown" category may refer to Europeans, but they could have also been Sinhalese or manumitted slaves. Cases involving Europeans, where they did not concern land matters outside the fort, would have been heard in the Civiele Raad of Galle. Yet, we see that Europeans were involved in property matters outside Galle Fort. The Landraad was a legal space that reached out to rural folk, but also had exclusive jurisdiction over land matters registered in the Galle thombos.

The literature has identified caste as a category through which the indigenous population could be rendered economically "useful" to the company.[50] Caste identities were hardly mentioned in the Landraad minutes, indicating the limited interest by the council in the social formation for its own sake. In some cases, it was possible to infer the caste from litigants' names or occasionally from the thombos, which generally provided caste information. A cross section of caste members came to the Landraad. We saw above how a hakuru caste woman was granted leave to appeal the Landraad's decision to the Raad van Justitie. *Radā* caste men, ritually associated with washing tasks, and men and women of the karāva and salāgama castes came to the Landraad.[51] Caste, because of its associated mandatory services to the company, was a way of "thinking about natives within the framework of

[50] See, for example, Dewasiri, *Adaptable Peasant*; Rogers, "Early British Rule and Social Classification."

[51] SLNA 1/6511, "Galle Landraad minutes," fols. 30r–31r, 9 Jul 1778.

productivity."[52] Yet, even more than caste, service categories were an important inclusion in land registers, which recorded a shareholder's service rendered in return for the property holding. This record was of importance in Landraad proceedings where the rendering of a service such as mayorāl, lascarin or grain measurer was at stake or litigants were threatened with demotion to coolie or nainde status. They were all assigned fixed amounts of *accommodessan* (maintenance grants), as seen in appendix III. Some services or titles were in practice seen across castes; service position or title-holding was not the exclusive prerogative of the goygama caste. Such positions were important for the economic activities of the colonial government. In land litigation, ethnicity and strict caste identifications were replaced by other categories of status such as title-holding and service.

Strikingly, 68 per cent of litigants were not assigned any social or occupational identity. We can assume that if they held a title it would have been claimed and recorded. This shows that the lack of status was not a setback in approaching the Landraad. Coolies, who performed menial labour and belonged to the subordinate ranks of the goygama caste or to low-status groups, came to the council and won. A dispute between two coolies and mayorāls resulted in a judgement in favour of the former, and in another case in my sample, the conclusion of which was not found, a coolie acted against the headman Sameradiwakere Jayasundara.[53] As litigants in the council, high-level local headmen may have been privileged, but this was not always the case.

In contrast, among the witnesses, a majority were persons of some status in a village. They would have been considered most capable of providing credibility to a litigant's claims. We can assume that litigants were aware of the advantages of bringing the testimony of rank and file to the council; almost forty per cent of witnesses were current or former headmen from both high and low ranks and persons of high standing in the village such as mayorāls, schoolmasters and schrijvers. The absence of a high ritual birth was occasionally remarked on – one witness was ridiculed by the opposing party for his occupation of tile-making and was asked if this was not a very low and hence disgraceful service for the "honourable" goygamas, to which he responded in the affirmative.[54] While some mudaliyārs and kōrālas also appeared, mayorāls appeared frequently as witnesses. Lascarins, kangāns and former kangāns, who had lower-level responsibilities in the village,

[52] Lauren Benton and Richard J. Ross, "Empires and Legal Pluralism: Jurisdiction, Sovereignty, and Political Imagination in the Early Modern World," in Lauren Benton and Richard J. Ross (eds), *Legal Pluralism and Empires, 1500-1850*, Kindle edition (New York: NYU Press, 2013), 11.

[53] SLNA 1/6511, "Galle Landraad minutes," fols. 5v–6v, 30 May 1778; 11r, 6 Jun 1778; 12v, 6 Jun 1778.

[54] SLNA 1/6534, "Galle Landraad Interrogations" (1778 to 1784), fols. 38r, 18 Dec 1778.

were frequently regarded as credible, accounting for 34 per cent of the witnesses. Landraad councillors also served as witnesses on occasion.

Status through caste and office played a significant role in pre-colonial legal and administrative orders. Officials had to be aware of a wrongdoer's caste before a punishment such as veläkma (see chapter one) was meted out, as persons of a higher caste and particular ranks were exempt from certain punishments. In the Kandyan kingdom, John D'Oyly wrote that corporal punishment was not inflicted on persons from noble families and on other high-level title holders, and they could not be imprisoned in the *Maha Hirage* (Great Prison). On the other hand, he said that headmen from subordinate ranks could be punished with the "open hand" and lower-level goygama caste members and persons of low caste were punished with rods called *ipal* (twigs).[55] The Landraad practised such corporal punishment with subordinate headmen – for example, when it found a mayorāl at fault in a case over a disputed land sale ola, the council directed that he be flogged after the meeting dispersed because they believed that it was quite likely that he had in fact signed the ola (which he denied) and, moreover, that he should know what took place in his village.[56] The Landraad had to repeatedly reprimand high-level headmen for non-cooperation with the thombo registration, but there is no evidence that corporal punishments were meted out for this. Evidently, headmen and service holders were not a monolithic body that was equally privileged.

In cases heard before the council, almost the entire spectrum of social groups appeared as principal parties or witnesses. The dominant story is of rural inhabitants who lived in thatched houses on their lands: a paddy-field with a harvest of a quarter acre of rice may be all that they had to defend. The costs of bringing an issue to the council were considerable, but litigants could apply for *pro deo*. Laymen appeared on a regular basis, including persons belonging to lower caste formations. The clergy do not appear in the sample cases; however, though they are traditionally not known to have private land holdings except as part of a temple, in 1794, a Buddhist monk asked for a garden and paddy-field that he had cultivated in 1786 and for which he had paid the required taxes to be registered in the thombo under his name.[57] As land ownership was divided among different ethnic groups, some cases involved cross-cultural litigation, particularly with Europeans who appeared in connection with property recorded in the thombo. Moors mostly filed claims against each other and occasionally against Sinhalese inhabitants. This is testimony to how social formations interacted in society, inevitably reflected in a judicial forum.

[55] John D'Oyly, *A Sketch of the Constitution of the Kandyan Kingdom*, ed. Lewis James Barnetson Turner, vol. 24, The Ceylon Historical Journal (Dehiwala: Tisara Prakasakayo, 1929; repr. 1975), 37.

[56] SLNA 1/6513, "Galle Landraad minutes," fols. 104r, 9 Sept 1780.

[57] SLNA 1/6517, "Galle Landraad minutes" (1794), fols. 116r, 22 Nov 1794.

Distance to the Council

In practice, how far did the jurisdiction of the Galle Landraad extend geographically? The ratione loci (by reason of place) I considered in the cases from 1778 to 1779 is the location of the paddy-fields and gardens under dispute. There were more dispute locations (93) than the number of cases involving land (83 of 99) as some cases dealt with fields and gardens in more than one village. The geographical origin of the disputes is as follows, arranged by sub-district: Four Gravets (36), Wellaboda (11), Gangaboda (12), Walallawiti (8) and Talpe (7). No cases were recorded from the Hinidum Pattuwa, while nineteen dispute locations remain unknown. The original residence of the litigants would be important in ascertaining how close to the centre of government they lived, but this information is not available for over 50 per cent of them. The high incidence of absentee ownership makes the residence of the litigants more important, as those who had moved closer to the seat of the Dutch government while retaining their rights to land in other villages may have been influenced towards initiating legal action. Such an analysis is beyond the scope of this study, but the recorded residence of witnesses gives us some indication of how accessible Kumbalwella was.

Proximity to the Dutch colonial centre was important in determining who came to the council. Galle Fort, and the sub-district of the Four Gravets within which Kumbalwella was the seat of the Landraad, the thombo office and the overseer of the Galle district were pivotal locations that connected Galle to Colombo, the centre of Dutch administration in Sri Lanka. They were relatively more "urban" than the surrounding hinterland. Many disputed lands were in the Four Gravets. Kumbalwella had at least ten dispute locations but is likely to have been a more populated and urban area within the Galle district. The contrast between a coastal urban area and the rural hinterland may apply here, although distinct categories of town and countryside as seen in European studies were of little consequence in Dutch Sri Lanka. Considerable parallels between the two were more likely than dissimilarities in life patterns. At the same time, the relationship between proximity to the Dutch government and legal action may be overrated. For instance, if witnesses were willing to travel the distances that they did, this is very likely representative of the distance that litigants could travel as well, although litigants are likely to have been more motivated to go the extra mile. The 264 witnesses in the period 1778–1781 resided in the following subdistricts: Four Gravets (54), Wellaboda (51), Gangaboda (49), Walallawiti (5) and Talpe (61).[58] No witnesses were recorded from the Hinidum Pattuwa.

[58] An "unknown" figure (44) includes villages that are located in two sub-districts, thereby making it impossible to know which part of the village the witness belonged to without accurately locating

The company instructed the Landraad to pay due regard to the distance litigants and witnesses had to travel to reach Kumbalwella.[59] Leonard Woolf, a British civil servant who also served as a magistrate in Sri Lanka, wrote on the difficulties of travelling in the region even in the early twentieth century.[60] In an eighteenth-century lawsuit, a group of eight witnesses were supposedly inconvenienced by the considerable distance to the council. First, the case was not taken up on the stipulated day in December 1779, as the Landraad had postponed the sitting for the next day. The witnesses were to be cross-examined by the opposing party, but they did not have a counter-interrogation ready. The litigant for whom they appeared pleaded that his witnesses could not remain because they lived far away and could not interrupt their services to the company. The commissioners who presided over the meeting asked the opposing party to be ready the next morning or within twenty-four hours "because the witnesses could not be delayed longer as they lived faraway in the country." However, they were forced to stay a third day as well.[61] On that day, the council's messenger said that the errant litigant had informed him that on leaving the hearing the day before, he had been attacked by piercing pains in the stomach and was still in confinement.[62] Yet, despite the distance, the witnesses reappeared twenty days later to be cross-examined.[63] These witnesses were from Amugoda-Keppitiyagoda (Gangaboda Pattuwa), Nagoda (Gangaboda Pattuwa), Thiranagama (Wellaboda Pattuwa), Katukolihe (Wellaboda) and Majuwana (Gangaboda Pattuwa), which are between 12 and 18 kilometres away (see Map 3). It is challenging to calculate how many days of travel such distances would have entailed as terrain difficulties are hard to gauge. The councillors and the litigant considered this to be a considerable distance, but the witnesses still appeared in the Landraad, as did other witnesses from locations further away.

The evidence suggests those living in the hinterlands bordering the Kandyan kingdom, where the Landraad's jurisdiction may have been contested, were less likely to have participated in colonial rule. In fact, the sub-districts of Wellaboda, Gangaboda, Talpe and Walallawiti had only around forty dispute locations in total,

him or her in the thombo. Fifteen of them were from Hinatigala, which is in both the Talpe Pattuwa and Four Gravets.

59 Hovy, *Plakkaatboek*, vol. 2; nr. 628, (II, 8), Instructions for the Landraden, including extracts from resolutions, 25 Jun 1789. See for translation S.A.W. Mottau, trans., "Instructions for the Respective 'Landraden' of this Government (Extract from the Dutch Political Council Minutes of 25th June 1789)," *Journal of the Dutch Burger Union of Ceylon* 55, no. 1–4 (1965).

60 Leonard Woolf, *The Village in the Jungle* (Oxford, Chennai: Oxford University Press, 1913; repr. 1981), 53–54, 60.

61 SLNA 1/6512, "Galle Landraad minutes," fols. 94v, 1 Dec 1779.

62 Ibid., fols. 95r, 2 Dec 1779.

63 SLNA 1/6521, "Galle Landraad draft minutes" (1779 to 1780), fols. 37v, 22 Dec 1779.

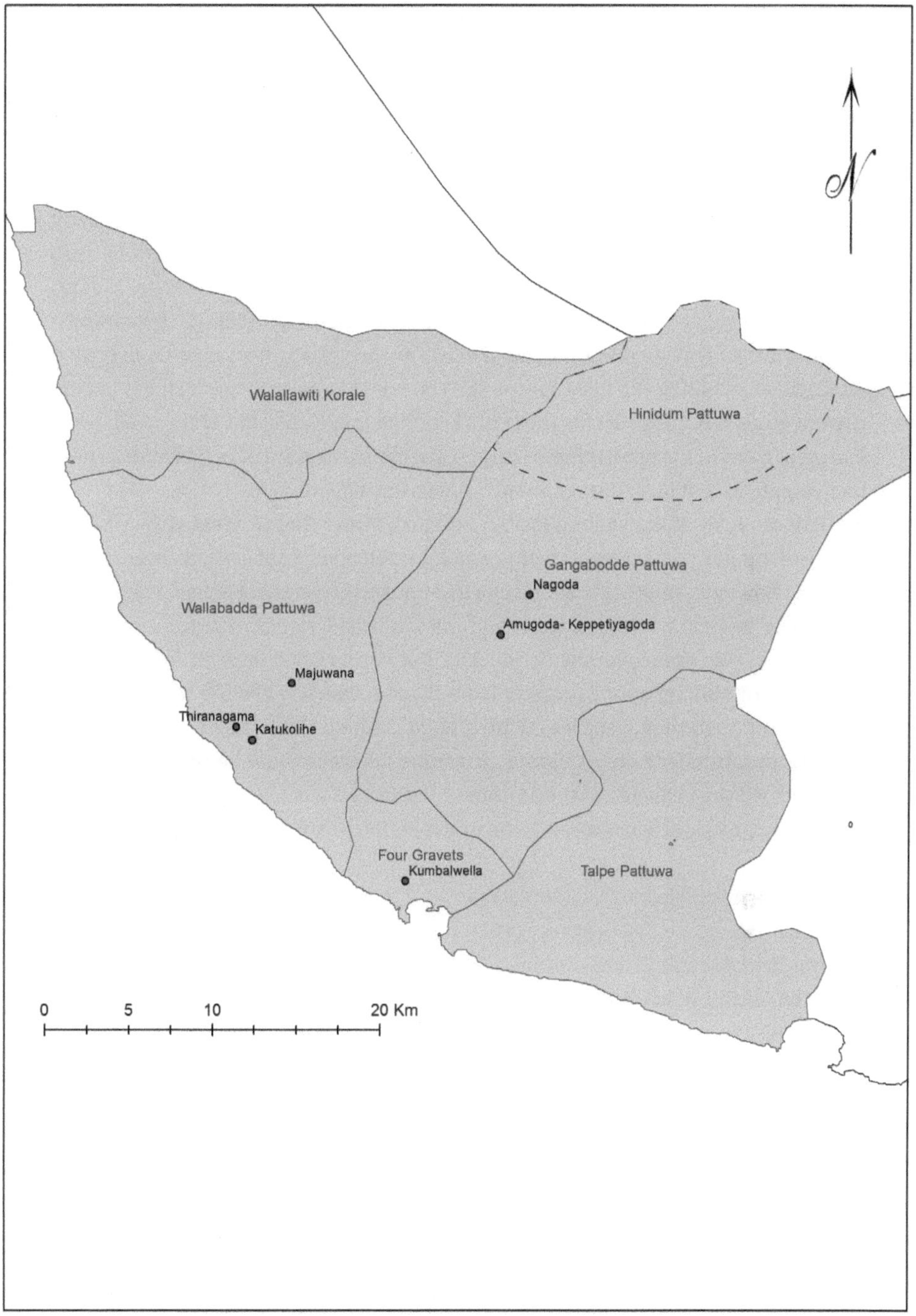

Map 3 Villages in Galle district (shown in grey) considered "far" by the Landraad located in Kumbalwella, all between 12 and 18 km away.

which almost equals the number of disputes from the Four Gravets. The population in the hinterland areas may have also been low. It is striking that there were no cases from the Hinidum Pattuwa – its considerable remoteness may be seen as an obvious reason for this. According to the available data, Hinidum also did not produce any witnesses. The area was remote from the administrative heart of Galle and lay on the border of the Kandyan kingdom. This indicates that if particularly long distances were involved, litigants were not keen to make representations to the Landraad. In all six well drawn up thombos of the Hinidum Pattuwa, I found no notations regarding council decisions on the ownership of lands. The commissioners, if they travelled to that sub-district for the registration, may have settled all disputes, avoiding the need for the full council to hear an issue.[64] This is in contrast to other thombos such as those of Dodampe and Ganegoda of the Wellaboda Pattuwa (close to the coast), where disputes arose at the time of registration. These two villages had at least ten recorded issues from 1780 to 1781.

This analysis of the ratione loci jurisdiction shows that in areas close to Galle Fort, the company's new legal regime and by extension its sovereignty were not in dispute. However, in other inaccessible locations that were less densely populated and closer to local powers, litigation at the Landraad was rare. If the company's jurisdiction was controversial, it was still not contentious enough for people to refrain from making a long journey from the sub-districts around the seat of the council, although they were less willing to go through thick jungle and other difficult terrain further north. Colonial litigation, where it could be relatively easily accessed, led the peasants to the Landraad in their efforts to secure justice.

Conclusion

During British rule, First Colonial Secretary Hugh Cleghorn, in the minutes of 1799 that are now infamous for promoting the "two-nation" theory of Sinhalese and Tamils, provided a glowing report of the Landraad. He said it was "extremely popular, and its decisions were generally respected."[65] Cleghorn may, however,

[64] It is not known if residents of the Hinidum Pattuwa travelled to the Landraad for the registration or whether commissioners went to that remote area. Given that they were all drawn up in the year 1760, and it would have been difficult to mobilise so many inhabitants to travel several miles, the latter is more likely. The Landraad minutes from 1760 have no references to the Hinidum villages. SLNA 1/6498, "Galle Landraad minutes" (1760). In contrast, there were cases from Mapalagama (Gangaboda Pattuwa), a thombo that was also drawn up in 1760. SLNA 1/7501, "Mapalagama (Gangaboda) Thombo" (1760).

[65] Ralph Pieris, "Administration of Justice and Revenue on the Island of Ceylon under the Dutch Government ('The Cleghorn Minute')," *Journal of the Ceylon Branch of the Royal Asiatic Society*, n.s., 3

have overrated the power of the mudaliyār, and in the process contradicted his statement on the popularity of the Landraad: "He [the mudaliyār] is the only judge in the first instance of the disputes among the natives, he is a constituent member of the Land Raad, and few of the natives venture to appeal from his decision to a court where one of the judges may have been their oppressor."[66] Cleghorn seems to have believed that the power of the mudaliyār was hardly ever challenged. By treating the Landraad's use of Sinhalese customary law as a given and stressing the regulation that made the presence of the headmen compulsory, Kotelawele also exaggerates their role in the Landraad, which he believes may have added to their power.[67] Yet, we know that headmen were not always present at meetings (see chapter two) and that locals were not reluctant to appear in the Landraad. The evidence proves that the Landraad and the thombo provided a means for the Dutch government to connect directly with the inhabitants of the Galle district.

Men and women participated extensively in the colonial legal system where distance was not a serious deterrent. Witnesses from locations considered to be "far" by the council (between 12 to 18 kilometres away) appeared on several occasions. Nonetheless, further away from the administrative heart of the south, participation in the Landraad decreased. It was not novel for women and lower-ranking persons to make claims at the Landraad, as they would have been accustomed to appealing to the pre-colonial legal system as well. The lack of title-holding was also not a deterrent in coming forward to face the law. If the company attempted to control the legal representation of women through their husbands, it could not be fully realised in a rural setting. Evidently, the Landraad had a wide social reach and became part of the imagination of the villagers. By investing in civil litigation, they were conscious agents in the pursuit of justice to recover or gain property. Taking an economic perspective on why people came to the Landraad, it can be said that the thombos fostered property litigation.

The recording of identities in the Landraad documents and thombos reflected the colonial preoccupations that eventually led to further essentialisation of such identities. While identifying litigants, service was mentioned more frequently than ethnicity, caste, religion and gender. Service and occupational categories were preferred to strictly caste classifications: it was more important, due to the legal implications in connection with land holdings, to explicitly mention a goygama villager's mayorāl status than his caste. Distinctions of rank, ranging from a lascarin to a mahamudaliyār, were important, and Dewasiri has shown how

pt. 2 (1953): 134.

[66] Pieris, "Administration of Justice," 145.

[67] D.A. Kotelawele, "Some Aspects of Social Change in the South West of Sri Lanka c. 1700–1833," *Social Science Review* no. 4 (1988): 96.

increased opportunities for land ownership for such groups under the colonial government gave rise to a new class formation.[68] Identities based on service to the company were a feature of the cultural order that emerged at the end of the eighteenth century. This focus reveals the economic interests of the VOC in the task of essentialising identities. The Landraad represented a colonial legal system that both responded to and reshaped cultural categories of identity. The purpose of the thombos to record taxation on property holdings, which in turn were closely related to service categories, ensured that occupations were recorded correctly. Peasants were keen to rectify mistakes on this front, as seen in the service issues described in chapter one. The public registry of the thombo was crucially linked to inheritance of land, and citizens invested in the Landraad to protect all-important land rights.

Kalegana Bastiaan Naidelage Maria's provocative fragment of resistance to the Landraad mentioned at the start of this chapter was short-lived; she had no choice but to subsequently appear in connection with her case in that very forum that ordered that she be flogged for her "impertinent expression." She was most probably punished on 1 April 1780 after the council adjourned for the day (we have no confirmation of the flogging itself). Coercive force would have been a determining factor in judicial participation, which in turn was a necessary evil to retain land rights. By the mid-eighteenth century, inhabitants were acquainted with the Landraad and its land registration processes, and used this knowledge in settling disputes. Litigants had to understand the strategies and best practices. For litigants with plural identities, the Landraad was a location of identification and a site for navigating a changing legal landscape.

[68] Dewasiri, *Adaptable Peasant*, 141–83.

CHAPTER 4

Marshalling Unseen Forces

Abstract

Colonial agents often saw the value of improvising the corporal form of the oath for the smoother functioning of judicial bodies. The VOC in Sri Lanka found that potential swearers were mostly nominal Christians who had few scruples about giving false oaths. This subtle resistance prompted the accommodation of local oath forms. Ultimately, the changes were of little use due to the mutual discrediting of potential oath-takers. A nominal Christian's refusal to take the Dutch oath and preference for the local oath would be criticised, as also an acceptance of the Dutch form. Plural forms of the oath thus did not always provide the desired effect but rebounded in unexpected ways. Such everyday judicial practices provide deeper insights into the navigation of pluralities.

Keywords: Oaths, evidence, pluralities, decisory oath, judicial oath, idolatry, Roman-Dutch law.

In the Landraad of Galle in 1782, twenty witnesses were asked if they knew the Ten Commandments, and particularly the Ninth Commandment. All of them had claimed to be Christians. Some were able to recall it, others could not. One witness said that he knew the Ten Commandments but could not recall the ninth. Another said that he did not know because from the time he was young he had been too busy working for the Dutch East India Company, and yet another said that he had not learned the Ten Commandments, only "Our Father."[1] This question aimed to prove that the witnesses should not take the oath if they did not know the commandment against false testimony. This is consistent with the principle underlying a legal oath, which is expected to bind the conscience of the swearer. Bereft of normative meaning, the oath loses its value and applicability. Unsurprisingly, European powers displayed an inherent lack of trust in colonised subjects. Testimonies, the oath, and a perception of trust were inherently interconnected.[2]

[1] SLNA 1/6534, "Galle Landraad Interrogations" (1778 to 1784), fols. 143v–144r, May and Jun 1782. Other reported answers were: "that he knows the Ten Commandments, and that the ninth commandment says not to give false testimony" and "that it has gone out of his memory."

[2] The dispute in North Carolina from 2003 over the Muslim form of the oath shows the continuing importance of the meaning attached to the oath as a legal practice for particular cultural groups.

Colonial agents often improvised the corporal form of the oath to enable the smoother functioning of judicial bodies. In eighteenth-century Sri Lanka, the Dutch colonial government found that potential swearers were mostly nominal Christians who had few scruples about giving false oaths. This subtle resistance prompted the Dutch to accommodate local customs. Thus, the change in the form of the oath from the Dutch form to a more local gesture was indirectly prompted by the colonised, who had subtly rejected the Dutch oath by being dismissive when delivering it. For the Dutch colonial government, such resistance meant that negotiating with local customs was inevitable. The need to establish the truth amidst perceived local mendacity was a source of anxiety. Ultimately, the adoption of local customs was of little use due to the mutual discrediting of potential oath-takers. A nominal Christian's refusal to take the Dutch oath and their preference for the local oath would be criticised, as also their acceptance of the Dutch form. As a result, the full function of the oath could not be realised. Thus, plural forms of the oath did not always provide the desired effect but rebounded in unexpected ways. This chapter argues that a closer reading of such mundane, everyday judicial practices is needed to gain deeper insights into the functioning of pluralistic colonial law.

The friction surrounding the administration of the oath shows the subtle dynamics at play in eighteenth-century colonial Sri Lanka. Dutch colonial ideas of local mendacity and idolatry connect with the relative failure of the Dutch Reformed Church in meaningfully converting the local population. Political and socioeconomic trends in relation to religion were important in driving potential swearers to engage in a subtle act of subversion. They claimed to be genuine Christians, but Dutch officials were mostly resigned to their duplicity. The indifferent attitude of the local population to Calvinism necessitated changes to the corporal form of the oath. Yet, tensions concerning the oath did not disappear the adoption of pluralities. In some ways, they were intensified.

First, I will examine the history of the oath in pre-colonial Sri Lanka and then analyse developments in Dutch times. I will examine articulations of trust in hitherto untouched records of the Galle Landraad as well as other administrative documents of the company. The interrogations (including the above question on the Ten Commandments) are written traces from the Landraad, and capture the social values of that time. They provide an invaluable source for social history as they record the voices of peasants. After a comprehensive account of the history and processes surrounding the oath, which is necessary to understand the subtleties involved, this chapter will then use interrogations of witnesses to examine the ways in which peasants and other colonial subjects subverted colonial power.

See Frederick B. Jonassen, "So Help Me: Religious Expression and Artifacts in the Oath of Office and the Courtroom Oath," *Cardozo Public Law, Policy & Ethics Journal* 12, no. 2 (2014): 350–53.

The Oath in Pre-Colonial Sri Lanka

Many premodern administrations attached great value to the oath, and the Sri Lankan experience was no exception. In pre-colonial legal spaces of the island, a decision was arrived at in two ways: by means of testimonial evidence – also referred to as trials by witnesses – or trials by oath. As in other premodern societies around the world, Sri Lankan trials invoked supernatural forces through the oath. In Sinhala, *diviya* (plural: *divi*) referred to a trial by oath where a dispute is settled through supernatural judgement. At times, the ceremony of the oath involved grave risks for the litigants, and such instances have been termed ordeals. The oath was deemed necessary if a case was complicated or if there were no witnesses to pursue a secular mode of trial. In local practice, if a diviya was admitted, the case was concluded through those means. Thus, it was a "decisory oath" that could be used to decide the case.

There were various forms of divi: oaths taken in the *dēvāla* (temple), by or upon paddy, by earthen vessels, by drawing white olas, by striking the earth and casting mud and water, and by kitul (palm) trees.[3] Not all can be described here, but the first, the oath made at the dēvāla, was a simple and possibly frequently practised form. In general, both the plaintiff and the defendant took the oath.[4] If their testimony was untrue, they sought for divine intervention to produce a sign in the form of some disaster or misfortune within a specific time frame. For example, Knox narrates an anecdote involving two parties, a slave and a merchant, who took such oaths at a temple. The slave himself burnt down the merchant's house as a "divine sign" of the merchant's guilt.[5] Other signs could involve the death of a relation, the loss of an animal, or damage to the harvest or house. In an early nineteenth-century case, it was said that the oath at the dēvāla "is considered as most binding on the conscience of persons professing the Buddhist religion."[6]

[3] F.A. Hayley, *A Treatise on the Laws and Customs of the Sinhalese* (New Delhi: Navrang, 1923; repr. 1993), 85–90; Ivor Jennings, "Notes on Kandyan Law Collected by Sir Archibald C. Lawrie LL.D," *University of Ceylon Review* 10, no. 3 (1952): 201–3; Ralph Pieris, *Sinhalese Social Organization: The Kandyan Period* (Colombo: Ceylon University Press Board, 1956), 160–63. *Caryota urens* is known as *kitul* in Sri Lanka.

[4] It appears that social hierarchies were preserved in this process: Ralph Pieris quotes two cases where the oath was not admitted as it was not customary for the nobility to swear with low-caste men. Pieris, *Sinhalese Social Organization*, 159, n. 62. See also Jennings, "Lawrie's Notes on Kandyan Law," 200.

[5] Robert Knox, *An Historical Relation of Ceylon* (Dehiwala: Tisara Prakasakayo, 1681; repr. 1966), 194–95.

[6] Pieris, *Sinhalese Social Organization*, 160. As an example of local accommodation of other forms of the oath, the mosque could take the place of the dēvāla. Jennings, "Lawrie's Notes on Kandyan Law," 201.

Conscience, however, may have had little to do with it; it was an instrumental fear that disaster would strike if one were to lie that made such oaths effective. This oath was closely connected to "acts of truth" (Sinhala: *satyakkriya*), which was a "belief that a solemn assertion of one's righteousness in a very particular respect can, by its truth, produce a specific desired result."[7] In essence, trials by oath relied on the intervention of a divine power to secure judgement. Evidently, this was effective because of a widespread belief that justice could be invoked through the supernatural.

A form of the oath involving blood relatives was common to certain parts of the country.[8] Reports requested by the Dutch governor from headmen (more on this below) reveal local practices relating to the oath practised in three areas, namely, Colombo, Galle and Matara.[9] A version of the oath involving relatives described in all three reports involved the children or other close relative of the oath-taker. This was the only type of oath reported among the "heathens" in Galle. First, the oath-taker had to purify themselves, wear new clothes and take one of their children to the special place stipulated for swearing. Standing opposite the child, they had to raise their right hand thrice to heaven, call the name of god and lay their hand on the child's head, saying: "what I said was the pure truth; if it is not so let god's righteous wrath and punishment befall upon me." The oath-taker would also specify a time limit for this divine intervention. If there was no child, any other next of kin could be produced. Versions of the same oath were mentioned in the reports sent from Colombo and Matara.[10] In the examples from Colombo and

[7] Vijaya Samaraweera, "An 'Act of Truth' in a Sinhala Court of Law: On Truth, Lies and Judicial Proof Among the Sinhala Buddhists," *Cardoza Journal of International and Comparative Law* 5 (1997): 133. Such acts of truth were in their most distinctive form plain statements of fact. K. de B. Codrington, "An Act of Truth in a Cingalese Court of Law," *Man* 33 (June 1933): 94, 95.

[8] It was also detailed by Ribeiro as an oath carried out under Portuguese rule. Joao Ribeiro, *The Historic Tragedy of the Island of Ceilao*, trans. P.E. Pieris (Colombo: The Ceylon Daily News, 1685; repr. 1948), 58–60.

[9] SLNA 1/93, "Governor in Council minutes" (1744), 24 Dec 1744; Pieter Sluijsken, "Eene beschryving van de landdienst op Ceylon: Zo uyt ondervinding als uyt oude papieren tezaemen gebragt (A Description of the Land Services of Ceylon: Compiled from both investigations and old papers)" (Colombo, 1784), vol. 1: 160-191, RP-31/32 Colonial Collection (KIT), Leiden University. See, for translations (I have used Kotelawele's free translation), "Alexander Johnston Papers" (1643 to 1817) (MssCol 1578, Manuscripts and Archives Division, The New York Public Library); D.A. Kotelawele, "Realms of Law: Judicial Procedures of the Low Country Sinhalese during Dutch Rule in Sri Lanka," *Modern Sri Lanka Studies* 2, no. 1 (1990): 117–20. These reports are possibly the only such records for southern and western local society on the subject from that time. Among other oaths, they describe the settling of boundary disputes in a ritual manner. Kotelawele briefly studies the incorporation of the native oath by the Dutch.

[10] Incidentally, the Matara report says that the oaths described were prevalent in the Kandyan kingdom as well.

Galle, the visitation of evil was wished upon the swearer, but in Matara, if the blood relative experienced misfortune, the swearer lost the case. Clearly, what would be perceived as irrational in trials today was considered legitimate in eighteenth-century Sri Lanka when secular methods failed. Such oaths involved passively waiting for divine judgement.

Other versions of the trial by oath included an ordeal.[11] Some ordeals included a red-hot iron, others a cobra or hot oil. Oath-takers would actively put themselves in physically harmful scenarios and await action by unseen forces. Emerging unscathed from such a physically challenging or near-impossible task or experience would be considered proof of innocence. In civil cases, both parties would take the oath, but in the case of robberies, the defendant alone had to take the oath.[12] Oaths that included an ordeal could also involve a visit to a dēvāla. Over time, the use of such ordeals went out of practice.[13] It is unlikely that they were in use in coastal Sri Lanka during Dutch rule, but there is one reference to it from the era of Portuguese rule. Ribeiro describes the ordeal of the red-hot iron being used in the Portuguese judicial forums of the marallas, or travelling courts.[14] In the reports commissioned by the Dutch in the eighteenth century, a local headman in Colombo described an oath administered while holding a hot iron, burning oil or cow dung with the note that he had never seen such an oath being performed or described in a Sinhalese book of laws, but had heard of it. Although the report from Matara referred to oaths involving ordeals that made use of hot oil, a hot iron, a snake and thorns, their use was not mentioned.

Oaths may have lost their divine connotation over time, but even in eighteenth-century Sri Lanka, perceptions of trust were connected to the supernatural. Belief in the divine associations of the law had written sanction in pre-colonial Sri Lanka, as seen in references to divine powers in property deeds.[15] Such written evidence shows the importance of the supernatural for the society of the time. The fear of divine power was so powerful that false accusations and false testimony were probably not easy options if they had to be supported with the oath. The fourth of the five precepts of good conduct in Buddhism, which had a powerful hold on the people, is to abstain from falsehoods. The concept of *divi-dōsa* (evils of false oaths) refers to the "awful misfortune that would befall individuals and their

[11] Hayley, *A Treatise on the Laws and Customs*, 85; John D'Oyly, *A Sketch of the Constitution of the Kandyan Kingdom*, ed. Lewis James Barnetson Turner, vol. 24, The Ceylon Historical Journal (Dehiwala: Tisara Prakasakayo, 1929; repr. 1975), 57.

[12] Pieris, *Sinhalese Social Organization*, 160.

[13] Hayley, *A Treatise on the Laws and Customs*, 90; Pieris, *Sinhalese Social Organization*, 160.

[14] Ribeiro, *Historic Tragedy*, 60.

[15] Pieris, *Sinhalese Social Organization*, 159–60.

immediate descendants as a consequence of falsely taking oaths."[16] Yet, if Knox's story of the slave and merchant were true, some swearers may have exploited the practice of the oath in the local judiciary. It was into this context that the Dutch entered in the seventeenth and eighteenth centuries.

The Dutch Oath in Sri Lanka

Two types of oaths were used for litigants and witnesses in The Netherlands in the eighteenth century.[17] For litigants, the Dutch had a decisory oath that in some ways mirrored local Sri Lankan practices, and witnesses were required to take a judicial oath. The eighteenth-century Landraad used both types of oaths. The Dutch jurist Johannes van der Linden says of the decisory oath: "Such an offer or tender of oath by one of the parties, does not become evidence in the cause before the judge has admitted it, but when it has been taken, the facts sworn to are held as proved between the parties."[18] The jurist Simon van Leeuwen says, "the oath having been taken, judgment at once follows thereon, for it is of such effect that the result of the case depends upon it."[19] Dutch jurists agree that the decisory oath was used by the plaintiff to support his evidence if it were incomplete, or by the defendant to strengthen his case when there was insufficient evidence against him.

The judicial oath was used to enhance the truthfulness of the witnesses in the eyes of judges but was not decisive in a case. It was used to authenticate (*bekrachtigen*) depositions or claims. At the time, the judicial oath supported a deposition or statement after it was made, although as practised in the modern world it precedes a testimony. There is no evidence of a judicial oath of that nature being required of witnesses at a lower level of the judicial hierarchy in pre-colonial Sri Lanka.

The Landraad allowed the decisory oath only on rare occasions. I found no mention of it being allowed in my sample of the minutes from May 1778 to August 1781, but I came across two examples from earlier years.[20] In 1769, Don Adriaan Gunawardena Ponnamperuma, the vocal mudaliyār of Bentota

[16] Samaraweera, "Act of Truth," 145.

[17] For example, see Simon van Leeuwen, *Simon van Leeuwen's Commentaries on Roman-Dutch Law*, ed. Cornelis Willem Decker and John Gilbert Kotzé, vol. 2 (London: Sweet and Maxwell, 1923), 477–85, 489–96.

[18] Johannes van der Linden, *Institutes of the Laws of Holland*, trans. Jabez Henry (London: J & W T Clerk, 1828), 263.

[19] Van Leeuwen, "Simon van Leeuwen's Commentaries," 494.

[20] The volumes SLNA 1/6511, 1/6512, 1/6513, 1/6514 contain the minutes of the Galle Landraad from 16 May 1778 to 28 August 1781.

who clashed with the European president of the Landraad in the 1740s,[21] took a decisory oath. He claimed that during the war with the Kandyan kingdom, he had lost the deed confirming a fifteen-year lease of a garden in Kumbalwella from a bookkeeper, Jurgen Ruijtenberg Bodijn, who had since died. Bodijn's children wanted to see the deed, but Ponnamperuma could only produce an entry in a diary in Sinhala referring to a lease for fifteen years for fifteen rixdollars in 1759. The Landraad allowed him to take the oath on the authenticity of the entry in the diary, and on that basis permitted him to hold the garden for the remaining period. The case was concluded when Ponnamperuma took the Dutch form of the oath (more on this later), on which occasion the Bodijns were not present, although they had been served the summons.[22] Another decisory oath, which was taken by a plaintiff to attest the sum of a debt, was recorded later in 1775. The plaintiff, Bastiaan Christobu, claimed that Don Apponsu Wannige Chintamunie Mohotti Appuhamy, a *vidānārachchi*[23] of Akmeemana, owed him 50 rixdollars. The defendant claimed that the due amount was only 40 rixdollars, but that if the plaintiff swore by the oath that he had lent him 50 rixdollars, he would return it. The plaintiff, a Chettiar who claimed to be of the Dutch Reformed Church, took the Dutch form of the oath. The decision followed immediately. The defendant had to pay 50 rixdollars, an interest of one per cent per month, and the costs of the lawsuit.[24] The decisory nature of this oath resembles the local usage except for the absence of a call for divine intervention. Ponnamperuma (and most likely Christobu) was of high social status and was perhaps thus deemed truthful and likely to be admitted to the oath.

In the records of the Landraad, the judicial oath was most frequently referred to in relation to validating depositions (*verklaring* or *depositie*)[25] by witnesses. The depositions were made by witnesses in the presence of the secretary to the Landraad at his residence. They were translated by a sworn interpreter. They did not have to be made before a judge or in the formal space of the council. As explained in chapter one, depositions were formally signed by the witnesses

[21] See chapter two.

[22] SLNA 1/6504, "Galle Landraad minutes" (1769), fols. 18r, 18 Feb 1769; 29r, 18 Mar 1769.

[23] A revenue collector in charge of one or more villages.

[24] SLNA 1/6509, "Galle Landraad minutes" (1775), fols. 53r–55v, 27 May 1775.

[25] Mottau mistakenly uses the word "affidavit" in his inventory, but they were not sworn statements as the term implies. The word deposition has also been used in the South African context, see S.A.W. Mottau, *Inventory of the Archives of the Dutch Government in the Divisions of Galle (Matara) and Jaffnapatnam 1640-1796* (The Hague: General State Archives, 1975); Nigel Worden and Gerald Groenewald, *Trials of Slavery: Selected Documents Concerning Slaves from the Criminal Records of the Council of Justice at the Cape of Good Hope, 1705-1794* (Cape Town: Van Riebeeck Society, 2005), xxiii. The word "depositie" was also used in the Landraad records in SLNA 1/6511, "Galle Landraad minutes" (1778), fols. 30r, 31r, 9 Jul 1778; 63r, 5 Oct 1778.

producing the deposition, two clerks (Europeans) as professional witnesses confirming the validity of the document, the secretary and the interpreter. Much of what was said, where repetitious, was omitted from the content. Each deposition contains interpretations from either Sinhala or Tamil to Dutch, as few declarants were conversant in the language. The interpreter's version had to be accepted by the document creator, who was usually the (European) secretary. Thus, the depositions were, in effect, third-person summaries of testimonies (as opposed to first-person accounts). It is important to understand that they were not written by the witnesses, but as reported speech by a clerical officer. A deposition typically begins by stating that the witnesses "declared as true as follows," and each witness is referred to in the order in which they were listed as the first, second, third etc. One example states: "The first witness [declared] that he knew very well that when Wadumeestrige Philippu had come to live in the garden Dombegahawatte there were only 15 to 20 old coconut trees, but since then it was planted by him and owned till his death and after his death his wife and children had possessed it to this date."[26] It is most likely that the reliance on proof through witness testimony in such depositions was greater than on a back-and-forth in a live council sitting. The depositions may reflect the voice of the witnesses, but it is difficult to know how closely the text followed the oral expression. Vijaya Samaraweera stresses the importance of knowing the local language in court, quoting James de Alwis, who said in 1852 that the Sinhala language was "the key to the heart of the native."[27] Every deposition usually ended by stating that the witnesses claimed to be stating the pure and genuine truth and promised to swear by it under oath.[28] The format of these depositions is similar to those made under the VOC at Cape Town.[29]

Council members were mostly careful about following procedure when admitting a witness to the oath. Either the councillors ordered the process of admittance to the oath (usually allocating fourteen days for the purpose) or the litigant requested it to be administered to their witnesses to strengthen their case. Most litigants complied. On one occasion, however, a party claimed that it could not ask their witnesses to swear as the witnesses were engaged in company work.[30] The process of admittance to the oath, however, was a complicated one. In the

[26] SLNA 1/6494, "Galle Landraad depositions" (1778 to 1781), fols. 8r, 22 Jul 1778.

[27] James De Alwis, *Sidath Sangarawa: A Grammar of the Sinhalese Language* (Colombo: W. Skeen, 1852), v, ccli; Samaraweera, "Act of Truth," 160.

[28] The full paragraph reads: "The witnesses ended their declaration which they stated contained the pure and genuine truth, indicating that the accuracy of their testimony is as given in the text, while being ready to further confirm what was attested to with the oath if necessary." In many depositions this was condensed to "Ending herewith etc...." See SLNA 1/6494, "Galle Landraad depositions."

[29] Worden and Groenewald, *Trials of Slavery*.

[30] SLNA 1/6514, "Galle Landraad minutes" (1781), fols. 115r, 28 Aug 1781.

language used in the minutes, one party would *inthimeeren* (offer) the oath of their witnesses to the opposing litigant. First, the deposition that was made earlier had to be read out aloud and confirmed, a step that was called *recollement*. The verb *recoleeren* (*recoleren* in modern Dutch) means re-stating and thereby confirming. If the statement was read aloud and followed by an oath taken by the defendant or witnesses, it would be *recollement onder eede* (confirmation under oath). The process was referred to as *in forma probanti te brengen* (to bring in the form of legal proof).[31] The language of "offering" the oath is significant in that the oath is offered at the judicial forum as verification of the evidence in the deposition. Heavy warnings on the enormity of the oath had to be given beforehand.[32] It was a formal procedure in which the reading out aloud of the text and the utterance of the oath stressed the oral process.[33]

Inevitably, the offer of the oath would be challenged by the opposing party. It was in the interests of the litigants to object by producing contra-interrogatorieën (counter-interrogations), which sought to prove the unsuitability of admitting the opposing party's witnesses to the oath.[34] Often, both adversarial parties interrogated each other's witnesses and objected to the oath on the basis that the interrogations proved that the depositions were false. First, the opposing party was invited to see the deposition introduced in *forma probanti,* and if they so wished, object to the oath by producing a counter-interrogation. In one Landraad case, the opposing party was sent a copy of the deposition well in advance for them to hand over a counter-interrogation. The opposition was also told that whether they appeared or not, the process would continue. Thus, it was stressed that the oath was a serious matter. But in practice, the Landraad was flexible. We see how the failure to produce a counter-interrogation was not condemned and was allowed to cause delays in the same case over many weeks.[35] If a party did not present a

[31] See Van der Linden, *Institutes of the Laws of Holland,* 473–74.

[32] Hovy, *Plakkaatboek*, vol. 2; nr. 628, (II, 27), Instructions for the Landraden, including extracts from resolutions, 25 Jun 1789. See for translation S.A.W. Mottau, trans., "Instructions for the Respective 'Landraden' of this Government (Extract from the Dutch Political Council Minutes of 25th June 1789)," *Journal of the Dutch Burger Union of Ceylon* 55, no. 1–4 (1965).

[33] This was not without parallels in the rest of the world. See Miles Ogborn, "The Power of Speech: Orality, Oaths and Evidence in the British Atlantic World, 1650–1800," *Transactions of the Institute of British Geographers* 36, no. 1 (2011): 109–125.

[34] I suspect that many, if not all, interrogations found in the two volumes of interrogations in the Galle records of the Landraad concern the stalling of the oath. SLNA 1/6534, "Galle Landraad interrogations,"; SLNA 1/6535, "Galle Landraad interrogations" (1785 to 1793).

[35] In October 1778, Matere Happuhannedige Johan twice pleaded that his party's procureur (Albertus Hissink) had fallen sick and therefore could not prepare a counter-interrogation. He was given three days initially and then eight days. But Johan failed to produce a counter at the next meeting of the commissioners as well and asked for another 14 days. The opposing party, led by Kahingellege

counter-interrogation of the opposing party's witnesses, this could be used against them. The procureur or process representative Albertus Hissink once proposed that the failure to present a counter-interrogation clearly established that the opposing party had no proof to challenge the witnesses.[36] Typically, however, the opposing party would produce a counter-interrogation[37] and try to prove the unsuitability of the witnesses.

These counter-interrogations were carried out in a clear, predetermined way. Two commissioners of the Landraad would lead the process by which the witnesses would be cross-examined. The questions were prepared in advance by the opposing party, most likely in consultation with a procureur. This differs from the more spontaneous nature of modern-day court room questioning. During the cross-examination of witnesses, the litigant for whom they were appearing was sent out of the room and recalled when the questioning was concluded. As each witness was asked the prearranged questions, it is possible that they were called in individually, but this is not mentioned in the sources. The answers were jotted down in reported speech next to the questions. The exercise aimed to prove that the witnesses were unsuitable candidates for the oath because of their impiety or vested interests. A standard objection (*reproche*) to the evidence of the counter-interrogation written out in the minutes over the years was: "And the opposing party accusing the witnesses of being corrupt people who in their depositions contradicted and refuted themselves, requested that they must not be admitted to the oath." To this, the litigant for whom the witnesses appeared attempted to redeem them (*salvation*) by

Matthees, requested that Johan not be allowed to present a counter-interrogation and that their witnesses be admitted to the oath as three deadlines had already passed. The council delegates deferred the matter to the full council, which decided that Johan and his party must bring *their* deposition in *forma probanti*, seeming to ignore the opposing party's own deposition and oath and Johan's failure to produce a counter-interrogation for it. SLNA 1/6511, "Galle Landraad minutes," fols. 63r, 5 Oct 1778; 71v, 10 Oct 1778; 76r, 21 Oct 1778; 89r, 28 Nov 1778. Unlike Johan and his party, the opposing party was prompt in producing a counter-interrogation and their offer of the oath was deferred to the full council. SLNA 1/6520, "Galle Landraad draft minutes" (1778 to 1779), fols. 53r, 18 Dec 1778; SLNA 1/6534, "Galle Landraad interrogations," fols. 32r–38v, 18 Dec 1778. Some six months later, Matthees's party handed over a counter-interrogation with answers, a deed of recollement and a written request (*dictum*). SLNA 1/6512, "Galle Landraad minutes" (1779), fols. 38r, 5 Jun 1779. No mention of the oath or the depositions was made thereafter in the records, let alone of Johan's failure to produce a counter-interrogation. The Landraad pronounced a sentence in 1783 in Johan's favour, but the matter concerning the costs of the case dragged on till 1794. SLNA 1/6524, "Galle Landraad draft minutes" (1783), fols. 79v, 15 Nov 1783; SLNA 1/6517, "Galle Landraad minutes" (1794), fols. 118r, 22 Nov 1794.

[36] SLNA 1/6514, "Galle Landraad minutes," fols. 9r, 6 Jan 1781.

[37] At times, the opposing party presented a dictum in response. SLNA 1/6512, "Galle Landraad minutes," fols. 94r, 1 Dec 1779; SLNA 1/6513, "Galle Landraad minutes" (1780), fols. 68r, 1 Jul 1780.

declaring that they were "men of honour" or "about whom there was nothing to be said" and requested admission to the oath.[38]

The turns and phrases of the language repeatedly used in seeking permission to take the oath may have escaped most litigants and witnesses but are testimony to the textual nature of the new practices of establishing truth. The Landraden are among Sri Lanka's first courts of record, and unlike the indigenous legal system, oral proceedings were recorded. The authorisation of evidence was thus experiencing a shift, from speech to standardised text in the Dutch legal arena.

To give an example from 1778, Pussewellege Johan and Ganegama Radāge Punchi were fighting over rights to a cow in the Galle Landraad. They requested that their witnesses be allowed to take the oath in support of their depositions. They presented counter-interrogations of each other's witnesses and objected to the Landraad admitting the oath on the basis that the counter-interrogations had proven that the depositions were false. After each counter-interrogation, the parties *persisteerd voor replicq* and *duplicq* (insisted on replies and rejoinders) and a decision on the oath was finally referred to the full bench of the Landraad.[39] But nothing more on the oath was found in the available records relating to the case. In the following months, the parties handed over a written statement, a condemnation of the witnesses, an answered counter-interrogation and *gerecolleerd verklaring* (confirmed declaration) with an *akte* (deed) of recollement.[40] The case ended the following year with the Landraad awarding the cow to Pussewellege Johan.

In over three years of Landraad records, the oath was not admitted to the witnesses despite it being offered on many occasions. As with the decisory oath, there was no mention of the Landraad allowing the judicial oath in the minutes from May 1778 to August 1781. Neither the two delegates who heard the interrogations nor the full council permitted the oath in this period. An example of two mayorāls offering the oath in support of a deposition was found from a later period (1784).[41] Such examples of the oath being performed are undoubtedly rare, being more the exception than the rule. On many occasions, the two councillors who heard the witness interrogations left the deposition under recollement only without allowing

[38] SLNA 1/6511, "Galle Landraad minutes," fols. 30r–31r, 9 Jul 1778. For this process in Roman-Dutch law, see Van Leeuwen, *Commentaries*, 2:482.

[39] SLNA 1/6511, "Galle Landraad minutes," fols. 30r–31r, 9 Jul 1778.

[40] Ibid., fols. 49r, 15 Aug 1778; 65r, 10 Oct 1778. Recollement of the deposition was documented in a deed.

[41] SLNA 1/6525, "Galle Landraad draft minutes" (1784 to 1786), fols. 57v, 11 Sept 1784; 58v–59r, 23 Sept 1784.

the oath,[42] or deferred the decision to the full bench.[43] When they deferred such cases to the full council, the decision was not in favour of the witnesses offering the oath. In one case, which was deferred to the council, the bench decided to circulate the case papers among the members, still without a favourable response.[44] Evidently, many people were not considered trustworthy enough to be administered the oath, but that does not seem to have led to a debarring of witnesses. In 1786, the Dutch Commander of Galle recommended that they avoid offering the oath as much as possible as the Sinhalese did not take the Christian oath seriously.[45] This is reflective of a general reluctance to allow the oath. It would be interesting to see how witnesses responded to a rejection of their offer to take the oath, but this is likely to be beyond the scope of the available sources. What such a rejection meant for the evidence produced by witnesses in the council is unclear. We may no longer think of an oath as a crucial part of legal action, but it was so in eighteenth-century Sri Lanka, at least conceptually. Yet, it was hardly ever allowed in the Landraad.

The attempted Dutch transplants and local practices had similarities and differences. In both, the decisory oath was a ritual act that decided the case. In the Dutch practice, swearing by god made the statement true. In the local practice, visitation of evil either passively or actively was the determining factor. The latter conceives of the gods or the supernatural as operating *through* the administration of the oath. The judicial oath of the Dutch for witnesses was, however, new to the locals. Given the decisory nature of the local oath of their experience, they may have wondered why witnesses and not the main parties involved were required to offer the oath,

[42] "The Hon. commissioned members decide to leave the declaration under recollement," SLNA 1/6520, "Galle Landraad draft minutes," fols. 51v (9 Dec 1778). See also SLNA 1/6513, "Galle Landraad minutes," fols. 18v, 14 Mar 1780. Other examples of the *Landraad* not allowing the oath: "The Hon. members decided to leave the declaration under recollement without admitting the oath," SLNA 1/6515, "Galle Landraad minutes" (1787 to 1793), fols. 145r, 29 Apr 1788. See also Ibid., fols. 179v, 4 Aug 1788; 182r, 25 Aug 1788; 249r, 27 Aug 1789.

[43] In one case where they had deferred the decision, the commissioners presented documentation of the recoleeren and an examination of the witnesses to the full council. The oath, however, was not permitted: "It was thus decided to leave the said evidence under recollement and the said Moor to be ordered to continue in principle." SLNA 1/6513, "Galle Landraad minutes," fols. 84r, 12 Aug 1780. In another example as well the witnesses were only allowed recollement: "so it was decided to keep the said witnesses under recollement." SLNA 1/6514, "Galle Landraad minutes," fols. 28r, 10 Feb 1781. After a counter-interrogation, the party in question may hand over the counter-interrogation with answers, the verified deposition with a deed of recollement and a statement or request. See, for example, SLNA 1/6512, "Galle Landraad minutes," fols. 42r, 19 Jun 1779. Another example of the commissioners deferring the decision to the council is SLNA 1/6515, "Galle Landraad minutes," fols. 115r-v, 10 Dec 1787.

[44] SLNA 1/6514, "Galle Landraad minutes," fols. 48r, 21 Apr 1781; 73r, 2 Jun 1781.

[45] SLNA 1/6225, "Scholarchale Vergadering minutes" (1786 to 1787), fols. 8v, 3 May 1786.

and if it was allowed, the litigants may have expected the case to be concluded on that basis. Other differences lay in the local practice being mostly oral, whereas the Dutch procedures were recorded. They were based on documents every step of the way.[46] In the transplant, there was also the requirement of counter-interrogations. That would have been difficult for the locals to conceive of without the help of the interpreters, in this case the sworn interpreter and the procureur. The historian Kotelawele, who does not mention the use of the decisory oath by the Dutch in Sri Lanka, says that the Dutch form of the oath was conceptually different to the local trial by oath. He believed that while the oaths played a different role in the local legal system – an oath invoking the gods was itself a form of trial – the Dutch oath was "merely the affirmation by the litigants to be truthful" or "merely a preliminary to a judicial procedure." Kotelawele calls this a "systematic misunderstanding" of colonial situations following Paul Bohannan.[47] Believing that the Dutch oath as practised in the courts of Sri Lanka was only a preliminary judicial oath, Kotelawele failed to realise that it was an oath offered on a deposition only if one was considered truthful enough to offer it. Moreover, as we saw above, the function of the decisory oath for litigants in the Roman-Dutch practice was not in conflict with the function of the trial by oath in local practice. It is thus important to study the legal practice in the donor country to fully understand its meaning and its transplantation to a foreign country.

What was mostly in conflict in the plural legal order of eighteenth-century Sri Lanka was the *form* of the oath. In the way of the Dutch Reformed Church, and as offered by Ponnamperuma and Christobu mentioned above, it involved holding up the second and third fingers of the right hand and saying, "so help me god almighty" (*so waarlijk helpe mij god almachtig*). Incidentally, this form of the oath is still in use in The Netherlands.[48] How it was changed when transplanted to eighteenth-century Sri Lanka will be discussed below.

[46] Oaths of office were recorded in writing as well, and the examples given above of Ponnamperuma and Christobu, who took decisory oaths, were recorded verbatim in the minutes. I have not found such a verbatim record of the individual oaths of witnesses.

[47] Kotelawele, "Realms of Law," 112; Paul Bohannan (ed), *Law and Warfare: Studies in the Anthropology of Conflict* (New York: Natural History Press, 1967).

[48] In the practice of oaths and affirmations in the courts of law today in The Netherlands, as in most other countries, a witness can choose between the oath and the promise. If the oath is chosen, he or she has to raise the second and third fingers of his right hand and say the words "*So waarlijk helpe mij god almachtig*" (So truly help me god almighty). A witness is also permitted to take the oath in a form prescribed by his religious identity. Apparently, this is made little use of in court today.

Disputing Form

The manner in which litigants or their witnesses offered the oath was of special concern to the company. For the Landraad councillors, we have seen that witness evidence was mostly inadmissible under oath. Sluijsken wrote in 1784 in his description of the land services of some territories in the island that "their complaints seldom saw a lack of witnesses, but even less seldom were there witnesses who could be approved, because when they profess to be Christians they are so flippant in the performance of the oath."[49] The company doubted the level of sanctity that natives attached to the Christian oath and their understanding of what it meant to be Christian. It was an issue that the company had been aware of for a long time. Questions of truth, Samaraweera says, were of less importance in the Gamsabhāva (village council) of the local system as there was "general familiarity of the assembly as a whole of the individuals and events that came before it."[50] For a foreign power, however, it was far more important.[51]

Many witnesses were ready to swear to the possession or cultivation of lands by others for the cadastral registration, but cultural differences lay at the base of the little

[49] Sluijsken, "A Description of the Land Services," vol. 1: 160.

[50] Samaraweera, "Act of Truth," 143.

[51] The issue of the oath form also came up in the seventeenth century in Jaffna. As far back as 1679, Laurens Pijl wrote: "Great care must be exercised in the administration of justice, because the people are a troublesome and dishonest race. They do not scruple to take a false oath to gain any profit, and the rich are able to get as many of the common people as they desire to give evidence in their behalf for their profit." This section written by Pijl to Ruthgaart de Heyde, his succeeding commander in Jaffna, appears with Governor Rijklof van Goens's memoir to Pijl, who was taking over as governor. Rijklof van Goens, *Memoir Left by Ryclof van Goens to Laurens Pijl*, trans. Sophia Pieters (Colombo: H.C. Cottle, Govt. Printer, 1910), 27–28. Knox's ideas of local mendacity perhaps prejudiced many Europeans as his work was available in print in Europe in different languages. Samaraweera points out that Knox's view was a result of the locals not being allowed to communicate to Knox on how to leave the Kandyan kingdom, where he was imprisoned for many years. See Knox, *An Historical Relation of Ceylon*, 120–21; Samaraweera, "Act of Truth," 137–38. In 1696, Colombo ordered two mudaliyārs of Jaffna to take their oath (as requested by a litigant in the Raad van Justitie of Jaffna) in "the heathen way." Commander of Jaffna Hendrick Zwaardecroon cites Pijl's statement as an explanation for why it was allowed "only in the heathen fashion, although this seemed out of keeping with the principles of the Christian religion (*Salva Reverentia*), as these people are recognised as baptised Christians, and therefore the taking of this oath is not practised here." Hendrick Zwaardecroon, *Memoir of Hendrick Zwaardecroon, Commandeur of Jaffnapatam, 1697*, trans. Sophia Pieters (Colombo: H.C. Cottle, Govt. Printer, 1911), 50. The local oath form was not officially accepted in Jaffna at the time, but Colombo was aware of the need for its use. Fifty years later, in 1746, Colombo banned the administering of the "heathen" oath form in Jaffna to baptised Christians who professed to be Christians in public. SLNA 1/98, "Governor in Council minutes" (1746), fols. 270r, 11 Jul 1746. This is different from the developments in Colombo explained in this chapter.

value they attached to the Christian oath. The flippancy with which the natives took the Dutch oath troubled the VOC. Yet, it is almost theatrical that the Dutch attempted to transplant an oath of holding up two fingers that was meaningless to the Sinhalese. This sense of absurdity was echoed in London in *Omychund v Barker* in 1744, when the issue of the "infidel" oath was debated: "it would be absurd for him to swear according to the Christian oath, which he does not believe; and therefore, out of necessity, he must be allowed to swear according to his own notion of an oath."[52] That same year, Governor Van Gollonesse in Sri Lanka called for a reform of the oath form.

Mistrust about who could effectively give their word prevailed, but rather than entirely barring witnesses from giving evidence because they were not true Christians, the company reached a compromise. The Governor in Council incorporated some local practices into the Landraad and all other judicial bodies and institutions after consulting native headmen. First, Governor Van Gollonesse called for reports on the oaths of the "Sinhalese heathens" from the headmen of Colombo, Galle and Matara.[53] In December 1744, two reports from Colombo and one each from Galle and Matara were submitted and the Landraden were asked for further advice. Having received this advice, local swearing-in practices that were acceptable to the "heathens" were adopted in 1745. It was obviously necessary to be able to accept evidence, which dictated a change in procedural aspects in the legal system as the early colonial state had appropriated the right to settle disputes among the natives.

The company thus began to accept plural forms of the oath.[54] The reports of 1744 described many practices but, as mentioned earlier, one common aspect

[52] *Omychund v Barker*, 1 Atkyn's Reports 22 (English Chancery 1744). This case had its origins in British Calcutta, and shows how imperial encounters prompted changes in the practice of the oath in the metropole. The case concerned a debt owed to an Indian, Omychund, by Barker, who was an East India Company official. Omychund filed a case in the Calcutta Mayor's Court. Barker fled India, and the case was eventually heard in the High Court of Chancery in England. Barker's defence moved to have the depositions of two Hindu witnesses taken in Calcutta dismissed because the witnesses had been sworn in by a Brahmin priest. The court in England held in favour of the plaintiff, Omychund, and thereafter, the testimony of witnesses sworn according to their own customs could be received as evidence in English courts. See Elizabeth Kolsky, *Colonial Justice in British India* (Cambridge: Cambridge University Press, 2010), 111–12. In arguing the case, Attorney-General Sir Dudley Rider for the plaintiff quoted the Dutch jurists Hugo Grotius and Johannes Voet to say that "the best writers of Christian morality have gone so far as to admit the oath to false gods." Omychund v Barker, 1 Atkyn's Reports at 28–29. *Omychund v Barker* led to the rationalisation of the oath into a legal practice, allowing the expansion of the admissibility of witnesses in court.

[53] SLNA 1/93, "Governor in Council minutes," fols. 147r, 21 Nov 1744.

[54] When a Mennonite refused to take the oath in the way of the Dutch Reformed Church before the *Raad van Justitie* (Council of Justice) in Colombo, the company adopted oaths that were acceptable to Roman Catholics, Mennonites and Jews in 1758. SLNA 1/125, "Governor in Council minutes" (1758),

was the inclusion of the children or other close relatives of the oath-taker. Other sources confirm the use of this oath as well. For example, petitioners to the Dutch Government appealed to the veracity of their statements by offering the oath on the heads of their children.[55] The company also eventually settled on this type of oath. On 24 December 1744, in order to do away with "many inconveniences" and "falsities" resulting from imposing the Dutch form, the governor proposed a new form of oath. Each "heathen" had to swear, after the usual cleansing process, and with their right hand on the head of one of their children, or if there were no children of another blood relative, saying out aloud the following words: "I swear by the true god of heaven and earth that so truly as I lay my hand at this moment on the head of my child (father, mother or other blood relative), that which I have declared and testified is true, and if I lie, the same god (in such and such a time) must punish me severely."

The governor asked the Landraden to consider the matter, and in March 1745, the proposal was made permanent.[56] A provision was also made to accommodate other forms of the oath that the locals practised.[57] But the one involving a relative

19 May 1758. An undated list of the oaths used in the Landraad for officials, litigants and witnesses includes the oath for Mennonites, Roman Catholics, Jews, Moors and "heathens." The oath of the Dutch Reformed Church was also the oath for Lutherans. SLNA 1/5666, "Miscellaneous Documents of the Galle Landraad Including Instructions" (1761 to 1789), fols. 20v–23v, n.d. An oath was not a part of Indian Islamic law (Kolsky, *Colonial Justice in British India*, 112–13) but the Dutch allowed it for the Moors of Sri Lanka. A Mohammedan had to swear with his "right hand lying on the Koran, in the presence of a Mohammedan priest, without saying anything." SLNA 1/5666, "Galle Landraad miscellaneous documents," fols. 23v, n.d.

55 Lodewijk Wagenaar, Personal communication on 21 Oct 2014; based on petition reports from Galle in 1758.

56 The words in Dutch of the accepted oath were: "*Ik zweere bij den waren God van hemel en aarde dat zo waarlijk als ik tegenwoordig mijne hand legge op het hoofd van mijn kind (vader, moeder of ander bloed verwant) zo waragtig is, het geene ik hebbe verklaart ende getuijgt, en zo ik liege, moet die zelve god mij (in zo of zo veel teijds) zwaarlijk straffen.*" SLNA 1/93, "Governor in Council minutes," 24 Dec 1744; SLNA 1/94, "Governor in Council minutes" (1745), 22 Mar 1745. The undated list of oaths mentioned in note 55 gives a slightly varied version, wherein punishment is invited upon both the swearer and the relative: "*Ik sweere bij den waeren God van Hemel en aarde, dat zoo waeragtig als ik mijn hand legge op 't hoofd van mijn zoon (of wie hij ook zijn mag) zoo waaragtig is 't geen ik heb verklaard, en indien ik in eenige deelen liege, moet die zelve God mij en deezen mijnen zoon (of wie hij anders zij) binnen korten swaarlijk straffen.*" SLNA 1/5666, "Galle Landraad miscellaneous documents," fols. 23v, n.d. An extract of the minutes of 24 December 1744 on the oath is also available in SLNA 1/5658, "Extracts of resolutions, orders, etc. regarding the Landraad and the thombo compilation" (1740 to 1745), fols. 17v–18r.

57 It was said: "But in places where the heathens are in the habit of swearing in a different way, the country's custom must be followed." SLNA 1/5666, "Galle Landraad miscellaneous documents," fols. 23v, n.d. It appears that the headmen's reports given in the December 1744 minutes were also approved, as for instance, Sluijsken copies them out verbatim in his account of the land services. Sluijsken, "A Description of the Land Services," vol. 1: 160-91.

became the standard form, and when a litigant or witness offered to take the oath in the "heathen" way, they had to appear before the council with family members. On one occasion, reference is made to two witnesses being required to produce their closest family members to take the oath in the "heathen" way. However, the oath was not allowed in this case.[58] It would not have been the Christian god, but the pantheon of gods that the locals worshipped, that they would have referred to if allowed to take the oath.[59] What mattered was that the witness believed in the god they were referring to; the expectation was that their belief would prevent false testimony. Paradoxically, this indigenous form of the oath was introduced primarily to address the issue of so-called Christians offering false oaths (more on this will follow). However, there are no references to the local form of the oath in practice in the Landraad.

Adopting the local form pricked the conscience of company officials. In 1790, the Governor in Council discussed the issue of Christians regarding the Dutch form of the oath with little reverence.[60] It consulted the church council on whether it would not be advisable to use local forms of the oath (evidently it was still a point of contention).[61] It is not clear why the church council was engaged at this point, especially as it was not called upon to comment in 1744, when the local oaths were initially adopted. However, the support of the church, for political and administrative reasons, may have been necessary.[62] The Governor in Council inquired of the Dutch Reformed Church consistory in Colombo as to whether it was in keeping with the Christian religion for local Christians to take the oath according to their own tradition, excluding idolatry ceremonies or those involving injury. The reports

[58] SLNA 1/6514, "Galle Landraad minutes," fols. 105r-v, 7 Aug 1781.

[59] As Samaraweera writes of the local oaths: "The god or goddess was chosen by the swearer, who then became the witness to the deed and acted as the arbiter of justice by determining whether the oath was false or not." Samaraweera, "Act of Truth," 145.

[60] See documents in this connection in SLNA 1/211, "Governor in Council minutes," 27 Nov 1790; SLNA 1/213, "Governor in Council minutes" (1791), 9 Feb 1791; Klaus Koschorke (ed), *The Dutch Reformed Church in Colonial Ceylon (18th Century): Minutes of the Consistory of the Dutch Reformed Church in Colombo*, trans. S.A.W. Mottau (Wiesbaden: Harrassowitz Verlag, 2011), 648–49, Extraordinary Meeting held on 14 Jan 1791, http://www.aecg.evtheol.lmu.de/cms/index.php?id=10. Accessed 12 August 2019.

[61] The Landraad instructions of 1789 also reflect this continuing concern in stating, "it is not so much the form of the oath or the manner in which it is taken, as in the act itself, and the terrible fate that awaits the person who dares to summon the Almighty God to witness any matter which they do not fully know, or, which is still worse, which they know to be untrue." Hovy, *Plakkaatboek*, vol. 2; nr. 628, (II, 27), 25 Jun 1789.

[62] The necessity for endorsement by the church council could have also been because the council discouraged converts from offering the non-Christian oath; however, this presumption must be supported by evidence.

of 1744 on Sinhalese oath forms and a report on how non-Christian Tamils swore were apparently attached with the query, but they are not in the extant records. The church council did not object to the idea but proposed a standard form of swearing by raising the hands up to heaven and lowering them to the ground, which was similar to the first form of the oath from Colombo, mentioned in the 1744 reports. But the Governor in Council recognised that this was not in common use among the "heathens," and would not be effective among Christians either. As such, they recommended maintaining the old practice. The advice of the church council was ignored in order to preserve the plural oath forms that were already recognised. The governing body realised that it could not compromise on the meaning of the oath for the people.

Questions on the form of the oath were not confined to the Dutch experience. The British, when they took over from the Dutch, were uncertain about which form of the oath to use in Sri Lanka. The multitude of local practices of the oath are also seen among the papers of Alexander Johnston.[63] Although Johnston had a translation of the 1744 reports, the British settled on other forms of the oath. They introduced the judicial oath of swearing before the evidence was given quite early in the littoral. Thus, the oath had different functions under British and Roman-Dutch law, but conflicts remained. The British retained a version of the trial by oath (divi) in the Kandyan provinces after 1815 but extended the judicial oath of the littoral to the interior in 1818, at least on paper.[64] In practice, the trial by oath, including the oath by hot oil, was a decisory process that individual judges in both the littoral and the interior continued to use. The Supreme Court looked on with disapproval, and by the late nineteenth century, deemed the decisory oath "as being both Contrary to law and against public policy."[65] The legislature, however, ruled otherwise and a litigant can still challenge an opposing party to take an oath under the Oaths Ordinance No. 9 of 1895.[66] This rather muddled state of affairs, as

63 "Alexander Johnston Papers (New York)."

64 Samaraweera, "Act of Truth," 147–48.

65 Hayley, *A Treatise on the Laws and Customs*, 92–93; Samaraweera, "Act of Truth," 151–53. See also: John D. Rogers, *Crime, Justice, and Society in Colonial Sri Lanka* (London: Curzon Press, 1987), 71–72.

66 See Section 8 of the ordinance and E.R.S.R. Coomaraswamy, *A Textbook of the Law of Evidence in Ceylon* (Colombo: Noel E. Hamer, 1955), 395–96. The last available reported case that refers to the decisory oath is from 1949: one party refused to take the oath when asked to do so by the opponent. As a result, an interesting question arose, as to "whether a judge in weighing the evidence is entitled to draw any inference from the refusal of a party, without sufficient reason, to take a decisory oath when challenged to do so by the opponent." The court was split on the matter: one judge, interpreting the law literally, responded in the affirmative, and the other did not. *Sinnapody et al. v Mannikan et al.*, 53 New Law Reports (1949).

in British India, reveals the uncertainties surrounding colonial authority that the coloniser experienced.

The British adopted forms of the judicial oath in Sri Lanka that were at times problematic. The insignia of the goddess Pattini was used in court for Buddhists to swear on. Basil leaves and water, symbolic of the Ganges, were used for Hindus, and Muslims swore on the Koran.[67] The anklets of Pattini were used for the decisory oath, but not all Sinhalese Buddhists in the country revered them.[68] Swearing on them outside of their ritual context meant little to the people. Incidentally, such conflicts between the oath form imposed by the colonial power and local beliefs were also seen in India, where, among other oaths, the British used basil leaves, water from the Ganges and the Koran in local courts. As a result of some practices, Indians believed that they would have to commit many wrongs in British courts.[69] In Bengal, for instance, the oath came into dispute – the Hindu oath on the Ganges was considered a sin and was also rejected on the grounds that it assumed equality across rank and caste through its impartial application. Ram Mohan Roy reportedly objected to swearing on water from the Ganges and asked that he be allowed to swear on the Vedas.[70] The ritualistic meaning attached to the oath was crucial to its successful use in court. As in Sri Lanka, the Hindus in India adopted the practice of swearing on one's children. In fact, using a relative to swear by may be a uniquely South Asian phenomenon.

Elizabeth Kolsky, in her study of the oath in British India, questions whether some corporal oath forms were "invented colonial traditions" and states that, at times, it "reflects how the colonial state reconstructed Indian society even as it

[67] John Whitchurch Bennett, *Ceylon and its Capabilities: An Account of its Natural Resources, Indigenous Productions, and Commercial Facilities* (New Delhi: Asian Educational Services, 1843; repr. 1998), 55.

[68] When he was a magistrate in the Galle district from 1823 to 1826, Bennet had been told by the local Buddhist priests that swearing on the insignia of the goddess Pattini was anything but sacred in the eyes of true Buddhists. He gives an example of a defendant who wanted the plaintiff to swear on the Buddhists' sacred books or under the sacred Bodhi Tree in a temple instead of on the insignia of the goddess Pattini. This had the desired effect of the plaintiff withdrawing his plaint – apparently, the defendant had known that the plaintiff did not follow Pattini (Ibid., 55-56). For an 1817 case in which Pattini's ornaments were used see Jennings, "Lawrie's Notes on Kandyan Law," 202–3. Incidentally, the insignia of Pattini is not described in the Dutch reports of local oath forms compiled in 1744. In the trial by oath of the local system, the swearer had to select the deity that they wanted to witness the oath. See Samaraweera who uses Obeyesekere's work to explore inherent issues in the adoption of the insignia of Pattini as the only oath form for Buddhists. Samaraweera, "Act of Truth," 154–58; Gananath Obeyesekere, *The Cult of the Goddess Pattini* (Chicago: University of Chicago Press, 1984).

[69] Kolsky, *Colonial Justice in British India*, 112–13.

[70] James E. Tyler, *Oaths, Their Origine, Nature, and History* (London: John W. Parker, 1835), 168.

endeavoured to rule in a fashion that was congruous with indigenous institutions."[71] She draws this conclusion as a result of the mirroring in the Indian corporal forms of the Christian oath, in which a swearer places their hand on the Bible. The British use of sacred Buddhist books in Sri Lanka further confirms this emulation, as this oath form is not found in accounts of the local oath or in Dutch sources.[72] Such significant transformations of the Sinhalese oath did not occur in Dutch Sri Lanka.

Colonial administrations commonly imposed ineffective forms of the oath. The disregard shown towards the Dutch form of the oath connects to a more general disrespect for colonial authority. The company attempted to standardise the local oath, but at the core of this effort was the acknowledgement of the relationship between faith and the truth. The Dutch Government may have expected the adoption of local oaths to foster a sense of inclusion and a commitment to the truth among the people. The profiles of witnesses and their professed Christianity as presented below reveal why this was necessary.

The Witnesses: Promising the Oath

Most witnesses in the Landraad were male, Sinhalese, and nominal Christians. They warrant special attention as they offered the oath more often than litigants. Producing witnesses was a primary form of legal proof and argumentation. Without witness narratives as reinforcement, many litigants could not have protected their property rights. These narratives helped them to regain or hold on to their land. In a breakdown of 264 witnesses in the Landraad between 1778–1781, most (244) were members of the Dutch Reformed Church; the rest were "heathen" (one), Muslim (five), Roman Catholic (three), and a handful (six) were described as belonging to the Kataragama belief (*Kataragamse geloof*), which is the worship of God Skanda or Kataragama, of the local Buddhist pantheon.[73]

The introduction of a non-Christian oath form, despite most witnesses being Christian, is paradoxical. So-called Christians were flippant when delivering the Dutch form of the oath. The contradictions inherent in adopting the Dutch oath were made apparent by the locals. Being an overwhelming majority in Galle,

71 Kolsky, *Colonial Justice in British India*, 113.

72 Nevertheless, this is likely to have held some value among Buddhists, perhaps signifying the influence of the use of the Bible by Christians.

73 SLNA 1/6494, "Galle Landraad depositions" 13 Jul 1778 to 14 Aug 1781. The religion of five witnesses with European names was not mentioned. See, for further details about the Kataragama cult: Gananath Obeyesekere, "Social Change and the Deities: Rise of the Kataragama Cult in Modern Sri Lanka," *Man* 12, no. 3/4 (1977): 377–96; Elizabeth Nissan, "Polity and Pilgrimage Centres in Sri Lanka," *Man*, n.s., 23, no. 2 (1988): 253–74.

"Christians" were in fact the primary targets of changes to the oath form. However, it was common knowledge that they were only nominal Christians; "Government Christians" and "Christian Buddhists" were among the terms used to refer to them under British rule in the nineteenth century.[74] In the Landraad, the conflict between theory (i.e., large numbers of conversions on paper) and practice (spiritual beliefs) had reached a climax. Ineffective Christianisation had led to a loss of trust; a gain in trust was sought by recognising local customs. Litigating parties used the issuing tension to their benefit, as shown below. Finally, hardly anyone was allowed to verify their statements with what would have been considered a sacred oath.

Most residents in Galle were baptised. Galle was one of three separate church communities on the island; the other two were Colombo and Jaffna. Members of the Dutch Reformed Church came from diverse ethnic and social groups. Europeans and Eurasians attended church services in Dutch, mostly in the forts, but the Reformed Church in Sri Lanka comprised of a much larger population of Portuguese-, Tamil- and Sinhala-speakers.[75] They came under a church council, which was not independent of company power. The Dutch initially attempted to obliterate the institutional structures of the Roman Catholic establishment (a legacy of Portuguese power) and replace it with Protestantism.[76] Yet by the late eighteenth century, the Catholic faith was hardly persecuted; maps from that time show a *Roomse Kerk* (Roman Church) on the high ground to the north-west of Galle Fort.[77] However, together with education, the reformed religion of Calvin was propagated. Schoolmasters played an important role in this process. G.J. Schutte points out that just as in the Moluccas, the schoolmasters had to conduct a church service

[74] Sir James Emerson Tennent, *Christianity in Ceylon* (London: John Murray, 1850), 89.

[75] G.J. Schutte, "Een hutje in den wijngaard: Gereformeerd Ceylon," in G.J. Schutte (ed), *Het Indische Sion: De Gereformeerde kerk onder de Verenigde Oost-Indische Compagnie* (Hilversum: Verloren, 2002), 179–80. The Moors alone, it appears, did not convert. Tennent, *Christianity in Ceylon*, 64.

[76] An early account of the rivalry with Roman Catholicism is found in Tennent, *Christianity in Ceylon*, 39 ff. The company attempted to persecute the Roman Catholic religion with penal laws in order to remove it from the island; however, such a policy could not be fully realised. By the late eighteenth century, the Dutch were resigned to the inevitable existence of Roman Catholics and allowed Catholic priests to reside in Dutch territory. In the archives of the Landraad, I found that the Dutch allowed the Roman Catholic oath of office and permitted Dutch Protestant or Lutheran marriage alliances with Roman Catholics upon production of a deposition that the offspring would not be raised as Roman Catholics, but rather, in accordance with the reformed religion. SLNA 1/125, "Governor in Council minutes," 19 May 1758; SLNA 1/5666, "Galle Landraad miscellaneous documents," 22v, n.d.; SLNA 1/6496, "Galle Landraad depositions" (1780 to 1799).

[77] Rob van Diessen, *Grote Atlas van de Verenigde Oost-Indische Compagnie: Deel IV: Ceylon* (Voorburg, Netherlands: Asia Maior, 2008), 200–201. This is the present-day St. Mary's Cathedral. Roman Catholicism was a tangible force, as it still is today. See also: J. van Goor, *Jan Kompenie as Schoolmaster: Dutch Education in Ceylon 1690–1795* (Groningen: Wolters-Noordhoff, 1978), 145–46.

on Sundays and read out a sermon. Ministers visited regularly for baptisms. The Calvinist Church in Sri Lanka was never as well staffed as the Roman Catholic Church, even in later Dutch times, but the late eighteenth-century saw a growth in the ecclesiastical body, due perhaps to the Eurasian and native element of the local population.[78]

Few scholars have attempted demographic studies of Dutch Sri Lanka in order to estimate the Christian proportion of the population. Pim de Zwart found that in 1684, the number of Christians in Galle appears to have been 56 per cent of the total population.[79] In both Galle and Matara, the Christians grew in numbers in the mid-eighteenth century from 25,827 in 1693 to 92,313 in 1753. Thereafter, their population declined to around 60,000 at the end of the century.[80] Due to the lack of demographic data from the Galle district, representing these figures as percentages of the population is not easy.[81] The thombos also do not provide reliable data on the population of Galle. They were the basis for the population estimate of 95,000 individuals,[82] but the Galle thombos have inherent characteristics (explained in chapter five) that question the reliability of this figure. Until more reliable data surfaces in the archives, it is sufficient to say that during the seventeenth and eighteenth centuries, the population of indigenous Christians in Galle, and in other Dutch-controlled areas, was undoubtedly large. Sir James Emerson Tennent says in the nineteenth century that there were "large districts in which it would be difficult to discover an unbaptised Sinhalese."[83] This predominance of Christians partly explains why most witnesses were Christian.

Conversions to Christianity and baptisms of children have been linked not to a true understanding of the religion, but to an interest in political and economic benefits such as holding high office and establishing property rights. One crucial reason for such high numbers of nominal Christians was a belief among the inhabitants that baptism was necessary in order for their property rights to be entered in the thombo. Yet this is not to say that all those who were entered in the Galle thombos were Christian. On the contrary, in some thombos of the Hinidum Pattuwa, out of 42 thombo groups (almost 500 individuals), 34 first-mentioned persons of a thombo group are described as "heathen" (and only three as Christian). Given that

[78] Schutte, "Een hutje in den wijngaard," 179, 186.

[79] Pim de Zwart, "Population, Labour and Living Standards in Early Modern Ceylon: An Empirical Contribution to the Divergence Debate," *Indian Economic & Social History Review* 49, no. 3 (2012): 378.

[80] Van Goor, *Jan Kompenie as Schoolmaster*, 160–61.

[81] De Zwart has attempted to represent the population of Ceylon. De Zwart, "Population, Labour and Living."

[82] Albert van den Belt, Jan Kok, and Kees Mandemakers, "Digital Thombos: A New Source for 18th Century Sri Lankan Family History," *The History of the Family* 16, no. 4 (2011): 484.

[83] Tennent, *Christianity in Ceylon*, 89.

their immediate families would have also been "heathens," this figure increases substantially. Yet, it is rare for the thombos to include an individual's religion. The Hinidum Pattuwa, however, was a remote area in the borderlands between Dutch and Kandyan rule, where control over religious beliefs was not always possible. Setting aside this exception, it is of course still possible that many of those who were included in the thombo were baptised. Tennent writes of a proclamation, to which there was a positive response, that no native could hold office or farmland unless he had converted. There also appears to have been a threat of losing one-third of one's property on failing to be baptised. The Sinhala term for baptisms was *christiani-karenewa* (Christian-making); it was not revered as a sacred process. In the minds of the local people, the process was intrinsically linked to the textual practice of the thombo. Parents could threaten their child with disinheritance, saying they would "blot out his baptism from the thombo."[84] Indeed, for peasants, baptism was synonymous with inheritance.

The history of Dutch persecution of local beliefs and engagement with conversions to Calvinism had its ups and downs. Initially, Dutch persecution of Roman Catholicism took precedence over interfering with local beliefs. With the resurgence of Buddhism in the eighteenth century and a desire not to anger the Kandyan king, the Dutch adopted a more tolerant attitude towards Buddhism.[85] A resurgence of Hinduism also occurred during the eighteenth century, perhaps inspired by the Buddhist revival in the Kandyan kingdom. The initial enthusiasm among the Dutch about conversion waned over time. It was considered important for baptised Christians to practise Calvinism regularly; at one point monetary fines were imposed on parents who did not send their children to church schools.[86] In 1700, the Classis of Amsterdam frowned upon such coercions, including the declaration that those who were not baptised would have to forfeit one-third of their property.[87] As Governor Van Gollonesse said, "[t]he aim...of holding together the native converts of the 17th Century and of keeping the Dutch community on the straight and narrow path of godly devotion"[88] took precedence in time.

The company did not regard many Christians among the witnesses as true believers and attempted to resort to methods such as imposing fines to produce and keep converts. Meanwhile, most converted inhabitants practised their local faiths. The Christian oath, in such a setting, could not have been one that the company

84 Tennent, *Christianity in Ceylon*, 45–46, 55–56, and 87–88.

85 Van Goor opines that "[t]here had never been any question of persecution whatsoever" of Asian religions. Van Goor, *Jan Kompenie as Schoolmaster*, 37.

86 Tennent, *Christianity in Ceylon*, 46–49.

87 Ibid., 55–56.

88 Julius Stein van Gollenesse, *Memoir of Julius Stein van Gollenesse*, 1751, trans. Sinnappah Arasaratnam (Colombo: Dept of National Archives, 1974), 38.

believed was taken with any sincerity. Intriguingly, adopting the Sinhalese oath form was an institutional necessity that gave official recognition to the nominal status of the Christians. This perception of native deceit was also evident in British Sri Lanka and British India; colonial officials in both territories often complained that the natives were quick to lie in court. In fact, belief in their mendacity was so pronounced that litigants used it to their advantage.

Mistrust, Idolatry and Local Mendacity

Judicial truth was not always connected to fact from the perspective of the litigants. Obeyesekere says, "Buddhist conscience, insofar as it contains a set of internalized norms, is not a punishing one, so that there is little in the literature that deals with a tormented religious conscience."[89] Richard Gombrich writes that the idea of truth as an autonomous secular value had no hold on Sinhalese villagers.[90] False testimony, according to John Rogers, "was not necessarily regarded as morally wrong.... False testimony in support of a just cause was moral; for an unjust cause it was immoral. In many cases, especially those which were related to long-standing feuds, both sides no doubt viewed themselves as in the right. In such instances court cases were like contests."[91] Borrowing from Clifford Geertz, Samaraweera says, "the Sinhala question of fact and law had to do with how to get them together, whereas the British saw it as having to do with how to tell them apart."[92] Such disregard for untruths may well have existed, but the threat of a binding oath was likely to have been a deterrent. In theory, if a swearer's conscience was to be pricked by the telling of a falsehood, it had to be followed by a meaningful oath. An oath that followed ritual held the threat of negative reprisals in the future, if not immediately, as reflected in the concept of divi-dōsa that was described earlier. VOC records show that the locals were more afraid of the native oath. In 1789, Diengihami told the *Scholarchale Vergadering* (School Board), which dealt with educational, ecclesiastical, and marital matters, that she would swear "even in the Sinhalese way" in order to prove that a certain man had fathered her out-of-wedlock children.[93] The locals are likely to have

[89] Gananath Obeyesekere, "Buddhism and Conscience: An Exploratory Essay," *Daedalus* 120, no. 3 (1991): 236.

[90] Richard F. Gombrich, *Buddhist Precept and Practice: Traditional Buddhism in the Rural Highlands of Ceylon* (Delhi: Motilal Banarsidass Publishers, 1971; repr. 1991), 263–64.

[91] Rogers, *Crime, Justice, and Society*, 74–75.

[92] Samaraweera, "Act of Truth," 162–63. See Clifford Geertz, *Local Knowledge: Further Essays in Interpretive Anthropology* (United States: Basic Books, 1983).

[93] SLNA 1/6226, "Scholarchale Vergadering minutes" (1789 to 1791), fols. 6v, 7 Oct 1789.

been aware of the ongoing conflict associated with the form of the oath that they took.

As locals were unwilling to use the local oath form, company officials had to encourage its use. Unexpectedly, this effort was unsuccessful. On a visit to schools in Galle and Matara, two European members of the Scholarchale Vergadering said that when litigants were asked to take the oath in the "heathen style" (*heijdensche trant*) , they answered, "We are Christians!" (*Wij zijn Christenen*). The board members said that the locals did not know what a Christian oath was because they were not Christian, and had no love or desire for it.[94] However, Sri Lankans saw the strategic advantage of opting for the Christian oath, which otherwise held no normative value for them.

It is likely that witnesses, to avoid telling the truth, opted for the Christian oath, since they did not believe in the Christian god. In the previously mentioned case involving a cow, we have counter-interrogations from 1778 that both litigants produced against the other's witnesses. In the counter-interrogation that was carried out against the five witnesses of Ganegame Radāge Puncha, who all professed to be Christian, three witnesses said that they preferred to take the Sinhalese oath. When asked what the *regtvaerdigen god* (just god) would do if they gave false evidence, three witnesses answered that they expected punishment from god, and two said that they expected it from both god and devils. To the next question, on what the Christian oath signified, three of them said it indicated that they spoke the truth, one did not "dare" to answer and another witness also did not answer. Clearly, the question had confused them. Then, they were asked why they were more afraid of the Sinhalese oath, which involved laying their hands on the heads of their children, than the Christian one. They all denied it. One witness, who had chosen the Sinhalese oath, claimed that he was not afraid to take the oath in any manner.[95] Evidently, the confused answers to the trap laid in the questions, which could potentially provide insights into witness psychology, indicate that they were unprepared for questions on the sanctity of their choice of oath form. The opposing party that asked the questions, knowing how sensitive Dutch officials were to false oaths, was keenly aware that their choice of oath form could expose the witnesses. This had the undesired effect (from the perspective of the company and judicial process), of the non-admittance of the oath and the failure of both oath forms.

Native litigants and their procureurs knew how to exploit the Dutch procedure and take advantage of the Dutch fear of irreverence. As most witnesses were Christians of a dubious nature, their degree of faith was a persistent issue of contention at the Landraad. Suspicion continued, and local litigants knew how to

94 SLNA 1/6220, "Scholarchale Vergadering minutes" (1768 to 1770), fols. 24r, 4 Jul 1770.

95 SLNA 1/6534, "Galle Landraad interrogations" fols. 11r–12v, 9 Jul 1778.

profit from it. Counter-interrogations prepared by opposing parties, which paid attention to the value that witnesses associated with the oath, continued well into the late 1780s. Questions about the sanctity of being admitted to the Christian oath were probably raised until the end of Dutch rule in coastal Sri Lanka. Proving that witnesses were not true Christians and, therefore, unsuitable to take the Christian oath, was in the interest of the opposing party.

Apart from issues of religion, character smears and potential bias as a result of being related to a litigant and other issues were also used to disqualify witnesses. In one case, the procureur Albertus Hissink asked the Landraad not to allow the oath as, apart from the witnesses having no knowledge of the case, one witness was an *aangehuwde zwager* (brother-in-law) of the opposing litigant.[96] In another case, the witnesses allegedly knew nothing about the case, so the commissioners refused to let them take the oath.[97] It is possibly also true that the company was faced with professional tricksters on property issues. Eight per cent of the sample of witnesses between 1778–1781 were likely to have attested in more than one deposition.[98] One witness was accused of being a fake because he was known to give false testimonies in exchange for alcohol.[99] False witnesses could get six years in chains.[100] But "professional" witnesses engaged in the truth business, which contributed to the general perception among company officials that the locals did not value truth.

Character assassination – throwing the beliefs of a witness into question – was the primary way to disqualify a potential swearer. Each litigating party usually questioned the witnesses of the opposing party on their sincerity in offering the oath in such a way that it would not be allowed. This manner of snide interrogation could begin with asking them if they knew of an all-seeing god who tests the hearts and souls of all men, observes all that they do and throws into eternal damnation those who are guilty of perjury and lies. In the fight over the cow, the first of six witnesses who appeared to testify for Pussewellege Johan claimed to be aware of it and said that he would speak to his heart when answering the questions. He was of the *boeddoese geloof* (Buddhist belief). The others, of the Christian faith, all answered in the affirmative. As in other counter-interrogations, the next question was whether, if they said yes to the first question, they were willing to keep that "frightening chief justice" before their eyes and answer the following questions truthfully. Ironically, but unsurprisingly, they all said yes.[101] Such a line

96 SLNA 1/6514, "Galle Landraad minutes," fols. 41r, 18 Apr 1781.

97 Ibid., fols. 100v, 31 Jul 1781.

98 See chapter three for more on this.

99 SLNA 1/6534, "Galle Landraad interrogations" fols. 133v, 14 Jan 1782.

100 SLNA 1/5658, "Galle Landraad, extracts of resolutions," fols. 9r, Extract resolution of 7 Mar 1744; 16r, Resolution of 14 Sept 1744.

101 SLNA 1/6534, "Galle Landraad interrogations," fols. 3r–6r, 9 Jul 1778.

of questioning was common. In 1789, the first four questions in an interrogation of four witnesses were about whether they knew the value of the oath, and the consequences of lying.[102] Most often, witnesses replied to questions with yes, no, or pleaded ignorance; occasionally, they answered in unexpected ways.

It was also often in question whether witnesses who offered the Christian oath were being honest about being Christian. In the case over the cow, one witness was asked whether he had been baptised, and if not, why he had claimed to be Christian when he was actually a "heathen". He was asked if he had imagined that such an "audacity" would go unpunished, and whether for that reason his deposition should be regarded as false. The witness in question declared that as he had been baptised, he had duly claimed to be a Christian.[103] It is possible that baptism records were examined to determine whether litigants and their witnesses were in fact Christians. One witness admitted that he had not been baptised because his father had died before marrying his mother.[104] In 1788, an opposing party had prepared to ask a witness (who failed to appear on the day of the hearing) if he was a "heathen," since he had not been baptised.[105] Baptism, though inconsequential to spirituality, was central to local understandings of Christianity.

Witnesses were closely questioned on their understandings of Christianity. In a counter-interrogation from 1780[106] that was meant to prevent six Christian witnesses from swearing on their deposition, they were closely questioned on their knowledge of the Christian religion. The first question was on what they understood by the word Christian. The first witness said that it referred to someone who lives truthfully and sincerely, another said that it meant having faith in god, and to three others, it tellingly meant *doop* (baptism). Other witnesses said that it meant attending school before marriage, attending church after marriage and baptising children. The witnesses were asked in whom Christians should have faith, their obligations as Christians, their knowledge of god's orders and whether they would go to heaven or hell if they did not abide by them. Some other questions and answers were:

> 6
>
> What is the command of the lord god?
>
> The first answered: to avoid all evil.
>
> The second answered to have not learnt so far to know this.
>
> The third answered: to do good and eschew all evil according to the Ten Commandments.

[102] SLNA 1/6535, "Galle Landraad interrogations," fols. 38r–39v, 27 Aug 1789.

[103] SLNA 1/6534, "Galle Landraad interrogations," fols. 12r-v, 9 Jul 1778.

[104] Ibid., fols. 105v, 18 Aug 1781.

[105] SLNA 1/6535, "Galle Landraad interrogations," fols. 26v, 29 Apr 1788.

[106] SLNA 1/6534, "Galle Landraad interrogations," fols. 89–91r, Mar and Jul 1780.

The fourth answered: to do good and abstain from all evil.
The fifth answered that those who do wrong will be punished.
The sixth answered: to give up the bad.

7
When Christians do not know the rites of god and his commandments, can they know about heaven or hell?
The first answered: those who do good will be rewarded with good and those who do evil will be punished with it.
The second answered: no.
The third answered: one cannot know this.
The fourth answered like the second.
The fifth answered like the first.
The sixth answered like the second.

8
If someone has no understanding of god or his injunctions, can we believe their claim that they are Christians or their testimonies?
The first answered that what he had declared contained the truth.
The second answered that he was not learned enough for such trick questions.
The third answered: no.
The fourth answered: ditto.
The fifth answered he did not know this.
The sixth answered that he had testified according to his conscience.[107]

The second witness above guarded himself against what he deemed a trick question. In general, witnesses did not lack boldness and even some audacity in creatively responding to questions, despite being unprepared.

Learning in the church school was considered a central requirement. One witness (mentioned at the start of this chapter) reported that he had not been able to learn the ninth commandment as he had had no time to attend school due to company work. In the interrogation quoted in the extract above, witnesses were asked if Christians are obliged to do the Christian work, to which they all answered in the affirmative. When asked what Christian work consisted of, one witness said he did not know, and another said it was to praise god.[108] In another interrogation from 1788, five Christians (one of them claimed to have been baptised in the Roman Catholic Church), were asked what their obligations as Christians were.

[107] SLNA 1/6534, "Galle Landraad interrogations," fols. 89v–90r, Mar and Jul 1780.
[108] Ibid., fols. 90v–91r, Mar and Jul 1780.

They all said that they had heard from their schoolmasters that they had to "do good and avoid evil."[109] These were standard answers, but the Governor in Council pointed out as late as 1790 that baptism was the only distinguishing characteristic of Christians on the island.[110]

The spectre of idolatry and heathenism loomed large for the company. The worship of heathen gods was banned, but not successfully implemented.[111] In a counter-interrogation from 1778, witnesses were called upon to declare what religion they *wezentlijk belijden* (actually professed). Although they all said they were Christian, one witness was asked whether he had not gone to the Kataragama temple for the last twenty-five years, to which he replied in the affirmative. He also confirmed that he had gone there the previous year with fellow believers.[112] This fact did not fall short of the witness's spiritual standards. He was either unaware of a need to hide idolatry worship or he simply wished to be truthful. Some witnesses clearly did not know what to lie about. In another case, witnesses were asked how they could be "so shameless as to claim to be Christians, when they are devoted to exorcisms of devils and other idolatrous ceremonies." They all denied these allegations. They were then asked if it was not true that there is some exorcism of devils in the Christian reformed religion as well, which they all negated. Next, they were asked whether it was not the case that in Buddhism as well such devil exorcisms were detested and completely forbidden. They all agreed, except for one witness who said that he did not know of such a thing. After questions about the case at hand, they were asked what they thought the evidence of such exorcists, drunkards and whores legally merited.[113] Questions on past associations with "heathenism" were also included. In one interrogation, witnesses were asked if it befit a Christian to become a "heathen" priest. The first witness rebelled at such questions, answering that he did not know but that those who have done such a thing should know. On whether a person who converted from Christianity to heathenism did not merit punishment, he said that the "gentlemen," probably referring to the councillors, should know. The issue was that the third witness had been a "heathen priest" at

[109] SLNA 1/6535, "Galle Landraad interrogations," fols. 24v, 29 Apr 1788.

[110] SLNA 1/211, "Governor in Council minutes," 27 Nov 1790.

[111] L. Hovy, *Ceylonees plakkaatboek: Plakkaten en andere wetten uitgevaardigd door het Nederlands bestuur op Ceylon, 1638–1796* (Hilversum: Verloren, 1991), vol. 1, nr. 145, Placard against heathen idolatry, 1 Jul/12 Aug 1682; 229, Placard forbidding idolatry, 6 Jun/11 Jul 1711.

[112] SLNA 1/6534, "Galle Landraad interrogations," fols. 26v, 31r-v, 9 Dec 1778.

[113] Ibid., fols. 32r–38r, 18 Dec 1778. The quoted extract reads: *"hoe zij zo onbeschaamd kunnen wezen om zig voor Christenen uijt te geven, daar zij aan duijvels banderijen en andere afgodische plegtigheeden verslaaft zijn."*

some point, to which he answered that he had been a priest for one year when he was young.[114]

The interrogations, examined for the first time here, bring out in reported speech the ways in which the locals navigated the murky waters of their real and professed belief systems in the new forum of the Landraad. The witnesses displayed a degree of irreverence and disrespect that did not go unnoticed by company officials. In eighteenth-century Sri Lanka, local litigants knew how to play on Dutch fears about whether witnesses were true Christians and whether they attached any value to the Christian oath. They were also able to show resistance to power in subtle but significant ways. I have attempted an exploration of the local experience of colonial authority through the subject of the oath. The colonial state was shaped by the interactions between government and subjects.

Conclusion

As a part of procedural law, the oath is an object of diffusion in comparative legal studies. Conflicts over the form of the oath illustrate debates on how far a "legal transplant" is a valid phenomenon. The study of the donor and recipient contexts of such a legal transplant is a comparative exercise, that is to say, it is "the study of the relationships of one legal system and its rules with another."[115] Pierre Legrand argues that it is impossible to have legal transplants because when rules are transferred to a new social context, they fail to retain the cultural meaning assigned to them in the donor country. All that would be displaced from the one jurisdiction to the other is a "meaningless form of words."[116] The adoption of the Dutch form of the oath in eighteenth-century Sri Lanka is an example of a rule that was rendered meaningless in the colonial context. As Jacques du Plessis says, "[t]he more foreign the new cultural environment (and especially legal culture), the greater the possibility that a rule will lose its meaning in such a new environment."[117] This occurred in eighteenth-century Sri Lanka as well, when the Dutch attempted to marshal the powers of the unseen world in a judicial council.

114 Ibid., fols. 141r, 7 Feb 1782. It is not clear if he was a Hindu or Buddhist priest.

115 Alan Watson, *Legal Transplants*, second edition (Athens: University of Georgia Press, 1993), 6. Quoted in Pierre Legrand, "What 'Legal Transplants'?," in David Nelken and Johannes Feest (eds), *Adapting Legal Cultures* (Oxford: Hart Publishing, 2001), 56.

116 Legrand, "What 'Legal Transplants'?," 63.

117 The question of whether to call a transfer of rules from foreign law a legal transplant or legal borrowing is mostly about terminology. Jacques du Plessis, "Comparative Law and the Study of Mixed Legal Systems," in Mathias Reimann and Reinhard Zimmermann (eds), *The Oxford Handbook of Comparative Law* (Oxford: Oxford University Press, 2006), 488.

The VOC was aware of the need to accommodate cultural differences. The stimulus to change the form of the oath came indirectly from the colonised themselves, when they subtly rejected the Dutch form. The colonised showed their resistance in subtle ways by being flippant and dismissive; it did not go unnoticed as it amounted to a rejection of the legal regime that the coloniser was attempting to introduce. Negotiating with the local normative order was then inevitable. The Roman-Dutch practice of the decisory oath had family resemblances to the local decisory oath, but this was a coincidence rather than an effort to incorporate a local judicial procedure. The judicial oath on the other hand was new to Sri Lanka. What appeared to particularly disturb company officials was that potential swearers were chiefly Christians who had few scruples about giving false oaths. Addressing the practical reality of the nominal status of such Christians led to the adoption of local forms of the oath. Establishing the truth amidst perceived local mendacity was a source of anxiety for the new rulers, and it is thus crucial to grasping the functioning of a plural legal system in colonial law.

This analysis of the oath in practice reveals that legal pluralism must not be studied just through major jurisdictional conflicts or codifications and law texts alone. In the end, the adoption of pluralities was of little use in connection with the oath. The mutual discrediting of potential oath-takers by litigant parties contributed to cementing a mistrust of natives. The oath was not a decisory factor in the final analysis, as it was hardly ever admitted in the Galle Landraad. The opposing party used the refusal by a "Christian" to take the Dutch oath and their preference for the local oath (itself a sign that its adoption was meaningful) to discredit the witness, in the full knowledge that any acceptance of the Dutch form would also be criticised. Neither Christianisation, nor the reluctant acceptance of its failure as evidenced by the adoption of the local oath forms, produced truthful subjects. The decision to include a native form of the oath appeared to have followed the path of least resistance in comparison to the contemporary case of *Omychund v Barker* in London in 1744, where long deliberations on the admissibility of witnesses who observed a different faith were held. Notwithstanding such adaptability, the full function of the oath could not be realised due to deserved or undeserved discrediting of those who offered it. The agency of the natives themselves in furthering this result is a perspective that is rarely observed, but the close reading of sources attempted here yielded such an insight. Pluralities thus adopted did not always provide the desired effect, but rebounded on both coloniser and colonised in unexpected ways.

CHAPTER 5

Defining Land Rights

Abstract

The primary task of the Landraad was to hear certain civil cases and maintain the thombo, through which it defined land rights and taxation. This chapter studies land rights by providing quantitative and qualitative evidence on the types of possession recognised by the VOC. The thombo and the Landraad were in effect the legal mechanisms by which the conversion of land, whether collectively or individually held, into alienable title was sought to be consolidated. Despite the complexities of the local land tenure system, the VOC attempted to enforce rules and regulations that would create a neat, circumscribed system. This was not always achieved in practice, indicating the important yet discreet role played by peasants in defining land rights in plural ways.

Keywords: Land tenure, land registration, thombo, land rights, planter's share, pluralities.

Any state, whether colonial or not, seeks to acquire a grip on its subjects and the resources under its jurisdiction. Creating a standard grid of land tenure involved looking at "exceptionally complex, illegible and local social practices," as James C. Scott observes.[1] Despite the difficulties in coding land tenure, it was a necessary step to render the terrain more understandable and its produce and subjects more controllable. This was the case with both local and foreign rulers in Sri Lanka. The Dutch power paid special attention to the standardisation of the legal aspects of land rights; however, this was not always achieved in practice. A cadastral survey was important for the VOC to understand and govern its subjects and resources in coastal Sri Lanka. Legality and simplicity were clearly difficult to ensure, yet diligently attempted by company officials as this chapter will demonstrate. The primary institution used for this was the Landraad, and its main instrument the thombo. The eighteenth-century agrarian regime in Sri Lanka included written and oral forms of the thombo, the Landraad, and the accompanying translation processes that such institutional developments gave rise to. The Landraad and the

[1] James C. Scott, *Seeing Like a State: How Certain Schemes to Improve the Human Condition have Failed* (New Haven: Yale University Press, 1999), 2.

thombo are said to have been necessary given the "infinite variety" of tenures in Sri Lanka.[2]

This chapter describes, for the first time, the discreet role that non-elite actors played in this process. Understanding land rights in eighteenth-century Sri Lanka has so far involved piecing together information from sources at a higher administrative level of company rule. Dewasiri was the first to innovatively study land rights through the thombo. Concentrating on some areas in western Sri Lanka, he proposes that the land tenure system was a platform for conflicts between peasants and the ruling class, including both the colonial rulers and native headmen.[3] This chapter introduces a legal turn and focuses on the agency of peasants, an aspect that is missing in existing literature, by exploring in greater depth the classifications of land rights and ownership in southern areas of Sri Lanka. I have considered the land rights of eight villages from two sub-districts in the Galle district, the Hinidum and Wellaboda Pattu, as case studies.

I have sought answers to the following questions. Through the legal intervention of the thombo and the Landraad, what local practices did the VOC attempt to standardise and how successful was that attempt? Next, how did the inhabitants of coastal Sri Lanka contribute to the legal discourse on land rights? First, I will introduce an important policy-level discussion on land rights in order to understand how they were classified and, thereafter, I will introduce the sample villages through the registers. Next, I will describe three classifications of land, stressing the continuation of pre-colonial practices and highlighting the inherited order through the thombo registration itself, while discussing the nature and organisation of the land registers and, thereby, their reliability. The chapter is thus supported by evidence from the thombos, Landraad documents and policy discussions.

The evidence suggests discreet interaction between colonial subjects and the process of determining the law in practice as villagers went about defining their land rights. The data are of Dutch origin but with unique traces left by peasant farmers and their headmen. The complex ensemble of the agrarian regime of that time and VOC regulations and mechanisms lay at the foundation of property rights in Dutch Sri Lanka.

[2] Ralph Pieris, "Administration of Justice and Revenue on the Island of Ceylon under the Dutch Government ("The Cleghorn Minute")," *Journal of the Ceylon Branch of the Royal Asiatic Society*, n.s., 3 pt. 2 (1953): 136, 138.

[3] Nirmal Ranjith Dewasiri, *The Adaptable Peasant: Agrarian Society in Western Sri Lanka under Dutch Rule, 1740–1800* (Leiden: Brill, 2008).

Discussing Land Rights

The company struggled to make sense of land rights. In 1745, at an ordinary meeting of the Landraad on a December morning in Galle, an important discussion on the compilation of the thombo and the question of paravēni, or ancestral rights, took place.[4] Nine European members and one *mudaliyār* were present at the meeting. The thombo commissioners, who were "both white and inland headmen," were also active participants, as they reportedly gave further advice.[5] Evidently, matters were deliberated carefully. The aim of the meeting, which was ordered by Van Gollonesse, was to make a "substantiated provisional decision together after good deliberation."[6] Letters from the VOC's Gentlemen Seventeen were quoted at the meeting, revealing that on intricate land matters, the Dutch government in Sri Lanka corresponded with The Netherlands, apart from its correspondence with Batavia.[7]

The discussion at the Landraad meeting confirms that it was difficult for villagers to grasp the ways in which the colonial government wished them to understand the title to their lands. The Landraad had little faith in those that came forward for registration on the grounds that they were ignorant, unwise and unwilling to talk. It was pointed out that most people were not aware of how their families came to possess land: "in general the inhabitants never or rarely knew (and nowadays even less) how their parents and forefathers had come upon those lands, or to whom, in whose names they had been gifted or purchased or how such cultivated lands are known."[8]

It is likely that nobody had asked such searching questions before of so many people in Sri Lanka. Further analysis is necessary to prove this, but it is possible that a similar combination of census-like aspects with a cadastral survey was absent in the Sinhala *lēkam miti* (a cadastre maintained by Sri Lankan kings), and in the Portuguese registrations which were precedents to the Dutch thombos.

[4] SLNA 1/2805, "Galle Landraad minutes (20 Dec 1745) and Governor's comments (5 Feb 1746)" (1745 to 1746). I have referred to parts of this discussion in chapter one.

[5] The councillors Robbert Cornelis Bagilet, Adriaan Oostdijk, Godfried Gerhard, Johannes de Moor, Johannes de Leeuw, Pieter Welbrink, Matthijs van Geijsen, Casper Dannen, Jan Willem Wickerman and the mudaliyār Robento De Silva [Dahanaike] were present at the meeting. The thombo commissioners were Johan François Obble, Jan François de Gonnon and local mohandirams Lanserot Volkertsz, Don Johan de Silva Wanigasekere, Don Bastiaan [Wijenaike] and Don Louis Livere [Wickremenaike Samarasinghe]. Ibid., 27r-v. A list of native headmen from another source confirms the full names of Robento and Don Bastiaan: SLNA 1/5046, "Galle Political Council minutes" (1743–1746), fols. 60r-v, 4 Dec 1744.

[6] SLNA 1/2805, "Galle Landraad minutes (20 Dec 1745)," fols. 27v.

[7] See for extracts from Batavian correspondence: SLNA 1/5658, "Extracts of resolutions, orders, etc. regarding the Landraad and the thombo compilation" (1740–1745), fols. 19r; "Extract of Letter Dated 24 Oct 1744 from Batavia to Colombo," 27r–28r; "Extract of Letter Dated 24 Sept 1745 from Batavia to Ceylon."

[8] SLNA 1/2805, "Galle Landraad minutes (20 Dec 1745)," fols. 40v–41v, 31r-v.

The Landraad discussion was an attempt to have clearly defined rules of private and feudal property. The minutes of the discussion were sent to Governor Van Gollonesse, who gave his decisions in February 1746. Officials in Galle had to strictly observe the governor's orders. Thus, it is clear that while the Landraad could discuss matters of policy and practical implementation, it was subject as a judicial body to the executive power of the governor. Yet Galle clearly had problems following orders when faced with the complexities of local customs. The governor, at times, did not agree with Landraad members and thombo commissioners in Galle, who were the men on the ground. The tension between practical realities at the grassroots level and perceived realities at higher levels of government is best seen in the thombos. Each thombo entry constituted a potentially unique situation, with certain common characteristics between entries in the attempted standardisation of the thombo, as described below.

Villages Viewed from the Thombos

Spatially the case studies of registration used in this chapter are from two sub-districts of Galle, the Hinidum and Wellaboda Pattu, which are roughly 40 kilometres apart. The Hinidum Pattuwa is more inland than the villages selected from the Wellaboda Pattuwa, remaining in the backwoods of the south well into the twentieth century. We have considerably more anthropological information about the Hinidum Pattuwa due to Obeyesekere's study of the village Mädagama which does not appear among the Dutch thombos but was included in that pattuwa in British times.[9] The relative isolation of the Hinidum Pattuwa made it an interesting region for Obeyesekere's field work in the 1960s, a fact that is even more relevant for the eighteenth century and for the other selected villages. We have thombos for

[9] Obeyesekere says that the inception of Mädagama was in 1790, just six years before the end of Dutch rule on the island. During British rule, the sub-district of Hinidum was considerably larger; this was a result of about fifteen villages to the north of the six villages recognised under Dutch rule, situated even closer to the Sinharaja rainforest, being incorporated into the Hinidum Pattuwa. These villages were previously a part of the Kandyan kingdom. This had some impact on the law because, as Obeyesekere points out, the inhabitants of the villages that were incorporated into the pattuwa later were permitted to marry under Kandyan law. Meanwhile, the villages previously in the low country came under the general law that was based on Roman-Dutch law. In practice, the general law gradually came to prevail, as most marriages were contracted between inhabitants of villages of both types. Obeyesekere concludes that Kandyan (Sinhalese) law was probably used throughout the pattuwa in pre-British times. Gananath Obeyesekere, *Land Tenure in Village Ceylon: A Sociological and Historical Study* (Cambridge: Cambridge University Press, 1967), 5–6. This is further testimony to the fact that there was no difference in the Kandyan and local low country marriage laws except for any impositions by the European powers.

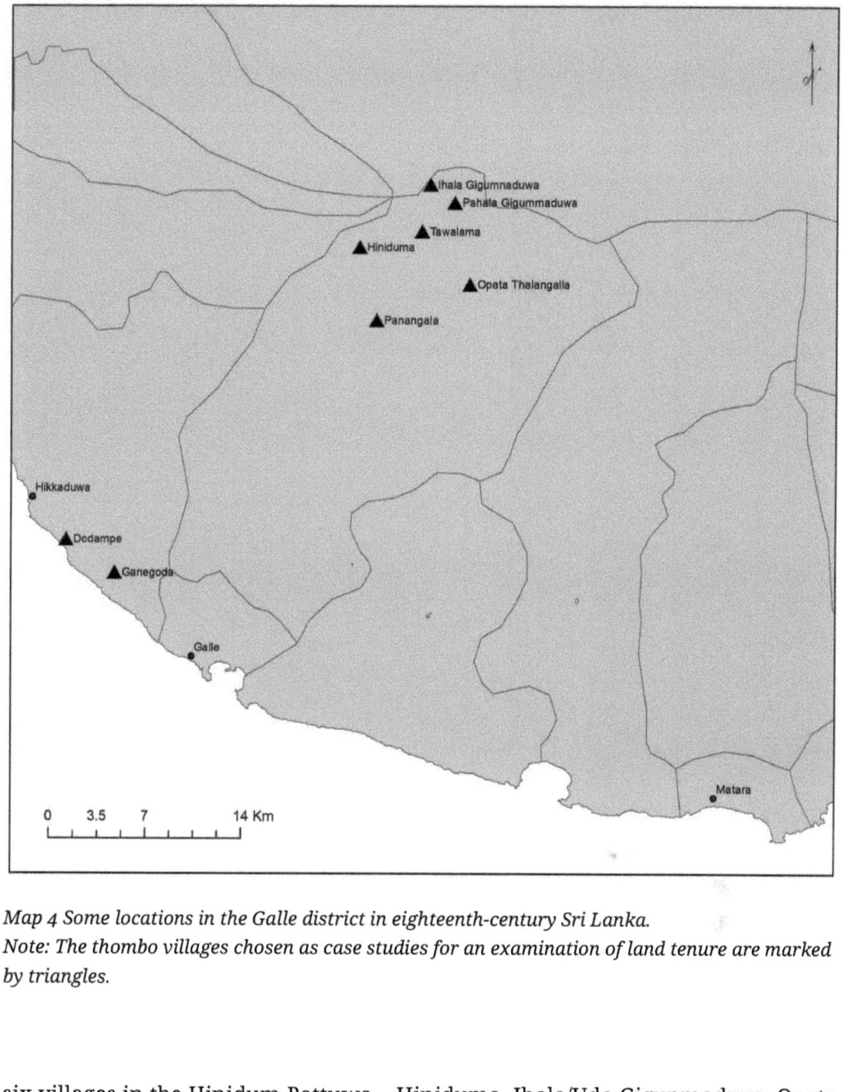

Map 4 Some locations in the Galle district in eighteenth-century Sri Lanka.
Note: The thombo villages chosen as case studies for an examination of land tenure are marked by triangles.

six villages in the Hinidum Pattuwa – Hiniduma, Ihala/Uda Gigunmaduva, Opata Thalangala, Pahala Gigunmaduva, Panangala and Tawalama – all drawn up in 1760 and for the most part carefully formulated according to regulations.[10] The larger villages considered in this chapter are Dodampe and Ganegoda of the Wellaboda

[10] SLNA 1/7462, 1/7472, 1/7519, 1/7569, 1/7542. These thombos have been certified, which I have not seen yet in other Galle thombos, but follow regulations stipulated in instructions given to the Landraad.

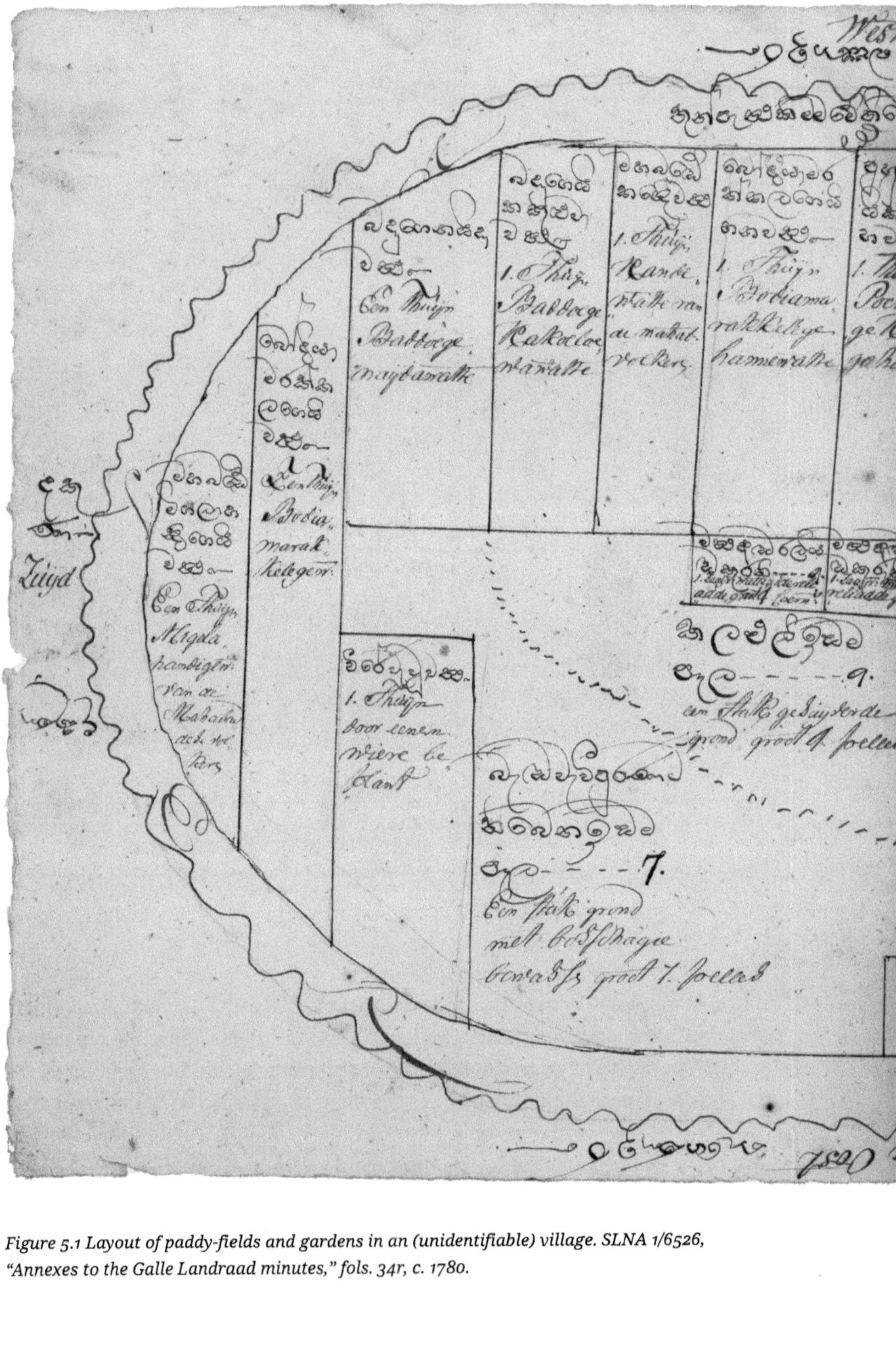

Figure 5.1 Layout of paddy-fields and gardens in an (unidentifiable) village. SLNA 1/6526, "Annexes to the Galle Landraad minutes," fols. 34r, c. 1780.

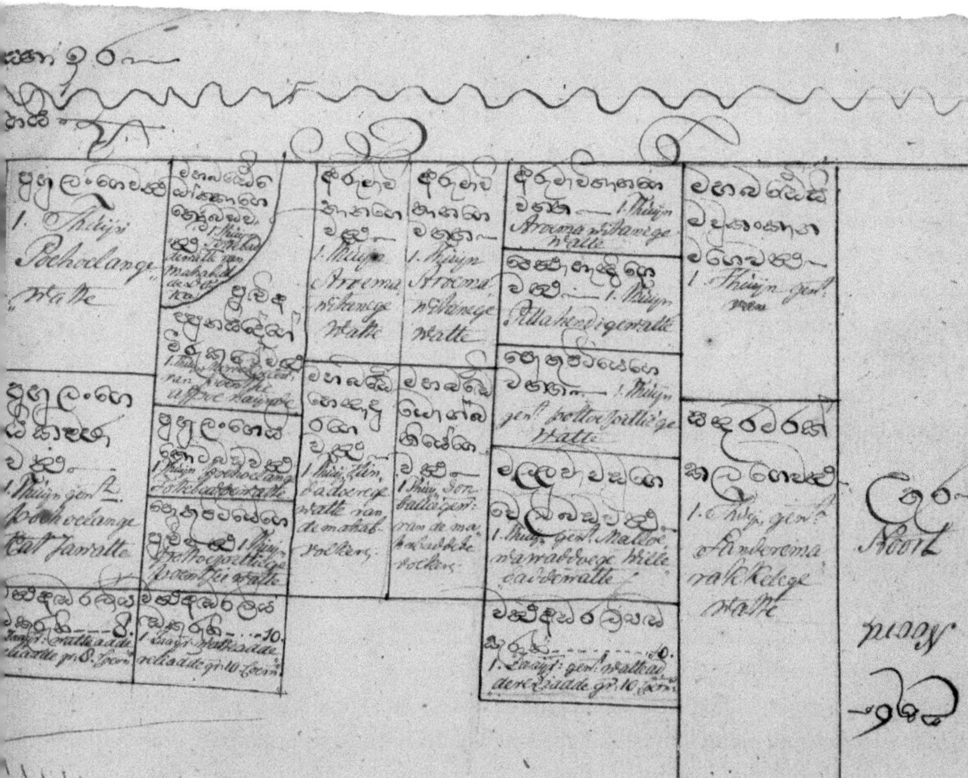
Noort
34

Pattuwa,[11] the thombos of which were drawn up in 1780 with a few additions in 1784 and 1785. Thus, temporally, the registrations are around twenty years apart. All sample thombos contain references to an older thombo, and villagers presented extracts from them in the council.[12] The Wellaboda Pattuwa villages were probably more prosperous and undoubtedly more accessible than the Hinidum Pattuwa due to their proximity to the sea. Map 4 shows the locations of the sample villages.

Most inhabitants of the Galle district are likely to have been registered in the thombos. It was the company's intention to record everyone living under Dutch territory: "in all civilized countries nothing is so proper and natural than that the particulars regarding one's own territory and subjects should be noted down in writing in such a manner that it would not be possible for a child to be born or a greybeard however old he may be to die without some mention being made thereof."[13] The thombos reveal that some villages in the district were disproportionately larger than others in demographic terms. A thombo village was closer to the idea of the Dutch village (*dorp*) in a modern administrative sense than to the Sinhalese concept of *gama*, which, as Codrington says, "normally signifies a village, but can also be applied to an estate or even to one field."[14] In Kandyan territory as well, it was applied to a single estate or field.[15] Obeyesekere proposes that gama could mean an estate or a parcel of rights, a hamlet with geographical boundaries and people within them, or a number of such hamlets loosely connected through kinship.[16] A plan found among the Landraad documents of Galle (see Figure 5.1) presents us with an idea of how paddy-fields and gardens would have been organised in a village. This image, with the names of plots in a mix of scripts and languages, may not indicate the actual size of the plots, but is likely to accurately indicate their boundaries.[17]

While the Colombo thombos consist of separate so-called "land" and "head" registers, those of the Galle district contain people's names, caste, service and relationships to each other (the "head" section), and their land holdings (the "land" section) alongside one another, on facing pages. A "thombo group" named persons who were either directly or indirectly connected to each other but did not always live together.

[11] SLNA 1/7428 and 1/7442.

[12] See for example SLNA 1/6513, "Galle Landraad minutes" (1780), fols. 150r, 2 Dec 1780.

[13] Jan Schreuder, *Memoir of Jan Schreuder, Governor of Ceylon, Delivered to His Successor Lubbert Jan Baron van Eck on March 17, 1762*, trans. E. Reimers (Colombo: Ceylon Government Press, 1946), 63.

[14] H.W. Codrington, *Ancient Land Tenure and Revenue in Ceylon* (Colombo: Ceylon Government Press, 1938), 1.

[15] C.J.R. Le Mesurier and T.B. Panabokke, trans., *Niti-Nighanduva or the Vocabulary of Law* (New Delhi: Navrang, 1880; repr. 1994), 119.

[16] Obeyesekere, *Land Tenure*, 13–14. See also Dewasiri, *Adaptable Peasant*, 43–47.

[17] I thank the anonymous reviewer of this book for pointing this out.

Dewasiri referred to the first-mentioned person of a group as the principal land holder (PLH), a practice that I follow.[18] The term PLH must be used carefully as often when a group lists a large number of people, there is no evidence that the first-mentioned person had a claim to all the recorded property. In reality, the PLHs in the Galle thombos did not have special rights to the shares mentioned in the thombo group; a number of people actually held the rights. In fact, in Landraad cases involving a few family members of a group, the PLH is not mentioned in the proceedings.[19] Since each person individually or jointly held the property rights mentioned within a group, I have used the term "land holdings group" (LHG) for at least the Galle thombos. The terms LHG or the less analytical "thombo group" are preferable to "household," as there is little evidence to support the use of the latter term in a uniform manner. A holdings group consisted of people related to each other, who were, therefore, part of an extended family unit. It represents a compound family, with nuclear families within the larger family. Within an LHG of the thombo, individuals or groups of individuals could hold exclusive rights to part of an estate. Dewasiri also uses the term "PLH group," but this unnecessarily focuses on the first-mentioned person. The "land" factor in both PLH and LHG is also disputable in light of "planter's shares," which exclude rights to the ground (more on this later); but this can be ignored for the sake of brevity. It is unclear if there was an intertwining of Dutch and local concepts in all this; at the very least it could be said that familial relationships had to be defined in the thombos for Dutch bureaucratic purposes. Such a record was necessary for tax purposes and for use in inheritance lawsuits.

The thombo commissioners are likely to have chosen a PLH if they were descendants of the founders of an estate.[20] Obeyesekere refers to how "in theory a hamlet comes into existence when a man, a founding ancestor, leaves his hamlet of origin, and with the permission of some traditional authority demarcates a space

[18] Dewasiri, *Adaptable Peasant,* 20.

[19] The Landraad makes no reference to the first-mentioned in the thombo group with the land in dispute in SLNA 1/6511, "Galle Landraad minutes" (1778)," fols. 50r, 15 Aug 1778. In another case, when a litigant claimed that two members of a family in Dodampe sold him their shares of a garden, the PLH of the thombo group did not appear in the Landraad, and no reference is made to him. SLNA 1/6513, "Galle Landraad minutes," fols. 47r, 20 May 1780; SLNA 1/7428A "Dodampe (Wellaboda) Thombo" (1780), 4–5, 15. The "ownership" rights of the principal land holder (PLH) are thus brought into question, as members of a thombo group could alienate their shares independent of the PLH.

[20] It is unlikely that the family member who was present at the registration was made the PLH, as some thombo entries indicate that this was not a rule. In the Hinidum thombos, individuals were recorded as "present," which probably meant present at the registration, but they were mentioned below the PLH. SLNA 1/7472A, "Ihala/Uda Gigunmaduwa (Hinidum) Thombo" (1760), fols. 4v; SLNA 1/7519A, "Pahala Gigunmaduwa (Hinidum) Thombo" (1760), 17, 19, 31; SLNA 1/7519B, "Pahala Gigunmaduwa (Hinidum) Thombo" (1760), 17, 19, 31; SLNA 1/7462A, "Hiniduma (Hinidum) Thombo" (1760), 7.

of forest or waste as his *gama.*"[21] Gama in Sinhala could also refer to a common estate. A connection to this ancestor could be established through the name of the PLH, which has a family name called the *vāsagama,* and usually has the suffix *ge.* It was shared by the other members except in the case of in-laws.[22] In the thombo, what mattered was that a PLH still bore the same vāsagama or was the widow of a man with that name. Thus, a connection to an ancestor from whom the lands were passed down was established. D'Oyly, an early nineteenth-century observer of Kandyan society said that in the Mahanaduva or great court of Kandy, "[i]n Land Cases, which are by far the most numerous, it is the General Practice to commence with the Original Proprietor, 3 or 4 Generations in Ascent, and thence to trace downwards by Inharitance or Transfer the Title of the Suitors."[23] As Obeyesekere says, "[a]ncestors are important in so far as they provided a charter depicting how and when a particular individual obtained his 'share.'"[24] Arumaperuma Achchige Johannes of Dodampe was thirty-five years old in 1780, and was given as the head of a family that possessed the service paravēni (lands held as subsistence in return for service) of his great-grandfather Arumaperuma Achchige Johan.[25] The old thombo was regarded as proof for the claim, which implies that relationship to a person mentioned in it was a qualification to become the PLH. Numerous examples of this kind refer to the old thombo. Dewasiri shows that persons with the same vāsagama in the Colombo thombos did not necessarily share a common estate or have a "charter of right," as Obeyesekere states, because those with the same vāsagama and with family connections were included in more than one LHG. This is seen in the Galle thombos as well. In most cases where two thombo groups in Galle had the same vāsagama, the connection between them is not mentioned, but can be imagined, as the groups also appear to have owned parts of the same lands.[26]

[21] Obeyesekere, *Land Tenure*, 17.

[22] Dewasiri, *Adaptable Peasant*, 55. Dewasiri's understanding of Obeyesekere's interpretation of a vāsagama group is that it involves a mythical ancestor and rights to a common estate. Dewasiri says that this does not fit the Colombo thombos because the PLH is alive in the thombos and, therefore, the bond between the PLH and the rest of the group is a living one. This is somewhat complicated in the Colombo thombos by the fact that the PLH hardly ever dies in the revision done roughly ten years later, around 1770. See Fabian F. Drixler and Jan Kok, "A Lost Family-Planning Regime in Eighteenth-century Ceylon," *Population Studies: A Journal of Demography* 70, no. 1 (2016): 99. Perhaps the intention was to retain reference to a senior member of the family, dead or alive, who may have had the same name as an ancestor who first owned the land. As a revision similar to that of Colombo did not occur in Galle, such a comparison is not possible for the Galle thombos.

[23] John D'Oyly, *A Sketch of the Constitution of the Kandyan Kingdom*, Lewis James Barnetson Turner (ed), vol. 24, The Ceylon Historical Journal (Dehiwala: Tisara Prakasakayo, 1929; repr. 1975), 33.

[24] Obeyesekere, *Land Tenure*, 162.

[25] SLNA 1/7428A, "Dodampe Thombo," 4.

[26] See for example LHGs 6 and 10 in Dodampe. Ibid., 4, 11.

Thus, an LHG was clearly not exclusively linked to a vāsagama, but LHGs with the same vāsagama are likely to have had kinship associations that were important in the organisation of labour and rituals.[27] The LHG indicates the division of estates and recognition of such divisions as separate groups of land holdings by the Dutch administration.

I argue that enumerating populations through the thombos is virtually impossible due to inherent characteristics and issues in the registration process. As mentioned before, according to Van den Belt et al, the Galle thombos record roughly 95,000 individuals and 30,000 shares of land.[28] The demographic patterns in the district were highly varied. Some thombos with over a hundred groups were Bope, Ettiligoda, Galupiadde, Kumbalwella (the seat of the Landraad), Ganegama, Salagama, Habaraduwa, Mipe, Bentota, Induruwa, Ambalangoda, Totagamuwa and Weragoda. Dodampe was an annex of Totagamuva, which was possibly the largest village in the Wellaboda Pattuwa, with more than 170 thombo groups. Akmeemana had ninety-nine groups so it can be considered a large village. Eight villages had just one LHG.[29] The number of LHGs in a village can give some impression of the population of the district, but it is a problematic figure for three reasons.

First, most thombos of Galle were not drawn up together or even within short periods of each other. This differs from the practice in Colombo, where at least the last two revisions were drawn up within ten years of each other. This facilitates the enumeration of the registered persons and an analysis of changes with a smaller margin of error. Among the eighteenth-century Galle thombos, the earliest thombos appear to be from 1742 (Bataduwa, Milidduwa and Wakwella of the sub-district of Four Gravets) and the latest from 1784 (Ambana, Degalle and Pitiwella of the Wellaboda Pattuwa, and Metiwiliya in the Walallawiti Kōralē). In some thombos, additions were made (usually at the end of a volume) as late as 1789.[30] This temporal disparity in the registration of villages naturally cannot provide credible census figures for individuals and holdings.

[27] Dewasiri, *Adaptable Peasant*, 56.

[28] Albert van den Belt, Jan Kok, and Kees Mandemakers, "Digital Thombos: A New Source for 18th Century Sri Lankan Family History," *The History of the Family* 16, no. 4 (2011): 484. These figures are estimates.

[29] These may be the neo-local residences that Obeyesekere describes, which he says are unusual because family help for cultivation would be limited, or the founding of a new hamlet and vāsagama. They occur, if at all, due to the scarcity of land combined with an abundance of people. Obeyesekere, *Land Tenure*, 59. Dewasiri also refers to how initially settlements may have been one-family villages. Dewasiri, *Adaptable Peasant*, 50–51.

[30] These changes are different to those made in the Colombo revision of 1766–1770. In the Galle thombos, a few new families were added but no changes were made to the existing groups.

The second reason is that providing an average figure for a rough calculation of the population of the district is problematic, as the number of people in an LHG could differ widely. For instance, in Dodampe of the Wellaboda Pattuwa, there were ninety persons mentioned in group number 30. This brings into question the composition of an LHG, and reflects the lack of a full understanding of a thombo group. How was such a group chosen? Those included had to have a legal claim to certain estates. Each individual mentioned in an LHG usually had a connection to the first-mentioned person. "First-named" (*eerstgenoemde*) is a phrase frequently used in the Galle thombos, whereas "head" (*hoofd*) is not used, although he or she is generally referred to as the "head" of a group in secondary literature. Yet "head" has associations with the concept of the head of the household or family, which LHGs do not fulfil. References were also made in the thombo to the second-mentioned, third-mentioned, etc. and those numbered in this manner in the thombo were usually of the same generation or older than the first-mentioned person. The PLH appears to have had a special connection to the property held by the LHG, mainly by virtue of being the senior-most member of a family with the same name as an ancestor from whom the lands were inherited.

The third reason for doubting the figures is that names were frequently repeated. Many were reported to belong to more than one thombo group within a village. For example, in Dodampe, of the roughly 470 names written down, almost ten per cent were repeated. The names that were repeated could range from the PLH to his or her more distant relatives.[31] At times, the first-mentioned person was repeated in other groups in the same village or in other villages. Such repetition across villages is connected to "absentee" landownership.[32] In short, it meant that the claimants lived outside the village of the registered land. Eliminating duplication is a difficult task, but may be possible if the data in the thombos are computerised. Keeping in mind these limitations of the registers, we can create a socio-economic snapshot through the thombos of the eight southern villages in the late eighteenth century.

Mobility in those times must have been fairly high, as absentee ownership was a common occurrence in the more densely populated villages. The PLH of an LHG frequently resided outside the village, as did other LHG members. Obeyesekere calls them "absentee shareowners" – those who own shares in the estate but do not cultivate the land.[33] Of the thirty-seven first-mentioned persons in Dodampe, only

[31] There was little interest in details about more distant relatives. Yet, it is possible to piece together information about such distant relatives from their different entries in separate LHGs.

[32] Dewasiri also refers to an "absentee PLH" in the Colombo thombos. Dewasiri, *Adaptable Peasant*, 114–16.

[33] Obeyesekere, *Land Tenure*, 165.

eleven persons or thirty per cent resided in that village.[34] As explained above, the first-mentioned person did not have exclusive rights to the land claimed by a group. In terms of population, the Dodampe thombo lists 432 persons, but only 155 lived in the village. Ganegoda had twenty-four LHGs, of which only eight (33 per cent) had PLHs who lived in that village; but its resident population was more than that of Dodampe, at 259 (out of 520 listed persons).[35] In 1760, the six villages in the Hinidum Pattuwa had forty-two thombo groups, of which twenty-nine (69 per cent) had first-mentioned persons who lived in the village in which they had holdings. Of those listed, 358 or around 75 per cent resided in the village where they held property. Relatively remote from the centre of Dutch government, peasants in the Hinidum Pattuwa lived and toiled on their only plots of lands more than others in the district.

All sample villages were inhabited by the Sinhalese. Dodampe had nineteen PLHs (51 per cent) who were goygama, the rest were durāva (12), European (2), āchāri (1), hakuru (1), radā (1) and hunu (1). The caste of the PLH, which is generally given in the thombo, usually applied to all members of the group.[36] The majority of residents were goygama (70 per cent), and the rest were durāva (26 per cent) and āchāri (4 per cent). Ganegoda had a larger majority of LHGs with goygama first-mentioned persons (70 per cent); the others were one durāva, radā and burger each, three karāvas and one person of European origin. All residents except for three radā caste members were goygama. In the Hinidum Pattuwa, most thombo groups (76 per cent) were headed by goygamas. The rest included three radā groups, five āchāri groups and two unknown groups. Two āchāri families lived outside the pattuwa, but forty-two villagers (almost 9 per cent) from the radā and āchāri castes lived in the pattuwa.

Interestingly, the Hinidum thombos contain a record of the religion of some PLHs. Most were "heathen" (31), as would be others in the same group unless otherwise mentioned as Christian. In the Hinidum village of Ihala Gigunmaduwa, one mayorāl, an important figure at the village level, was recorded as a "heathen". Another unique feature of the Hinidum Pattuwa thombos is that occasional marriages in the "heathen way" have been recorded as such and thereby given

[34] Individuals whose ages are recorded in the thombos were generally those who resided in the registered village. The number of residents thus obtained was tallied at the end of the thombos of the Hinidum Pattuwa.

[35] Incidentally, two groups in Ganegoda had the same female PLH: SLNA 1/7442A, "Ganegoda (Wellaboda) Thombo" (1780), 35–37; 63–67; SLNA 1/7442B, "Ganegoda (Wellaboda) Thombo" (1780), 33–35; 61–63. Others were also frequently repeated, so the figures on the number of persons listed in a thombo do not reflect the number of unique persons.

[36] There were exceptions to this generalisation. In Gintota, a particularly interesting inter-caste marriage appeared in one family: three nephews and a niece of the PLH had their caste listed as visser, being the offspring of a visser father and goygama mother. The PLH and other members were listed as goygama. SLNA 1/7445B, "Gintota (Four Gravets) Thombo" (1745).

sanction. This analysis of the Hinidum thombos indicates that imposing Calvinism and marriages sanctioned by the company (more on this in chapter six) in remote areas was a difficult task. It was likely to have been an area to which company control could not be easily extended.

The extent to which the language of the law reached such areas varied. Apart from the socio-economic analysis that the Galle thombos can enable, significant entries were made in the margins of the thombos, citing Landraad decisions in lawsuits. Dodampe and Ganegoda were not short of action on the legal front, but no references to Landraad cases are found in the Hinidum Pattuwa thombos. Yet the thombo registration itself was an expression of the law: inhabitants recognised that each entry was legally binding on them. Naturally, conflicts occurred within this process of cross-cultural translation, as reflected in policy-level discussions as well. Certain commonalities exist in the attempted standardisation, divided into the three classifications given below.

Classification One: By Cultivation

The company wished to be able to separate property shares into neat, clearly defined plots. All land holdings groups had descriptions of land rights, and each description could be referred to as a holding (in Sinhala: *panguva*; plural: *pangu*), if only as a quasi-legal category.[37] It may even be similar to the *panku* of south India that Dirks refers to as shares of land held by a group of family or lineage members, or by a dominant caste (or castes) of a locality.[38] Such usufruct and hereditary rights were legally recognised through a title obtained from the thombo and were also contested and discussed in the council. The thombo registrars described a share along with its history of ownership or possession. As shown in Table 5.1, Dodampe and Ganegoda had 174 and 315 holdings respectively in the 1780s, while the Hinidum villages, drawn up in 1760, had a total of 235 holdings.

Each holding can initially be separated according to whether it is a field (*kumbura*), garden (*watte*), swidden cultivation (*hēn*) or meadowland (*owiti*). The latter two were recorded in the Hinidum Pattuwa thombos, but were not important categories in the sample villages closer to the sea. The extent of the sowing field (*zaaiveld* in Dutch), usually paddy, was given in *amunu* and *kuruni*, measurements of sowing capacity. "Garden" is a literal translation of the Dutch *tuin*, which in turn would have been a translation of *gevatte*, or home-garden, in Sinhala. These

[37] See Codrington on pangu in *Ancient Land Tenure*, 3–5.

[38] Nicholas B. Dirks, "From Little King to Landlord: Property, Law and the Gift under the Madras Permanent Settlement," *Comparative Studies in Society and History* 28, no. 2 (1986), 310.

Table 5.1 Distribution of holdings in some Galle villages 1760 and 1780

Village	Fields	Gardens	Swidden	Meadows	n/a	Total
Wellaboda Pattuwa (selected)						
Dodampe	36	137	-	-	1	174
Ganegoda	205	110	-	-	-	315
Hinidum Pattuwa (all villages)						
Tawalama	12	6	4	6	-	28
Panangala	19	10	-	-	-	29
Opata Thalangala	43	53	3	3	-	102
Ihala/Uda Gigunmaduwa	8	9	5	1	-	23
Pahala Gigunmaduwa	7	5	3	-	-	15
Hiniduma	20	18	-	-	-	38
Hinidum Pattuwa Total	109	101	15	10	-	235
Total for eight villages	350	348	15	10	1	724

Sources: SLNA 1/7542, 1/7569, 1/7519, 1/7472, 1/7442 and 1/7428

gardens surrounding houses were spacious, but the term "tuin" is also used in the thombos for larger estates on the scale of plantations (*watte* or *watu* in Sinhala).[39] The amount of coconut trees, jak trees and areca nuts in such gardens was registered in the thombo. This was how the land was measured. The highlands of a village saw swidden cultivation and meadowland occasionally cultivated with paddy. In addition, taxes were generally fixed and mentioned in the thombo: one-tenth of the produce (*otu*), one-half (*ande*) or a garden tax (*watubadde*) for coconut and areca nut.[40]

In addition to the classification of fields, gardens, swidden cultivation and meadowlands, other ways of classifying lands were used in the thombos. Included in the thombo before the extent of the holdings and after the family information, were details on how members of a thombo group had acquired a share and who held it. These descriptions will be looked at next.

[39] In modern-day Dutch "tuin" means garden, but in the eighteenth-century it referred to a fence, hedge or enclosure around a piece of land. Hence, it is not surprising to see it being used in relation to plantations as well. I thank the anonymous reviewer of this book for drawing this to my attention.

[40] Going by the figures in the thombo, for holdings with one to six coconut trees, the tax appears to have been ¼ stivers but regulations state that there could be great variation depending on the condition of the tree and soil. On taxes, see D.A. Kotelawele, "Agrarian Policies of the Dutch in South-West Ceylon, 1743–1767," *A.A.G. Bijdragen* 14, no. 8 (1967), 30–31.

Classification Two: Contracting on Land

The categories of land tenure emerged from the colonial subjects themselves. As precisely as possible, the terminology used in the Galle thombos defined why a property right was being claimed. This included the status of the land in relation to the company and private rights to land. As the "legislators" at the time, the VOC agreed to regard such terminology as the law. Details of various categorisations of holdings, which determined the tax or services due to the government, are given in the thombos. The VOC used traditional terms in their original Sinhala form even in internal correspondence at higher levels and seemed to have made no attempt to translate them into Dutch, an exercise that would have been futile.

Regulating Crown Land

The terms *ratmahara* and *'s Compagnies grond* (company's land) occur often in the sample villages. The term ratmahara was quite simply described as the "company's empty land" by Pieter Sluijsken.[41] Literally, ratmahara or the older *ratmāsara,* meant the great thicket that belonged to the king.[42] It was one of roughly five kinds of land that belonged to the "lord of the land" (*bhupati*), at one time the king, a role assumed by the VOC in the eighteenth century. The other terms found in the thombos are *malapālu, nilapālu, muttettu* and 's Compagnies grond. Malapālu were lands escheated by the death of their possessor,[43] and nilapālu were lands that had reverted to the crown at the end of the tenant's service obligation due to the lack of male heirs or termination of the service or office.[44] Malapālu and nilapālu occur only in the thombos of the sample villages from the Hinidum Pattuwa, while the term muttettu, a demesne sown for the king or other owner[45] does not occur. These five types of land can be referred to as crown land.

[41] Pieter Sluijsken, "Eene beschryving van de landdienst op Ceylon: Zo uyt ondervinding als uyt oude papieren tezaemen gebragt (A Description of the Land Services of Ceylon: Compiled from both Investigations and Old Papers)" (Colombo, 1784), vol. 1, 353, RP-31/32 Colonial Collection (KIT), Leiden University.

[42] Codrington, *Ancient Land Tenure*, 8. An early nineteenth-century document among Alexander Johnston's papers in New York states that the original term may be *radamahara,* with *rada* meaning king: "The proper derivation of the word is unknown. It is said that it should be spelled Radamaharra, from Rada – king and that it means uncultivated king's or crown lands, brought into a state of cultivation or capable of being so." "Alexander Johnston Papers" (1643 to 1817) (MssCol 1578, Manuscripts and Archives Division, The New York Public Library).

[43] Schreuder, *Memoir*, 65.

[44] Codrington, *Ancient Land Tenure*, 25.

[45] Ibid., 23.

The intricacies of traditional terms of land tenure were hard to grasp for some company officials. Galle Landraad members at the 1745 meeting believed that all lands that had no owners anymore had to be registered as belonging to the company. They said that such land must also be understood as being malapālu or "feudal" lands. Van Gollonesse corrected them, saying that malapālu and nilapālu were feudal property before their owners died or deserted the land, but as soon as they became malapālu and nilapālu, they could not be called feudal property anymore. "On the contrary, they belong among the company's possessions and domains till they are handed over again to others," he added.[46] Understanding terminology was seen as important for the production of a legible cadastre.

Crown land, when acquired by peasants, was taxed and handed down the generations. Although malapālu and nilapālu were company lands, in practice, the produce of such lands was "owned" by the locals. In the Hinidum Pattuwa, twelve of 235 holdings were malapālu and nilapālu lands held by villagers. A tax of otu or one-tenth on the produce of such acquired lands was levied.[47] Ratmahara and company lands were also frequently acquired by people. Following a practice from pre-colonial times, for such gardens cultivated with permission, the company's share was one-third. If cultivated without permission, it was half. For paddy lands, an annual tax of one-tenth of the produce for land cultivated with permission and one-half without was imposed.[48]

The payment for gardens was not always made, as seen in the Galle thombos. With respect to many such holdings, the sample thombos stated that the company's share of one-third was not extracted. In order to increase cinnamon production, its primary interest on the island, the VOC at one time restricted the expansion of private gardens that threatened the supply of cinnamon. This led to rebellions, and the company had to curtail the adoption of such harsh measures.[49] In practice, therefore, the company could not always implement its regulations, as it would disturb the peace.[50] At times, the company granted its share of ratmahara lands in

[46] SLNA 1/2805, "Galle Landraad minutes (20 Dec 1745)," fols. 38v.

[47] See SLNA 1/7472A, "Ihala/Uda Gigunmaduwa Thombo," fols. 6v, 9; SLNA 1/7519A, "Pahala Gigunmaduwa Thombo," 27–28.

[48] Kotelawele, "Agrarian Policies," 18–19.

[49] D.A. Kotelawele, "The VOC in Sri Lanka, 1658–1796: Social and Economic Change in the Maritime Regions," in K.M. de Silva (ed), *University of Peradeniya, History of Sri Lanka (From c. 1500 to c. 1800)*, vol. 2 (Peradeniya: University of Peradeniya, 1995), 422–26.

[50] In the Colombo Dessavony, the category of company ground became a potentially contentious issue. Dewasiri says: "*Tombo* commissioners did not take for granted tenants' claims to each holding and in many cases they ignored tenants' claims that their holdings were *paravēni* or purchased lands." He gives an example of 479 holdings registered in the village of Mapitigama (Hina/Gangaboda), of which 216 were claimed as paravēni by their tenants, but only 116 were accepted as such. The remaining holdings were declared company lands, he says, and taxed accordingly. Dewasiri, *Adaptable*

certain villages to the salāgamas or cinnamon peelers.[51] In a matter discussed in more detail in chapter six, a division of land in Gamage Livina's case showed that a one-third share was demarcated for the salāgamas. In another inheritance issue that came up in the Landraad, a salāgama kangān and three other parties claimed a land plot, the former on the basis that it was malapālu land to which the salāgamas had rights in that village, and the latter on the basis that it was their paravēni property.[52] Dewasiri believes that in the traditional system, cinnamon peelers received the right to cultivate lands in return for working for the sovereign, and that the progressive disengagement with peasant agriculture and the practice of granting them the revenue of villages (which he identified with regard to the *lascarins*) was new.[53] A description of lands in the Galle district found among Alexander Johnston's papers states: "old Ratmahera Gardens pay no duty only certain villages wherein 1/3rd in Ratmahera Gardens had been allowed a accommodessan to the cinnamon peelers during the Dutch Government. The Ratmahare Gardens in some of such villages pays 1/3rd at present."[54]

The company and the people grappled for control over crown land. Fishermen from Ambalangoda, whom the thombo commissioners had referred to the Galle Landraad, asserted that their lands were paravēni and not ratmahara lands, as recorded by the commissioners, by virtue of a gift from a king of Kandy to their ancestors at a time before Portuguese rule.[55] Litigants also came to the council to petition that since they had cultivated and paid taxes for ratmahara lands for many years, they were entitled to be included in the thombos as the rightful owners of such lands. Ratmahara land, if cultivated for at least ten years by a cultivator who had paid taxes on it, could be entered in the thombo under that cultivator's name.[56] Councillors reported on such cases after consulting the village headmen.[57] The transformation of crown land into private property was thus permitted within limits.

Peasant, 112. Yet in Mapitigama as well, a significantly high proportion of the company's share appears to have remained unpaid.

51 See SLNA 1/151, "Governor in Council minutes" (1767), 2 Jun 1767.

52 SLNA 1/6506, "Galle Landraad minutes" (1771), fols. 68v, 3 Aug 1771.

53 Dewasiri, *Adaptable Peasant*, 96–97.

54 "Alexander Johnston Papers (New York)."

55 This example is from Alexander Johnston's papers, which includes a translation from the Galle Landraad meeting of 24 April 1773. Incidentally, this volume of minutes is not available among the Dutch records. Ibid. Perhaps this translation being among Johnston's papers explains the absence of the original, as Johnston was collecting information about the country from various sources.

56 The prescription for this was determined in 1744 as ten years. SLNA 1/92, "Governor in Council minutes" (1744), fols. 247r-v, 26 Sept 1744.

57 SLNA 1/6516, "Galle Landraad minutes" (1793), fols. 5r-v, 58r-v.

Managing Paravēni Rights

Van Gollonesse wrote in his marginal comments to the minutes of the Galle Landraad that all paravēni has been reduced to three classes, namely, purchase, gift or service paravēni. He clearly recognised the hereditary nature of such rights: "While the word paravēni itself means hereditary, it is unnecessary to add the same in the Dutch language to it, because it is never disputed and in fact is known to everyone, that it is hereditary."[58] This shows sensitivity towards the task of translating terminology from one system to another. Even as the new judicial system imposed many legal terms on the locals, the VOC attempted to understand local terms. In practice as well, the company recognised the hereditary nature of paravēni rights.

Yet, the hereditary nature of service paravēni included some customary restrictions. It was linked to a service that had to be rendered to the company or community in return for the holding. Such lands were also referred to as *accommodessan* in Dutch (mostly in the Colombo thombos) and *divel* (as in some Galle thombos). The extent of land granted in exchange for each service was fixed, one list of such fixed services is provided in appendix III. Service paravēni, according to custom, could not be divided among heirs (unlike purchase and gift paravēni), as it could only devolve on the eldest son or the person who, "according to the customs of the country," undertook to perform the service instead of the father.[59] In one case, the Landraad denied a woman's claims to a garden and three paddy-fields till there was a male in her family who could perform the required mayorāl service.[60] Sluijsken and others have confirmed the need for a male heir to take over the service.[61] People, services and land were closely interconnected, and the company wished to retain land to give it out in return for services. Service tenure holders were, at times, burdened with more work by the company, but this led to rebellion, as in Matara.[62]

At the same time, other supposedly fixed characteristics of paravēni rights were not utilised in a way that was detrimental to the people. For instance, it was

58 SLNA 1/2805, "Galle Landraad minutes (20 Dec 1745)," fols. 39r.

59 Hovy *Plakkaatboek*, vol. 2; nr. 355, Instructions for the commissioners of the Landraad who are responsible for drawing up the new land- and headthombo of the Colombo and Matara dessavonys and of the Galle kōralē, 15 Nov 1745, 18. See for translation, S.A.W. Mottau, trans., "Documents on Ceylon History (2): Documents Relating to the Tombo Registration of the Dutch Administration in Ceylon: Instructions Issued to the Tombo Commissioners," *The Ceylon Historical Journal* 3, no. 2 (1953): 181.

60 SLNA 1/6513, "Galle Landraad minutes," fols. 89r, 12 Aug 1780.

61 Sluijsken, "A Description of the Land Services," vol. 1, 158. See also Codrington, *Ancient Land Tenure*, 19.

62 Kotelawele, "The VOC in Sri Lanka," 434–36.

frequently publicised through plakkaten that service paravēni must not be mortgaged or transferred.[63] However, they could be sold on the condition that the new owner rendered the relevant service. Alienation of land held for service was also seen in pre-colonial times.[64] The inconsistency between the policy decisions taken by the VOC and actual practice on the ground is not surprising. Accommodating such flexibility at a higher level, Van Gollonesse wrote:

> [...] it is completely untrue that we would have ordered, as it is said, that most people would inevitably lose their gardens and estates as a result of the lack of sufficient proofs. On the contrary, we have ordered that each person may and must keep his service paravēni on the conditions that 1) they provide services for them and 2) that it is not bigger than what the regulation dictates.[65]

He acknowledged that the company "may well suffer" and added that when the holdings were larger than the size permitted for that service, "the surplus shall also stay in that family if the family is unusually large, on the condition that those on whose names the land has been registered should come to increase the number who render their services."[66] So, in short, if the family was "unusually large" – and it's not clear what that meant for the VOC – the extra lands could be retained on the condition that more family members served the company.[67] This has been demonstrated in the sample village Ganegoda, where paddy-fields and gardens were held free of otu tax for the mayorāl or coolie service and lands that exceeded the stipulated extent for a particular service were held on the payment of otu tax.[68] The excess lands, which were more than the permitted extent for a particular service (based on the hierarchy of officers), were effectively private property with no obligatory service attached to them.

63 See for example SLNA 1/93, "Governor in Council minutes" (1744), 226r-v, 10 Dec 1744.

64 W.I. Siriweera, *History of Sri Lanka: From the Earliest Times upto the Sixteenth Century* (Colombo: Dayawansa Jayakody & Co, 2002), 148.

65 SLNA 1/2805, "Galle Landraad minutes (20 Dec 1745)," fols. 34v–35r.

66 Ibid., fols. 35r–35v.

67 It would be interesting to try to determine if a "family" meant a thombo group for the governor. See discussion on how to analyse a thombo group earlier in this chapter.

68 In one thombo entry, a garden and six paddy-fields were held "in common" by an LHG on payment of garden tax and otu, but two other paddy-fields were held by the mayorāls in the thombo group free of tax. In yet another LHG, one amuna from the paddy-fields and two gardens were held for providing coolie service free of tax, but otu had to be paid for the other paddy-fields. Another thombo entry read: "All [holdings] according to the old thombo the paravēni of the first-mentioned person's great-grandfather also called Happoetantrige Joan, mayorāl; the garden was held for the payment of tax from old times, and the two last-named paddy-fields were free of otu, but for the other paddy-fields they must pay otu." SLNA 1/7442A, "Ganegoda Thombo," 5, 31, 45.

If, as Governor Van Gollonesse clarified, malapālu and nilapālu were feudal when they were still held as subsistence by those rendering a service, then service paravēni was also understood as part of a feudal agreement. The governor believed that in disputes between private parties, which he said were the majority of disputes heard by the council, the parties failed to realise that the land actually belonged to the company and not to them. He complained that no one wished to speak of the right of the company in such cases out of either ignorance or self-interest. It was still fresh in his memory, he wrote, how those who according to their sworn oath and obligation should execute the company's interests had given away and sold company lands like it was booty. Yet, it would not be very complicated, he added, if the company made a proper distinction between lands that belonged to someone as a result of legal purchase and gift, and hereditary paravēni that someone possessed for his service. For the governor, that was the foundation of the whole matter.[69] Evidently, it was essentially the tension between feudal and private ownership of land that was under discussion.

Planter's Shares

Another "right" and local custom hitherto undisclosed in the thombo literature was the ownership of cultivated trees. Known as planter's shares, this right was exercised frequently in the Galle thombos. In brief, it means that a planter who cultivates fruit-bearing trees in a piece of land with the owner's knowledge retains the right of possession to the trees by right of cultivation. Its inclusion in the laws of Sri Lanka continues today. One lawyer, arguing in the Supreme Court in 1892 for a respondent who claimed a planter's share, said that "[n]o one would buy planted land without enquiring into or allowing for and protecting himself against planters' rights." Judge C.J. Burnside said in that case:

> A custom has prevailed throughout the Maritime Provinces, the origin of which is perhaps coeval with the ownership of land, whereby estates in land have been created and known as 'planters' shares' in first or second 'plantations.' A cultivator with the leave of the owner of the land would plant a portion or perhaps all of it with coconut, jak, areca, or other trees of that character, of slow growth and long lived, upon an agreement or understanding that when they came into bearing the planter should have such an interest in them as might be agreed on. In some cases the planter would have a certain number of the trees with the ground on which they stood and with right to live on the land and to go over it to take care of the trees and pluck the fruit. In some cases the planter's share would be a certain portion of the fruit itself. In some cases he would have the right to retain the trees, which

[69] SLNA 1/2805, "Galle Landraad minutes (20 Dec 1745)," fols. 37r-v.

> he had planted, until he had been paid at a stipulated price for each by the owner of the land, and, in fact, often upon some customary rule which applied to these plantations. But in all cases the interest acquired by the planter has been recognised as a right of property in the land separate from and adverse to that of the owner, to be dealt with by the planter at his own will, to be sold by him, inheritable by his heirs, subject to his devise and to his creditors for his debts in all respects, as any other property.[70]

Burnside points out that the custom had become interwoven with actual possession of land, despite statutory laws that challenged it. Cooray states that the local custom of the planter's share was recognised as a *jura in re aliena* within the framework of the Roman-Dutch law of property.[71] Marleen van den Horst argues that the planter's share or right is particular to Sri Lanka and that "[t]he rights of the planter and the extent of his share are determined by the agreement between him and the landowner and may differ depending on the customary rules of the various districts."[72] I am yet to come across a discussion on this remarkable acceptance of local law in the records of the VOC.

It was a customary right acquired by cultivating long-standing fruit-bearing trees in gardens. In the thombos, planter's shares or interests are identifiable by the phrases *over moeite van aanplanting* (for the trouble of planting) and *over/wegens aanplanting* (as a result of planting). This appears to be a translation of *vev mahansiya pinisa* in Sinhala, which means, literally, "for the trouble of planting" and is a term found in nineteenth-century land deeds.[73] Another Dutch term used in the Landraad, *aanplantings deel*, is closer to the English translation of planter's share.[74] Witnesses at the Landraad confirmed the existence of this local custom in 1778. Asked why a stranger was permitted to plant on an already appropriated land, and if it were not true that this could never happen among the Sinhalese,

[70] *Jayasuria v. Omar Lebbe Marcar*. 1892. H.L. Wendt and T.E. de Sampayo, eds., *The Ceylon Law Reports: Being Reports of Cases Decided by the Supreme Court of Ceylon* (Colombo: Ceylon Examiner Press, 1892), vol 2, no. 3, 7.

[71] L.J.M. Cooray, "Common Law in England and Sri Lanka," *International & Comparative Law Quarterly* 24, no. 3 (1975): 556.

[72] Marleen H.J. van den Horst, *Compensation for Improvements: The Roman Dutch Law in Sri Lanka* (Amsterdam: Free University Press, 1989), 164.

[73] When one Sophia de Saram Wiresinghe Siriwardene Lama Eteni bought a garden share from Cornelis de Saram, the transfer deed from 1853 refers to the exclusion of two coconut trees and a jak tree planted by Salman Fernando of Wolvendaal. She resold it in 1885, again with the exclusion of Fernando's three trees. A last will of 1846 also refers to the bequest of a planter's share. I thank H.F. Rupesinghe for bringing these deeds, which are among the private papers of Lorna Seneviratne of Galkissa, to my attention.

[74] SLNA 1/6512, "Galle Landraad minutes" (1779), fols. 80r, 20 Nov 1779; SLNA 1/6513, "Galle Landraad minutes," fols. 11r, 5 Feb 1780.

they answered that if the land was empty it could occur.[75] The people thus asserted a local custom. The Dutch were in all likelihood baffled by it, but were forced to accept it.

Planter's shares were hereditary and taxable, as seen in references in the thombo to inheritance from those who had planted trees. Yet, contrary to Burnside's references to owning the land, the Landraad excluded planter's rights to the ground. In 1775, one of three holders of an inherited planter's share in Piyadigama appeared in the council with an extract from the thombo. He requested permission to sell his share. The owner of the land had agreed to take over the share at a price of 30 rixdollars. The owner of the planter's share stated that a schoolmaster had offered the same price, but he had not committed to him. The Landraad approved the sale with a significant remark that "the trees that someone owns in another man's garden for the trouble of having planted them may be sold, but not the ground." But the council ruled that the owner of the garden, when he was willing to pay the same price as a third party, was legally entitled to exercise his right of first refusal.[76] Other issues brought up in the Landraad also confirm the exclusion of rights to the ground. The executors of the estate of the late Adam Hendeling asked the Landraad in 1779 for two commissioners of the council to estimate the planter's share of one of his gardens. Two European members, August Charles de Marin and Daniel Gerrardus Kersse, and one native member of the council, Augustinus Ferdinandus Wiresinghe, submitted a report recommending compensation of almost seventy rixdollars to three Moors for their planter's shares in that garden. A secretarial certificate in this respect had to be prepared.

The evaluation was done, it was said, according to a resolution of the Governor in Council on 15 September 1772.[77] In the 1778 lawsuit in which the witnesses quoted above testified to the custom, the Landraad stated that when a certain garden was auctioned and the proceeds divided among the heirs, the new owner should compensate the planter.[78] Further confirming that planter's shares were well-recognised and excluded rights to the ground, a Landraad sentence assigning ownership of a garden to one party added that any shares due to those who the thombo commissioners may find in the future to have also planted on it should be

[75] SLNA 1/6534, "Galle Landraad interrogations" (1778 to 1784), fols. 22r-v, 9 Dec 1778.

[76] SLNA 1/6509, "Galle Landraad minutes" (1775), fols. 10r, 7 Jan 1775. A note on the sale was made on 22 January 1776 on the Piyadigama thombo. SLNA 1/7534A, "Piyadigama (Four Gravets) Thombo" (1744), 1; SLNA 1/7534B, "Piyadigama (Four Gravets) Thombo" (1744), 3.

[77] SLNA 1/6512, "Galle Landraad minutes," fols. 80r, 20 Nov 1779; SLNA 1/6513, "Galle Landraad minutes," fols. 11r, 5 Feb 1780.

[78] SLNA 1/6511, "Galle Landraad minutes," fols. 74r, 17 Oct 1778.

registered in the thombo under such a right.[79] It is thus clear that planters and their heirs could not lay claim to more than their share in trees.

Of the fifty-six such holdings of trees in Dodampe, which were held because they had been planted or were inherited from planters, individuals held the most (thirty-five). Six were inherited shares. Only four planter's shares were clearly held by the whole family mentioned in the LHG. Groups of two or more people held the rest (seventeen). In Ganegoda, of fifty-nine such planter's shares, individuals held at least thirty-seven, and the rest were held jointly (some may have included the whole family, but that has not been explicitly stated). People related to the owner, or at least those who lived in the same village, held most planter's shares. All such holdings of coconut and jak trees, with one mention of areca nut trees in Dodampe, were liable to pay the garden tax. Planter's shares in coconut ranged from a single tree to fifty-six trees in Dodampe and up to thirty-six in Ganegoda. At times, such shares also had up to twenty-four jak trees. In the Hinidum Pattuwa, of eight planter's shares, four were held by individuals, three jointly and one by the family in common. In essence, the land belonged to someone else, but you could hold on to certain trees on it.

Classification Three: By Ownership

The third approach to classification touched upon above is to analyse who "held" a share. Here, we resort to a greater degree of interpretation of phrases used in the sample thombos. The phrases used are: *in 't algemeen gepossideerd* ("possessed in general"), *door deze familie gepossideerd* ("possessed by this family") or *de gantsche familie competeerende* ("belonging to the whole family"). They are categorised here as "in common." Such holdings of gardens and paddy-fields involved the rights of multiple people, and the phrases were generally used in thombo groups of more than one individual. The land was held "in common" in that the members of the group were joint heirs or shareholders and had a connection to the PLH. It must not be confused with a communistic type of ownership.[80] The rights of the individual can be expressed in terms of a portion of an original ancestral estate.[81] These

[79] SLNA 1/6514, "Galle Landraad minutes" (1781), fols. 93r, 21 Jul 1781. Walgamage Jantje et al. v Henadirage Christobu et al.

[80] Obeyesekere quotes Baden-Powell who says of the joint village in India: "'joint ownership' does not involve the idea of possessing land 'in common,' if by this is meant 'something of a communistic type as regards property in land'; and most certainly 'collective ownership has nothing to do with the social community of goods.'" B.H. Baden-Powell, *The Indian Village Community* (London: Longmans, 1896), 3; Obeyesekere, *Land Tenure*, 277.

[81] Obeyesekere, *Land Tenure*, 38.

fractions can at times be quite minute. It may appear that the possession or holding of shares in a particular tenure is different to "ownership" as we use the term today. However, such boundaries are porous, and as we have seen above, evidence of absolute rights in property in eighteenth-century Sri Lanka is not lacking.

Table 5.2 shows how twenty per cent of holdings in Dodampe, fifteen per cent in Ganegoda and twenty per cent in the Hinidum Pattuwa were held by families in common in the 1760s and 1780s. Lands held thus were cultivated according to the *tattumāru* system, which Obeyesekere found was still prevalent in the Hinidum Pattuwa some two hundred years later.[82] In tattumāru, stakeholders rotated the cultivation of their undivided shares to ancestral lands. The Landraad noted that when the fields were so big that they were divided into three, for instance, each owner would be assigned one-third of it on rotation year after year. The council said that disputes were settled in that way "according to the customs of the country and as customary among most inhabitants."[83] The surveyor, it further declared, could not divide the land. The Dutch use of the term *beurt wisseling* (changing turns), in relation to the rendering of the service and cultivation of the land, connects to tattumāru.[84]

Tattumāru was probably the way in which relatively large LHGs "shared" holdings. Inheritance by males and a patrilineal residential aggregation of males facilitated the system.[85] The nuclear family that lived on the land may also have had special rights. When a family was exceptionally large with many members living outside the village in which the land was located, it is hard to imagine that they all had an equal share of the produce. In an LHG of ninety people in Dodampe, the first recorded property mentioned was held in common.[86] "In-residents" who lived in the village would have had special rights to such property. An anonymous and undated document among Johnston's papers in New York confirms that the Sinhalese held their lands "for the most part in common according to the ancient custom and usage amongst themselves," adding that fragmentation had a negative effect on cultivation.[87] It was clearly stated that it was not a Dutch custom.[88]

[82] Obeyesekere, *Land Tenure*, 18–36.

[83] SLNA 1/6525, "Galle Landraad draft minutes" (1784 to 1786), fols. 39v, 19 Jun 1784.

[84] See, for example, how two brothers shared "3 gardens and 1 sowing field freely owned for the service of mayorāl and possessed by changing turns." SLNA 1/7531A, "Pitigala (Walallawiti) Thombo" (1778), 1.

[85] Obeyesekere, *Land Tenure*, 134.

[86] SLNA 1/7428A, "Dodampe Thombo," 30.

[87] "Alexander Johnston Papers (New York)." This quotation is an answer from a single question and answer sheet, the question being "Do the Singalese people possess their lands in common according to any Dutch custom or according to any custom or law of their own and what effect has it on the cultivation of lands?"

[88] For an extensive explanation of the *tattumāru* system, see Obeyesekere, *Land Tenure*, 18–36.

Such distinctions were determined based on who obtained the produce from the land. Dewasiri says that the pangu recorded under one PLH can be called his estate.[89] This implies ownership by the PLH but, as said before, it is unlikely that the PLH in the Galle thombos had special rights to the holdings mentioned in an LHG. A variety of people actually held the rights to the holdings, which included general rights to fields and gardens together with other joint and individual rights. Furthermore, the difference in the structure of the Colombo and Galle thombos could be due to different understandings of the significance of the first-mentioned person regarding ownership. The land information in the Colombo thombos it should be recalled was given in a separate thombo. As the PLH in the head (family) thombo was repeated in the land thombo, a natural correlation between the estate and the PLH was created. Thus, it is not difficult to conclude that he or she "owned" the estate as well. Such a conclusion is almost impossible to arrive at with regard to the Galle thombos, which have land information alongside details of people, and many references to common and individual ownership are made. It is perhaps a difference in the nature of land rights in Galle that led to different formats of thombos, but this must remain conjectural. Further complicating the picture, in one thombo entry, it was said that although some lands belonged to the family in common, one or two persons in the family actually owned it.[90] Tenurial illegibility to that degree was rare. Yet, this could mean a shift to more individual rights.

Table 5.2 shows that holdings that were held in common were infrequent. Individuals or small groups of two or more people whose names appeared under a particular LHG held most holdings in the sample villages. Such "joint" ownership was by specific individuals and did not refer to the whole family as in possession in common. The function of the thombo in this mutual recognition was crucial as individuals and joint owners established distinct rights to specific shares through it. For example, a thombo entry may stress individual ownership as "in possession of the first-mentioned person only."[91] In another case, Makkundagamage Christina's request for a certificate of ownership over a large property gifted by her grandfather shows the assertion of individual rights. She appeared before the Landraad in 1779 with an extract from the "new thombo" of the village Gintota, a

[89] Dewasiri, *Adaptable Peasant*, 109.

[90] "Mahagedarewatte according to the old thombo, service paravēni of the first-mentioned's mother-in-law or wife of the aforementioned Pasquaal de Silva, belonging thus to this family in common, was however in the possession of the third-mentioned and his brothers and sisters…." Also, "Nilawatte, according to the old thombo service paravēni of the first mentioned person's mother-in-law or wife of the aforementioned Pasquaal de Silva, belonging thus to this family in common, was however in the possession of the two last-named persons, Arruma Peruma Achchige Johannes and Johanna under payment of tax." SLNA 1/7428A, "Dodampe Thombo," 30.

[91] SLNA 1/7442B, "Ganegoda Thombo," 21.

village in Galle not among the sample villages in this chapter. Recognising that she had legal possession to the garden, the council agreed to her request.[92]

Table 5.2 Frequency of holdings held in common in Dodampe, Ganegoda and Hinidum Pattuwa

	Dodampe	Ganegoda	Hinidum
Fields	17	38	33
Gardens	20	10	15
Total	37 (20 %)	48 (15 %)	48 (20 %)

The thombo extract found among the papers of the above case is from a registration done in 1745. The Gintota thombo, made in 1745/46, has had insertions added to it over time, even as late as 1804.[93] According to the thombo, Christina was the granddaughter of Makkundagamage Francisku. The extract, dated 9 July 1779, had been obtained by Christina's cousin's son. The garden in question, which according to the 1745 thombo had 180 coconut trees, six jak trees and 728 areca nut trees, had been bought by Francisku at a company auction, as proven by a certificate from the year 1716. Twelve years prior to the thombo description made in 1745, Francisku had favoured and gifted away (*vereerd en weggeschonken*) the garden to his granddaughter Christina, according to evidence provided by the rest of the family. In 1745, Christina was living in Horangalla/Walallawiti Kōralē. In the description of Horangalla village made in 1778, she is likely to be the same person listed as Makkundagamage Christina, wife of Ududollewattege Domini.[94] Thus, although she appears to have married virilocally (more on this follows in chapter six), her rights to the land were protected through the gift.

Whether individual and joint rights mark a break with the past is debatable. Dutch conceptions of private property may have seeped into local society. Yet, it is more likely that the individual rights we see in the thombos reflect an indigenous practice; the idea that colonialism led to the creation of private rights to landed

92 A stamped extract from the Landraad session, followed by the thombo extract, and a signed copy of the certificate (marked *certificaat*), most probably made up on 4 July 1780 (the last digit of the year is not clear) appear in SLNA 1/6491, "Registers of Deeds Affecting Land, Galle" (1780 to 1791), fols. 6r–8r. The relevant thombo entry is in SLNA 1/7445B, "Gintota Thombo," 41.

93 SLNA 1/7445, "Gintota Thombo," loose unnumbered pages. Later additions included notes on the transfer of lands.

94 SLNA 1/7467A, "Horangalla (Wellaboda) Thombo" (1778), 7; SLNA 1/7467B, "Horangalla (Wellaboda) Thombo" (1778), 5. Christina was seventy years old in 1778, ten years older than her husband, which means she would have been thirty-seven years old at the time the Gintota thombo description was made (as is common for those who lived outside the estate, her age is not given in the Gintota entry), and the bequest would have been made in the early 1730s.

property is an enduring myth.[95] The VOC continued customary practices of land ownership, given the evidence for individual and joint rights to land in pre-colonial Sri Lanka as well.[96]

It is not clear how such holdings, held in common and individually, converged in practice. Obeyesekere analyses how in the twentieth century, "out-residents" created occasional conflict with a core group of "in-residents" who enjoyed the rights in common. This is likely to have occurred in Dutch times as well, given the high numbers of absentee owners.

Conclusion

This chapter explored the intricacies of the thombo registration in all its implications for land rights. Sluijsken's declaration that the thombo was the "essential law book" and the ultimate reference for property disputes is amply illustrated when considered together with Landraad cases.[97] The thombo was the law, he argued. We need hardly entertain any doubts about the importance of the thombo in practice, which continued to be legally relevant in the nineteenth century under British rule. Today, the thombo is a document that is used to a limited extent in legal cases. Generated at a lower administration level, it was, in essence, drawn up in conversation with peasants.

Given the presence of a foreign power that found the prevalent system of land tenure a novelty, the Landraad provided a space within which ideas and practice could merge in written form on the question of land rights and entitlements. It provided the opportunity for peasants to be more assertive in southern Sri Lanka. The contact zone of coloniser and colonised in Galle produced acclimatised ideas of land rights that diverted from higher-level discussions on land tenure involving the governor, whose involvement was a part of the quest to consolidate authority. At the grassroots level, the making of a single thombo entry engaged the practical realities that lower-level officials had to contend with. I argue that there was fluidity and flexibility in practice which corresponds with the work of Lauren Benton on colonial law.[98] The discursive struggles centred and finally settled around the text of the cadastre, despite moves by higher officials to appropriate the production

95 David Washbrook, "Sovereignty, Property, Land and Labour in Colonial South India," in Huri Islamoglu (ed), *Constituting Modernity: Private Property in the East and West* (London: I.B. Tauris, 2004), 69.

96 See for example Siriweera, *History of Sri Lanka*, 146–60.

97 Sluijsken, "A Description of the Land Services," vol. 1, 307, 367–368.

98 Lauren Benton, *Law and Colonial Cultures: Legal Regimes in World History, 1400-1900* (Cambridge: Cambridge University Press, 2001), 259.

of knowledge on categories of rights. The Landraad and by extension the Dutch government in Sri Lanka may have constituted the legal platform on which tenurial rights could be discussed, but the realities lay further out in the field.

On the subject of contractual relationships with fellow countrymen or the rulers of a land, the language of the people was the law. What they spoke was law, what was translated was law, and what was written down in the end product of the thombo was supposedly the law as well to both coloniser and colonised. On categories of tenurial rights, the perspective of the indigenous inhabitant was taken into account, indicating an active engagement with the conflicting view. In essence, this was bottom-up lawmaking. At the same time, the act of making representations to the Landraad on land matters may have affirmed that the company was in charge and was the arbiter of justice. Significantly, the peasants appear to have had considerable faith in the company's power to fix and regulate land rights, as shown in the number of cases that came up, which I will demonstrate more clearly in the next chapter. In a colonial setting, it is to be expected that there would be difficulties in translating terms cross-culturally. This chapter focused on how the VOC went about deciphering local land tenure in practice.

The early colonial power regulated land use carefully, making it seemingly impossible to escape the long arm of the law. At the same time, the thombo itself is testimony to the fact that the policies of the VOC were flexible on the ground. They maintained the status quo, and subject to extra taxes, they allowed excess land to be held by service caste members and native officials. Other irregularities such as the appropriation by private parties of the full produce of company lands and wasteland were also permitted, as were planter's shares and undivided shares held in common. The locals renegotiated "custom"; where possible, they had no wish to adhere to rules if aspirations to absolute property rights ran high. The thombo and the Landraad were, in effect, the legal mechanisms by which the conversion of land, whether collectively or individually held, into alienable title was sought to be consolidated. That history of land tenure in the countryside had remained untold till now.

In such a context, it is difficult to detect an overpowering domination in colonial state formation, as colonial subjects, both elite and non-elite, were involved in the process. Lawmaking in coastal Sri Lanka was most significant in agrarian rights, determined to a large extent by the locals themselves. The mundane practices through which property holdings were classified on an everyday basis relied heavily on the subjects. Through the new discursive platforms of the Landraad and the thombo, colonial officials used the law to control each share of land. In spite of the complexity of tenurial rights, the new platforms, they believed, would render the agrarian countryside administratively controllable in a process that made room for pluralities of practice.

CHAPTER 6

On Inheriting Land

Abstract

Diverse practices in relation to inheritance laws, marriage and nonmarital children can be observed in eighteenth-century Sri Lanka. Family law was an area in which the attempt to transform local practices was conspicuously present, but not fully achieved. The VOC faced a normative order that was characterised by ritual underpinnings. The Dutch practice of registering marriage was linked to conversion and to inheritance of property. Yet, the two-step process of reading the banns and subsequent marriage ceremony created confusion and locals still followed customary practices for forging unions. Assimilation is seen in the European concept of illegitimacy seeping into family life, while situational judging led to the adaptation of local concepts of inheritance. The perseverance of local practices of inheritance is testimony to the lived experience of pluralities in practice.

Keywords: Inheritance law, marriage, pluralities, situational judging, colonial family law, nonmarital children

Pilane Godakandege Gimara of Galle did not deny that her husband had been born out of wedlock, and neither did his biological mother. However, in 1788, years after his death, Gimara was brought to the brink of economic ruin when her husband's relatives challenged his inheritance rights. Illegitimacy laws introduced by the Dutch East India Company threatened her right to retain her land rights. She did not deny the circumstances of Daniel's birth, but objected to a rescinding of property rights on those grounds. Why, it was asked in her appeal to a higher court, had her husband's relatives brought up the issue only now? How did ordinary men and women like her respond to new laws concerning nonmarital children in late eighteenth-century Galle? This was a period in which Dutch laws had potentially the most effect. In a final twist of events, Gimara's opponents were also denied any added inheritance. Marriage and inheritance, transactions of everyday life, were affected by the company's requirement for either a recognised customary marriage or registered marriage, without which births would be considered nonmarital.

Land ownership, inheritance and kinship are inseparable elements in the Sri Lankan context. A legal approach necessarily involves all three aspects. Observing family life and inheritance together is an expected outcome. Forms of land tenure, i.e., particular agreements relating to the land that people had, reflected on inheritance and, by extension, on kinship. The law of family inheritance is the subject of this chapter, an important issue due to its implications for the individual. Who inherits within a family and in what proportions are key questions. An important question in early modern and modern litigation in Sri Lanka was how an ancestral estate was to be divided after a death. Unsurprisingly, intestate succession was an issue that resulted in the Landraad hearing a fair number of cases in the eighteenth century.

As preceding chapters have shown, the mixed legal system had far-reaching impacts through the Galle Landraad, the traces of which must be read in close accompaniment with the thombos. All those who received title to land through the thombos were engaging with their legal rights at the registration. If the thombo commissioners could not decide, cases were brought to the Landraad and shareholders attempted to prove their rights. The entries in the thombos are, in fact, the ultimate reference for studying inheritance patterns, but that would require extensive computerisation of data and a monographic work of its own.

I have examined the question of whether the inheritance law applied in Landraad decisions reflected Dutch or local legal customs, starting by retracing the steps of an inheritance issue brought up by one Claas Fontijn in 1780. A detailed exploration of the case requires a discussion of traditional inheritance norms and the Roman-Dutch law of inheritance. Which law was used in Dutch judicial councils? I have not attempted a comprehensive introduction to Dutch or Sinhalese inheritance laws in this chapter – aspects of these are discussed in the cases I provide as examples.[1] I have also used cases to show how principles of Sinhalese law settled through situational judging, such as the concept of familial assistance, local modes of marriage, and the rights of widows, also came up in the Landraad. Most strikingly, the Landraad displayed a trend towards bilateral inheritance. In

[1] For a discussion of local inheritance laws, see Gananath Obeyesekere, *Land Tenure in Village Ceylon: A Sociological and Historical Study* (Cambridge: Cambridge University Press, 1967); Nur Yalman, *Under the Bo Tree: Studies in Caste, Kinship, and Marriage in the Interior of Ceylon* (Berkeley & Los Angeles: University of California Press, 1967); Edmund Ronald Leach, *Pul Eliya: A Village in Ceylon* (Cambridge: Cambridge University Press, 1961). On the Roman-Dutch law of inheritance, see: L.M. Rollin Couquerque, *Het Aasdoms- en Schependomsrecht in Holland en Zeeland, in verband met het erfrecht der naburige provinciën* ('s Gravenhage: Nijhoff, 1898); Robert Warden Lee, "The Intestate Succession of Husband and Wife in Roman-Dutch Law," *Journal of the Society of Comparative Legislation* 12, no. 310 (1911); Melius de Villiers, "Succession *Unde Vir Et Uxor*," *South African Law Journal* 33 (1916): 158–61; C. Graham Botha, "Intestate Succession," *South African Law Journal* 34 (1917): 172; Robert Warden Lee, *An Introduction to Roman-Dutch Law*, fourth edition (Oxford: At the Clarendon Press, 1946).

addition, the records of the Scholarchale Vergadering or School Board draw a picture of marriage and nonmarital children in eighteenth-century Galle, providing a better understanding of their potential bearing on inheritance matters. Some locals embraced Dutch concepts of illegitimacy, which was at times diligently recorded in the thombos, and engaged in litigation in the Landraad to exclude others from inheritance as is evident from the case of Pilane Godakandege Gimara. This is by no means a comprehensive attempt to understand all aspects of family inheritance, but illustrates some aspects through empirical data.

Claas Fontijn's Claim

In 1780, Claas Fontijn, a sieve-maker and burger in the company's service in Kumbalwella (Four Gravets), inherited property in a village in the Galle district through his father's second wife. He had no blood relationship with the rest of the family in Dodampe (Wellaboda Pattuwa), to which his father Hendrik's second wife Johanna Floorman belonged. Since the land in Fontijn's matter required a registration in the thombo, he had to appear before the Landraad. His case serves as an introduction to the question of intestate law.

The thombo entry in question, illustrated in Figure 6.1, ran thus.[2] The principal landholder (PLH) in the thombo group is Arumaperuma Achchige Johannes, the great-grandson of Arumaperuma Achchige Johan. Johannes was 35 years old in 1780 and lived in Dodampe with his wife, son and two daughters. Of the goygama caste and a lascarin, Johannes had a sister named Johanna who lived in Tellumbura and an aunt named Maria Bouman who lived in Kumbalwella.[3] The thombo mentions Claas Fontijn as the stepson of Maria's cousin (mother's sister's daughter), Johanna Floorman. The thombo and Landraad records also state that one lascarin named Arumaperuma Achchige Johan was the grandfather of both

[2] SLNA 1/7428A, "Dodampe (Wellaboda) Thombo" (1780), 4–6. Another thombo entry made thirty years earlier in Hinatigala probably represents the generation of the grandfather of the Dodampe PLH, but I have not included them in the family tree, as they do not appear directly in reference to the case heard in 1780. SLNA 1/7460B, "Hinatigala (Talpe) Thombo" (1750), 13.

[3] Maria is recorded as "nicht," meaning niece or cousin, and is described as Johannes's grandfather's sister's daughter. However, corresponding references to the same persons indicate that Maria Bouman is indeed an aunt of Arumaperuma Achchige Johannes. Discrepancies in recorded relationships and names are common in the thombo. The father of Johanna and Johannes is called Arumaperuma Achchige Michiel (and not Allensu) in another thombo group to which they have family connections. SLNA 1/7428A, "Dodampe Thombo," 30. One Jacob Floorman is referred to as Maria's "neef" in Ibid., 15; SLNA 1/6513, "Galle Landraad minutes" (1780), fols. 47r, 20 May 1780. By May 1780, Jacob had died. "Neef" in Dutch could indicate that he was either a cousin or a nephew. He was probably Johanna Floorman's brother, but he could have also been a brother's son.

Maria and Johanna. Thus, Maria and Johanna were the offspring of two sisters whose father was Arumaperuma Achchige Johan, who, according to the thombo, was also PLH Arumaperuma Achchige Johannes's great-grandfather. This made Johanna Floorman the aunt of the PLH as well. Thus, the stepson of the aunt of a PLH in a thombo group was included as a fellow inheritor in a decision made in the Landraad, the details of which I will discuss here.

Claas's stepmother Johanna died giving birth to the son she had with his father Hendrik, and, according to written reports, the son died a few hours later as well. Claas's argument in his request to the Landraad on 3 June 1780 was brief: "because the lands of Arumaperuma Achchige Johan belonged to his granddaughter Johanna Floorman, and by her death to her son and as a result of his [the infant's] death to his or the supplicant's father, who had also died since then, the supplicant held the stance that this share should be transferred to him."[4] He asked that his share (*aandeel*) be recorded under his name in the new thombo, which was drawn up for the village that same year. The Landraad asked the thombo commissioners to ascertain if the supplicant had a legal right to the said shares of the land and, if so, to insert the same in the new thombo.[5]

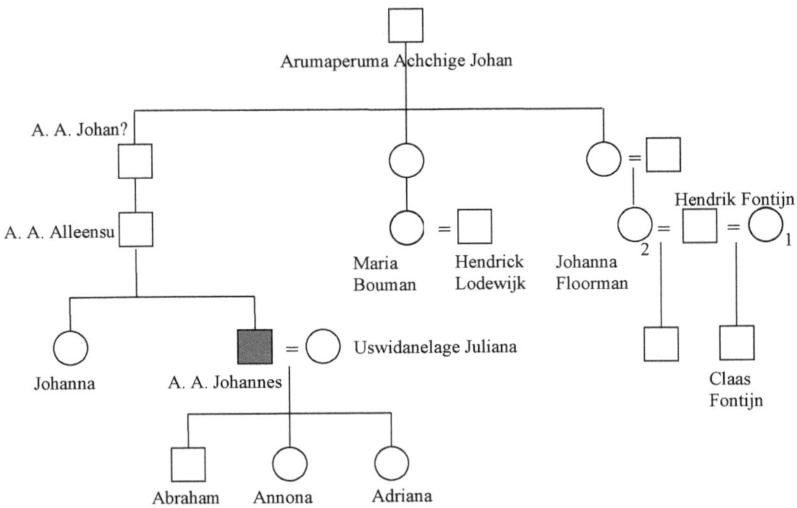

Figure 6.1 Family details of PLH Arumaperuma Achchige Johannes of Dodampe

4 SLNA 1/6526, "Annexes to Galle Landraad minutes" (1780 to 1782), fols. 56r-v, n.d.

5 SLNA 1/6513, "Galle Landraad minutes," fols. 52r, 3 Jun 1780.

Arumaperuma Achchige Johannes's family held shares in the inherited land held in common, a type of ownership that was customary in Dodampe.[6] These shares included one-third of a garden named Tannewierewatte; one-half of a garden named Arumaperuma Achchiwatte; and one paddy-field named Kundeniyekumbura, the sowing capacity of which was one amuna and ten kuruni, or more than two acres of land. The thombo says they were "[a]ll service paravēni of the first-mentioned person's great-grandfather Arumaperuma Achchige Johan, lascarin according to the old thombo and in the possession of this family under payment of tax and otu." They also held in common another paddy-field of fifteen kuruni, Ihale Kalugalle, but this was Ratmahara land. The two gardens they held in common were not large[7] – they had sixty-four coconut and twelve jak trees between them. Within the same landholdings group, exclusive individual rights were also recognised. Arumaperuma Achchige Johan had cultivated one field (approximately a quarter of an acre), which was held by his granddaughter Maria Bouman. Arumaperuma Achchige Johannes and his sister Johanna jointly held another, slightly smaller field, which was company ground that their father had cultivated without consent. Johannes also had rights to a small garden with ten coconut trees, ratmahara (wasteland) that he had cultivated without consent. In 1787, two litigants unsuccessfully challenged some of the family's holdings, claiming an error in the thombo.[8] This proves yet again that the thombo, with its information about holdings and shareholders, was a living document that villagers took seriously. Claas Fontijn was requesting a share of these lands in Dodampe.

The thombo commissioners, Christian Huijbertsz, Albert Christoffel Luijk and Johan Casper German, submitted a report to the Landraad on 12 August 1780. They confirmed the family relationships between the persons concerned and that Johanna Floorman had died some years ago and that her infant had died shortly after. Moreover, they queried whether Claas's request to be a fellow inheritor in place of his father could be considered, because according to reports (which were probably oral), neither father nor son had occupied the lands left behind by Arumaperuma Achchige Johan.[9] So they could not use long-term possession as an added qualification. Claas and his father were not among the "in-residents" of the thombo group or among the "out-residents" who had been previously

[6] SLNA 1/7428A, "Dodampe Thombo," 4.

[7] Dewasiri's definition of a plantation having more than 200 trees serves as a guide here. *The Adaptable Peasant: Agrarian Society in Western Sri Lanka under Dutch Rule, 1740–1800* (Leiden: Brill, 2008), 83.

[8] SLNA 1/6515, "Galle Landraad minutes" (1787 to 1793), fols. 36r-v, 24 Mar 1787; 231r-v, 30 May 1789; 257v, 26 Sept 1789.

[9] SLNA 1/6526, "Annexes to Galle Landraad minutes" fols. 23r, 12 Aug 1780.

acknowledged. The commissioners were clearly uncertain on whether to enter Claas's name in the thombo.

The council's response was to order Claas to show through a deposition that "the infant had lived longer than the mother."[10] This request, as we will see, is crucial for a thorough understanding of the case. The implication inherent in it is that if the infant had not lived longer than his mother, Claas Fontijn could not have inherited her share. We will consider below the possibilities of what may have followed if she had died after the infant. We can imagine that the order was preceded by a discussion in the council; unfortunately, we are not privy to it through the extant minutes and other documents. It is also possible that Fontijn had some knowledge of the law and that such a request would be made. If so, he may have already assembled a group of supporting witnesses. He also undertook the task of providing evidence when he first presented his case to the Landraad.[11]

To fulfil the order, a deposition by five witnesses was made before Landraad Secretary Petrus Jacobus Roosmale Cocq six days later, on 18 August 1780. Claas, an inconspicuous sieve-maker, had moved fast, which further suggests that the deposition had been pre-arranged. He proved himself well able to muster the support of five witnesses, including four women. Johannes Philipsz, a thirty-six-year-old burger, declared that when he heard that Claas's stepmother had died in childbirth, he had gone to the house around seven in the evening, and stayed the night when asked to. He said the just-born son had also died that night or early in the morning. Four women corroborated Johannes's deposition. They were Elizabeth van der Hoeven, the sixty-five-year-old widow of the master sailmaker Eldert Brink; Magdalena Dias, the sixty-one-year-old widow of the soldier Arij Liere; Catharina de Silva, the thirty-six-year-old widow of the cooper Nicolaas Jochem Kok and Francina Joosten, fifty years old, described as an orphan (*weesdochter*). Van der Hoeven, Brink, Kok and Joosten are all names of people who lived in Galle.[12]

[10] SLNA 1/6513, "Galle Landraad minutes" fols. 88r, 12 Aug 1780.

[11] The initial request reads thus: "Claas Fontijn, sieve-maker in the company's service here [in Galle], your honour's humble servant, respectfully shows that the granddaughter of a certain lascarin Aruma Peruma Achchige Joan, called Johanna Floorman, married to the supplicant's father Hendrik Fontijn, has died, leaving a small son by the mentioned father of the supplicant, who also died shortly after the mother, and the supplicant undertakes to prove the same with credible evidence." SLNA 1/6526, "Annexes to Galle Landraad minutes," fols. 56r, n.d.

[12] See the index of names in Lodewijk Wagenaar, *Galle, VOC-vestiging in Ceylon: Beschrijving van een koloniale samenleving aan de vooravond van de Singalese opstand tegen het Nederlandse gezag, 1760* (Amsterdam: De Bataafsche Leeuw, 1994). Most depositions list the residence and religion of the witnesses, but this information is absent in this case. It is most likely that they were either Dutch Protestant or Catholic and lived in the Four Gravets or Galle Fort.

The decision (*appoinctement*) of the Landraad was given on August 26. The council ordered the thombo commissioners to include Claas Fontijn, in place of his late father Hendrik Fontijn, as a fellow inheritor of the lands of Arumaperuma Achchige Johan in the new thombo. The case was heard and decided within about three months in 1780. After the baby's death, the council regarded Hendrik as the next of kin with inheritance claims. On Hendrik's death, the Landraad decided that Claas was the rightful heir to Johanna's share of her maternal paravēni. They provided no judicial reasoning for the judgement.

Thus, on the strength of the fact that his infant stepbrother outlived his mother Johanna, and as the Landraad thereby established that Hendrik had inherited his deceased child's property, Claas was entered as a fellow inheritor of a land holdings group (LHG) in Dodampe. Fellow LHG members do not appear to have challenged his inheritance. Claas had died by 1786, a few years after the judgement in 1780, but his family retained an active interest in the lands. His daughter Cornelia Clara appeared in the Landraad in 1786 and obtained permission in 1787 to sell her late father's share of the lands in Dodampe.[13] Her husband Johannes Westerman was also a sieve-maker like her father, and they were undoubtedly not wealthy burgers.[14] Cornelia and her husband were apparently in a hurry to sell the land, as they were moving to Colombo.[15] She produced a copy of the 1780 Landraad decision and an extract of the thombo made that year. The Landraad granted her permission to sell one-fourth each of two lands held in common with the rest of the family and a similar portion from another land if the council decided a case in progress regarding it in their favour.[16] The Landraad is very clear that Cornelia had inherited through her father the one-fourth share of the garden, Arumaperuma Achchiwatte, the paddy-field, Kundeniyekumbura, and another paddy-field called Ihale Kalugalle. The latter, however, was under dispute at the time. Cornelia did not receive the rights to alienate a share of the garden Taniwierawatte. It is possible that Johanna Floorman and Maria Bouman, the daughters of two sisters, had

[13] SLNA 1/6525, "Galle Landraad draft minutes" (1784 to 1786), fols. 207v, 2 Dec 1786; SLNA 1/6515, "Galle Landraad minutes," fols. 80v, 8 Sept 1787; 130r, 16 Feb 1788.

[14] At the time of their marriage in 1782, Westerman was recorded as having been a carpenter in the militia. New No. 5/2, "Marriage Register, Dutch Reformed Church, Galle" (1774 to 1789), Christian Reformed Church.

[15] This internal migration is confirmed by the baptism of their two children at the Dutch Reformed Church in Wolfendaal in 1789 and 1793. S.A.W. Mottau, "Index to the Baptisms Registered in the Baptism Registers of the Dutch Reformed Church at Wolfendaal" (1709 to 1952), 1: 582, Dutch Reformed Church at Wolvendaal. Accessible on www.familysearch.org.

[16] This may be the case referred to earlier where two litigants claimed an error in the thombo.

already forfeited their rights to that garden.[17] Later, in 1788, Cornelia reappeared in the council with the "widow of Abraham Mamboer"[18] to retrieve the 1780 judgement and thombo extract that she had produced in 1786, and they both signed with marks on the register to indicate that they had obtained them. Perhaps this implies that Mamboer's widow was the new owner, but no revision was made in the thombo itself. If Mamboer's widow became the owner, the share was alienated to a non-agnatic and non-vāsagama person, for the second time since Claas Fontijn. The reference to one-fourth of the lands held in common clearly indicates that Johannes, his sister Johanna, his aunt Maria Bouman and Claas Fontijn were the four shareholders identified in 1780. However, no mention is made of the performance of the *lascarin* service originally rendered by Johanna's grandfather and PLH Arumaperuma Achchige Johannes.

Claas approached the Landraad because he believed that his right to the property was under dispute. No references to succession inter vivos or a testament were made, it was clearly a matter of intestate succession. The PLH in the thombo, whom we can assume was largely responsible for providing information about shareholders, had not included him. The headmen of the village, who were supposedly accountable to the thombo commissioners assigned to register the lands of the village, also did not include Claas. The thombo of Dodampe was being drawn up at the time Claas's case was heard, and we will see below that other cases from the village were also heard around the same time. The headmen of the village were also required to assist in the investigation by the three European commissioners appointed by the Landraad after Claas made his claim.[19] Presumably, the village headmen did assist the European commissioners. Perhaps they were expected to explore Sinhalese jural norms in their investigation but found none. The field investigation drew up an inconclusive report for unknown reasons.

[17] In 1771, Maria Bouman and her "neef" Jacob Floorman – very likely Johanna's brother who had died by 1780, which was the time of the registration – had sold (or leased) two-thirds of Taniwierawatte. They claimed that this was the share that they had received from their mothers – Maria's mother and Jacob's mother, both daughters of Arumaperuma Achchige Johan, who had married Europeans. The PLH Arumaperuma Achchige Johannes and his family had retained the remaining one-third share of Taniwierawatte. Maria and Jacob, with or without Johanna's consent (if she had had a say in the matter), had already alienated their shares of Taniwierawatte. SLNA 1/6513, "Galle Landraad minutes," fols. 47r, 20 May 1780.

[18] Abraham Mamboer was born in Galle, and his first appointment was in 1745 as a sailor. He was made a blacksmith in 1761. S.A.W. Mottau, "Alphabetical Index to the Registers of the Acts of Appointments of Company's Servants of the Dutch East India Company Issued at the Galle Secretariat (1645–1796)" (n.d.), Research Room, Sri Lanka National Archives.

[19] For example, see the advice on the registration of lands in Matara in 1770 and 1776. SLNA 1/5660, "Extracts of resolutions, orders, etc. regarding the Landraad and the thombo compilation" (1740 to 1770), fols. 60r ff.

We are also in the dark about what role the indigenous headmen in the council played in the decision-making process. The councillors were initially reluctant to establish the conditions under which Claas Fontijn would be able to inherit, instead assigning the responsibility for the investigation to the European commissioners. An equal number of European and local members of the council were present on the two most important days of the hearing: the day on which Claas was asked to prove that the infant had lived longer than his mother and that of the final decision. The members present on both days[20] were the president Abraham Samlant, Andreas Everhardus de Lij, Christiaan Huijbertsz, Petrus Jacobus Roosmale Cocq, Johan Casper German, Mahamudaliyār Nicolaas Dias Abeysinghe Amarasekera, Korālē Mudaliyār Adriaan de Silva Jayatilleke Seresinghe, titular Mudaliyār Augustinus Ferdinandus Wiresinghe, Mohandiram Don Philip de Silva Wickremesinghe Dahanayake and Mohandiram Don Matthijs de Silva Abeyewardene Wijeyesekere. They were also present when Claas first came to the council with his petition. Comments on Claas's claim from the local members were not recorded on any of these occasions.

Many interesting questions now arise. In the final decision, did the council apply a principle of Roman-Dutch law or an aspect of inheritance law that was recognised by the Sinhalese? Whose norms were the Landraad most likely to follow in Claas's case? We may never know conclusively, but the case provides an entry point to discuss the differences in the intestate laws of the two systems. Claas's stepmother Johanna Floorman is likely to have had a burger father, in which case the Roman-Dutch law presumably applicable to her, Claas's father and himself was applied. We can also imagine that the council made some attempt to adhere to Sinhalese law, since the matter affected Sinhalese peasants as well. The local members of the Landraad may have pointed this out as a necessity. According to nineteenth-century sources of Kandyan/Sinhalese laws of intestate inheritance, property usually reverts to origin. Hence, if Johanna Floorman had died after her son, her blood relations alone would have inherited her shares; then it becomes necessary to determine at which point she died. As seen below, according to certain Dutch intestate laws as well, her share would have then reverted to her family. This case is of special interest for the Sinhalese-burger alliance that we see, and is a foundation from which to explore differences in intestate laws. This discussion, and I caution that it is only an experimental discussion, is further complicated by the ambiguity of what we know about Sinhalese law at the time, provincial differences in inheritance laws in the Dutch Republic, and the uncertainty about Dutch laws supposedly in operation in Sri Lanka at the time. Further complicating the picture are the resemblances among legal traditions of law in relation to intestate succession.

[20] 12 August 1780 and 26 August 1780.

Local Jural Norms

First, let us consider Claas Fontijn's inheritance issue through established understandings of Sinhalese law. We do not have written sources recording the Sinhalese intestate laws of the area. We are in the dark about the extent to which Sinhalese law was clearly defined, let alone how uniform it was across the island. Inheritance laws in Sabaragamuva have been recorded as being different, but we are unable to identify local inheritance laws that were applicable to the coastal areas of the south. Going by the premise that the principles of Sinhalese intestate succession were fundamentally the same, I studied this case considering the application – or non-application – of the principles described by nineteenth-century British writers. I will, for the most part, use Obeyesekere's account of Sinhalese inheritance law, which he bases on the available sources mentioned in chapter one of this book. The Sinhalese jural norms dealt with here are of the ideal type. Principles aside, we must also remember that the situational character of judging on a case-by-case basis was seen in the local system. No ideal type of inheritance law in Sinhalese law was applicable to every case – we are not dealing with a black box.[21] Yet, most authorities do agree on some fundamental rules.

Two seemingly contradictory principles governed Sinhalese rules of intestate succession.[22] The first was that property should revert to its source; the second was bilateral inheritance, where property was divided equally among both male and female children. The solution to this contradiction was linked to the two types of marriage recognised in Sinhalese law. In *dīga* marriages, the woman left her family home to live virilocally with her husband. In *binna* marriages, a man lives uxorilocally in the wife's family home or settles down with her in her property. The offspring of a binna marriage were entitled to the maternal grandfather's estate, but the offspring of a dīga marriage were not. According to the first principle, which protects the rights of the line (vāsagama), when a wife died intestate, her widower and their offspring were excluded from inheriting her parents' paravēni property if she had married in dīga. Through a dīga marriage she rescinded her rights to a deceased parent's paravēni. Often, she received gifts at the time of marriage; this dowry was considered an alternative to inheritance of ancestral land. If she returned to her family home after her husband's death or divorce, she was entitled to maintenance during her father's lifetime. In the special cases I discuss below, under the concept of familial assistance, she could also claim a part of her parents' property.[23]

[21] See Obeyesekere, *Land Tenure*, 48–49; Yalman, *Under the Bo Tree*, 121.

[22] Obeyesekere, *Land Tenure*, 41.

[23] For a discussion of types of marriages, see Ibid., 43–47; Yalman, *Under the Bo Tree*, 122–30; Ralph Pieris, *Sinhalese Social Organization: The Kandyan Period* (Colombo: Ceylon University Press

In Claas Fontijn's case, if Johanna Floorman legitimately inherited her grandfather's property, under Sinhalese law, does her husband Hendrik Fontijn inherit through her son, who survived her for a few hours after her death? As Johanna's son died without descendants, the ancestral property would revert to the parents, in this case, the surviving Hendrik, and on his death, to Johanna's son's half-brother, Claas.[24] Familial rights, rather than unilinearity that retains paravēni shares in the vāsagama, would then have been recognised. But the crucial question in Sinhalese law would be whether virilocal or uxorilocal marriages had been contracted. Johanna Floorman and her mother were most probably married through registrations in church and were subject to Roman-Dutch law conditions of the community of property and divorce. Moreover, Roman-Dutch law applied to their husbands and offspring. Dīga and binna distinctions are hardly likely to have applied to them. Johanna's husband Hendrik Fontijn was from Amsterdam and had already been married to one Clara Ferdinando, with whom he had had several children, including Claas.[25] The other children, if they were alive and in Sri Lanka during Claas's claim in 1780, were not mentioned in the case or on subsequent occasions, when Claas's daughter appeared before the Landraad.

Under Sinhalese law, Johanna Floorman's inheritance would depend on what type of marriage her mother had contracted. The lands in question were Johanna's maternal grandfather's paravēni. Johanna's mother would have almost automatically withdrawn her claims to the property in Dodampe if she had married in dīga, possibly to a soldier named Pieter Floorman from Bergen-op-Zoom.[26] If she had received a dowry from her father, it would have been a "conversion of her interest

Board, 1956), 203–4. Yalman says people of the lowest economic background did not apply the rules of dīga and binna, and were possibly even unaware of them.

24 As Obeyesekere says: "It is only when a man has no descendants, that the ancestral property reverts to his parents, and on their death to their male children and *binna* married females, that is, the intestate's brothers and sisters." *Land Tenure*, 48.

25 Hendrik's first appointment was in 1724, and he became jailor and provost in 1744 and a free trader in 1747. Mottau, "Alphabetical Index, Galle"; SLNA 1/5690, "Register of acts of appointment of company's officials" (1742 to 1747), fols. 48r, 11 May 1744; f. 114v, 15 Mar 1747.

26 Annona, with likely connections to the Dodampe family, is recorded as the widow of Pieter Floorman, a former soldier. In 1750, she was living in Galle Fort. SLNA 1/7460B, "Hinatigala Thombo," 13. One Pieter Floorman from Bergen-op-Zoom, whose first appointment was in 1715 and who was appointed midshipman in 1728, may have been the same person. Mottau, "Alphabetical Index, Galle"; SLNA 1/5684, "Register of acts of appointment of company's officials" (1728 to 1729), 16v, 4 Sept 1728. In all likelihood, Johanna had also settled down in Galle Fort. We must remember, however, that virilocal residence alone did not make a marriage dīga. It was, as Hayley says, "not dependent on any particular form or ceremony, but on the intention of the parties and their parents." F.A. Hayley, *A Treatise on the Laws and Customs of the Sinhalese* (New Delhi: Navrang, 1923; repr. 1993), 194. See also Obeyesekere, *Land Tenure*, 45.

in the landed property into cash, jewelry and other movable and non-paravēni property."[27] If Johanna's mother had given up her rights to the Dodampe property by marrying in dīga, according to Hayley, she "severs her connection with her father's people" and "[w]hatever claim she has to a share of her property is satisfied by her dowry, and neither she nor her children have henceforth any claim in competition with brothers and sisters who may have not so left the family abode."[28] As I have said before, Claas's claim does not refer to any will or deed of gift, so going by Sinhalese law, this norm of excluding dīga-married daughters should have applied.

However, during the course of the Landraad proceedings, no effort is made to ascertain the type of marriage. If Johanna's father lived uxorilocally, for instance, his children could have claimed the mother's paravēni. Incidentally, I found no references to dīga or binna marriages in late eighteenth-century Landraad records or other Dutch records. Johanna's mother and Floorman marrying in binna, however, would have been highly irregular, for as a burger to whom Roman-Dutch law applied, Floorman was hardly likely to have passively accepted the subordinate position of a binna husband. Restrictions to inheritance through dīga marriages also do not seem to have been applied, for we know that Johanna's mother and Maria's mother both inherited property from their fathers. Maria and Jacob had sold their two-thirds share of their grandfather's garden, Taniwierawatte. Johannes had inherited the remaining one-third. Maria still owned paddy land in Dodampe as well.

The principle of retaining property within the patrilineal line is in contradiction, as I have said before, with the second principle of bilateral inheritance in Sinhalese law. Obeyesekere shows that this was resolved through the recognition of permanent and temporary rights to the paravēni property. Males who carried the patrilineal name had permanent rights, while females whose children had a different patrilineal name had temporary rights. In this way, "while all members of the family are a man's immediate heirs, the rights of some heirs are restricted in a manner that will ensure the continuity of the ancestral line, and the convergence of property among a body of agnatic kinsmen."[29] Daughters held temporary rights while they resided in their family homes, as did widows when they had a life interest in the paravēni of their deceased husband. Divorcées and destitute widows, who had the right to return to their family homes for support, also claimed these rights, but as Sawers says, their children had "no rights of inheritance in the estate of their mother's parents."[30] Thus, assuming this may have happened in Johanna's

[27] Obeyesekere, *Land Tenure*, 43.

[28] Hayley, *A Treatise on the Laws and Customs*, 166.

[29] Obeyesekere, *Land Tenure*, 42.

[30] Simon Sawers, *Digest of Kandyan Law* (Colombo: 1826), 4. Quoted in Ibid.

mother's case, Johanna still had no rights to the estate, as her mother's rights would have been temporary. Yet, her rights were not being disputed. The commissioners did ask, however, how Claas Fontijn and his father could inherit if they had not possessed the land for so long. This indicates that there could have been some opposition at the village level.

Another factor that serves to disinherit the Floormans under local jural norms is that in families dealing with undivided shares (referred to as rights held in common, as I have explained in more detail in chapter five), the in-residents of the village were most likely to hold cultivation rights on the understanding that the out-residents would not interfere.[31] The in-residents in this case were the PLH Arumaperuma Achchige Johannes, his wife and three children, who in all likelihood retained cultivation rights to the lands. If Johannes's grandfather's two sisters had married in dīga, and his sister Johanna had lived virilocally, Johannes would have had full cultivation rights. In such a situation, Claas Fontijn's claims deviated from local norms. Other explanations based on Sinhalese law may well be possible, but no ready solution appears to have been applicable through the ideal type of Sinhalese law.

Roman-Dutch Intestate Law

When faced with ambiguity in the Sinhalese system, the Landraad had leave to proceed with the laws of the Dutch Republic. Was the Roman-Dutch law of inheritance applied to the Sinhalese in Sri Lanka? A. St. V. Jayewardene was one of the first to deal with this question comprehensively in 1901. Without studying legal records, but by focussing on an index of Dutch legislative enactments that the British had translated, he speculated that except where the Sinhalese laws were silent and unsuitable, the Dutch had used them. He says: "The Roman Dutch Law of succession, inheritance, fidei commissum, and contracts does not seem to have been imposed on the Sinhalese. The laws of the Sinhalese seem to have been left intact."[32] However, Walter Pereira says the law of inheritance was Dutch.[33]

An 1817 report written by the judge H. Wright on inheritance in Matara, found among Alexander Johnston's papers, is likely to reflect laws in Galle as well due to

[31] Obeyesekere, *Land Tenure*, 167–68.

[32] Adrian St. Valentine Jayewardene, *The Roman Dutch Law: As it Prevails in Ceylon, How Much of it is Applicable, and in What Localities?* (Colombo: Ceylon Examine Press, 1901), 5.

[33] James Cecil Walter Pereira, *Institutes of the Laws of Ceylon*, vol. 1 (Colombo: H.C. Cottle, Govt. Printer, 1901), 13.

geographical proximity.[34] He gives a concise account of Dutch inheritance laws, which can serve here as an entry into the question of Claas's inheritance from the point of view of Dutch law. We must note, however, that his account may reflect British impositions of Dutch law from 1796 onwards. Wright signed the report as a provincial judge, so he should have had authoritative knowledge of the topic.[35] He says the inheritance laws that he described were Dutch in nature. One paragraph in particular gives a succinct explanation that can be applied to the decision in Claas Fontijn's case:

> As the whole estate is the joint property of both [husband and wife], if either die leaving children half the estate becomes the property of the children equally divided, whether male or female who can do what they like with their respective shares; and upon the death of the other parent the remaining half devolves in like manner upon them. But in case any of the children die in the interim without issue, the share to which the deceased child was entitled in right of father or mother deceased, reverts to the surviving parent as the nearest relation.[36]

This echoes the 1661 charter on intestate law that was enacted in the Netherlands Indies (more on this below). According to Wright's explanation, for the short time that her son was alive, Johanna Floorman's share of her grandfather's property devolved to him. When he died, his share reverted to the nearest relation – the surviving parent, Hendrik Fontijn.

Let us now explore in more detail whether interpretations of Dutch law from The Netherlands apply to this case. The principal succession laws in the Dutch Republic were the Schependoms law of South Holland and the Aasdoms law of North Holland. The river Hollandse Ijssel formed the boundary line between the two regions. There has been some dispute as to which version of Dutch law was applied in Sri Lanka. A judgement in 1822 favoured the North Holland law while another in 1871 expressed the opposite view. Lee was in favour of the law of South

[34] This Wright may be the same "agent of government" that S.B.D. de Silva refers to in *The Political Economy of Underdevelopment* (London: Routledge & Kegan Paul, 1982; repr. 1984), 216. Wright wrote an account of the land tenure in the district and his opinions on inheritance. Wright had sent his original manuscript, which was promptly copied and returned to him. "Alexander Johnston Papers" (1643 to 1817) (MssCol 1578, Manuscripts and Archives Division, The New York Public Library).

[35] Elsewhere in the report, he admits conscientiously to the possibility that he could make mistakes. On whether land tenure or inheritance in the district would facilitate or obstruct the introduction of a quit rent to replace the proportionate land tax, he expresses the hope that allowance will be made for his "inexperience in subjects of this nature." Wright refers to the people's "aversion to any innovations on their customs," doubting whether the transformation would be successful.

[36] "Alexander Johnston Papers (New York)."

Holland; more on this will follow an exploration of whether either of the two systems applies to Claas Fontijn's case.

Under Schependoms law, as stated in the Political Ordinance of Holland of 1580, children have first rights to a deceased parent's property. Johanna then rightly passed on her property to her infant son. However, the guiding principle of Schependoms law is that "the property goes to the side from which it came."[37] If she had died after her son, which as we know the council established was not the case, her parents and, failing them, her collaterals or their descendants, would have inherited the property. Failing them, her grandparents and their issue would have inherited her share, and we know that Maria Bouman, for instance, was a surviving cousin and another cousin's children and grandchildren were also still alive. Johanna thus had other relatives who could inherit by this law. Under Schependoms law, failing even these relatives, the inheritance would be passed on to the issue of the eight great-grandparents.

However, we know that the council had established that Johanna had died before her son, thus making him the sole inheritor. Then, we arrive at the question of how *his* intestate property would be disposed of under South Holland law. Under this law, in the absence of children, both parents could succeed to the property. However, if only one parent was alive, the estate would devolve on the children of the deceased parent, i.e., to the brothers and sisters of the intestate, whether of whole or half blood. Claas was not Johanna's son, so he did not fall into this category. In fact, even as the baby died after Johanna, by Schependoms law, Maria Bouman and other descendants of Arumaperuma Achchige Johan the senior would inherit Johanna's share. The sole surviving parent at the time of the infant's death would not inherit; distant relatives could inherit over him or her.[38] Thus, Schependoms law effectively ruled out Hendrik and Claas, who did not have a claim under it. Thus, an intention to apply Schependoms law could not have been what drove the council to ask Claas to prove that the child had lived longer than the mother.

It could, however, have been the recognition of a surviving parent's rights under Aasdoms law that led the council to ask Claas for proof that the baby had outlived his mother. Under the Aasdoms law of North Holland, as the plakkaat of 18 December 1599 in The Netherlands mentions, descendants, or, in their absence both (living) parents, had first rights. Its guiding principle was that "the nearest blood inherits the property."[39] If one parent survived with no brothers or sisters

[37] "Het goed gaat van waar het gekomen is." Couquerque, *Het Aasdoms- en Schependomsrecht*, 4; Botha, "Intestate Succession," 175; Villiers, "Succession *Unde Vir Et Uxor*," 160.

[38] Lee, "Intestate Succession," 318; Botha, "Intestate Succession," 174.

[39] "Het naaste bloed erft het goed." Couquerque, *Het Aasdoms- en Schependomsrecht*, 6; Villiers, "Succession *Unde Vir Et Uxor*," 160; Botha, "Intestate Succession," 175.

who are the issue of the deceased parent, the surviving parent had exclusive rights. By the law of North Holland, Maria Bouman would have been the next of kin eligible to Johanna's share, if Johanna's infant son had died before her. Because he died after her, Hendrik was the sole inheritor of his share. Thus, by Aasdoms law, it was important to establish when the son had died, and the final decision was compatible with the use of this law. Under Aasdoms law, it was not important where the property came from.

However, the practice in 1822 in various provincial courts in Sri Lanka indicates the use of the law of South Holland.[40] In reality, the provincial successorial differences in the Dutch Republic were not directly important *per se* in the colonies during Dutch rule. Scholars have agreed that it was Schependoms law, as modified by a charter of 1661 that contained a part of the law of North Holland, or, in other words, a mix of Schependoms and Aasdoms law, that was in use in Sri Lanka. In fact, while the charter issued by the States General in 1661 and promulgated in Batavia in the same year stipulated that Schependoms is the law of succession, it only deviates from it in admitting the sole surviving parent as inheritor, much like the Aasdoms law. The Political Ordinance of 1580, which enacted the Schependoms law, does not admit a surviving parent to the inheritance of a deceased child.[41] However, the charter of 1661 states that if the intestate had one surviving parent but no children and no siblings or their offspring (or offspring of deceased half-brothers and half-sisters being related to the intestate on the side of the deceased parent), the surviving parent inherited the whole estate. He or she would be preferred to all collateral relatives.[42] So, if we accept that we must only concern ourselves with the part of Aasdoms law that was in operation in the Dutch Indies, the question of applicability of the entire succession law of North Holland does not arise. Incidentally, it is ironic that in present-day Sri Lankan law, the North Holland law applies.[43] But the charter of 1661, like the Aasdoms law, facilitates an understanding of how Hendrik inherited from his deceased infant son, and how Claas inherited from Hendrik thereafter.

Over the years, there has been some confusion regarding whether it was Schependoms law, Aasdoms law or simply the charter of 1661 that was used in Sri Lanka under Dutch rule. To answer this question, Lee refers to the resolutions

[40] Lee, "Intestate Succession," 320.

[41] Ibid., 318.

[42] Lee, *Introduction to Roman-Dutch Law*, 341–42.

[43] The Matrimonial Rights and Inheritance Ordinance No. 15 of 1876 (and amendments) regulates intestate matters in the island today. It states that where the ordinance is silent, "the rules of the Roman-Dutch law as it prevailed in North Holland are to govern and be followed" (s. 26). An appeal dismissed in 1936 refers to the law of North Holland as the common law of the country, and cites the Aasdoms law. *Vanderstraaten v Eaton*, 37 New Law Reports 294 (1936).

of the Governor in Council in Colombo in the eighteenth century and to nineteenth-century court cases. In a case decided in 1822, Chief Justice Sir Hardinge Giffard, delivering the judgement of the Court of Appeal, hesitantly ruled in favour of North Holland law. Some fifty years later, in 1871, the same court, then presided over by Chief Justice Sir Edward Creasy, ruled in favour of Schependoms law.[44] It is a resolution by the Governor in Council of Colombo on 20 December 1758[45] to promulgate the charter of 1661 that holds within it a contradiction that has added to the confusion. For, a 1599 plakkaat from Holland – an amendment to the Aasdoms law – was annexed with other documents relating to Schependoms law. It is believed that the attachment was a mistake.

One wonders at the state of confusion that prevailed with regard to intestate law prior to the resolution being passed, as it says that Governor Schreuder leafed through the *plakkaten* of the Netherlands and found the charter of 1661. He also extracted other documents that he believed belonged to the charter and should be annexed with it. Among those listed in the resolution were the political ordinance of 1580, an interpretation of the 1580 ordinance in 1594, and the "plakkaat on the subject of intestate succession bearing the same date."[46] The plakkaat that was actually attached was in fact the contradictory plakkaat of 1599 from Holland that contained the new Aasdoms law. It may have been Schreuder who had made the mistake of attaching the wrong plakkaat. Schreuder wished to know if there were other laws that were relevant to the 1661 charter. The Governor in Council members, having confirmed that they did not know of any changes or additions to it – and that the law was certainly given to them by the sovereign (the States General) – decided that they should follow the charter. They failed to see the contradiction in the attached 1599 plakkaat. Yet, it is clear that whatever the attached documents may have been, it was the intention of the Governor in Council to enact the charter. Furthermore, and most importantly for this discussion, the resolution said that it should be observed everywhere on the island ("alomme op dit eijland").

This could mean that the 1758 resolution was applied in the Landraad as well.[47] The resolution's stated intention was to place intestate law on a firm footing. It was said at the 1758 meeting that not only the Raad van Justitie, the Civiele Raad, the

[44] Lee, "Intestate Succession," 319.

[45] NL-HaNA, VOC 2927, "Resolutions of the Governor in Council" (1758), 20 Dec 1758; SLNA 1/127, "Governor in Council minutes" (1758), 20 Dec 1758. Translated into English in, National Archives at Kew, CO 416/13 F6 pp. 82-90 and published in English in J.W. Vanderstraaten, *The Decisions of the Supreme Court of Ceylon Sitting in Appeal from 1869 to 1871* (Colombo), app. i-xxi.

[46] NL-HaNA, VOC 2927, "Resolutions," 20 Dec 1758; SLNA 1/127, "Council Minutes," 20 Dec 1758.

[47] Incidentally, the volumes of extracts of orders belonging to the Galle Landraad archives do not include references to this resolution. SLNA 1/5658, "Extracts of resolutions, orders, etc. regarding the Landraad and the thombo compilation" (1740 to 1745); SLNA 1/5659, "Extracts of resolutions,

Orphanage and procurators, but also the provinces in Sri Lanka should receive a copy of the resolution and its annexes. The Landraad was not mentioned. However, if the procurators were notified, could that mean that it was the law that they knew and passed on to the public? Justinus Rutgard Visser, a sworn procureur, drew up Claas's request and we can assume that Visser knew of the law by 1780. Did Claas and Visser know before they made their initial petition that the council would exclude the spouse, as in Johanna's case, if she had died after her son? Were they aware of the clear line of succession from his stepbrother to his father and then to him, as his initial request indicates? Visser's name appears in many council minutes and documents of the Galle Landraad; he also held power of attorney in some cases. Clearly, it was not immediately obvious to the council that the charter should be applied. If the Landraad did adopt the charter in this case, it is possible that it was a case of lawmaking by the procurator that the councillors subsequently adopted.

In other former Dutch colonies as well, the charter was held as law. A South African Chief Justice ruled fully in favour of the 1661 charter in 1914: "The Charter granted by the States-General to the Dutch East India Company, on the 10th January 1661, regulates the law of succession *ab intestato* in this Colony. That Charter adopted as the law of succession the provision of the Political Ordinance of 1580, as interpreted by an edict of the States bearing the date 13th May 1594, with one modification."[48] He believed, therefore, that it was a mistake to refer to both North Holland and South Holland law as the law of the South African colony, and this is likely to be applicable to Sri Lanka as well. In fact, it is possible that the 1661 charter was born of a necessity to accommodate several single parents facing the deaths of their children in the colonies.

The charter appears to have dropped out of use in Sri Lanka in the course of the nineteenth century, when references to the laws of North and South Holland were made. The question is of purely academic interest today as the law of the country is now clearly defined. But it is important to remember that questions regarding the substance of law are inherently questions about law and society, and in this particular case from Sri Lanka, colonial law. Whether or not Roman-Dutch law was used to adjudicate matters relating to the locals is a question about whether a colonial state endeavoured to impose foreign laws or incorporated customary laws. A judgement itself, however, was not the end of the matter. Arumaperuma Achchige Johannes, the first-mentioned person and other members in the thombo group do not appear to have protested Claas's inheritance through an intestate case. Were they aware of it? Maria Bouman, at least, was not shy of the Landraad, having appeared before it

orders, etc. regarding the Landraad and the thombo compilation" (1743 to 1744); SLNA 1/5660, "Galle Landraad, extracts of resolutions."

[48] Botha, "Intestate Succession."

in 1780.[49] Did she accept Claas as a fellow inheritor? Her father, however, was most probably European, since she had the name Bouman, and she was married to one Hendrick Lodewijk. Did she choose not to object to Claas's inheritance for reasons of familial affinity? Was there a general acceptance that the Roman-Dutch law should apply to the case, because it involved the rights of a burger? Did Claas Fontijn and his family obtain their share of the produce from the lands held in common after so many years of not appearing on the land? In what manner did they do this? How did the family resident in the village respond to him using a legal provision to obtain a share that the rest of the family had not initially recognised? They appeared to have allowed Maria Bouman, however, to own a ratmahara paddy land with five kuruni in Dodampe, which her grandfather (the great-grandfather of the PLH) had cultivated without consent from the company. It is likely that these and other questions will remain unanswered. We only know that the Landraad upheld his inheritance because his daughter sold his share some years later.

Other second-hand accounts of inheritance law in colonial Sri Lanka contradict each other at times, but they mostly agree that the Dutch law of inheritance was in use. François Valentijn, who produced another early account of Sri Lanka, said: "The immovable goods are inherited by the children but not just the oldest son alone, or, if this happens, he must maintain the mother and the children."[50] Perhaps Valentijn recognised the bilateral nature of Sinhalese inheritance while also referring to the permanent rights of male heirs. When he wrote his account in the 1720s, based on company papers, historical works and travel accounts, the use of Dutch inheritance laws was probably not discussed (the charter was enacted in 1758). Much later, in 1784, Sluijsken referred to the dowry given to daughters before the death of her parents, and that daughters inherited in equal measures to sons, but did not inherit service paravēni.[51] In 1803, Joseph Greenhill said briefly that the law of inheritance was certainly Dutch: "The Dutch have granted numerous freeholds to the inhabitants especially those of the... conquered provinces. These being divided and subdivided according to the Dutch laws of inheritance, instead of industry a habit of constant litigation has been produced."[52] The imposition of

[49] SLNA 1/6513, "Galle Landraad minutes," fols. 47r, 20 May 1780.

[50] Francois Valentijn, *Francois Valentijn's Description of Ceylon*, trans. and ed. Sinnappah Arasaratnam, vol. 149, Hakluyt Society 2 (London: Hakluyt Society, 1978), 169.

[51] Pieter Sluijsken, "Eene beschryving van de landdienst op Ceylon: Zo uyt ondervinding als uyt oude papieren tezaemen gebragt (A Description of the Land Services of Ceylon: Compiled from both investigations and old papers)" (Colombo, 1784), vol. 1: 158-159, RP-31/32 Colonial Collection (KIT), Leiden University.

[52] Joseph Greenhill, "On Ceylon" (British Library, 1803), fols. 12r, Add MS 26568, ADVERSARIA Indica. I thank Manjusha Kuruppath for transcribing Greenhill's account at the British Library.

bilateral inheritance without the system of temporary rights that the Sinhalese had devised to cope with the pressure on the land would have led to such a situation.

Towards Bilateral Inheritance

Notwithstanding the lack of a well-defined answer to the question of intestate law in Claas Fontijn's case, the final decision shows a clear recognition of bilateral rules of inheritance, a feature of Roman-Dutch law that gradually seeped into local society.[53] Except in principle, the local system was not bilateral. Bilateral inheritance was not sustainable in the long run, as it led to the fragmentation of shares. The British judge Wright criticised the modes of inheritance that he certainly did not regard favourably as a result of their adverse effects on agriculture. He gave an extreme example of fifty heirs who held a small field that yielded about two handfuls of paddy for each shareholder:

> as soon as a man dies leaving 5 or 6 children they take possession of half his estate – this is often too small to make it worth their while entering into a division of it and the customary practice in such cases is for each to possess the whole alternately for a year thereby feeling no interest in extending the limits of what he is only to possess once in 5 or 6 years and if he did he would be obliged to divide the produce of the spot so enlarged upon or added to the former extent if it formed part of the heritable property among all the other heirs. I confess that I am not aware of a remedy for this knowing them to be scrupulously tenacious of the smallest piece of ground to which they have any claims – a stronger instance of this perhaps cannot be given than one I know of in the Wellebaddepattoe of this district where there is a small field in the possession of about 50 inheritors, each of whom at the harvest receives for his share about two hands full of paddy, and this he would rather take, than dispose of his right in that field. But it is only cultivated by one or two of them – who therefore receive half as the planter's share and divides the other half with the 48 other proprietors. Hence arise innumerable disputes.[54]

[53] Obeyesekere shows how bilateral inheritance on intestate succession became an empirical reality in Mädagama in the early twentieth century. Obeyesekere, *Land Tenure*, 135. I thank the anonymous reviewer of this book who drew my attention to how bilateral inheritance is not a common expression in legal scholarship in relation to succession by descendants in Europe. However, the term has been used in this sense by anthropologists in the Sri Lankan context to refer to equal sharing of property between sons and daughters.

[54] "Alexander Johnston Papers (New York)."

Wright adds that "[p]eople of a higher class generally make a distinct division of any property they inherit."[55] We saw how in the local normative order, daughters did not usually inherit land "as is customary" but received a dowry.[56] However, in intestate succession, the Landraad appeared to almost consistently impose the law of bilateral inheritance following the practice of Roman-Dutch law.

Gamage Livina, a litigant who had returned to her father's village on the death of her husband, insisted on bilateral inheritance.[57] The dispute between Gamage Livina and her cousin Gamage Dinees was about the ownership of a ratmahara garden named Dollemegodawatte. As Livina and Dinees, inhabitants of Dodampe and Pedinnoruwa respectively, belonged to a holdings group consisting of ninety persons in Dodampe, the family tree drawn in Figure 6.2 includes only those whom the Landraad records mention in connection with the case. Livina, the widow of a kangān with two sons and three daughters, came to the council in 1780 to challenge the inclusion of what she claimed was her share of the garden within the land assigned to Gamage Dinees in the new thombo. She recognised that the company's share was one-third (because it was ratmahara planted without consent) but that another one third should go to her as her father, together with Dinees's father, had planted it. However, she claimed that Gamage Dinees had had two-thirds of the garden registered under his name alone. Dinees either engaged in "genealogical amnesia"[58] by conveniently leaving Livina out of the thombo or genuinely believed that through her marriage, which took her to Akmeemana, she had rescinded her rights to the land. But Livina's witnesses claimed that on being widowed eight years ago, she had returned to her father's village. Destitute widows were permitted to return to their villages but we do not know the circumstances of Livina's return.

Gamage Dinees said the garden had been listed under his name after an investigation conducted by the thombo commissioners. He clearly claimed the authority of the Landraad in his favour. Livina said their forebears had planted the garden together, and the council asked her to prove this.[59] Both sides called witnesses, and the Landraad ordered two of its members to carry out an investigation.[60] Before Livina's deposition was made, Gamage Dinees (together with his brothers Bastiaan, Matthijs and Johan) produced six witnesses on his behalf. Some of Dinees's brothers thus asserted their rights as well, although his sister Annika, who was married and living in Pedinnoruwa, and brother Adriaan, who also lived in Pedinnoruwa, were

[55] "Alexander Johnston Papers (New York)".

[56] Pieris, *Sinhalese Social Organization*, 200–201.

[57] SLNA 1/6513, "Galle Landraad minutes," fols. 92r, 26 Aug 1780.

[58] Obeyesekere, *Land Tenure*, 163.

[59] SLNA 1/6513, "Galle Landraad minutes," fols. 102r, 9 Sept 1780.

[60] Ibid., fols. 132v, 4 Nov 1780.

not named in the deposition. They may have renounced their cultivation rights. The first witness said that the parents of the four brothers had planted and owned the garden, and that after their death, their children had cultivated the garden further. He added that it was the father of their mother, Gamage Setuhamie, who had planted and owned it at first, and after his death, she had owned it. The second witness said that Gamage Dinees's father, Dodampe Gamage Simon, had planted and owned the garden, and that after his death, his children had owned it. He said he didn't know of anyone else having planted any trees in the garden. The third and fourth witnesses agreed with him. The fifth and sixth witnesses agreed with the second witness, adding that the sons had continued to cultivate the garden after their father's death.[61]

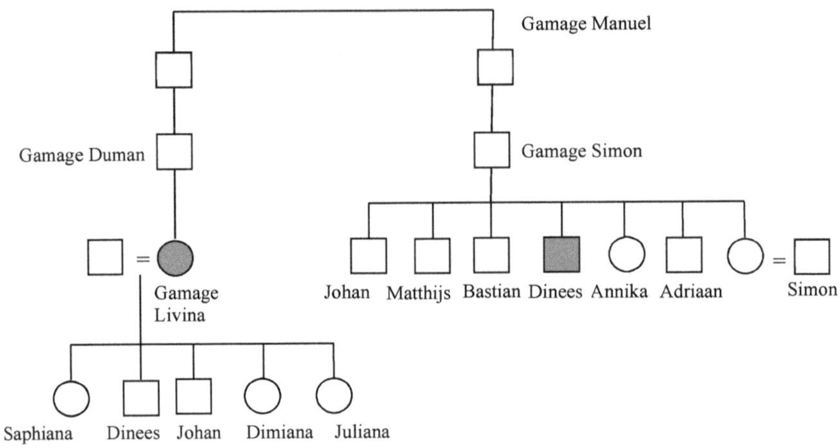

Figure 6.2 Family details of Gamage Livina and Gamage Dinees of Dodampe

Three witnesses produced a deposition on behalf of Gamage Livina. The first witness, twenty-five-year-old Wijetunga Arachchige Don Salomon de Silva, vidāne of Totagamuva and inhabitant of Wewelle, said that two years previously, during the overseer Diederick Thomas Fretz's term of office, the inhabitants of the village Dodampe had requested that their ratmahara gardens be parcelled out because the salāgamas extracted tax from them in excess. He said that he, together with two *nanayakkārayo*,[62] three kangāns of the Cinnamon Department and the mayorāls of the village, were appointed to the task, and that they had divided all the ratmahara lands, including the garden planted by Livina's father Gamage Duman

[61] SLNA 1/6494, "Galle Landraad depositions" (1778 to 1781), fols. 84r, 20 Sept 1780.

[62] Permanent native commissioners who inspected gardens and fields.

and Dinees's father Gamage Simon. It had been divided into three parts: one for Livina, one for Gamage Simon's heirs, and the other for the salāgamas. The second witness, seventy-one-year-old Mohottie Philippu, nanayakkāraya and inhabitant of Mipe, said that Livina's father Duman and his cousin Simon had planted the ratmahara garden, and since Duman and Livina had settled in Hinatigala, the garden had been occupied by Simon, who had paid rent money (*huur penningen*) for it. Furthermore, he said that Livina had since been living in Dodampe for eight years, while retaining half of the garden. The third witness, sixty-two-year-old Runage Andriku, *wildschutter* (huntsman) and inhabitant of Yakgaha, said that Livina's father Duman and his cousin Simon had planted the garden and owned it for forty years. He said that Livina had married a kangān and lived in Akmeemana, and that after her husband's death, she had lived in the garden under dispute in Dodampe for eight years, owning half of it.[63]

Haartel and Huijbertsz handed in their report on 6 January 1781, and the case documents were circulated among the members of the Landraad. The Landraad concluded on 27 January 1781 that it appeared from the circulated papers that Gamage Duman, Livina's father, and Gamage Simon, Dinees's father, had both planted the garden, and that therefore Livina was entitled to her half share of the trees.[64] According to the thombo, the garden had fifty-two coconut trees and nine jak trees.[65] Duman and Simon were cousins, and their children inherited in equal shares. Livina became an in-resident again even though her marriage may be perceived as dīga due to her change of residence, but she was allowed to return with her family to claim her father's property after her husband's death. While this case displays the application of bilateral inheritance, it is also an example of the VOC practice of dealing with the wasteland claimed by the people and granting the company's share to caste groups for their services.

Concept of Familial Assistance

In general, in cases similar to Livina's, it was considered necessary to prove that the child rendered assistance to the parents on returning to the village in order to claim a part of the property held by the parents. The Landraad recognised the concept of familial assistance, which was important in Sinhalese law. Under this concept, Obeyesekere says, "any person who had rendered assistance to an intestate was

[63] SLNA 1/6494, "Galle Landraad depositions" fols. 85r, 5 Oct 1780. It is possible that the witnesses meant the "half" of what was left after the company's share of one-third was extracted from it.

[64] SLNA 1/6514, "Galle Landraad minutes" (1781), fols. 7r, 6 Jan 1781; 20v, 27 Jan 1781.

[65] SLNA 1/7428A, "Dodampe Thombo," 32.

'entitled' morally to a share of the intestate's estate, even if the person so entitled was a non-agnate or outsider."[66] He further says that in the Sinhalese system, such situations were judged on a case-by-case basis. A dīga married daughter who returned to her family home to render assistance to a parent would be entitled to a share of paravēni property if the parent wished it. For such a bequest, rendering assistance was essential. Land could also leave the agnatic source in this way to a person outside of the family, and "such bequest will be perfectly valid, although the donor had not reserved any portion of his lands for his children and did not expressly disinherit them – it being premised that the donor's children were adults, and had wilfully neglected their duty to their said parent."[67]

Inheritance laws (*inter vivos*) recognised assistance as a reason as "perfectly valid": gift olas quoting it were not uncommon.[68] In one issue, heard in 1779, two men appeared in the Landraad and asked for their names and those of their children to be registered in the thombo against property gifted to them by one Kodawege Michiel. Other parties technically eligible to shares also appeared in the council that day and declared that they had nothing against the request of the two heirs. But one Kodawege Annika claimed a share because her son had provided "much assistance" to the said uncle Michiel. The council ruled that the gift ola that the two men produced was not written by a qualified person, but since the other family members had no objection they approved shares for the two men after separating a share for Annika.[69] Recognition of Annika's claim, although unsupported by an accepted deed of gift, shows the Landraad's recognition of familial assistance. This is an indication of the situational character of judgements, as was the practice in indigenous courts. The case also demonstrates the strong family ties that existed in eighteenth-century Sri Lanka.

Other cases of familial assistance proved harder to resolve. In 1780, family members challenged a mother's gift to one of her daughters, made on the grounds of assistance rendered to her in her old age. Kosmulage Lisa de Silva claimed that her mother had favoured her with a gift of a garden excluding her siblings. The disinherited sisters objected on the grounds that the garden belonged to their father, and therefore they should also have a share. The council asked the thombo commissioners to examine the thombo and report if the mother could gift the land.[70]

[66] Obeyesekere, *Land Tenure*, 49.

[67] John Armour, *Armour's Grammar of the Kandyan Law*, ed. Joseph Martinus Perera (Colombo: Examiner Press, 1861), 106. See also Obeyesekere, *Land Tenure*, 49–51.

[68] See SLNA 1/5969, "Galle Translations of Olas" (1780 to 1784), fols. 25r, 2 Jun 1780; f. 58r, 20 Jan 1781; 65r, 28 Apr 1781.

[69] SLNA 1/6512, "Galle Landraad minutes" (1779), fols. 92v, 27 Nov 1779; SLNA 1/6514, "Galle Landraad minutes," fols. 55r, 5 May 1781.

[70] SLNA 1/6513, "Galle Landraad minutes," fols. 59v, 24 Jun 1780.

They reported that the garden called Kobeiwatte in Hinatigala was held in common by the whole family, and that she owned one-seventh of it, which she had gifted to Lisa. Catharina (the eldest of Lisa's sisters), two daughters of her second sister Christina and the third sister Juliana's husband made submissions to the commissioners opposing the gift. Lisa may have been the youngest of all her siblings. They claimed that they had been ignorant of the gift, and because the garden had been planted by their father and grandfather, whose paravēni it was, they requested that their shares be recognised. A third daughter of Christina, however, backed her aunt Lisa, saying that Lisa alone had supported her grandmother and borne many costs till her death. Lisa claimed she could produce witnesses to that fact, and that she had possessed the garden freely thus far.[71] The gift deed, referred to as a "gift and donation inter vivos," was dated ten years before the matter was taken up by the council and Lisa's husband had obtained an extract of the thombo entry a few weeks prior to the hearing.[72] The council asked Lisa to prove that she had supported her mother and that she alone had owned that part of the garden over the years without encumbrances.[73] It had been ten years since the gift ola was drafted in 1770, so the Landraad was possibly also seeking to establish the rule of prescription.

Lisa's husband was a vidāne of Hinatigala, which was also the location of the garden, and all her witnesses were men from the same village – two mayorāls, a grain measurer and a lascarin. The first witness said that Lisa had supported her mother financially for twenty years since her father's death without the presence or help of the other children. Nine months before her death, he added, Lisa's mother had called for him and declared that she had not received any assistance from any children apart from Lisa. Therefore, he said, she had gifted the thirty coconut trees and fifteen jak trees that her husband had planted in Kobeiwatte to Lisa, and because he had not been present on that occasion, she had requested him to bear testimony to it and added that the other lands would be owned equally by all her children together. He said that after her mother died, Lisa had had her buried and borne the cost, without any contribution from or the presence of the other children. The second and third witnesses confirmed the first witness's account. The fourth witness, a lascarin, also claimed that Lisa had looked after her mother for twenty years and then buried her upon her death, bearing the cost alone. He said he had dug the grave, for which Lisa had paid him, and that none of the other children had been present or contributed in any way.[74] The council recognised the gift deed and instructed the thombo commissioners to register one-seventh of Kobeiwatte under Lisa's name in the

[71] SLNA 1/6526, "Annexes to Galle Landraad minutes," fols. 109r, 4 Nov 1780.

[72] Ibid., fols. 158r–159r, Thombo extract dated 23 Feb 1770; 160r, Gift ola, 28 Apr 1770.

[73] SLNA 1/6513, "Galle Landraad minutes," fols. 137r, 4 Nov 1780.

[74] SLNA 1/6494, "Galle Landraad depositions" fols. 97r-v, 22 Mar 1781.

thombo.[75] Many believe that rendering assistance to elders is ingrained in Sri Lankan culture, and Lisa's claim was strengthened by her niece's support.[76] It is unlikely that challenges to such bequests are unique to the colonial situation, although the trend towards bilateral inheritance would have encouraged the plaintiffs.

Yet another disagreement connected to the concept of assistance occurred around the same time. Kallu Appu cited the concept of assistance in the Landraad with regard to his mother's bequest to his adopted brother.[77] Kallu Appu's mother, the widow of Peditantrige Ediri Appu, had bequeathed her husband's paravēni property through a Sinhala gift ola dated 11 July 1765. She transferred one-third to her adopted son Omeri and two-thirds to her two biological sons. Kallu Appu (who spoke at the Landraad for his mother's other biological son as well) and Omeri wanted the ola approved. Kallu Appu said he had no objection to the gift, but that their mother had made the bequest on the understanding that she would enjoy "some assistance" from the adopted Omeri. Omeri said that he had mortgaged his section for three sacks of paddy and given the same to their mother. Kallu Appu refuted this, claiming that Omeri had only given 7 *medieden*[78] to his mother. The council rejected Kallu Appu's claims as baseless and fully approved the gift ola because he himself said that he had nothing against it. It is not clear what the two biological sons wished to achieve by bringing up the issue of promised assistance. As far as the record goes, they were not explicitly asking for the adopted brother to be disinherited. In the local system, that was possibly something that only the donor could do if she felt neglected by the donee. Perhaps the Landraad recognised this. John Armour states that if the donee neglected the donor, a deed of gift became null and void if the donor resumed possession of the land and refused further assistance from the said donee, or if the donor voluntarily left the donee's premises and took up abode elsewhere.[79] However, this Landraad case did not refer to these conditions.

Litigants were clearly willing to invoke the concept of familial assistance in the Landraad. It was a space within which they could present the idea, while its strictures were determined by a mixed body of councillors. Three local members

[75] SLNA 1/6514, "Galle Landraad minutes," fols. 86r, 7 Jul 1781. The thombo entry in question could not be found.

[76] It is considered unthinkable to leave the elderly to fend for themselves in modern-day Sri Lanka. Carla Risseeuw, "Urban Middle-Class Elderly in Sri Lanka and the Netherlands: Everyday Sociality and Ways of Keeping Company," in Brigitte Röder, Willemijn de Jong, and Kurt W. Alt (eds), *Alter(n) anders denken: Kulturelle und biologische Perspektiven* (Cologne: Bohlau Verlag, 2012).

[77] SLNA 1/6511, "Galle Landraad minutes" (1778), fols. 4r, 23 May 1778.

[78] A *medied* was a measure of weight. Four medieden were equal to one *kuruni*. S.A.W. Mottau, "Glossary of Terms Used in Official Correspondence of the Government of Sri Lanka Compiled from Records at the National Archives," *The Sri Lanka National Archives* 3 (1985 to 1986): 157.

[79] Armour, *Armour's Grammar*, 92.

and five European members were present in the Kodawege family case. Local and European members were present in equal numbers on the day Kosmulage Lisa de Silva was asked to prove that she had supported her ailing mother. When her witness testimony was produced and the gift from her mother was approved, there were three local members and eight European members present. Nicolaas Dias Abeysinghe Amarasekera, Augustinus Ferdinandus Wiresinghe, Don Johan de Silva Wanigasekere and Don Philip de Silva Wickremesinghe Dahanayake were present at the meeting that Kallu Appu and Omeri attended, and they equalled the number of European members present. Evidently, European councillors did not object to the recognition of familial assistance.

The above analysis focuses on how the Landraad dealt with the technical aspects of inheritance through the navigation of the pluralities of law in the local context. For a fuller analysis, we would need to observe the eighteenth-century family in southern Sri Lanka, as many issues surrounding inheritance arose as a result of changes in family law. Marriage and the concept of illegitimacy went through significant changes during this period.

Marriage, Divorce and the Rights of Widows

Monogamous, legitimate marriage was emphasised under Dutch rule in eighteenth-century Sri Lanka, but not fully achieved. Marriage registration laws intended to transform local practices were conspicuously present.[80] Dutch efforts to register marriages saw a baffling confusion of mutual agreement, putting up the banns and solemnisation in church, as I go on to describe, through plakkaten, documents of the Landraad, and the minutes of the Scholarchale Vergadering. These sources are replete with stories of adultery, promiscuity and broken promises that are the stuff of scandal.[81]

Within the space of the Scholarchale Vergadering, matters of religious and secular education, registration and, as it appears, morality, were regulated. The board was required to perform some ecclesiastical tasks aside from those carried out by clergymen. It dealt with the predominantly Sinhalese population of the south, among whom a large number were nominal converts to Dutch Protestanism.[82] Set

[80] This tension between rules and practice was also present in the eighteenth-century in The Netherlands. Manon van der Heijden, *Huwelijk in Holland: Stedelijke rechtspraak en kerkelijke tucht, 1550–1700* (Amsterdam: Bert Bakker, 1998), 261–64.

[81] For a more extensive article by me on this topic using the records of the Scholarchale Vergadering, see Nadeera Rupesinghe, "Navigating Pluralities Reluctantly: The Marriage Contract in Dutch Galle," *Itinerario* 42, no. 2 (August 2018): 220–37.

[82] See chapter four for more details of the religious composition of Galle society.

up in 1663, the board consisted of a *predikant* (ordained pastor), a senior official of the Galle Commandment as president and other members of the Galle Political Council, who were referred to as *scholarchen*.[83] It sought the approval of the commander of Galle for its resolutions. Its tasks included inspecting schools, compiling the school thombos and recommending the appointment of schoolmasters at the parish level.[84] Marriage and divorce matters among local Christians also came under the purview of the Scholarchale Vergadering.

Outside the forts, Protestant churches, many of which also functioned as schools, were set up in the former Catholic churches of the Portuguese. Ministers would visit villages regularly to conduct baptisms and solemnise marriages. Native schoolmasters taught the principles of the reformed religion and reading and writing. They also registered births, marriages and deaths among the peasants.[85] Such registrations were important in connection with inheritance disputes.

The Dutch practice of registering marriages was alien to Sri Lankans. However, the locals are likely to have been somewhat familiar with demands to solemnise marriages in church, as Portuguese rule would have required this of Catholic converts as well. Portuguese Captain Ribeiro went so far as to say in 1685 that Sinhalese marriages were a "ridiculous matter."[86] Knox reported on what he regarded as private "whoredom" surpassing public prostitution.[87] In later times, one British judge saw marriage relations among the locals as "established with a wink and cancelled with a kick."[88] Despite this laxity in sexual relations, family attachments were strong, as Davy noted in the early nineteenth century.[89] Locals

83 In the records from 1770 to 1780, Albertus Homoet, the second in command of the Galle Commandment, was also the president of the Scholarchale Vergadering. He was followed by Mattheus van der Spar, his successor as second in command. Mottau writes that the number of members fluctuated, as is evident from Galle. S.A.W. Mottau, "Education under the Dutch," in *Education in Ceylon (From the Sixth Century BC to the Present Day): A Centenary Volume*, vol. 1 (Colombo: Ministry of Education and Cultural Affairs, 1969), 305, n8.

84 For example, see the Galle Scholarchale Vergadering documents. Also L. Hovy, *Ceylonees plakkaatboek: Plakkaten en andere wetten uitgevaardigd door het Nederlands bestuur op Ceylon, 1638–1796* (Hilversum: Verloren, 1991), vol. 1; nr. 74, Instructions for the scholarchen who are in charge of the schools in the districts of Colombo, Jaffna and Galle, 25 Dec 1663.

85 In the towns and areas to which they could travel, church officials did the registrations.

86 Joao Ribeiro, *The Historic Tragedy of the Island of Ceilao*, trans. P.E. Pieris (Colombo: The Ceylon Daily News, 1948), 50.

87 Robert Knox, *An Historical Relation of Ceylon* (Dehiwala: Tisara Prakasakayo, 1681; repr. 1966), 173–75.

88 T. Berwick, *Judicial Report (Administration Reports)* (Kandy: Ceylon Government, 1870), 51, quoted in Pieris, *Sinhalese Social Organization*, 195.

89 John Davy, *An Account of the Interior of Ceylon, and of its Inhabitants* (London: Longman, 1821), 216.

had no difficulty regarding cohabitation as marriage because it was "recognised by everyone as such on the village level."[90] Men and women could find their own partners, or their parents could give them away in marriage. Higher ranks in society had elaborate celebrations that were largely absent among peasants. Ralph Pieris writes that rituals were followed only to "symbolize the conclusion of a relatively permanent union, contracted with a view to raising a family."[91] Simple cohabitation by a man and woman of the same rank also automatically legitimised the marriage and children. Pieris points out that there was a "remarkable vagueness as to the essentials of a legal marriage, and the line which distinguished marriage from concubinage was faint indeed."[92] But mutual agreement to cohabit was no longer considered legally sufficient under colonial rule.

The earliest available Dutch plakkaat relating to marriages among native Christians in Galle dates from 1647.[93] It said that either from ignorance of the law, or because they did not consider each other true couples, many alliances were not registered during recent wars. Considered whoredom or concubinage, they were given two months within which to register their marriages, failing which they faced a fine. In those early years, villagers in the countryside could give notice of their marriages to their vidāne and mayorāl, who were required to make public proclamations in the village on three successive Sundays. This was the putting up of the banns (*ondertrouwen*), which was supported by an ola to that effect, after which the marriage had to be solemnised in the church in town or when church officials visited three or four times a year. If you were marrying outside of your village, each side had to produce at least two closely related or associated witnesses and the mayorāl of the village where the banns were put up. Later, schoolmasters took over such matrimonial duties in the countryside.[94] In 1780, couples in the

[90] Obeyesekere, *Land Tenure*, 140.

[91] Still, even after performing various rituals or after the first fortnight of cohabitation, the marriage could be annulled. Pieris, *Sinhalese Social Organization*, 200–201.

[92] Ibid., 197.

[93] Hovy, *Plakkaatboek*, vol. 1; nr. 15, Ordinance on the legalisation of illegal marriages between native Christians and on the registration and ending of marriages; punishments against concubinage, separation and adultery, 1 Aug 1647. For other relevant ordinances, see Ibid., vol. 1; nr. 195 Regulations on the church and school obligations of native Christians, 15 May 1699; 543 Plakkaat regulating the formalities for proclaiming the banns and the marriage solemnisation... 24 Dec 1776; 684, Concept-mandate of the Scholarchale Vergadering in Galle... 19 May 1795.

[94] A plakkaat stipulates this in 1776, but the schoolmaster's role is mentioned in the Galle Scholarchale Vergadering minutes of an earlier time and in seventeenth-century plakkaten. Hovy, *Plakkaatboek*, vol. 2; nr. 543, 24 Dec 1776; SLNA 1/6221, "Scholarchale Vergadering minutes" (1770 to 1773), fols. 31r–33r, 5 Sept 1770; 35v, 3 Oct 1770. See also Hovy, *Plakkaatboek*, vol. 1; nr. 187, Plakkaat binding the native Christians in the southwest of Ceylon to register their pledges of dowries... 13 Jun 1692.

Galle Commandment who could afford it had to pay six stivers for the banns and marriage.[95] By the 1790s, it was recognised that no marriage could take place among native Christians without the approval of the schoolmasters. They maintained separate books to record marriage notices.[96] Although not always achieved in practice, all headmen and inhabitants, "excluding no one," had to attend the Sunday service and the public proclamations of marriage notices that followed it.[97] If a betrothal was not challenged, the marriage could be solemnised the first time a predikant or proponent came to the district. If they wished to have the marriage confirmed immediately, they could go to the nearest company town with attested proof that the banns had been read out without obstacles.[98] Except under special circumstances, it is likely that couples in Galle rarely married outside the church, although in Holland couples could marry before municipal authorities.[99] Baptism, therefore, was crucial, and meant greater control of marriage by the Dutch Reformed Church. Objections could be brought up after notice of marriage or in church. At one solemnisation in church, a sibling of the bridegroom claimed that the bridegroom was an illegitimate child and had not been baptised.[100]

Often, locals did not consider the second step of solemnising the marriage necessary, but failure to do so was a punishable offence.[101] For many couples, the banns meant they could start living together. This is not surprising due to the importance of public recognition in both, the mutual agreement of the local practice and the reading of the banns in the Dutch practice. A dispute heard in the Scholarchale Vergadering in 1790 suggests that couples were likely to have been dressed well when putting up the banns. A female witness said that the woman had dressed up in the jewels and clothes of a bride in her (the witness's) house. The couple had returned to her house after putting up the banns and she had welcomed them in the Sinhalese way and sprinkled them with rose water and flowers.[102] It is likely that as far as the couple was concerned, they were thereby married to all intents

[95] SLNA 1/6224, "Scholarchale Vergadering minutes" (1779 to 1783), fols. 23v, 2 Aug 1780. The plakkaat warned officials that this would be a new practice for the locals.

[96] These records have not survived. The Christian Reformed Church in Wellawatte holds some records of marriages among Europeans, Eurasians and the indigenous elite, originally from the Dutch Reformed Church of the Galle Fort.

[97] See Hovy, *Plakkaatboek*, vol. 2; nr. 684 (3, 15), 19 May 1795.

[98] Ibid., vol. 2; nr. 543, 24 Dec 1776.

[99] Heijden, *Huwelijk in Holland*, 37–38.

[100] SLNA 1/6221, "Scholarchale Vergadering Minutes," fols. 53r-v, 5 Nov 1772; 55r–56r, 6 Jan 1773; 59r–v, 60r–64r, 2 Sept 1773; 71v–72r, 4 Dec 1773.

[101] For more details of the process, see the plakkaat of 1776. Hovy, *Plakkaatboek*, vol. 2; nr. 543, 24 Dec 1776.

[102] SLNA 1/6226, "Scholarchale Vergadering minutes" (1789 to 1791), fols. 29r, 5 May 1790.

and purposes. After the parties gave notice of marriage, they commonly cohabited and procreated, although this was illegal before the actual marriage.

The Scholarchale Vergadering in Galle wanted parents to guard daughters from their bridegrooms.[103] The Dutch considered virginity at marriage socially important, while the locals had a more relaxed attitude towards it. As the scholarchen complained at one meeting, many Sinhalese regarded the publishing of the banns to be "as good as the marriage" and did not "bother themselves" with the second step of confirming the marriage.[104] If the locals did appear for the solemnisation, they clearly did not take it seriously, as it seems they were often late to the occasion – and the Dutch imposed fines that increased depending on how late they were. If they arrived after the minister had already climbed the stool and started to preach, the fine was ten rixdollars, and at the end of the prayer it was twenty rixdollars. If they were unable to pay, they had to serve in the public works.[105]

Some women were rudely awakened to the necessity of confirming their marriages after the deaths of their partners. A couple who had announced the banns in the school in Talpe had lived together as husband and wife in the "Sinhalese way" for seventeen years and had two children. Eighteen years after the man's death, his surviving partner, Kobeiwattege Annika, was likely to have been caught unawares by the law when she heard that her partner's children by a previous marriage sought to disinherit her daughter. She asked the Scholarchale Vergadering in 1770 to recognise their daughter as legitimate so that she could be registered in the thombo. Annika's request was granted.[106] The secretary of the Scholarchale Vergadering was also the Landraad secretary, and the records of both bodies appear to have been maintained together.[107] Swift communication between the two institutions in this case was thus facilitated. Annika was able to bring forward witness testimony to reinforce her claim, so she did not lack support from those around her. If the failure to confirm a marriage was taboo, which is highly unlikely, few witnesses would have come forward to legitimise the child. Indeed, the widespread cooperation of witnesses on issues surrounding marriage indicates that there was little or no censure from friends and family on such matters. Another woman, Mellegodage Simange Anna, faced a similar predicament when her intended husband died five years after they

103 Hovy, *Plakkaatboek*, vol. 2; nr. 684, 19 May 1795.

104 SLNA 1/6220, "Scholarchale Vergadering minutes" (1768 to 1770), fols. 27v, 4 Jul 1770; SLNA 1/6221, "Scholarchale Vergadering Minutes," fols. 41r, 23 Sept 1771.

105 Hovy, *Plakkaatboek*, vol. 2; nr. 458, Resolution in order to make known that those who come for the marriage solemnisation in church too late must pay fines in favour of the military cashier, 3 June 1760.

106 SLNA 1/6220, "Scholarchale Vergadering Minutes," fols. 27r-v, 4 Jul 1770.

107 S.A.W. Mottau, *Inventory of the Archives of the Dutch Government in the Divisions of Galle (Matara) and Jaffnapatnam 1640–1796* (The Hague: General State Archives, 1975), 63.

proclaimed the banns in 1758 without confirming the marriage contract. She had gone to the Landraad with their son in 1774, many years after the proclamation of the banns, to have their names inserted in the land register under the family of her late partner, whose brother strongly denied the notice of marriage. The Landraad had referred the matter to the Scholarchale Vergadering.[108] Failure to solemnise the marriage could at times lead to legal encumbrances years later, but it was an error that the authorities were willing to overlook. The Galle thombos often recorded a status of *ondertrouwden* (having put up the banns) for individuals. Where cohabitation had once sufficed to establish a conjugal bond, the colonisers imposed complicated new requirements that are likely to have baffled many inhabitants.

The company could not control interpersonal relationships in the village exactly the way it wished. Women often complained that their men did not honour the banns. In 1772, a Sinhalese woman complained to the Scholarchale Vergadering that her "bridegroom" was living in concubinage with another woman despite having had three children with her after proclaiming the banns ten years previously. She was not seeking a separation – she wanted him back and the marriage confirmed.[109] In 1771, the Scholarchale Vergadering allowed two men to marry their deceased brothers' intended wives (their brothers having passed away after notice of marriage) on proving with credible witness testimony that the women had not had sexual intercourse with their first bridegrooms. Two other men were permitted to marry the sisters of their deceased wives-to-be (with whom they had proclaimed the banns) after they produced testimony in support of their claims that they had not slept with the deceased women.[110] The Dutch were anxious about the local practice of polygamy, which was prevalent in Sri Lanka until at least the middle of the twentieth century. The company was unable to rout out the practice. Fraternal polyandry, the marriage of one woman to two brothers, or parallel cousins, was the most common arrangement of joint husbands.[111] In another issue taken up at the Scholarchale Vergadering, a man who wished to marry his wife's sister was flogged and jailed, as it was considered an "incestuous" relationship.[112] Yearly orders published since 1773 banned such affinal alliances and couples who

108 SLNA 1/6222, "Scholarchale Vergadering minutes" (1774 to 1778), fols. 8v, 9r-v, 5 Oct 1774; 24v, 7 Dec 1774. Anna's betrothed was to be summoned to appear before the Scholarchale Vergadering at the next meeting, but I found no mention of the case thereafter.

109 SLNA 1/6221, "Scholarchale Vergadering Minutes," fols. 48r, 11 Aug 1772.

110 Ibid., fols. 38v, 6 Feb 1771; 42r-v, 23 Sept 1771.

111 For work on polyandry see S.J. Tambiah, *Polyandry in Ceylon, with Special Reference to the Laggala Region* (Social Scientists' Association, 2011); Pieris, *Sinhalese Social Organization*; Yalman, *Under the Bo Tree*.

112 SLNA 1/6220, "Scholarchale Vergadering Minutes," fols. 29v, 4 Jul 1770.

were closely related to each other.[113] An individual had the option of marrying the sibling of their deceased partner if the relationship with the deceased partner had not been consummated and confirmed. The deciding power over these issues lay with the Scholarchale Vergadering.

Despite the regulations on marriage registration, the Landraad and the Scholarchale Vergadering grudgingly recognised a "Sinhalese way of marriage". We can understand this phrase in two ways: cohabitation as husband and wife after the banns were read or cohabitation without legal betrothal. In the Landraad, customary unions were recorded and recognised as such. "Married in the heathen way" (*op de heidense wijse getrouwt*) was recorded against a few names in the Galle thombos that the council maintained.[114] We can imagine that during the thombo registrations, unions that were public knowledge in the village were easily recognised.[115] We saw in chapter one how Witānachchige Bastiaan had his son Jantje by his first wife, whom he claimed he had married in the Sinhalese way, registered in the new thombo as a mayorāl by petitioning the Landraad.

It is not clear if de facto spouses were treated in the same way as registered spouses for the purpose of intestate inheritance. In a case heard in 1778, the Landraad upheld the inheritance rights of the surviving spouse and children based on a deed of gift. A Sinhalese woman, Bussa Āchārige Kalu Nachera, produced a gift ola by which the man she had married *na de Singaleese wijze* (in the Sinhalese way) had gifted her and their children property and other goods. Her husband's relatives, however, appeared in the council and said that they knew neither of the gift nor that Kalu Nachera had married their brother in the Sinhalese way. The Landraad ignored them and approved the gift and entry in the thombo of Kalu Nachera's ownership rights.[116] She had the advantage of the gift ola. However, more research is required to fully understand the inheritance rights of men and women who had married in the Sinhalese way.

113 Hovy, *Plakkaatboek*, vol. 2; nr. 528, Notice concerning the forbidden grades of blood relationship by marriage or out of wedlock relationships, 28 May 1773. See also Ibid., vol. 2; nr. 530, Notice against all possible crimes, 1 Jul 1773; 684, 19 May 1795. In the Dutch Republic, as marriage was considered permanent, unions between people related by marriage were considered incestuous and criminal. Gerald Groenewald, "'A Mother Makes No Bastard': Family Law, Sexual Relations and Illegitimacy in Dutch Colonial Cape Town, c. 1652-1795," *African Historical Review* 39, no. 2 (2007): 78.

114 See for example SLNA 1/7569, "Panangala (Hinidum) Thombo" (1760), 9, 11; SLNA 1/7424, "Degalle (Wellaboda) Thombo" (1784), fols. 3v.

115 As there is much variation between thombos regarding marriage, they must be more comprehensively studied.

116 SLNA 1/6511, "Galle Landraad minutes," fols. 92r, 5 Dec 1778; SLNA 1/7491C, "Kumbalwella (Four Gravets) Thombo" (n.d.), 143.

The company is likely to have had difficulties distinguishing between promiscuity, concubinage and cohabitation. The Dutch imposition of marriage registrations clearly baffled the inhabitants of the south. Old ways of life held fast in the face of the new theological messages of Protestantism. The company employed another term similar to our understanding of the "Sinhalese way of marriage": *massebaddoesschap,* which seemed to refer to unions where even the banns had not been announced. These unions were frequently condemned in the Scholarchale Vergadering.[117] In Sinhala, the word *massebāduva* is a Portuguese-origin word meaning rape,[118] which is significant, as the Dutch use massebaddoesschap to refer to how native men had led local women astray. Clergymen and laymen of the board who inspected village schools listed couples who lived in *massebaddoe.* Couples who lived in concubinage had to marry or face punishment.[119] Given their relative intimacy with villagers, radā caste members, whose traditional occupation was washing clothes, had to report to schoolmasters on Christians partnering with non-Christians and those who had married in the Sinhalese way. Schoolmasters were required to stop marriages in the Sinhalese way, and, if they were unsuccessful, to inform the predikant.[120]

Some percentage of unions in villages thus remained unregistered and unconfirmed, but notifying the schoolmaster became a regular practice over time. The less serious manner in which one could break the law was by omitting the extra step of consecrating the marriage which many considered unnecessary. While the VOC overlooked this, the locals had reluctantly begun to accept that they were required to put up the banns. Obeyesekere describes how, well into the twentieth century, Mädagama villagers regarded the "absence of registration as rendering a marriage *legally* invalid."[121] They were unaware of the laws relating to validity of marriage solemnised according to customary rituals and that the proof of marriage was cohabitation and repute. This may have been due to repeated enforcement of legislation requiring the registration of marriage since early colonial rule and

117 See SLNA 1/6219, "Scholarchale Vergadering minutes" (1766 to 1768), fols. 13v, 6 Feb 1767. See also the plakkaat in Hovy, *Plakkaatboek*, vol. 2; nr. 684, 19 May 1795. During a school visit in 1770 it was noted that many natives everywhere lived in *massebādu.* SLNA 1/6220, "Scholarchale Vergadering Minutes," fols. 23r, 4 Jul 1770.

118 Charles Carter, "Massebāduva," in *A Sinhalese-English Dictionary* (Colombo: M.D. Gunasena & Co. Ltd, 1924; repr., 1965), 484. The word is not in common usage today. In Dutch, "oe" sounds like "oo" in tooth.

119 Hovy, *Plakkaatboek*, vol. 1; nr. 39 Ban on concubinage, 19 Nov 1658; 195, 15 May 1699; 257 Translation of a Sinhala mandate ola by which the native headmen and other inhabitants of the dessavonij Colombo and the commandment Galle were ordered . . . to follow Christian obligations, 4 Apr 1732; vol. 2; nr. 457, Resolution to forbid concubinage between non-Christian men and Christian women by notice in the usual languages of the country, 3 Jun 1760.

120 Ibid., vol. 1; nr. 257, 4 Apr 1732; vol. 2; nr. 684, 19 May 1795.

121 Obeyesekere, *Land Tenure*, 139–41.

the growing understanding that inheritance and legal marriage were linked. If it could not establish even a local customary marriage, the thombo recorded a child born to either an unmarried woman or an adulterous married man or woman as a nonmarital birth. The child was then forced to accept a lower status of nainde and a reduced land grant, about which I will say more later. Economic factors thus contributed to the growing awareness of registration, but the accommodation of customary marriages created a plural structure of family norms in the eighteenth-century south.

Men and women came to the Scholarchale Vergadering for cancellation of the banns or to obtain a divorce. Banns, once put up, were cancelled by the board, often many years later.[122] Separation that occurred after notice of marriage and dissolution were meant to ensure that a legal second marriage could take place. The Landraad did not deal with marriage dissolution among the locals. Given that the Scholarchale Vergadering met just twice in certain years, formal divorce procedures under Roman-Dutch law – requiring proof of malicious desertion or adultery – could not have been widely applied among the local population. According to early Dutch regulations, legally married native couples who subsequently separated had to pay a fine.[123] Laguruge Jantje, a goygama inhabitant of Hikkaduwa, claimed in 1770 that he had been legally married (in Dutch terms) to Tottege Siekuge Christina for fifteen years, but that she had since left him and had children by other men. He wanted the registration cancelled and requested permission to marry another woman. The board decided that the woman in question should be summoned. At the same meeting, Nagahawatte Clara of Bope complained that her husband, to whom she was legally married, had left her and taken up residence with another woman. In such a case, Clara's grounds for divorce would be adultery. Two other cases heard at the same meeting in 1770 had grounds of desertion. Witanege Simonge Gimara of Kodagoda said she had not heard from her husband, who had been absent for twenty-five years. Ellepitti Baddehellege Diogu, a pottery maker from Bentota, said his wife had deserted him fourteen years ago and that he had since heard that she had died in the Seven Kōralēs of the Kandyan kingdom. In both cases, the allegedly aggrieved parties wished to remarry. They had allowed many years to pass before taking action – in all likelihood, they wished to legitimise new unions to ensure their children's inheritance, but the schoolmasters or other officials would have sounded them on the legal obstacles they faced. The board ordered

122 Both men and women asked the board to cancel notice of marriage. See SLNA 1/6221, "Scholarchale Vergadering Minutes," fols. 34v–35r, 3 Oct 1770; 49r, 51r-v, 2 Sept 1772; 60r, 70r, 2 Sept 1773; 72r, 75r, 4 Dec 1773.

123 Hovy, *Plakkaatboek*, vol. 1; nr. 15, 1 Aug 1647.

that the absconding husband and wife in the two separate cases be summoned by tom-toms.[124]

It is doubtful that the practice of approaching the Scholarchale Vergadering to obtain separations was widespread. If the Sinhalese way of marriage was accepted, it can be safely assumed that couples parted for the most part in a relatively uncomplicated way as well, without having to resort to the Roman-Dutch law of marriage dissolution. Divorce, as Ralph Pieris says, was a common event and a man could divorce his wife simply "by taking her back to her village."[125] It is likely that mutual consent or the will of either party (as seen in Kandyan law) was the basis for separation. In contrast, divorce in the Roman-Dutch fashion was a cumbersome and expensive procedure. If a divorce came through, disputes over the division of property could have been heard in the Landraad, but I did not find such lawsuits.

In terms of the disposal of intestate property, the above discussion on marriage and its dissolution is of special interest. Christian registration propelled a couple towards Dutch jurisdiction and new laws of intestate inheritance. Under Roman-Dutch law, husband and wife pooled their resources in a community of property, but this was not a feature of Kandyan law. Under local jural norms, men married in binna (matrilocally) had no power over their wives' property; and if they were married in dīga (patrilocally), their wives lost the right of inheritance to their paternal paravēni. Widows had no absolute interest in their husband's paravēni property. Obeyesekere points out that Armour, the *Niti-Nighanduva,* D'Oyly and Sawers agree on this point.[126] But one lawsuit I discussed above illustrates that widows in Dutch times had deciding power on how a husband's paravēni property was divided. In Kosmulage Lisa de Silva's case, her mother was bequeathing property that had been acquired by her husband, so it does not fall into the category of paravēni property, but in the case of the mother with three sons including an adopted son, she prepared a deed of gift for her husband's inherited property. "Historical sources," as Obeyesekere says, "disagree as to whether on the death of a man, his sons and *binna* married daughters take over the *pravēni* at once or whether their rights remain in 'abeyance' until the death or dīga marriage of the widow."[127] The mother appeared to hold temporary rights to the property till her death.

[124] The cases are from SLNA 1/6220, "Scholarchale Vergadering minutes," fols. 29r-v, 4 Jul 1770. The decisions have not yet been found. Incidentally, Diogu did not know his wife's name.

[125] Pieris, *Sinhalese Social Organization*, 200.

[126] Obeyesekere, *Land Tenure*, 51. He was referring to Armour, *Armour's Grammar*; C.J.R. Le Mesurier and T.B. Panabokke, trans., *Niti-Nighanduva or the Vocabulary of Law* (New Delhi: Navrang, 1880; repr. 1994); John D'Oyly, *A Sketch of the Constitution of the Kandyan Kingdom*, Lewis James Barnetson Turner (ed), vol. 24, The Ceylon Historical Journal (Dehiwala: Tisara Prakasakayo, 1929; repr. 1975) and Sawers, *Digest of Kandyan Law*.

[127] Obeyesekere, *Land Tenure*, 51.

Significantly, Kosmulage Lisa de Silva's sisters who challenged their mother's bequest of a garden said that since their father had planted it, they had rights to it. They implied that their mother did not have absolute interests in that property although it may not have been a paravēni holding. If the children recognised the mother's temporary rights to the land, they believed that on her death it reverted to them, and that she did not have the right to bequeath it as she pleased. The available sources are contradictory on this issue; while Armour says that the mother is heiress to all acquired property of her husband, D'Oyly and Sawers do not agree.[128] The thombo commissioners, who were asked to examine the thombo to ascertain whether the mother had the right to gift the land, ruled in her favour. This recognition was not contrary to local practice. As Obeyesekere says, "[w]idows and mothers in several instances can inherit acquired property absolutely, since such property is not associated with the patrilineal ideology of the society."[129] It is likely that such cases were judged situationally, as in the local practice. A group of owners of a paddy-field in Kalegana came to the Landraad and asked that they be allowed to sell the land, but the Landraad would not let one of them, a widow, sell her share because her minor son, Godage Aberan, was still alive.[130] Here, the council upheld the rights of the child. Such situational judging by the Landraad reveals a sensitivity towards native practices of inheritance and attention to the details of individual cases.

The rights of widows as recognised in the Landraad were considerably greater than expected in local law. The laws of Sabaragamuva, as recorded by George Turnour could shed more light on this matter. They differed from the rest of Sinhalese law as described in Turnour's 1826 account. Obeyesekere treated the pre-British jural rules of Hinidum Pattuwa, for instance, as though they conformed with those of Sabaragamuva. As Sabaragamuva adjoins the Galle district, this fairly early description from British rule could play a part in our understanding of inheritance laws to the south of the area in Dutch times. Turnour writes, "[i]f the widow had children she had full managerial control of the husband's estate." The children could institute proceedings against her to have the land divided, in which case the land would be divided equally between the mother and the children. If such a division occurred, the widow could alienate her portion in any way she liked till she contracted a subsequent dīga marriage. Turnour's sources were six prominent chiefs from the Sabaragamuva province, who said the increased rights of widows were "compensation for the loss of a woman's rights in her own paternal *pravēni*

[128] Obeyesekere, *Land Tenure*, 52.

[129] Ibid.

[130] SLNA 1/6522, "Galle Landraad draft minutes" (1780 to 1781), fols. 128r, 21 Oct 1780.

due to *dīga* marriage."[131] The difference between the Kandyan and Sabaragamuva laws has not been fully explained through research.

The British assumed that the Sabaragamuva province had come under the influence of Roman-Dutch law. Obeyesekere rejects this explanation, as Sabaragamuva was not part of Dutch territory and because he believed that Roman-Dutch law was unlikely to have prevailed in the maritime provinces, or that it influenced the Hinidum Pattuwa. He further points out that the rights of widows in Sabaragamuva were considerably different to the practice of Roman-Dutch law. "Finally," he says, "it is highly doubtful whether the Roman-Dutch law would have influenced the rights of widows, whereas the other aspects of the legal system so offensive to Roman-Dutch law, like polyandry, *binna* marriages etc. remained unaffected."[132] His explanation for the difference in Sabaragamuva is the existence of strong marriage ties and an ideology of wifely devotion to the husband. Yet this is unworkable as an explanation as a plausible comparison with Kandyan areas on this question is not feasible. As S.B.D. de Silva argues, "geographically or culturally, there was no sharp dividing line between the Kandyan territory and the extensive tracts comprising the Sabaragamuwa district."[133] He believes that Sabaragamuva had connections with the maritime provinces as well. Such links make it difficult to rule out the possibility of the influence of southern practices, including the residues of Dutch practice.

On the matter of marriage, it is possible that covert efforts were made to adjudicate under Dutch laws in the late eighteenth century. Attempts to incorporate Dutch legal principles and customs were not uncommon. The plakkaat forbidding marriages and extramarital relationships between "undesirable" parties, including blood relatives of one's partner, was published many times from 1773.[134] The reason for the publication of the plakkaat in the Wanni in 1787 was that men married three or four women and left them, leading to many disputes over inheritance. The governor in council recommended that the commander did not investigate the marriages himself, but in case of complaints, settled it "in such a way that it gradually tallies with

[131] I have used Obeyesekere's interpretation of Turnour here. Obeyesekere, *Land Tenure*, 53. Turnour's account is in John D'Oyly, *A Sketch of the Constitution*, 162–64.

[132] Obeyesekere, *Land Tenure*, 54.

[133] De Silva, *Political Economy*, 217. He further says: "The district in turn was contiguous with several other districts in the extreme South and on the West coasts of Sri Lanka, such as the Giruwapattu of Hambantota, Morowakorle or Matara and Gangabode Patto of the Galle district and the Pasdun, Raigam and Hewagam Korles of the Colombo district…The inhabitants of the Sabaragamuwa district, while being essentially Kandyan and governed by Kandyan law, had 'adopted many of the habits and customs' of the maritime provinces."

[134] See note 113 above.

the Dutch laws."[135] This appears to have been the policy with regard to other matters of inheritance as well, particularly with regard to complaints over illegitimacy.

Navigating Illegitimacy

The Galle branch of the Scholarchale Vergadering often deliberated on the issue of "illegitimate" (Dutch: *onecht*)[136] children. The Governor in Council in Colombo referred the matter to the Landraad of Colombo to report on how such children were registered and the service due from them to the company in Colombo.[137] The company thus determined the law relating to such children and assigned the male children of goygama caste parents the status of nainde, a husbandman who performed menial work.[138] The extent of paddy land assigned to such a person was twenty *kuruni* (or one acre), which was equivalent to that given to messengers, village smiths, washermen, and drummers, among others.[139] Being assigned the nainde status was considered a demotion. The Dutch also legislated that where the parents were from different castes, the illegitimate son would be assigned the lower caste. The order, which was supposed to be published widely, did not specifically refer to female illegitimate children. The definition of illegitimacy in this context is ambiguous. The use of the word "onecht" in the Dutch records can be linked to the issue of adultery, temporary unions, unregistered marriages, or ondertrouwden – those who had put up the banns but not had their marriages solemnised. The threat of children being made illegitimate is among the punishments meted out for not solemnising a marriage.[140]

135 See note in Hovy, *Plakkaatboek*, nr. 528, 28 May 1773.

136 One meaning of the Dutch word *echt* is "real," and "onecht" is literally "un-real" or fake.

137 SLNA 1/160, "Governor in Council minutes" (1770), 2 Aug 1770. Colombo Landraad minutes and correspondence for the year 1770 are no longer extant.

138 Ibid., 21 Aug 1770; SLNA 1/5660, "Galle Landraad, extracts of resolutions," fols. 64r, Extract from letter dated 5 Sept 1770 from Colombo to Galle. See also Hovy, *Plakkaatboek*, vol. 2; nr. 513, Resolution to instruct the Galle officials that illegal children of parents of the Wellale caste shall be regarded as naindes…, 21 Aug 1770. Goygama inhabitants of the Walallawiti Corle in Galle who had, out of ignorance, not contracted a Christian marriage were exempt from the status demotion of their children in 1775. Ibid., vol. 2; nr. 537, Resolution by which the Wellales in the Walallawiti Corle (Galle Commandment) who from ignorance have not contracted a christian marriage, shall not be punished with the status demotion of their children to the subcaste of the naindes…, 4 Jul 1775. See also SLNA 1/5895, "Draft of annual compendium sent to Colombo" (1774 to 1775), fols. 29v–30r, 13 Dec 1776.

139 See appendix III.

140 Hovy, *Plakkaatboek*, vol. 2; nr. 543 (4), 24 Dec 1776.

The sources for a study of illegitimacy laws in local society are limited. This lacuna, as it were, leads one to the *Niti-Nighanduva,*[141] a late eighteenth- or early nineteenth-century source on Kandyan law that must be read with caution as its applicability to the maritime provinces is doubtful. Yet it corroborates other sources that link inter-caste unions to illegitimacy, and gives details of other deviating unions in relation to differences of rank. Sinhalese law recognised the concept of illegitimacy in some circumstances, as in the case of children of women who had married beneath their caste. A higher-caste woman who had an alliance with a lower-caste man was subject to much censure, potentially even death at the hands of her kin.[142] Children born of such unions were considered illegitimate. Issue from an "equal" union of a man and woman of equal caste and rank in a recognised union was not considered illegitimate and could inherit their father's property. In general, ranks within a caste refrained from marrying into an inferior rank than their own. The *Niti-Nighanduva* states that the children of a man of higher caste who married a woman of a lower caste, or a woman within the prohibited degrees of relationship, or a woman of unequal rank, without the consent of his parents, could claim only the father's acquired property. Similarly, when a woman who had entered a matrilocal marriage later cohabited and had a child with a man of a lower caste, that child was only entitled to a share of her acquired property. Illegitimacy in local society appears not to have been linked to the lack of a marriage or union per se, but was rather more connected to the rank and caste of the cohabiting individuals and to forbidden relationships. Thus, it is doubtful if the more modern term "nonmarital birth", preferred to "illegitimate", would be meaningful in the local context. I have used both terms in this book.

Illegitimacy under the Dutch was linked to the formal registration of marriage, which the local system did not have. Thus, the concept of illegitimacy that was dependent on it was new. Yet it could be argued that the principal of registration, if it is taken to be the declaration of an intention to form a definite alliance, was not entirely new. In local customs, such intentions, and the concordance of the wishes of the families were sufficient to form a permanent union.[143] Since this practice held an element of public recognition of a permanent union, illegitimacy was also linked to the lack of a recognised marriage in the local system. In that sense, it was similar to the European concept of nonmarital children, but was not linked to formal marriage registration practices introduced by a government.

Within the new understanding of nonmarital children, based on the registration requirement imposed by the VOC, "illegitimate" persons appeared often in

141 Le Mesurier and Panabokke, *Niti-Nighanduva*, 13–15.

142 Pieris, *Sinhalese Social Organization*, 177–78.

143 Ibid., 202–3.

the Galle thombos. In the villages of Dodampe and Ganegoda, the occurrence of nonmarital birth was around seven per cent. But it could be that another thombo of the same subdistrict does not list a single nonmarital birth. The frequency of nonmarital children is almost impossible to measure, as each thombo registration could have been unique to the clerk or thombo-keeper. In Dodampe, the service of most resident nonmarital males was listed as nainde.[144] In 1780, Simon was registered as the fifty-year-old illegitimate son of the widow Liyana Āchchige Catharina. Gamage Punchi Ettena, a niece of the PLH Gamage Gimara, was forty years old in 1780, and is referred to as the illegitimate *ondertrouwd* widow of Maddugodage Punchi. She belongs to a new category of ondertrouwd widow because her betrothal had not been solemnised. The two youngest of her four sons, Se-appuwa (aged twelve years) and Annurappa (aged seven years), were also listed as onecht. Henadirege Kattona, a woman of another thombo group in Dodampe, was unmarried and had a nonmarital son and four nonmarital grandsons. Christina, who was Kattona's sister's daughter, was also illegitimate and had an illegitimate son. In Ganegoda, Bastiaan was illegitimate but was recognised by a thombo group that had his father's brother as the PLH. Incidentally, his mother's name is also mentioned. Also in Ganegoda, Christobu had three nonmarital sons and one nonmarital daughter.[145] Most nonmarital offspring, however, are mentioned alongside their mothers, with no mention of the father.

The above was an account of illegitimacy in two southern villages at one point in the late eighteenth century, but the thombos offer a rich source of information for a more comprehensive analysis of the phenomenon, whether invented or real. Its moral and legal implications in Dutch and later British times can be explored in more detail. Here, I only attempt an introduction to its use in Dutch Galle.[146] The thombos can reveal who the parents of such nonmarital children were, whether it was a more urban or non-urban phenomenon,[147] what happened to such children, and what status in society they were accorded in the official records. The enforcement (or lack thereof) of new understandings of the concept was, of course, heavily

144 It is unclear why all of them were not listed as nainde. The following examples from Dodampe are from SLNA 1/7428A, "Dodampe Thombo," 1, 21, 27.

145 SLNA 1/7442A, "Ganegoda (Wellaboda) Thombo" (1780), 3, 27; SLNA 1/7442B, "Ganegoda (Wellaboda) Thombo" (1780), 3.

146 It is possible that the recording of "illegitimacy" was more common in the Galle thombos than in the Colombo thombos, as revealed through a preliminary comparison with the database of the Hina Korle (Mäde Pattuwa) and Hapitigam Korle (Udugaha Pattuwa) thombos, sponsored by Jan Luiten van Zanden of Utrecht University and Jan Kok of Radboud University.

147 "Urban" or "non-urban" would be in the sense of proximity to the centre of Dutch administration in Galle.

influenced by both the experience of the colonisers in early modern Europe and the necessary negotiations on the ground.

When the new laws on the consequences of nonmarital birth were published, villagers must have become aware of how to utilise them for the purpose of (dis) inheritance. I have illustrated this through Gimara's case, which I briefly described at the start of this chapter. Many of the supporting documents of this case have survived.[148] In 1788, two Sinhalese men said that their brother-in-law Kottegodage Daniel, Gimara's husband, was "illegitimate" and therefore not an heir. They produced a thombo extract from Mipe and said that Daniel should have been mentioned in it as onecht. The thombo had been drawn up in 1751, and Daniel had been entered as a son of Kottegodage Philippu. Philippu himself was said to have been present at the thombo registration and included Daniel as his son. At the time, Philippu was described as a forty-three-year-old goygama lascarin. His wife was thirty-eight years old and Daniel was eight years old. He also had three daughters who were older than Daniel, two of whom were living away, while the other was twelve years old and appeared to be living with her parents.[149] Johan de Silva, a former vidāne of Pilane, and Melagodege Jantje were married to the two older daughters and made their claim after Daniel's death. Two European and two local members were present at the commissioner's meeting of the Landraad when they made the claim. They decided that in order to ascertain whether Daniel was an inheritor, the matter should be investigated by the thombo-keeper, the *toerbeurds* (rotating) members of the Landraad, the village heads and all the heirs.[150]

It was revealed during the course of the inquiry that Daniel was "no legitimate son of Kottegodage Philippu, but an illegitimate son of his, conceived by his sister-in-law or wife's sister Manege Johange Jibika."[151] Jibika confirmed this, adding that Philippu and her sister had entered Daniel as their legal son in the thombo. Daniel's brothers-in-law, who had filed the case, were also present and produced an extract from the school thombo, showing that he had been baptised under his mother's name. They claimed that she had not known till after Philippu and his wife's death that Daniel had been entered in the thombo as their legal son. They wanted the lascarin service and lands held for that service by Daniel, and thereafter his sons, to be transferred to them. Daniel's widow was also present at the inquiry and showed a lascarin deed and a trump card – a Sinhala report from the sabandar mudaliyar,

148 SLNA 1/1514, "Galle Political Council minutes," 29 Oct 1789; SLNA 1/6515, "Galle Landraad minutes," fols. 167r, 2 Jul 1788; 197v, 24 Jan 1789; 229v, 30 May 1789, 280v, 27 Feb 1790. We have more details of cases that went up for appeal like this.

149 SLNA 1/7447A, "Mipe Thombo" (1751), 109.

150 SLNA 1/6515, "Galle Landraad minutes," fols. 167r, 2 Jul 1788.

151 SLNA 1/1514, "Galle Political Council minutes," 29 Oct 1789, Report by Landraad commissioners dated 24 Jan 1789.

who was most probably the Landraad councillor, Don Balthasar Dias Abeysinghe. The councillors Pieter Simon Cadenski, Justinus Christiaan Trek and Bernhard Hendrik van Bergheim, signed the report of the inquiry, the first two agreeing that the lascarin service and associated lands could be held in turns by Daniel's children and his brothers-in-law, while the third signatory believed that Daniel's children alone should hold the privilege. That report, together with a new land and family thombo extract, an extract from the school thombo of Talpe, and a lascarin deed of Kottegodage Philippu, dated 28 April, 1769, were produced at a subsequent Landraad meeting. The council sent the papers around before deciding on the matter.[152]

The council approved the proposal by Cadenski and Trek to provide the rights in turns to both parties. The thombo-keeper was instructed to insert a note in the thombo, stating that Daniel was a nonmarital son of Kottegodage Philippu's sister-in-law, Manege Johange Jibika. He also had to add that from now on, the service of lascarin would be carried out by the men and descendants of Philippu's legitimate daughters and Daniel's children (as Daniel was no longer alive), who would enjoy the lands belonging to that service in turns.[153] This decision was duly entered in the thombo on 1 July 1789, but was subsequently struck off and followed by yet another new note.

For, soon after, the case came up in appeal in the Raad van Justitie of Galle. Pilane Godakandege Gimara, Daniel's widow, together with their children, Dinees and Mathees, wished to revert to what they believed were their exclusive rights to the service and associated lands. Their plaint claimed that Daniel, being Philippu's only son, had performed the lascarin service till his death and cultivated the lands attached to the service. It was only after his death that his sisters' husbands had brought up the issue of his illegitimacy, the plaint further claimed. Invoking an emotional argument, it was asked in the plaint why they had not prevented Daniel's entry in the thombo at the time of registration,[154] when he was eight years old, but had only brought up the issue around a year ago, after having waited so long till he was dead and could no longer answer for himself. It is plausible that that anomaly would have struck Gimara and her sons, although we do not know to what extent the content of the plaint was the opinion and argumentation of a process representative who drew up the document. Despite Daniel being an illegitimate son of Philippu, the plaint said it was fully apparent that Philippu had recognised him as a legitimate child, as he himself had had Daniel registered as

[152] SLNA 1/6515, "Galle Landraad minutes," fols. 197v, 24 Jan 1789.

[153] Ibid., fols. 229v, 30 May 1789.

[154] In fact, it was not unusual for fathers to come forward to register sons in the thombo in their service. For instance, see the story of Witānachchige Bastiaan in chapter one.

such, for which he would have had his reasons.[155] As the paterfamilias, Philippu's decision was honoured, and the plaint implied that it should not be questioned. In fact, one Landraad record refers to Daniel as Philippu's adopted son.[156] His three other children, it must be considered, were daughters, two of whom had already moved away; he might have had concerns about who would continue to perform the service obligations and farm the land. Philippu's relationship with his sister-in-law suggests polygamy, accepted in local society but condemned by the Dutch. It is very likely that Daniel posed no issues to his family or local society in terms of acceptance; the imposition of a new law by a colonial power in that situation would have been difficult for villagers to fathom. Daniel's brothers-in-law, however, had other ideas. The initial report submitted to the Galle Commander Kraijenhoff on the appeal mentions that the Landraad's first decision was in full contradiction of the 1770 resolution to assign nonmarital goygama children the nainde service. Subsequently, the commander had asked the Landraad to report on the history of the case.

This report of the Landraad is of special interest, as it provides an example of how European and indigenous councillors judged a case. It reveals how the Landraad arrived at a decision. The councillors Pieter Arend de Moor, Dirk François van Gijsel and Coenraad Otto voted in favour of the majority decision in the commissioners' field report. The president and a councillor, referred to as the sabandaar mudaliyar, who could only have been Balthasar, were of the opinion that Daniel's children alone should be entitled to the lascarin service and its associated gardens.[157] Balthasar may have wished to turn the tide in favour of Daniel's widow, who may also have been hopeful, but more powerful authorities came into play.

Nicolaas Bernadus Martheze and Pieter de Vos, members of the Raad van Justitie of Galle, were assigned the task of providing further advice on the case. They said that the Galle Landraad had not observed the "laws and orders of the country, which were fixed and pre-assigned on this subject."[158] They commended the Landraad for recognising that Kottegodage Daniel was "born of incest" (*uit bloedschande gesprooten*), which, they said, the village headmen and the mother

[155] "And certainly the father Philippu would have known the reasons best." SLNA 1/1514, "Galle Political Council minutes," 29 Oct 1789; Plea dated 9 Sept 1789 from Pilane Godakandege Gimara.

[156] SLNA 1/6515, "Galle Landraad minutes," fols. 197v, 24 Jan 1789.

[157] SLNA 1/1514, "Galle Political Council minutes," 29 Oct 1789, Report of Landraad dated 29 Sept 1789. It is not clear here whether Balthasar had a vote. Cadenski and Trek wrote the initial report on the investigation, so their votes are not mentioned. The councillor Adriaan Hendrik Lourensz is recorded as being present at the meeting, but his vote is also not mentioned. No mention is made of the opinion or votes of the two other local members present at the meeting. The report of 29 September 1789 was signed by Don Balthasar Dias Abeysinghe as well.

[158] Ibid., Report dated 19 Oct 1789.

had herself attested to without restraint. But they said he could have no right to inherit or possess through the father's line. As I described previously, the Dutch government had banned the practice of partnering with a deceased spouse's sibling. However, this situation was different. As his wife's sister was officially considered to be his sister, Daniel was conceived by Philippu with his "sister," making Daniel an "overwonnen" child – a child that is conceived by adultery or incest. Thus, Philippu's incest with his sister-in-law and their child were anathema to the Raad van Justitie councillors.[159] They disapproved of the Landraad's decision to allow Daniel's children to perform the lascarin service together with Daniel's sisters' husbands. They stated that Daniel had had no right to the privilege during his lifetime and was "no lascarin due to his illegitimate birth." They remarked that since Philippu was not survived by male heirs, his lascarin service had to be regarded as vacant as the service could not be transferred to his daughters, because their husbands also had their separate obligations. In response to the reports, the Galle Political Council referred to the 1770 order and demoted Daniel's sons to the nainde service. They requested approval from Colombo, and the decision was communicated to the Galle Landraad.[160]

Accordingly, on 17 April 1790, another note was entered below the earlier note in the thombo. It refers to a letter from the Governor in Council dated 31 December 1789.[161] The note also referred to the children of (the deceased) Daniel as illegitimate. Thus, Daniel's illegitimacy was appended to his children as well.[162] They were to be registered as naindes and the service lands of Kottegodage Philippu were to be absorbed by the company as malapālu, as lands escheated on the death of the owner. The sons were only allowed the portion that was ascribed to a nainde. Referring to the 1770 resolution on nonmarital children, the earlier judgement was considered a mistake, as Daniel's children also needed to be disinherited if he were to be disinherited; this was the rectification as it were. The Landraad, especially when considering the minority opinion of the president and Balthazar, had ignored the 1770 resolution and judged the case more in accordance with local

[159] Incidentally, Martheze and de Vos were present at the Scholarchale Vergadering, when the issue of nonmarital children was taken up. SLNA 1/6220, "Scholarchale Vergadering minutes," 4 Jul 1770.

[160] SLNA 1/6515, "Galle Landraad minutes," fols. 280v, 27 Feb 1790.

[161] SLNA 1/5315, "Inward Letters, Colombo to Galle" (1789), fols. 308r, 31 Dec 1789, Letter from Governor in Council to Galle Political Council. Also in SLNA 1/1565, "Outward Letters, Colombo to Galle" (1789), 31 Dec 1789, Letter from Governor in Council to Galle Political Council.

[162] The children, it is possible, were considered nonmarital in accordance with the scriptures. "Deuteronomy prohibits bastards and their seed from the assembly of the Lord." John Witte, Jr., *The Sins of the Fathers: The Law and Theology of Illegitimacy Reconsidered* (Cambridge: Cambridge University Press, 2009), 45.

customs, which did not always penalise nonmarital children. But the higher Dutch judicial body reconfirmed the lower status given to nonmarital children and their disinheritance under Dutch intestate laws.

In this case, two litigants believed they could capitalise on illegitimacy. They would have been aware of the 1770 order that had been published in the village schools.[163] We see here how the lower judicial body, with the influence of headmen, attempted a judgement that was more consensual in nature, yet problematic. Such situational judging without regard for new rules, served to make the judicial forum more powerful. But its efforts were overturned by the higher authority, where there was no representation by local headmen. The Raad van Justitie of Galle also imposed a judgement that left both parties bereft, the "illegitimate" party more so than the other.

Why did Gimara's close family members suddenly invest in the law, seeking to actively confront and disinherit her on the basis of her late husband's nonmarital birth? Exploring the motives of her opponents in challenging her land rights allows for "speculative exploration of the legal imaginary of peasant litigants."[164] More generally, the question concerns the reception of a colonial law that was introduced to the local inhabitants. As Daniel Lord Smail shows, disputes based on animosity and hatred are common to all social fabrics, and the answer may lie in such an explanation.[165] The pursuance of emotional satisfaction may explain how laws that are seemingly new seeped down to the very heart of family life in a colonised population. Emotional motivations may have played a key role in the acceptance of legal transformations, despite the new law having little significance in the local normative system.

With no personal narrative of her own, we hear Daniel's wife's voice vaguely; yet strongly in her actions. Gimara fought the case against her, likely made supplications to a prominent local headman on the Landraad to support her and appealed the decision when it was made to her disfavour. She perhaps saw herself as a competent legal subject freely engaging in lower and higher judicial spaces, led to believe that the colonial justice system would give her just dues, even in appeal. Gimara may have been unaware of the new laws of illegitimacy; it is more likely that she believed that the local laws would prevail. That in itself may be

163 SLNA 1/6221, "Scholarchale Vergadering Minutes," 39v, 23 Sept 1771. It was supposed to be published in Matara as well: SLNA 1/5660, "Galle Landraad, extracts of resolutions," fols. 64r, Extract letter dated 8 Sept 1770 from Galle to Matara.

164 Jane Burbank, *Russian Peasants Go to Court: Legal Culture in the Countryside, 1905–1917* (Indiana: Indiana University Press, 2004), 32.

165 Daniel Lord Smail, *The Consumption of Justice: Emotions, Publicity, and Legal Culture in Marseille, 1264–1423* (Ithaca, NY: Cornell University Press, 2003), 89.

extraordinary yet it is expected in an environment where local officials served on the judicial body that she first faced.

Did the Dutch colonial power try to impose a European idea of nonmarital children, and if so, were they successful? Why would the locals embrace such a law if it were not a part of their customs? Gimara's dilemma must be seen not in isolation, but in the context of other cases heard in the Landraad as well. The rights of nonmarital children if stipulated by inheritance inter vivos were safeguarded against challenges and, at times, they were also the principal land holders of thombo groups. In a Landraad session on 21 June 1794, Madegamage Adriaan and his sister Madegamage Babiana are described as the *onegte kinderen* (illegitimate children) of the late Abittegodage Don Philippu, a Sinhalese inhabitant of the village Ganegama.[166] Abittegodage Johan challenged their rights to parts of gardens and paddy-fields in Horeganpita, Piyadigama and Ganegama,[167] but the council validated the deed of gift from 1760 that the children had received from their father Philippu. Johan, the opposing party, was charged the costs of the investigation conducted by the thombo-keeper Trek and another member of the Landraad. The Ganegama thombo entry made in 1760 for Abittegodage Don Philippu, listed as a goygama lascarin, does not mention the two nonmarital children; neither is he listed as married.[168] Yet, Don Philippu thought it important enough to establish that it was his two "illegitimate" children who would have the rights to his property in the year the thombo was compiled. These rights were upheld even when challenged in the Landraad. A note in the thombo refers to the deed of gift that he made and the 1794 case. In yet another case heard in 1787, the Landraad allowed Haupe Hewage Simon to gift all his property ("houses, gardens and fields") with life interest to his brother's "illegitimate son."[169] The necessity to secure their inheritance indicates how a belief that nonmarital children could be disinherited through the thombo and the Landraad if their rights were challenged had seeped into the peasants' concept of family.

166 SLNA 1/6517, "Galle Landraad minutes" (1794), fols. 68r, 21 Jun 1794.

167 Johan's exact relationship to Philippu is uncertain. According to the thombo entry, Johan may have been Philippu's father's brother's son who was married and living in Horaganpitiya.

168 SLNA 1/7441A, "Ganegama (Gangaboda) Thombo" (1760), 113, group nr 47. An extract of this thombo also appears in the Landraad annexes: SLNA 1/6526, "Annexes to Galle Landraad minutes," fols. 181–183r.

169 SLNA 1/6515, "Galle Landraad minutes," fols. 106r-v, 1 Dec 1787.

Conclusion

Family law was an area in which the intention to transform local practices was conspicuously present but not fully achieved. We saw in chapter four how conversions were ensured by their relationship to thombo registrations; baptism was also linked to marriage, which in turn was linked to inheritance. Economic forces were more likely to bring about transformations in customary laws than moral grounds. Unlike in nineteenth-century Hawai'i, where American missionaries closely regulated matters of sexuality,[170] the company did not proactively attempt to reform family life, an area where the government could not easily dictate terms. It is doubtful that the Scholarchale Vergadering could achieve change in a significant way, given the limited nature of its operations. It may have made a small dent, as the requirement for registration and (to a lesser extent) legal marriage dissolution appears to have seeped into local society, but evidence of customary marriages from areas far from the centre of southern government, such as the Hinidum Pattuwa, shows us its reach was limited. The enduring nature of marriage registration can nevertheless be seen over the nineteenth and twentieth centuries, when registration practices were further streamlined and came to be preferred despite the legal recognition of customary marriages. The association of legal marriage with land ownership was not consistently emphasised in the Landraad but came to be a lasting legacy of Dutch rule.

Other areas of family life were also beginning to be affected by Dutch rule in the eighteenth century. Landraad officials looked at issues of nonmarital children benevolently, but such decisions were liable to be overturned by higher authorities that were exclusively European. The decision of the Landraad in Pilane Godakandege Gimara's illegitimacy case discussed in this chapter, was overturned and judged as incorrect by the higher court, which restricted the inheritance of nonmarital children. Litigants adapted to the laws introduced by the company and reflexively redefined their own traditional ideas of some aspects of the family for economic benefit. Thus, the adoption of new laws had the potential to cause conflicts between individuals and the company.

This process would have been perplexing, to say the least, for most of peasant society. Some awareness, not necessarily critical, of Daniel's unorthodox birth would have existed in the family. Daniel's widow, Pilane Godakandege Gimara, and his mother did not attempt to hide his "illegitimacy" – it was a part of their everyday reality that was hardly dishonourable, given that the father recognised Daniel as his son. Acknowledged by his father, Daniel himself experienced no constraints

170 Sally Engle Merry, *Colonizing Hawai'i: The Cultural Power of Law* (Princeton, NJ: Princeton University Press, 2000).

on his inheritance. Yet, the colonial state was instrumental in transforming that. It imposed illegitimacy laws, legal missiles, that the "legitimate" part of the family learned they could exploit, long after Daniel's death. His wife and children, whose agency in this case warrants close attention, were thus rudely awakened to a colonial state affecting their everyday reality. Ordinary persons actively contributed to remaking and transforming the family norms of pre-colonial society through their appropriation of the legal order of the colonial state. Gimara's appeal contains an emotional plea, asking why her opponents had waited till her husband was no more to bring up the dispute. The language of emotions naturally drives men and women across cultures to process opportunities for competitive gain. In eighteenth-century Sri Lanka, the judicial institution available to express that emotion had changed, and the acceptance of the colonial power was driven by the use of the forum and its laws by the people.

By going up in appeal, Gimara's case displays the intersection of the Landraad with higher legal bodies, that of the Raad van Justitie of Galle and the main political administration of the Governor in Council in Colombo. Illegitimacy laws, as the VOC defined them, had not yet become pervasive in the everyday lives of the peasant, but Gimara's case shows us the eighteenth-century origins by which they entered society. We see a gradual shift in public understandings of the legal implications of illegitimacy. In time, illegitimacy laws reshaped the consciousness of a family unit together with individual conduct. The case describes how one family initially ignored, then used, and finally came to terms with colonial law. We see a concrete implication of colonial law, almost irretrievable in Gimara's case, as the final decision had come from the Governor in Council and was unlikely to be further entertained in the High Court of Colombo. This preliminary study of marriage practices and nonmarital birth in late eighteenth-century Galle shows how the early colonial state began to change the lived experience of peasant family life. Over time, peasants were compelled to transform how they regarded their family units.

In some areas of family law, the company faced an institutionalised normative order characterised by ritual underpinnings. Yet this did not extend to all aspects of inheritance law. The absence of strict rules and the practice of situational judging in Sinhalese law, when faced with the rules of a legal system that was more clearly defined, led to the dominance of Dutch laws. In that sense, the creation of Dutch judicial forums, meant that the early colonial experience saw the beginnings of restricting rather than expanding pluralism. Claas Fontijn's case strongly suggests that in complex intestate cases, Dutch laws were in use. Less ambiguously, the Landraad used Dutch laws of bilateral inheritance on a consistent basis. Although local jural norms recognised bilateral inheritance, other principles, such as virilocal and uxorilocal marriages, served in retaining the lands in the original family. Gamage Livina's case shows us how a woman who is likely to have married virilocally asserted her rights to her share through the Landraad and the thombo on returning to the village. Fragments of Sinhalese law are also visible in the Landraad: the concept of familial assistance, wherein the daughter or son who cares for a parent is favoured for inheritance, received sanction. Such recognition of the local normative order, which would have been a direct result of the presence of native councillors, was possible through situational judging but went unrecognised in official law. In all this, the emerging dominance of company rules in family law is unmistakable.

The microhistorical approach to the issue of change in family law attempted in this chapter, gives us a perspective of how individuals faced legal transformation in Dutch Sri Lanka. Deconstructing the role of the litigants indicates how new colonial laws could have been used reflexively by the people in a way that would have had long-term effects towards redefining some aspects of the family. The Dutch legal records of lower-level judicial forums that lie in the National Archives of Sri Lanka provide hundreds of microstudies, which are a valid way to open a window of understanding to the everyday lives of the past. This approach is unique in Sri Lanka's historiography, as earlier studies using Dutch sources of the eighteenth century have focused on macro-level phenomena. The legal issues reflect broader contexts but can also be studied purely for the intrinsic value of each individual story.

CONCLUSION

Revisiting Colonial Legal Practice

Abstract

The Landraad was a space in which agency was multifarious. The nuances of everyday judicial practices as studied in this book reveal both rejection and manipulation by local actors. This in turn informs us of everyday life in early-modern colonialism. The Landraad adopted the local practice of situational judging on a case-by-case basis. A choice of laws came into play, that choice being significant at varying degrees for different areas of the law such as evidence, inheritance, land and family law. While there was inevitable conflict, in practice the local normative order was as much a social fact for early colonial rulers as Roman-Dutch law, leading to the navigation of pluralities in an early colonial encounter.

Keywords: Legal pluralism, pluralities, Dutch colonial law, colonialism, Sinhalese law, Roman-Dutch law.

Legal pluralism is closely related to the fragmented nature of colonial rule. Contested arguments over change in early colonial society have largely overlooked the practical realities of pluralities as they manifest in everyday life. This book contributes to an open debate of over 200 years on the extent to which Dutch and Sinhalese laws were applied to the Sinhalese of the maritime provinces in Sri Lanka. Cooray has opined that the question of the application or non-application of Sinhalese customary law remains purely academic today, as it is the Roman-Dutch law that is now applied to the low country (coastal) Sinhalese.[1] For, whatever the outcome of a study of Dutch legal records, Roman-Dutch law is here to stay in Sri Lanka as its proponents would say that "it continues to be of great value to the legal system."[2] Developments under the British in the nineteenth century could be even more important in understanding present-day law, but the foundation for such

[1] L.J.M. Cooray, *An Introduction to the Legal System of Sri Lanka* (Pannipitiya: Stamford Lake, 2003; repr. 2009), 69.

[2] A.R.B. Amerasinghe, "The Dutch Influence on the Legal System of Sri Lanka," in Saman Kelegama and Roshan Madawela (eds), *400 Years of Dutch-Sri Lanka Relations 1602–2002* (Colombo: Institute of Policy Studies of Sri Lanka, 2002), 321.

developments was laid before their rule. The study of the application of Sinhalese law is of more relevance when one considers that, as Elizabeth Kolsky states, the legacy of Partha Chatterjee's "rule of colonial difference" is that "difference, exclusion, and exemption might still define how states and structures continue to behave."[3] Thus, "the legal history and relevance of colonialism does not lie dormant in the archives."[4] New developments in the field of socio-legal studies of legal pluralism warrant paying further attention to the Sri Lankan example.

The British legacy of its understanding of Dutch rule is still with us today. Legal pluralism is said to be practised in modern Sri Lanka. A modified version of the *Thesavalamai,* which is a codification of the customary laws of the Tamils of Jaffna that the VOC commissioned and produced in 1707, forms part of official Sri Lankan law. The British also instituted as statute law some local practices that they believed to be exclusive to the up-country "Kandyan" residents. Yet, the pluralism of British times, and that of today's world, is a much-reduced version of the pluralities in practice under early colonial rule.

In legal matters, British moves to make Roman-Dutch law statute law in many areas marked a break from the more plural manner in which the Dutch approached the local normative order. Claims of a rupture that the British created in the legal arena can be contextualised in an important debate on either evolutionary or revolutionary change in nineteenth-century colonial rule. The question is whether late colonial rule was transformational, marking an epistemological break with an earlier period when the East India companies were operating, or merely a change of guard. For Sudipta Kaviraj, Chatterjee and Gyanendra Pandey, the dynamic and fluid nature of social relations changed in the nineteenth century.[5] For others, such as C.A. Bayly and Susan Bayly, the continuities of late colonial rule, rather than its radically transformational effects, are more striking.[6] Further study of the British legal

[3] Partha Chatterjee, *The Nation and its Fragments: Colonial and Postcolonial Histories* (Princeton, NJ: Princeton University Press, 1993), 10, 18; Elizabeth Kolsky, "A Note on the Study of Indian Legal History," *Law and History Review* 23, no. 3 (2005): 703–6.

[4] Kolsky, "A Note on the Study of Indian Legal History."

[5] Sudipta Kaviraj, "On the Construction of Colonial Power: Structure, Discourse, Hegemony," in Dagmar Engels and Shula Marks (eds), *Contesting Colonial Hegemony: State and Society in Africa and India* (London: British Academic Press, 1994); Chatterjee, *Nation and its Fragments*; Gyanendra Pandey, *The Construction of Communalism in Colonial North India* (Oxford: Oxford University Press, 2006). Pandey argues that colonialism played a significant role in the creation of religious communalism in India. Other works stress a similar, transformational nature of nineteenth-century developments: Nicholas B. Dirks, *Castes of Mind: Colonialism and the Making of Modern India* (Princeton: Princeton University Press, 2001); Arjun Appadurai, *Worship and Conflict under Colonial Rule* (Cambridge: Cambridge University Press, 1981).

[6] C.A. Bayly, *Origins of Nationality in South Asia: Patriotism and Ethical Government in the Making of Modern India* (Oxford: Oxford University Press, 1998), 44–49, 210–37. He argues that communalism

arena in Sri Lanka is necessary to determine the full extent of its transformational role. In contrast to nineteenth-century British understandings of the imposition of Roman-Dutch law, this study reveals a story of how Dutch law intertwined with local legal orders in the eighteenth century. Within the social arena of Dutch-controlled Galle, social actors from both elite and non-elite groups identified more than one source of law, a situation that was mutually recognised, if not successfully followed.

Navigating Pluralities

The Dutch set up an institutional legal structure through the Landraad that peasants approached for mediation. In Jeremy Ravi Mumford's words, "[j]udging the colonized population was both a claim to legitimacy and a major part of the colonizers' job." [7] Sri Lankan peasants faced courts of record for the first time through the Dutch legal system, as the textual proceedings of the Landraad were novel within the local normative order. Boosting judicial efficiency was not far from the intentions of the Dutch Government, but efforts to bring down costs of litigation or improve local participation were not always successful. The Galle Landraad can be seen as a site for negotiation between the Sinhalese, other locals and the VOC rather than simply an instrument for colonial domination. Yet, this process was mired in uncertainty and confusion, and lacked a clear trajectory.

In a racialised hierarchy, dominant "white" members were pitted against "black" councillors in the Landraad. As in the Landraad in Java, which also had local councillors, there was never a local chairman or majority on the bench. The Indonesian and Sri Lankan sides were thus subordinate to the Dutch side – ultimately a sign of direct rule.[8] Local headmen were powerful, but clearly less so than company officials; peasant farmers had even less power. Yet we must consider the interdependence, however uneven, among the parties concerned. The locals wielded independently created entitlements and could use tools, such as the petition or riot, to compel the stronger coloniser to enter into negotiations over rule-making. Without the native department of the bureaucracy, the indirect rule of the company had little hope of survival; for their provision of labour services, including the collection of the prized cinnamon, the inhabitants were

during the colonial period had its origins in the eighteenth century. Susan Bayly argues that caste was a distinct part of Indian life, one that evolved from the pre-colonial period, in *Caste, Society and Politics in India from the Eighteenth Century to the Modern Age* (Cambridge: Cambridge University Press, 2001).

[7] Jeremy Ravi Mumford, "Litigation as Ethnography in Sixteenth-Century Peru: Polo de Ondegardo and the Mitimaes," *Hispanic American Historical Review* 88, no. 1 (2008): 5–40.

[8] Daniel S. Lev, "Colonial Law and the Genesis of the Indonesian State," *Indonesia*, no. 40 (1985): 57–74.

indispensable to both local and foreign elite formations. While the company held the threat of coercion and, if necessary, violence in establishing "collaboration," locals had the recourse of turning to the Kandyan kingdom and harming the company's economic interests. The relative bargaining powers of the company, local elite and peasant groups are indeterminable and are unlikely to have been spatially and temporally static. Men and women of high and low ritual status groups across cultures and economic standing strove for justice in the Landraad, which engaged in the task of essentialising identities based on caste that were linked to labour services. The litigants and witnesses who appeared in the Landraad – presented in this book in a hitherto unseen manner in Sri Lankan historical literature – were not necessarily undiscerning collaborators who simply affirmed the legitimacy of the colonial judicial forum. As Lauren Benton says, drawing on Pierre Bourdieu, "[i]t is possible simultaneously to use imposed law (thereby reaffirming it) and to seek to undermine its authority."[9] Authority, through recognition of plural authorities of law, could also contain features of the local normative order, achieved through a process of navigation. This can be seen in both the subtle and more evident processes that I analysed in this book.

The Dutch believed that property rights, clearly defined through the implementation of the land registration process, had obvious economic benefits and helped individuals live together in peace and prosperity. Indigenous practices of land tenure and fixing property boundaries, pre-existing and emerging practices of registering lands, Dutch and local practices of surveying and traditional means of communicating information via tom-tom beaters were combined with a new institutional legal framework for dispute settlement. On entering the local framework, the Dutch colonial power sought to establish a legal foundation for the exercise of authority, based on both Roman-Dutch legal procedures and laws and local normative orders. Traditional forms of ordering society were then faced with different forms of knowledge and institutional practices in the assigning of meanings. In seeking to combine written records, such as deeds of gift and sale, and the oral evidence and memories of the inhabitants in a new legal forum, new forms of ordering knowledge emerged. But this was not purely an imposition of a foreign system – the one in place in the eighteenth century grew out of multiple systems of knowledge. For the VOC there was a need to define laws on property, and the thombo and the Landraad were the central instruments used for that purpose. At times, procedural rules and practical experience were in conflict; processes had to be adapted during the course of the registration of land. Governance had to be on a stable footing, but the primary aim of the thombo was to know who owned what and how much was due to the

[9] Lauren Benton, *Law and Colonial Cultures: Legal Regimes in World History, 1400–1900* (Cambridge: Cambridge University Press, 2001), 257–58.

company in cash or crop shares. In the end, it was a means by which Dutch possession could become more profitable through a coherent and functional basis for revenue collection. It had also to have meaning ideologically – the definitions of land tenure, while having their foundations in the local normative order, also needed to have meaning for the new European rulers. Despite the complexities of the local land tenure system, the VOC attempted to enforce rules and regulations that would create a neat, circumscribed system that followed specific legal procedures and written forms. This was not always achieved in practice, indicating the important yet discreet role played by peasants in defining land rights.

The ideas and practices of the agrarian regime at the time were navigated in the formal, legal spaces of the thombo registration and the Landraad, an effort that involved both officials and shareholders in the process of lawmaking. Their interdependence would have been a key factor in negotiations. The law was central to controlling the lands of the colonised – or economically powerless groups – and incorporating plural legal orders was often a part of this effort. In the end, the law has to be productive, not repressive or limiting. The texts of law had to be made real in the courtroom, where they could be received or rejected. In a colonial setting, one can expect difficulties in translating terms cross-culturally. Chapter five focused on how the VOC went about deciphering local land tenure in practice. It dealt with the continuation of local customs and the flexibility of rules, given that an expectation of colonialism as a "great watershed"[10] of change is no longer tenable.

A reading of legal narratives from eighteenth-century Galle shows that the local inhabitants regarded the company and its legal system as a means of affirming ownership and resolving land disputes. This was rendered necessary through the registration process. We can imagine that the compilation of the thombos gave out a clear signal to the citizens as to who controlled the coast and its hinterland. The interplay between colonial and indigenous needs would eventually lead to a compromise. Chapter five showed how the thombo and the Landraad were sites of interaction or negotiation for both Europeans and locals, and simultaneously a means of colonial domination. They battled out on the cadastre their own particular understandings of property rights, and these battles come alive in the succession disputes of the Landraad, which I have analysed in chapter six. By the mid-eighteenth century, the local inhabitants were at least reasonably knowledgeable of the Dutch forms of law and used this knowledge to their advantage in navigating the law. Some saw the pluralities of law as opportunities. To others, they signified the imposition of baffling judgements. In inheritance law, pluralities of rules could be oppressive or accommodating.

[10] Nicholas B. Dirks, "From Little King to Landlord: Property, Law and the Gift under the Madras Permanent Settlement," *Comparative Studies in Society and History* 28, no. 2 (1986): 307–33.

Exactly which aspects are borrowed or rejected between foreign and local legal orders cannot be easily predicted, but the dominance of inheritance, land and marriage law in socio-legal studies of legal pluralism gives some indication. Not all attempts at assimilation were fully realised; aspects of evidence law, such as the decisory oath, were unsuccessful in practice. The oath in Dutch Sri Lanka was a judicial site in which religious differences between the cultural spaces of Europe and Asia were both passionately and dispassionately denied, debated and endorsed within the platform of the Landraad. The decisory function of the Dutch oath had an accidental congruence to the local practice, as did the bilateral laws of inheritance I explored in chapter six. We can also see more conscious adoption or adaptation of local practices, as in the acceptance of the Sinhalese forms of the oath, local land tenurial practices, the concept of familial assistance in inheritance cases, and the Sinhalese way of marriage or consensual decision-making in the case of the inheritance of nonmarital children.

In eighteenth-century southern Sri Lanka, the European concept of illegitimacy seeped into family life through colonial rule. A lawsuit initially heard in a lower court, which then went to appeal in Galle, revealed how a woman and her two sons were rudely awakened to the possibility of their property rights being rescinded through a new law on nonmarital children imposed by the VOC. Others in the family sought to gain more land by citing the new legal consequences of nonmarital birth. Yet, the birth was not registered as onecht at the registration of the thombo. The Landraad with its mixed body of local and European officials, which operated at a lower level of the hierarchy of judicial fora, looked at the issue of nonmarital children more benevolently. But their decision was overturned and judged as incorrect by a higher court that was exclusively European. This micro-study compellingly shows how some colonial laws could strike at the heart of the family. Family members would have invested in such litigation due to personal motivations. The new laws may have been perplexing to peasant society, but could be reflexively "consumed" in a way that would have had long-term effects on redefining some aspects of the family. Thus, the emerging dominance of company rules in family law is unmistakable.

Through this discussion, I question the notion of the enforcement of distinctly defined cultural boundaries in jurisdiction and suggest that accommodation, negotiation and resourcefulness are more appropriate concepts for understanding the legal interactions that occurred in eighteenth-century Sri Lanka. The coloniser would negotiate on rule-making "because he believes himself morally obliged to do so, or, more pragmatically, because he believes that establishing rules by the sheer use of power may entail undue costs."[11] Resistance by the locals would impose

[11] Melvin Aron Eisenberg, "Private Ordering through Negotiation: Dispute-Settlement and Rulemaking," *Harvard Law Review* 89 (1976): 675.

costs that would make the colonial enterprise on the island economically unviable. Recognising the local normative order was conducive to the company, yet they did it within limits. In family law, the Sinhalese way of marriage, the concept of familial assistance, or the inheritance of nonmarital children, were normative practices to which the locals were able to induce the compliance of the Landraad. Distinct knowledge of the law, as opposed to intuitive groping in the dark, as it were, characterised indigenous legal participation. Furthermore, the Dutch Government recognised land tenurial agreements for their obvious economic benefits. On the adoption of Sinhalese laws, the company found the middle ground between strict and permissive extremes through a process of navigating pluralities.

Discerning Pluralities

The conventional legal literature in Sri Lanka has tended to draw a sharp line between the use of Sinhalese and Roman-Dutch law. The underlying assumptions of the discussion have seen a mostly dichotomous solution to the problem. This early debate can benefit from the developing legal literature on "pluralism as a central concept in studies of diffusion or transplantation of law."[12] The cultural twist in the discussion about the lack of a Sinhalese code is hard to shed, but I emphasise moving away from culturalist arguments. For the inhabitants of Galle, the law could have simply been a means to an end, and the use of customary laws, or the lack thereof, would have assumed a secondary role with the local population, at least in certain areas. The people were provided with a "durable, if flexible resource,"[13] and it would enhance our understanding to be conscious of a "hodge-podge of courts and norms operating side by side" and of "various complex mixtures and combinations, and mutual influences"[14] within the whole legal system, let alone within the operation of the Landraad. This warrants a refashioning in the way the story is told in legal education in Sri Lanka. Legal pluralism and its functioning should be emphasised, despite the conventional suspicions that lawyers hold about legal pluralists.[15]

[12] William Twining, "Normative and Legal Pluralism: A Global Perspective," *Duke Journal of Comparative & International Law* 20 (2009): 487.

[13] Lauren Benton and Richard J. Ross, eds., *Legal Pluralism and Empires, 1500–1850*, Kindle edition (New York: NYU Press, 2013), 3.

[14] Brian Z. Tamanaha, "Understanding Legal Pluralism: Past to Present, Local to Global," *Sydney L. Rev.* 30 (2008): 375.

[15] William Twining refers to how lawyers can be resistant to the idea of legal pluralism in "Normative and Legal Pluralism," 476. For a fuller account see Roger Cotterrell, *Law, Culture and Society: Legal Ideas in the Mirror of Society Theory* (Hampshire: Ashgate Publishing, 2006).

The Galle Landraad exemplified a forum where a choice of laws came into play; that choice was significant in varying degrees for different areas of the law. The councillors were asked to adjudicate according to local custom but also told they had the option of resorting to Dutch laws when local laws were unclear or unreasonable. The Landraad shows the tension of two apparently competing sets of norms within a single system. It is no surprise that the likes of Kalegana Bastian Naidelage Maria of Galle said that even her dog would not appear before the Landraad.[16] Nominal Christians in Galle rejected the Dutch form of the oath, yet, at the same time, they used its non-acceptance to their advantage in preventing opponents from being admitted to the oath. Pilane Godakandege Gimara collided more visibly with the Dutch Government in appealing the loss of her inheritance due to her late husband's nonmarital birth, which she did not seek to hide. Resistance, however subtle, was unavoidable and served to undermine the company's state-like power. At the same time, the company was careful to ensure subordination and widespread recognition of their authority. Litigants employed strategies of both adaptation and resistance to the colonial power. We must also remember that the higher judicial councils are likely to have prioritised Dutch law. Where possible, this predominance was also imposed on the Landraad. But at times, their efforts to recognise the local normative order were also successful. The exclusion of such adaptability between legal orders from the concept of legal pluralism is not viable, as it would exclude the lived experience of inter-legality within the Dutch legal regime. The local normative order was as much a social fact as Roman-Dutch law, and early colonial rulers understood that it could not be ignored.

We may use an "ism" in the term "legal pluralism," but Paul Halliday is right to say "in the living of laws in the past, they were simply pluralities." As in this study, in the hands of historians, "pluralism has become pluralities."[17] Thus, the sources of all laws are hardly likely to be acquired rather than existing normative practices. Pluralities, both imposed and existing, operated within the council or in the codifications of the laws of ethnic and religious groups in Sri Lanka. They demonstrate how the inhabitants of southern Sri Lanka experienced the early colonial world. It is not the intention of this study, however, to romanticise the notion of pluralism.[18] I have, as Halliday advocates for historians, observed pluralities. The observation of pluralities, however, must not be an endpoint: I have shown that when discerned

[16] See chapter three.

[17] Paul Halliday, "Laws' Histories: Pluralisms, Pluralities, Diversity," in Lauren Benton and Richard J. Ross (eds), *Legal Pluralism and Empires, 1500-1850*, Kindle edition (New York: NYU Press, 2013), 262.

[18] Santos and others have warned against such romanticisation. See Twining, "Normative and Legal Pluralism," 502; Boaventura de Sousa Santos, *Toward a New Legal Common Sense: Law, Globalization, and Emancipation* (Cambridge: Cambridge University Press, 2002), 89.

in practice, they might fail, as they could be either supported or contested. This is evident, for example, in the ultimately unsuccessful adoption of the local form of the oath, and in the Landraad's more consensual stance on the inheritance of nonmarital children backfiring at a higher level of legal authority. Studies of this nature can thus provide in-depth analyses of legal pluralism in practice.

This in turn informs us about the nature of early colonial rule. Benton rightly says, "[c]olonial states did not in an important sense exist *as* states in the early centuries of colonialism. They did not claim or produce a monopoly on legal authority or on the assignment of political and legal identity." She points out that there was an undeniable dominance, "but both colonizing factions and colonized groups were not irrational or deluded when they sought advantage in the fractured qualities of rule."[19] As explained in the introduction, I have presented the "nuanced historical analysis of legal pluralism," that Benton and Ross have lamented the loss of, but state is not as practicable as a focus on jurisdictional conflict that shows structural changes.[20] This work uniquely gestures towards a nuanced history from below of the headmen and peasants involved in lawmaking through an approach that integrates socio-legal studies, the nature of colonial rule and peasant studies. An emphasis on jurisdictional conflicts alone would have skewed our understanding of legal pluralism and colonialism in Dutch Sri Lanka.

The incorporation of existing practices and ideologies into the enterprise of colonialism makes it less of a rupture than Dirks contended.[21] The practice of law in Dutch times further emphasises that the transformative role of colonialism as it trickled down to peasants was not consistently dissonant with the local normative order. The legal structure had to come to terms with existing norms and legal practices. Yet, the transplant, as it were, also sought to disrupt the existing order. The pluralities of the system in practice would invariably bring about a seemingly unsatisfactory association of both change and continuity, as David Washbrook argues.[22] The tempered normality of the recognition of pluralities would inevitably lead to such an association, as other means of managing the diversity of laws that were encountered would not be feasible. As Benton and Ross state, "[i]mperial officials could regard jurisdictional complexity as acting to reinforce state power rather than unleashing transformative conflicts. The dynamics of legal pluralism, they show, extended well beyond the end point of the mid-nineteenth century...

19 Benton, *Law and Colonial Cultures*, 259. Emphasis as in original.

20 Benton and Ross, *Legal Pluralism and Empires*, 5–6.

21 Nicholas B. Dirks, *The Hollow Crown: Ethnohistory of an Indian Kingdom* (Michigan: University of Michigan Press, 1993).

22 David Washbrook, "South India 1770–1840: The Colonial Transition," *Modern Asian Studies* 38, no. 3 (July 2004): 479–516.

and beyond any other artificial marker separating 'early modern' and 'modern' worlds."[23] The Landraad in Galle exemplifies the early colonial practices of legal pluralism, which in turn arguably had its origins in a much earlier time, under the local normative order, through the practice of situational judging. This is in contrast to optimistic calls for one law for all in popular Sri Lankan politics today. Colonial experiences of law instruct us in the adoption of an inclusive approach in law reform, structural adjustment programmes and human rights advocacy.

The company's extensive penetration into local society is evident through the Landraad, which is a rich source for understanding the intersection of local and external normative orders. This book is one step towards an in-depth study of a colonial judicial forum, but a vast unexplored territory still lies buried in the archives, waiting to be noticed.

[23] Benton and Ross, *Legal Pluralism and Empires*, 14.

APPENDIX I

European Members at the Galle Landraad 1759–96[1]

Name	*Birthplace*	*First appointment*	*Record in meetings*	
			First	*Last*
Aldons, Hendrik	Galle	1768	22 Jun 1782	25 Sept 1784
Aldons, Jacobus	Galle	1767	29 Apr 1786	24 Jul 1787
			5 Jan 1788	21 Mar 1789
Anthonisz, Steven	Galle	1762	31 Mar 1781	12 Dec 1795
Bergh, Adrianus van den	Dordrecht	1768	15 Jul 1769	7 Jan 1775
Bergheim, Bernhard Hendrik van	Colombo	1783	16 Feb 1788	21 Mar 1789
Brakel, Hendrik	Colombo	1737	14 Jul 1764	19 Dec 1772
Busing, Eijlert	Oldenburg	1760	21 Feb 1767	21 Mar 1772
Cadenski, Johan Pieter Simon	Jaffna	-	25 Oct 1786	28 Jun 1793
Cock, Cornelis de	Emden	1755	5 Sept 1767	30 Dec 1769
Conradie, Johan Fredrik	Kirchheim	1772	16 May 1778	9 May 1779
Cramer, Hendrik	Galle	1742	20 Jul 1763	16 Aug 1766
Engelbregt, Harmanus	Galle	1737	9 Jul 1768	30 Apr 1785
Engelbregt, Johannes	Galle	1738	21 Mar 1772	13 Feb 1776

[1] The Landraad councillors are given here in alphabetical order, with the dates indicating when they appeared for the first and last occasion in the available meeting records. At times their first day in the Landraad is corroborated by a letter of appointment from the Galle commander and formal introductions at the meetings. A few records of earlier meetings exist but these are intermittent. Councillors who served for short periods from 1759 to 1796 may have escaped this list as some meeting data during this period is also missing. It must be kept in mind that some members were absent for long durations, citing reasons mentioned in chapter two. The "last" date is the day on which the member is listed for the last time in the available meeting records, but it does not mean that he was always present at that meeting. On some occasions, his death was announced on that day. The "generale land- en zeemonsterrollen" of the VOC's Amsterdam chamber and S.A.W. Mottau's indexes of acts of appointments from Galle and Colombo provided information on birthplace and first appointment in the East. Family trees published in the *Journal of the Dutch Burgher Union* and the database of VOC sea voyagers (https://www.nationaalarchief.nl/onderzoeken/index/nt00444) were also useful in drawing up this table.

Name	*Birthplace*	*First appointment*	*Record in meetings*	
			First	*Last*
Evaristo, Jean	[Spain]	-	9 Oct 1790	12 Dec 1795
Franken, Johan Harmanus	Heusden	1764	14 Oct 1775	25 Jul 1778
Fretz, Diederick Thomas	St Goar	1764	24 Feb 1770	2 Mar 1782
Frits, Roelof	Karlskron	1745	26 Apr 1760	30 Dec 1763
German, Johan Casper	Hildersheim	1766	9 Dec 1779	11 Oct 1783
Gijsel, Dirk François van	Colombo	1763	20 Apr 1786	12 Dec 1795
Graaff, Adriaan Sebastiaan van de	Huissen	-	14 May 1785	24 Mar 1787
Gratiaan, Johannes Franciscus	Bruges	-	14 Apr 1787	5 Apr 1788
Haan, Johannes de	Galle	1736	29 Sept 1759	30 Dec 1769
Haartel, Christian Hendrik	Altenberg	1757	16 May 1778	2 Jun 1781
			20 Apr 1786	14 Apr 1787
Hingert, Hendrik Johannes	Galle	1760	5 Jan 1788	28 Jun 1788
Huijbertsz, Christiaan	Galle	1745	21 Feb 1767	1 Dec 1787
Johnson, Hendrik Anthony	-	-	10 May 1793	12 Dec 1795
Jolles, Lourens	Jaffna	1760	31 Mar 1781	12 Dec 1795
Kersse, Daniel Gerardus	Colombo	1750	6 May 1775	31 Mar 1781
Koene, Hendrik	Amsterdam	1756	20 Jul 1771	12 Mar 1774
Kroner, George Michiel	Pappenheim	1760	25 Jul 1778	15 Jun 1782
Lasge, Nicolaas	Galle	1734	29 Sept 1759	25 Sept 1779
Leembruggen, Robbertus Henricus	Matara	-	9 Oct 1790	10 May 1793
Leeuw, Johannes de	Galle	1730	29 Sept 1759	6 Dec 1760
Lij, Andreas Everhardus de	Colombo	1778	24 Dec 1779	12 Oct 1782
Loose, Jan	Bremen	1752	25 Jul 1778	29 Jul 1780
Lourensz, Adriaan Hendrik	Galle	1762	19 Apr 1788	18 Feb 1792
Marci, Adolph Fredrik	Lubeek	1751	17 Sept 1762	6 Aug 1764
Marci, Paulus	Cochin	1760	14 Jul 1764	14 Feb 1767

Name	*Birthplace*	*First appointment*	*Record in meetings*	
			First	*Last*
Marin, August Charles de	Celle	1774	25 Jul 1778	21 Oct 1780
Martheze, Nicolaas Bernardus	Galle	1737	27 Jun 1767	5 Sept 1767
			7 Jan 1775	21 Sept 1776
			11 Mar 1780	15 Jul 1780
Mazius, Sixtus	Colombo	1737	14 Jul 1764	14 Feb 1767
Medeler, Hendrik Anthonij	Colombo	1751	21 Feb 1767	28 Nov 1767
Meurling, Johannes	Westerwijk	1745	20 Nov 1779	
Moor, Pieter Arend de	Colombo	1761	20 Apr 1786	12 Dec 1795
Nagel, Harmanus	Amsterdam	1749	8 Dec 1770	22 Jun 1771
Oosterlo, Maurits	Varnholte	1723	29 Sept 1759	6 Dec 1760
Otto, Coenraad	Mannar	1751	21 Mar 1789	2 Aug 1793
Poulier, Aarnout	Galle	1740	14 July 1764	6 Aug 1764
Poulier, Adriaan	Galle	1770	21 Apr 1781	15 May 1784
Prevo, Coenraad	-	1733	14 Jul 1764	8 Mar 1766
Ranzow, August Christian Anthon Graaf van	Oldenburg	1788	23 Aug 1793	12 Dec 1795
Rooij, Jacobus de	Galle	1740	9 Mar 1765	7 Jan 1775
Roosmale Cocq, Petrus Jacobus	Leiden	1764	16 May 1778	19 Aug 1785
			11 Dec 1790	12 Dec 1795
Runstoff, Casparus	Matara	1766	19 Aug 1785	14 Jan 1786
Samlant, Abraham	Colombo	1769	24 Dec 1779	12 Nov 1788
Schreuder, Johan Fredrik	Erfurt	1775	12 May 1787	1 Sept 1787
Schuler, Pieter William Ferdinand Adriaan van	Utrecht	1780	12 Nov 1788	23 Oct 1790
Sieling, Casper	Galle	1755	4 Jul 1772	25 Jul 1772
Silva, Pieter Simonsz de	Galle	1761	28 May 1785	12 May 1787
Sluijsken, Pieter	Amsterdam	1758	15 Jan 1766	14 Mar 1772
Stein, Johannes	Halle	1745	29 Sept 1759	15 Jul 1775
Strehl, Johan Theodoor	-	-	29 Sept 1759	22 Oct 1760
Stroebbe, Balthazar Hendrik	Osnabrück	1748	14 Jul 1764	27 Apr 1776

Name	*Birthplace*	*First appointment*	*Record in meetings*	
			First	*Last*
Stroebbe, Balthazar Nicolaas	Galle	1760	29 Jul 1775	21 Sept 1776
Swieten, Floris van	Leiden	1736	12 Jul 1760	15 Oct 1762
Teylingen, Theodoris van	Negapatnam	1784	24 May 1788	12 Nov 1788
Tekenborg, Jan David	Nijmegen	1763	21 Feb 1767	19 Dec 1772
Toussaint, Johannes	Colombo	1732	29 Sept 1759	6 Dec 1760
Trek, Justinus Christiaan	Colombo	1775	11 Jul 1787	12 Dec 1795
Velde, Egbert van de	Galle	1734	29 Sept 1759	6 Dec 1760
Velzen, Adriaan van	Batavia	1746	21 Feb 1767	26 Nov 1768
Vos, Pieter de	Colombo	1742	8 Jun 1765	21 Mar 1772
			16 Nov 1782	2 Feb 1793
Wahlberg, Johannes	Kalmer	1787	10 May 1793	12 Dec 1795
Wijnants, Gerrits Jansz	-	-	15 Aug 1772	21 Sept 1776
Zitter, Wilhelmus Gijsbert van	Galle	1766	8 Jul 1786	-

APPENDIX II

Rulers of Kandy and Dutch Governors

Kings of Kandy 1591–1815	
Vimaladharmasuriya I	1591–1604
Senerat	1604–1635
Rajasingha II	1635–1687
Vimaladharmasuriya II	1687–1707
Narendra Singha	1707–1739
Sri Vijaya Rajasingha	1739–1747
Kirti Sri Rajasingha	1747–1782
Rajadhi Rajasingha	1782–1798
Sri Vikrama Rajasingha	1798–1815

Dutch Governors of Ceylon 1640–1796	
Willem J. Coster	1640
Jan Thyszoon	1640–1646
Jan Maatzuyker	1646–1650
Jacob van Kittensteyn	1650–1653
Adriaan van der Meijden	1653–1660
Rijklof van Goens	1660–1661
Adriaan van der Meijden	1661–1663
Rijklof van Goens	1663
Jacob Hustraart	1663–1664
Rijklof van Goens	1664–1675
Rijklof van Goens Jr.	1675–1780
Laurens Pijl	1680–1692
Thomas van Rhee	1693–1697
Gerrit de Heere	1697–1703
Cornelis Jan Simons	1703–1707
Hendrik Becker	1707–1716
Isaac Augusteijn Rumpf	1716–1723
Johannes Hertenberg	1723–1726
Petrus Vuyst	1726–1729
Stephanus Versluys	1729–1732

Jacob Christiaan Pielat	1732–1734
Diederik van Domburg	1734–1736
Gustaaf Willem Baron van Imhoff	1736–1739
Willem Maurits Bruyninck	1739–1742
Daniel Overbeek	1742–1743
Julius Valentijn Stein van Gollonesse	1743–1751
Gerard Jan Vreelandt	1751–1752
Johan Gideon Loten	1752–1757
Jan Schreuder	1757–1761
Lubbert Jan Baron van Eck	1762–1765
Iman Willem Falck	1765–1785
Willem Jacob van de Graaff	1785–1794
Johan Gerard van Angelbeek	1794–1796

APPENDIX III

List of Accommodessan Grants

	amunu	*pela*	*kuruni*
To a *maha* or first *mudaliyār* of the governor's gate	20		
To a second *mudaliyār* of the governor's gate	18		
To a *mohotiaar*[1]	14		
To a *mohandiram* of the guard of the governor's gate	14		
To a *mudaliyār* of the *dessave* called *atapattu mudaliyār*	12		
To the *mudaliyārs* of the *kōralēs* each	12		
All *mohandirams* each	8		
All *ārachchis* each	6		
All *kangāns*	4		
All *lascarins*	2		
The *kōrālas* of the Hewagam en Salpity *kōralēs**	10		
A *mahavidāne* of the gold- and silversmiths gets**	6		
To a *vidāne* of a *pattu*	4		
To a *atukōrāla*[2]	3		
To a *mohotti* of the *kōralēs* or secretary	3		
To a village writer	2		
To a village *vidāne*	1		
To a *terikōrāla* or servant of the *atukōrāla*		3	
To a *saparamādu* or permanent commissioner	3		
To a *mayorāl*	2		
To a *nainde*		2	
To a *kuruwerāle* or master of the elephant hunt	10		
To a *pantiya ārachchi* or chief of the elephants' stable	3		

[1] A clerk or secretary.

[2] An assistant to a *kōrāla*.

	amunu	*pela*	*kuruni*
To a *baddena ārachchi* or assistant of an elephant catcher	2		
To a *mahapannikila* or chief of the elephant drivers	2		
To a *kudapannikila* or assistant of a *mahapannikila*	1	2	
To a *kornak* or elephant driver	1		
To a *mahaduraya* or head of the *pannayas*		2	
To a *liyanaduraya* or writer of the *pannayas*		2	
To a *kudaduraya* or assistant of the *mahaduraya*		2	
To a *hulawaliya* or messenger		2	
To a *dekumkaraya* or attendant of the elephant stables		2	
To a *pannaya* or grass-cutter		3	
To a head of the gold- and silversmiths in Colombo	6		
To a head of the stone-cutters	4		
To a head of the goldsmiths in the *kōralēs*	3		
To a head of the iron smiths	2		
To a head of the carpenters	2		
To a head of the gold smith		3	
To a *gamachāria* or smith of the villages		2	
To a carpenter		2	5
To a *porovakāraya* or woodcutter		3	
To a *kangān* of the *pottebakkers*	1		
To a *pottebakker*		3	
To a *vidāne* or *pēdiya* of the *wassers*	1		
To a *wasser*		2	
To a *tamblinjero*	1		
To a *tamblinjero* of the villagers or *berewase*		2	
To a grain-measure called *mananna*	3		
To a coolie	1		
To a *vidāne* of the barbers	1		
To a barber			
To a *kangān* of the huntsmen	1	2	
To a huntsman	1		
To a horn player or *kambukāraya*	1		

	amunu	*pela*	*kuruni*
To a *schalmij*[3] player or *horiyākaraya*	1		
To a provider of provisions for Kandyan ambassadors	6		

**Note in original: But the kōrālas of the other kōralēs should maintain themselves from the usual pehindums or the obligatory pingos, which the mayorāls should bring to them monthly... The wibadde vidānes, or collectors of the company taxes also get nothing, but they should manage with the 5 per cent excess and 2 parras paddy per month that the company allows them, apart from those who are also ārachchis over some lascarins for whom the company then allows land.*

***Note in original: But the other mahavidānes of the gold- and silversmiths receive nothing.*

Source: Sluijsken, "A Description of the Land Services," (1784) p. 249-257. He refers to the Colombo Dessavony in this list, but implies in his description of Galle that it applies to that district as well.

3 A type of horn.

Bibliography

Unpublished Primary Sources

Sri Lanka National Archives (SLNA)
Lot 1: VOC Records

Governor in Council minutes:
1/78 (1740); 1/92 (1744); 1/93 (1744); 1/94 (1745); 1/98 (1746); 1/104 (1748); 1/125 (1758); 1/127 (1758); 1/149 (1766); 1/151 (1767); 1/160 (1770); 1/165 (1772); 1/188 (1784); 1/191 (1785); 1/192 (1785); 1/193 (1786); 1/211 (1790); 1/213 (1791); 1/214 (1791); 1/226 (1794).

Galle Landraad:
Galle Landraad minutes (20 Dec 1745) and governor's comments (5 Feb 1746): 1/2805 (1745 to 1746).
Copies of proceedings of Galle and Matara Landraden sent to Colombo: 1/3215 (1747 to 1748); 1/3216 (1749 to 1752).
Extracts of resolutions, orders, etc. regarding the Landraad and the thombo compilation: SLNA 1/5658 (1740 to 1745); 1/5659 (1743 to 1744); 1/5660 (1740 to 1770).
Miscellaneous documents of the Galle Landraad including instructions: 1/5666 (1761 to 1789).
Digest of orders and extracts from council minutes etc. received by the Galle Landraad: 1/6204 (1745 to 1779).
Registers of deeds affecting land, Galle: 1/6491 (1780 to 1791).
Galle Landraad depositions: 1/6492 (1760 to 1770); 1/6494 (1778 to 1781); 1/6495 (1783 to 1793); 1/6496 (1780 to 1799).
Galle Landraad minutes: 1/6497 (1759); 1/6498 (1760); 1/6499 (1760 to 1763); 1/6500 (1763 to 1764); 1/6501 (1765 to 1766); 1/6502 (1767); 1/6503 (1768); 1/6504 (1769); 1/6505 (1770); 1/6506 (1771); 1/6507 (1772); 1/6508 (1774); 1/6509 (1775); 1/6510 (1775); 1/6511 (1778); 1/6512 (1779); 1/6513 (1780); 1/6514 (1781); 1/6515 (1787 to 1793); 1/6516 (1793); 1/6517 (1794).
Galle Landraad drafts minutes: 1/6519 (1775 to 1776); 1/6520 (1778 to 1779); 1/6521 (1779 to 1780); 1/6522 (1780 to 1781); 1/6523 (1781 to 1782); 1/6524 (1783); 1/6525 (1784 to 1786).

Annexes to Galle Landraad minutes: 1/6526 (1780 to 1782); 1/6527 (1782 to 1785).
Notes of inquiries by Galle Landraad commissioners in cases of theft and other offences: 1/6532 (1784 to 1793); 1/6533 (1795).
Galle Landraad interrogations: 1/6534 (1778 to 1784); 1/6535 (1785 to 1793).
Inward letters, Galle Landraad: 7/2353 (1778 to 1801).
Miscellaneous documents of the Galle Landraad with conditions of auction sales, notices etc, 7/2354 (1776 to 1779).

Galle Thombos:
1/7419, Dadalla (Four Gravets), 1782 to 1784.
1/7424, Degalle (Wellaboda), 1784.
1/7428, Dodampe (Wellaboda), 1780.
1/7441, Ganegama (Gangaboda), 1760.
1/7442, Ganegoda (Wellaboda), 1780.
1/7445, Gintota (Four Gravets), 1745.
1/7447, Mipe (Talpe), 1751.
1/7460, Hinatigala (Talpe), 1750.
1/7462, Hiniduma (Hinidum), 1760.
1/7467, Horangalla (Wellaboda), 1778.
1/7472, Ihala/Uda Gigunmaduwa (Hinidum), 1760.
1/7491, Kumbalwella (Four Gravets), 1741 to 1750.
1/7501, Mapalagama (Gangaboda) (1760)
1/7512, Naranowita (Walallawiti), 1778.
1/7519, Opata Thalangala (Hinidum), 1760.
1/7519, Pahala Gigunmaduwa (Hinidum), 1760.
1/7569, Panangala (Hinidum), 1760.
1/7531, Pitigala (Walallawiti), 1778.
1/7534, Piyadigama (Four Gravets), 1744.
1/7542, Tawalama (Hinidum), 1760.
1/7557, Unawatuna (Talpe), 1748.

Scholarchale Vergadering minutes:
1/6219 (1766 to 1768); 1/6220 (1768 to 1770); 1/6221 (1770 to 1773); 1/6222 (1774 to 1778); 1/6224 (1779 to 1783); 1/6225 (1786 to 1787); 1/6226 (1789 to 1791)

Other:
Governor in Council draft ordinary minutes: 1/273 (1747).
Galle Political Council minutes: 1/1514 (1789); 1/5046 (1743 to 1746).
Outward letters, Colombo to Galle: 1/1565 (1789).
Considerations by Governor Van Imhoff on the management of the island: 1/2784 and 1/2785 (1740).
Inward letters, Colombo to Galle: 1/5315 (1789).
Register of acts of appointment of company's officials: 1/5684 (1728 to 1729); 1/5690 (1742 to 1747).
Register of acts of appointment of native officials: 1/5713 (1767 to 1775).
Draft of annual compendium sent to Colombo: 1/5895 (1774 to 1775).
Galle translations of olas: 1/5969 (1780 to 1784).
Modder, Earle. Memoranda of the laws of inheritance &c., and notes on Sir John D'Oyly's exposition of the Kandyan law by Simon Sawers: SLNA 25. 98/4.

National Archives of The Netherlands
Archives of the Verenigde Oost Indische Compagnie (VOC): 1.04.02
NL-HaNA, VOC 2927. Resolutions of the Governor in Council. 1758.
NL-HaNA, VOC 5208–5238. Generale land- en zeemonsterrollen of the VOC's Amsterdam chamber (1760–1790).

Rijksmuseum

Brandes, Jan, *Cornelis de Cock with Sinhalese Officers in Hulftsdorp, Colombo, Seated in His Verandah to Settle the Affairs and Disputes of the Natives*, November 29, 1785, Watercolour over sketch in pencil, 19.5 x 15.5, November 29, 1785, Rijksmuseum, Amsterdam, https://www.rijksmuseum.nl//en/collection/NG-1985-7-1-9

Reimer, Carel Frederik. *Ontvangst van de Gezanten van de Koning van Kandy Door Gouverneur Imam Falck*, 1772, h 280 mm × b 430 mm, 1772, Rijksmuseum, Amsterdam, https://www.rijksmuseum.nl/nl/collectie/RP-T-1904-18.

New York Public Library

Alexander Johnston Papers (1643 to 1817), MssCol 1578, Manuscripts and Archives Division, The New York Public Library.

National Archives at Kew

CO 54/124. Ceylon Native Laws and Customs, Part 2, Presented by Sir Alexander Johnston. 1770. National Archives, Kew.

Christian Reformed Church, Wellawatte

Baptismal register of Galle (1677 to 1807).

New No. 5/2, Marriage Register, Dutch Reformed Church, Galle (1774 to 1789).

Alphabetical index to the marriage registers of Galle (1748 to 1833).

Leiden University Library

Sluijsken, Pieter, Eene beschryving van de landdienst op Ceylon: Zo uyt ondervinding als uyt oude papieren tezaemen gebragt (A Description of the Land Services of Ceylon: Compiled from Both Investigations and Old Papers). Colombo, 1784. RP-31/32 Colonial Collection (KIT). Leiden University.

Private Collection

Inventory of Nicolaas Dias Abeysinghe, 1797. Private collection of Siran Deraniyagala at Ekneligoda Walauwa, Kuruvita.

Databases, Dictionaries, Indexes & Inventories

Carter, Charles, *A Sinhalese-English Dictionary* (Colombo: M.D. Gunasena & Co. Ltd, 1924; repr. 1965).

Jurriaanse, Maria Wilhelmina, *Catalogue of the Archives of the Dutch Central Government of Coastal Ceylon, 1640–1796* (Colombo: Ceylon Government Press, 1943).

Wordenboek Nederlandse Taal. www.gtb.inl.

Mottau, S.A.W., *Inventory of the Archives of the Dutch Government in the Divisions of Galle (Matara) and Jaffnapatnam 1640–1796* (The Hague: General State Archives, 1975).

———, "Glossary of Terms Used in Official Correspondence of the Government of Sri Lanka compiled from Records at the National Archives," *The Sri Lanka National Archives* 3 (1985–1986).

———, "Alphabetical Index to the Registers of the Acts of Appointments of Company's Servants of the Dutch East India Company Issued at the Galle Secretariat (1645–1796), (n.d.)" Research Room, Sri Lanka National Archives.

———, "Index to the Baptisms Registered in the Baptism Registers of the Dutch Reformed Church at Wolfendaal (1709 to 1952)." Research Room, Sri Lanka National Archives.

National Archives, The Hague, "VOC Sea-Voyagers." Accessed December 5, 2014. https://www.nationaalarchief.nl/onderzoeken/index/nt00444.

Source Publications

Armour, John, *Armour's Grammar of the Kandyan Law*, ed. Joseph Martinus Perera (Colombo: Examiner Press, 1861).

Becker, Hendrick, *Memoir of Hendrick Becker, Governor and Director of Ceylon for His Successor Isaac Augustyn Rumpf, 1716*, trans. Sophia Anthonisz (Colombo: H.C. Cottle, Government Printer, 1914).

Bennett, John Whitchurch, *Ceylon and its Capabilities: An Account of its Natural Resources, Indigenous Productions, and Commercial Facilities* (New Delhi: Asian Educational Services, 1843; repr. 1998).

Bertolacci, Anthony, *A View of the Agricultural, Commercial, and Financial Interests of Ceylon* (London: Black, Parbury and Allen, 1817).

Burnand, Jacob, "Fragments on Ceylon," *Asiatic Journal* 12 (June 1821), 553–61.

The Ceylon Law Reports: Being Reports of Cases Decided by the Supreme Court of Ceylon (Colombo: Ceylon Examiner Press, 1892).

Chijs, Jacobus Anne van der, *Nederlandsch-Indisch plakaatboek, 1602–1811*, vol. 6 (1750–1754), (Batavia: Landsdrukkerij, 1885).

Daniel Silva v Johanis Appuhamy, 67 New Law Reports 457 (1965).

Davy, John, *An Account of the Interior of Ceylon, and of its Inhabitants* (London: Longman, 1821).

De Alwis, James, *Sidath Sangarawa: A Grammar of the Sinhalese Language* (Colombo: W. Skeen, 1852).

Diessen, Rob van, *Grote Atlas van de Verenigde Oost-Indische Compagnie: Deel IV: Ceylon* (Voorburg, Netherlands: Asia Maior, 2008).

D'Oyly, John, *A Sketch of the Constitution of the Kandyan Kingdom*, ed. Lewis James Barnetson Turner, vol. 24, *The Ceylon Historical Journal* (Dehiwala: Tisara Prakasakayo, 1929; repr. 1975).

Forbes, Jonathan, *Eleven Years in Ceylon*, 2 vols., (London: R. Bentley, 1841).

Galletti, A., *The Dutch in Malabar: Being a Translation of Selections Nos. 1 and 2* (Madras: Government Press, 1911).

Geiger, Wilhelm, *The Mahāwamsa* (Colombo: Government Press, 1986).

Goens, Rijklof van., *Memoir Left by Ryclof van Goens to Laurens Pijl*, trans. by Sophia Pieters (Colombo: H.C. Cottle, Government Printer, 1910).

Gollenesse, Julius Stein van, *Memoir of Julius Stein van Gollenesse* 1751, trans. Sinnappah Arasaratnam (Colombo: Department of National Archives, 1974).

Hayley, F.A. *A Treatise on the Laws and Customs of the Sinhalese* (New Delhi: Navrang, 1923; repr. 1993).

Heydt, Johann Wolffgang, *Heydt's Ceylon*, trans. R. Raven-Hart (Colombo: Ceylon Government Information Department, 1952).

Hovy, L., *Ceylonees plakkaatboek: Plakkaten en andere wetten uitgevaardigd door het Nederlands bestuur op Ceylon, 1638–1796*, 2 vols. (Hilversum: Verloren, 1991).

Imhoff, Baron van, *Memoir Left by Baron van Imhoff to His Successor, 1740*, trans. Sophia Pieters (Colombo: H.C. Cottle, Government Printer, 1911).

Karonchihami v Angohami, 2 New Law Reports 276 (1896).

Karonchihami v Angohami, 8 New Law Reports 1 (1904).

Knighton, William, *The History of Ceylon from the Earliest Period to the Present Time* (London: Longman, 1845).

Knox, Robert, *An Historical Relation of Ceylon* (Dehiwala: Tisara Prakasakayo, 1681; repr. 1966).

Koschorke, Klaus (ed), *The Dutch Reformed Church in Colonial Ceylon (18th Century): Minutes of the Consistory of the Dutch Reformed Church in Colombo*, trans. S.A.W. Mottau (Wiesbaden: Harrassowitz Verlag, 2011).

Leeuwen, Simon van, *Simon van Leeuwen's Commentaries on Roman-Dutch Law*, ed. Cornelis Willem Decker and John Gilbert Kotzé, vol. 2 (London: Sweet and Maxwell, 1923).

Linden, Johannes van der, *Institutes of the Laws of Holland*, trans. Jabez Henry (London: J. & W.T. Clerk, 1828).

Loten, Joan Gideon, *Memoir of Joan Gideon Loten, Governor of Ceylon, Delivered to His Successor Jan Schreuder, 1757*, trans. E. Reimers (Colombo: Ceylon Government Press, 1935).

Mesurier, C.J.R. Le, and T.B. Panabokke, trans. *Niti-Nighanduva or the Vocabulary of Law* (New Delhi: Navrang, 1880; repr. 1994).

Mottau, S.A.W. (trans), "Documents on Ceylon History (2): Documents Relating to the Tombo Registration of the Dutch Administration in Ceylon: Instructions Issued to the Tombo Commissioners," *Ceylon Historical Journal* 3, no. 2 (1953), 173–89.

———, (trans), "Instructions for the Respective 'Landraden' of this Government (Extract from the Dutch Political Council Minutes of 25th June 1789)," *Journal of the Dutch Burger Union of Ceylon* 55, no. 1–4 (1965), 1-16.

———, "Education under the Dutch," in *Education in Ceylon (From the Sixth Century BC to the Present Day): A Centenary Volume*, vol. 1 (Colombo: Ministry of Education and Cultural Affairs, 1969).

Omychund v Barker, 1 Atkyn's Reports 22 (English Chancery 1744).

Overbeek, Daniel, *Memoir of Daniel Overbeek, Governor of Ceylon*, trans. K.D. Paranavitana (Colombo: Department of National Archives, 2009).

Paulusz, J.H.O., *Administration Report of the Government Archivist for 1951* (Colombo: Ceylon Government Press, 1952).

Paviljeon, Anthony, "Memoir by Anthony Paviljoen to His Successor, 1665," in *Instructions from the Governor-General and Council of India*, trans. Sophia Pieters (Colombo: H.C. Cottle, Government Printer, 1908).

Perera, S.G. (ed), *The Tombo of the Two Korales* (Colombo: Ceylon Government Press, 1938).

Pieris, Ralph, "Administration of Justice and Revenue on the Island of Ceylon under the Dutch Government ('The Cleghorn Minute')," *Journal of the Ceylon Branch of the Royal Asiatic Society*, n.s., 3 pt. 2 (1953), 125–52.

Pieters, Sophia (trans), *Instructions from the Governor-General and Council of India to the Governor of Ceylon, 1656 to 1665* (Colombo: H.C. Cottle, Government Printer, 1908).

Pridham, Charles, *An Historical, Political, and Statistical Account of Ceylon and its Dependencies*, 2 vols. (London: T. and W. Boone, 1849).

Ribeiro, Joao, *The Historic Tragedy of the Island of Ceilao*, trans. P.E. Pieris (Colombo: The Ceylon Daily News, 1948).

Saparamadu, S.D. (ed), *A True and Exact Description of the Great Island of Ceylon by Phillipus Baldaeus*, trans. Pieter Brohier, vol. 42, *The Ceylon Historical Journal Monograph Series* (Dehiwala: Tisara Prakasakayo, 1960; repr. 2012).

Schreuder, Jan, *Memoir of Jan Schreuder, Governor of Ceylon, Delivered to His Successor Lubbert Jan Baron van Eck on March 17, 1762*, trans. E. Reimers (Colombo: Ceylon Government Press, 1946).

Silva, Chandra Richard de, "The First Portuguese Revenue Register of the Kingdom of Kotte, 1599," *The Ceylon Journal of Historical and Social Studies* 5 (1975), 69–153.

Sinnapody et al. v Mannikan et al., 53 New Law Reports (1949).

Tennent, Sir James Emerson, *Christianity in Ceylon* (London: John Murray, 1850).

———, *Ceylon: An Account of the Island*, 2 vols., fourth edition (London: Longman, Green, 1860).

Tieken, Herman, *Between Colombo and the Cape: Letters in Tamil, Dutch and Sinhala Sent to Nicolaas Ondaatje from Ceylon*, vol. 6, Dutch Sources of South Asia (New Delhi: Manohar, 2015).

Tyler, James E., *Oaths, Their Origine, Nature, and History* (London: John W. Parker, 1835).

Valentijn, Francois, *Francois Valentijn's Description of Ceylon*, trans. and ed. Sinnappah Arasaratnam, vol. 149, Hakluyt Society 2 (London: Hakluyt Society, 1978).

Vanderstraaten, J.W., *The Decisions of the Supreme Court of Ceylon Sitting in Appeal from 1869 to 1871* (Colombo: Catholic Orphan Press, 1871?).

Vanderstraaten v Eaton, 37 New Law Reports 294 (1936).

Worden, Nigel, and Gerald Groenewald, *Trials of Slavery: Selected Documents Concerning Slaves from the Criminal Records of the Council of Justice at the Cape of Good Hope, 1705–1794* (Cape Town: Van Riebeeck Society, 2005).

Zwaardecroon, Hendrick, *Memoir of Hendrick Zwaardecroon, Commandeur of Jaffnapatam, 1697*, trans. Sophia Pieters (Colombo: H.C. Cottle, Government Printer, 1911).

Secondary Sources

Abeyasinghe, Tikiri, *Portuguese Rule in Ceylon, 1594–1612* (Colombo: Lake House, 1966).

Abhayawardena, H.A.P., *Lekam Miti Vimarshanaya (A Critical Study of Lekam Miti)* (Colombo: Department of National Archives, 2009).

Amerasinghe, A.R.B., *The Legal Heritage of Sri Lanka* (Colombo: Royal Asiatic Society of Sri Lanka, 1999).

———, "The Dutch Influence on the Legal System of Sri Lanka," in Saman Kelegama and Roshan Madawela (eds), *400 Years of Dutch-Sri Lanka Relations, 1602–2002* (Colombo: Institute of Policy Studies of Sri Lanka, 2002).

Andaya, Barbara Watson, *The Flaming Womb: Repositioning Women in Early Modern Southeast Asia* (Honolulu: University of Hawai'i Press, 2006).

Anthonisz, R.G., *Report on the Dutch Records in the Government Archives at Colombo* (Colombo: H.C. Cottle, Government Printer, 1907).

———, "Governor Falck's Audience with the Kandyan Ambassadors," *Journal of the Dutch Burger Union of Ceylon* 2, no. 4 (1909), 147–52.

Appadurai, Arjun, *Worship and Conflict under Colonial Rule* (Cambridge: Cambridge University Press, 1981).

Arasaratnam, Sinnappah, *Dutch Power in Ceylon, 1658–1687* (Amsterdam: Djambatan, 1958).

———, "Introduction," in Julius Stein van Gollenesse, *Memoir of Julius Stein van Gollenesse* (Colombo: Department of National Archives, 1974).

———, "Social History of a Dominant Caste Society," in *Ceylon and the Dutch, 1600–1800: External Influences and Internal Change in Early Modern Sri Lanka* (Brookfield, Vt.: Variorum, 1996).

Ariyapala, M.B., *Society in Mediaeval Ceylon: The State of Society in Ceylon as Depicted in the Saddharma-Ratnāvaliya and Other Literature of the Thirteenth Century* (Colombo: Department of Cultural Affairs, 1956; repr. 1997).

Attygalle, Nicholas (ed), *University of Ceylon, History of Ceylon: From the Earliest Times to 1505*, vol. 1 (Colombo: Ceylon University Press, 1959).

Baden-Powell, B.H., *The Indian Village Community* (London: Longmans, 1896).

Bayly, C.A., *Origins of Nationality in South Asia: Patriotism and Ethical Government in the Making of Modern India* (Oxford: Oxford University Press, 1998).

Bayly, Susan, *Caste, Society and Politics in India from the Eighteenth Century to the Modern Age* (Cambridge: Cambridge University Press, 2001).

———, *Saints, Goddesses and Kings: Muslims and Christians in South Indian Society, 1700–1900* (Cambridge: Cambridge University Press, 1989).

Belt, Albert van den, *Het VOC-bedrijf op Ceylon: Een voorname vestiging van de Oost-Indische Compagnie in de 18de eeuw* (Zutphen: Walburg Pers, 2008).

Belt, Albert van den, Jan Kok, and Kees Mandemakers, "Digital Thombos: A New Source for 18th Century Sri Lankan Family History," *The History of the Family* 16, no. 4 (2011), 481–89.

Benton, Lauren, *Law and Colonial Cultures: Legal Regimes in World History, 1400–1900* (Cambridge: Cambridge University Press, 2001).

———, "Historical Perspectives on Legal Pluralism," *Hague Journal on the Rule of Law* 3, no. 01 (2011), 57–69.

Benton, Lauren, and Richard J. Ross, "Empires and Legal Pluralism: Jurisdiction, Sovereignty, and Political Imagination in the Early Modern World," in Lauren Benton and Richard J. Ross (eds), *Legal Pluralism and Empires, 1500–1850*, Kindle edition (New York: NYU Press, 2013).

———, (eds), *Legal Pluralism and Empires, 1500–1850*, Kindle edition (New York: NYU Press, 2013).

Biedermann, Zoltán, *The Portuguese in Sri Lanka and South India: Studies in the History of Diplomacy, Empire and Trade, 1500–1650* (Wiesbaden: Harrassowitz Verlag, 2014).

Bosma, Ulbe and Remco Raben, *Being "Dutch" in the Indies: A History of Creolisation and Empire, 1500–1920*, trans. Wendie Shaffer (Singapore: NUS Press, 2008).

Botha, C. Graham, "Intestate Succession," *South African Law Journal* 34 (1917), 172–92.

Brohier, R.L., *De Wolvendaalsche Kerk* (Colombo: Consistory of Wolvendaal Church, 1957).

Burbank, Jane, *Russian Peasants Go to Court: Legal Culture in the Countryside, 1905–1917* (Indiana: Indiana University Press, 2004).

Chatterjee, Partha, *The Nation and its Fragments: Colonial and Postcolonial Histories* (Princeton, NJ: Princeton University Press, 1993).

Chiba, Masaji, "Legal Pluralism in Sri Lankan Society: Toward a General Theory of Non-Western Law," *Journal of Legal Pluralism and Unofficial Law* 25, no. 33 (1993), 197–212.

Codrington, H.W., *Ancient Land Tenure and Revenue in Ceylon* (Colombo: Ceylon Government Press, 1938).

Codrington, K. de B., "An Act of Truth in a Cingalese Court of Law," *Man* 33 (June 1933), 94–96.

Coomaraswamy, E.R.S.R., *A Textbook of the Law of Evidence in Ceylon* (Colombo: Noel E. Hamer, 1955).

Cooray, L.J.M., "Common Law in England and Sri Lanka," *International & Comparative Law Quarterly* 24, no. 3 (July 1975), 553–64.

———, *An Introduction to the Legal System of Sri Lanka* (Pannipitiya: Stamford Lake, 2003; repr. 2009).

Cotterrell, Roger, *Law, Culture and Society: Legal Ideas in the Mirror of Society Theory* (Hampshire: Ashgate Publishing, 2006).

Couquerque, L.M. Rollin, *Het Aasdoms- en Schependomsrecht in Holland en Zeeland, in verband met het erfrecht der naburige provinciën* ('s Gravenhage: Nijhoff, 1898).

Dewaraja, Lorna S., "The Muslims in the Kandyan Kingdom (c. 1600–1815): A Study of Ethnic Integration," in M.A.M. Shukri (ed), *Muslims of Sri Lanka: Avenues to Antiquity* (Beruwala: Jamiah Naleemia Institute, 1986).

———, *The Kandyan Kingdom of Sri Lanka, 1707–1782*, second edition (Colombo: Lake House, 1988).

Dewasiri, Nirmal Ranjith, *The Adaptable Peasant: Agrarian Society in Western Sri Lanka under Dutch Rule, 1740–1800* (Leiden: Brill, 2008).

Dirks, Nicholas B., "From Little King to Landlord: Property, Law and the Gift under the Madras Permanent Settlement," *Comparative Studies in Society and History* 28, no. 2 (1986), 307–33.

———, *The Hollow Crown: Ethnohistory of an Indian Kingdom* (Michigan: University of Michigan Press, 1993).

———, *Castes of Mind: Colonialism and the Making of Modern India* (Princeton: Princeton University Press, 2001).

Drixler, Fabian F. and Jan Kok, "A Lost Family-Planning Regime in Eighteenth-century Ceylon," *Population Studies: A Journal of Demography* 70, no. 1 (2016), 93–114.

Dulm, Frits van, *"Zonder eigen gewinne en glorie": Mr. Iman Wilhelm Falck (1736–1785), gouverneur en directeur van Ceylon en onderhorigheden* (Hilversum: Verloren, 2012).

Duve, Thomas, "Global Legal History: A Methodological Approach," Social Science Research Network (SSRN Scholarly Paper ID 2781104), (2016), http://papers.ssrn.com/abstract=2781104. Accessed 28 August 2016.

Eisenberg, Melvin Aron, "Private Ordering through Negotiation: Dispute-Settlement and Rulemaking," *Harvard Law Review* 89, no. 4 (1976), 637–81.

Es, W.J.L. van, *Het eedsvraagstuk* (Leiden: Eduard Ijdo, 1911).

Flores, Jorge (ed), *Re-Exploring the Links: History and Constructed Histories between Portugal and Sri Lanka* (Wiesbaden: Harrassowitz Verlag, 2007).

Gaastra, Femme S., *The Dutch East India Company: Expansion and Decline* (Zutphen: Walburg Pers, 2003).

Geertz, Clifford, *Local Knowledge: Further Essays in Interpretive Anthropology* (United States: Basic Books, 1983).

Genet, Jean-Phillipe, "Cultural History with a Computer: Measuring Dynamics," in Terry Coppock (ed), *Information Technology and Scholarship: Applications in the Humanities and Social Sciences* (Oxford: The British Academy, 1999).

Gombrich, Richard F., *Buddhist Precept and Practice: Traditional Buddhism in the Rural Highlands of Ceylon* (Delhi: Motilal Banarsidass Publishers, 1971; repr. 1991).

Goonetilleke, Janaka, (ed), *Atapattu Walawwa: Residence of the Gooneratne & Dias Abeyesinghe Families of Galle* (Galle: Atapattu Walawwa, 2012).

Goonewardena, K.W., *The Foundation of Dutch Power in Ceylon, 1638–1658* (Amsterdam: Djambatan, 1958).

———, "Some Comments on Robert Knox and His Writings on Ceylon," *University of Ceylon Review* 16 (1958): 39–52.

———, "Muslims under Dutch Rule up to the Mid-Eighteenth Century," in M.A.M. Shukri (ed), *Muslims of Sri Lanka: Avenues to Antiquity* (Beruwala: Jamiah Naleemia Institute, 1986).

Goor, J. van, *Jan Kompenie as Schoolmaster: Dutch Education in Ceylon 1690–1795* (Groningen: Wolters-Noordhoff, 1978).

Gordley, James, "Comparative Law and Legal History," in Reinhard Zimmermann and Mathias Reimann (eds), *The Oxford Handbook of Comparative Law* (Oxford: Oxford University Press, 2006).

Griffiths, John, "What is Legal Pluralism?" *Journal of Legal Pluralism and Unofficial Law* 18, no. 24 (1986), 1–55.

Groenewald, Gerald, "'A Mother Makes No Bastard': Family Law, Sexual Relations and Illegitimacy in Dutch Colonial Cape Town, c. 1652-1795," *African Historical Review* 39, no. 2 (2007)

Gunawardana, R.A.L.H., "'Necessary Evil': The Growth of a System of Judicial Courts and the Responses it Evoked among the Buddhist Monastic Community in Ancient Sri Lanka," *Buffalo Law Review* 55, no. 2 (2007).

Haks, Donald, *Huwelijk en gezin in Holland in de 17de en 18de eeuw (Marriage and Family in Holland in the 17th and 18th Centuries)*, second edition (Utrecht: HES Uitgevers, 1985).

Halliday, Paul, "Laws' Histories: Pluralisms, Pluralities, Diversity," in Lauren Benton and Richard J. Ross (eds), *Legal Pluralism and Empires, 1500–1850*, Kindle edition (New York: NYU Press, 2013).

Heijden, Manon van der, *Huwelijk in Holland: Stedelijke rechtspraak en kerkelijke tucht, 1550–1700* (Amsterdam: Bert Bakker, 1998).

Horst, Marleen H.J. van den, *Compensation for Improvements: The Roman Dutch Law in Sri Lanka* (Amsterdam: Free University Press, 1989).

———, *The Roman Dutch Law in Sri Lanka* (Amsterdam: Free University Press, 1985).

Huxley, Andrew, "Studying Theravada Legal Literature," *Journal of the International Association of Buddhist Studies* 20, no. 1 (1997), 63–91.

Israel, Jonathan I., *Democratic Enlightenment: Philosophy, Revolution, and Human Rights 1750–1790* (Oxford: Oxford University Press, 2011).

Jacob, Sir Jack I.H., *The Fabric of English Civil Justice* (London: Stevens & Sons, 1987).

Jayawardena, Kumari, *Nobodies to Somebodies: The Rise of the Colonial Bourgeoisie in Sri Lanka* (London: Zed Books, 2000).

Jayawickrama, Sarojini, *Writing that Conquers: Re-Reading Knox's an Historical Relation of the Island Ceylon* (Colombo: Social Scientists' Association, 2004).

Jayewardene, Adrian St. Valentine, *The Roman Dutch Law: As it Prevails in Ceylon, How Much of it is Applicable, and in What Localities?* (Colombo: Ceylon Examine Press, 1901).

Jennings, Ivor, "Notes on Kandyan Law Collected by Sir Archibald C. Lawrie LL.D.," *University of Ceylon Review* 10, no. 3 (1952), 185–220.

Jennings, Ivor and H.W. Tambiah, *The Dominion of Ceylon: The Development of its Laws and Constitution* (London: Stevens, 1952).

Jonassen, Frederick B., "So Help Me: Religious Expression and Artifacts in the Oath of Office and the Courtroom Oath," *Cardozo Public Law, Policy & Ethics Journal* 12, no. 2 (2014), 303–73.

Kan, J. van, "Bataviasche statuten en de buitencomptoiren," *Bijdragen tot de Taal-, Land- en Volkenkunde van Nederlandsch-Indië* 100 (1940), 255–82.

Kanapathipillai, Valli, "Dutch Rule in Maritime Ceylon 1766–1796," PhD dissertation, University of London, 1969.

Kaviraj, Sudipta, "On the Construction of Colonial Power: Structure, Discourse, Hegemony," in Dagmar Engels and Shula Marks (eds), *Contesting Colonial Hegemony: State and Society in Africa and India* (London: British Academic Press, 1994).

Kemper, Steven, "The Buddhist Monkhood, the Law, and the State in Colonial Sri Lanka," *Comparative Studies in Society and History* 26, no. 3 (1984), 401–27.

Kleinhans, Martha-Marie and Roderick A. Macdonald, "What is a Critical Legal Pluralism?" *Canadian Journal of Law and Society* 12, no. 2 (1997), 25–46.

Kolsky, Elizabeth, "A Note on the Study of Indian Legal History," *Law and History Review* 23, no. 3 (2005), 703–6.

———, *Colonial Justice in British India* (Cambridge: Cambridge University Press, 2010).

Kotelawele, D.A., "Agrarian Policies of the Dutch in South-West Ceylon, 1743–1767," *A.A.G. Bijdragen* 14, no. 8 (1967), 3-33.

———, "Nineteenth-Century Elites and Their Antecedents," *Ceylon Historical Journal* 25, no. 1–4 (1978), 204–12.

———, "Muslims under Dutch Rule in Sri Lanka," in M.A.M. Shukri (ed), *Muslims of Sri Lanka: Avenues to Antiquity* (Beruwala: Jamiah Naleemia Institute, 1986).

———, "Some Aspects of Social Change in the South West of Sri Lanka c. 1700–1833," *Social Science Review* no. 4 (1988), 53–100.

———, "Realms of Law: Judicial Procedures of the Low Country Sinhalese during Dutch Rule in Sri Lanka," *Modern Sri Lanka Studies* 2, no. 1 (1990), 112–20.

———, "The VOC in Sri Lanka, 1658–1796: Social and Economic Change in the Maritime Regions," in K.M. de Silva (ed), *University of Peradeniya, History of Sri Lanka (From c. 1500 to c. 1800)*, vol. 2 (Peradeniya: University of Peradeniya, 1995).

Kramer, Hans Martin, Jenny Rahel Oesterle and Ulrike Vordermark, *Labeling the Religious Self and Others: Reciprocal Perceptions of Christians, Muslims, Hindus, Buddhists, and Confucians in Medieval and Early Modern Times* (Leipzig: Leipziger Universitatsverlag, 2010).

Le Bailly, Marie Charlotte, *Recht voor de Raad* (Haarlem & Hilversum: Historische Vereniging Holland & Uitgeverij Verloren, 2001).

———, *Staatse Raad van Vlaanderen te Middelburg (1599–1795): De hoofdlijnen van het procederen in civiele zaken voor de Staatse Raad van Vlaanderen, zowel in eerste instantie als in hoger beroep*, Procesgids 6 (Hilversum: Verloren, 2007).

———, *Hof van Holland, Zeeland en West-Friesland*, Procesgids 7 (Hilversum: Verloren, 2008).

Leach, Edmund Ronald, *Pul Eliya: A Village in Ceylon* (Cambridge: Cambridge University Press, 1961).

Lee, Robert Warden, "The Intestate Succession of Husband and Wife in Roman-Dutch Law," *Journal of the Society of Comparative Legislation* 12, no. 310 (1911), 310–23.

———, "Bynkershoek's Observationes Tumultuariae," *Journal of Comparative Legislation and International Law*, Third Series, 17, no. 1 (1935), 38–46.

———, *An Introduction to Roman-Dutch Law*, fourth edition (Oxford: At the Clarendon Press, 1946).

Legrand, Pierre, "What 'Legal Transplants'?" in David Nelken and Johannes Feest (eds), *Adapting Legal Cultures* (Oxford: Hart Publishing, 2001).

Lev, Daniel S., "Colonial Law and the Genesis of the Indonesian State," *Indonesia*, no. 40 (1985), 57–74.

Lewis, J.P., "Dutch Extracts and the Dutch Company in the Matara District," *Journal of the Dutch Burger Union of Ceylon* 1, no. 4 (1908), 195–203.

Ludden, David, *Peasant History in South India* (New Jersey & Surrey: Princeton University Press, 1985).

Merry, Sally Engle, "Legal Pluralism," *Law and Society Review* 22, no. 5 (1988), 869–96.

———, *Colonizing Hawai'i: The Cultural Power of Law* (Princeton: Princeton University Press, 2000).

———, "Colonial Law and its Uncertainties," *Law and History Review* 28, no. 4 (2010), 1067–71.

Morris, Robert J., "Occupational Coding: Principles and Examples," *Historical Social Research* 15, no. 1 (1990), 3–29.

Mumford, Jeremy Ravi, "Litigation as Ethnography in Sixteenth-Century Peru: Polo de Ondegardo and the Mitimaes," *Hispanic American Historical Review* 88, no. 1 (2008), 5–40.

Munasinghe, Indrani, *Sri Lankan Woman in Antiquity (Sixth Century B.C. to Fifteenth Century A.C.)*, trans. S.B. Herath (Colombo: Author Publication, 2004).

Nadaraja, T., *The Legal System of Ceylon in its Historical Setting* (Leiden: Brill, 1972).

Nierstrasz, Chris, *In the Shadow of the Company: The Dutch East India Company and its Servants in the Period of its Decline (1740–1796)* (Leiden: Brill, 2012).

Nissan, Elizabeth, "Polity and Pilgrimage Centres in Sri Lanka," *Man*, n.s. 23, no. 2 (1988), 253–74.

Obeyesekere, Gananath, *Land Tenure in Village Ceylon: A Sociological and Historical Study* (Cambridge: Cambridge University Press, 1967).

———, "Social Change and the Deities: Rise of the Kataragama Cult in Modern Sri Lanka," *Man* 12, no. 3/4 (1977), 377–96.

———, *The Cult of the Goddess Pattini* (Chicago: University of Chicago Press, 1984).

———, "Buddhism and Conscience: An Exploratory Essay," *Daedalus* 120, no. 3 (1991), 219–39.

———, "On Buddhist Identity in Sri Lanka," in Lola Romanucci-Ross and George De Vos (eds) *Ethnic Identity: Creation, Conflict and Accommodation* (California: AltaMira Press, 1995).

Ogborn, Miles, "The Power of Speech: Orality, Oaths and Evidence in the British Atlantic World, 1650–1800," *Transactions of the Institute of British Geographers* 36, no. 1 (2011), 109–25.

Pandey, Gyanendra, *The Construction of Communalism in Colonial North India* (Oxford: Oxford University Press, 2006).

Pereira, James Cecil Walter, *Institutes of the Laws of Ceylon*, 2 vols. (Colombo: H.C. Cottle, Government Printer, 1901).

Pieris, P.E., *Notes on Some Sinhalese Families: Being the Diary of Adirian de Alwis Goonetilleke Samaranaike*, vol. 3 (Colombo: The Colombo Apothecaries Co., 1911).

———, *Notes on Some Sinhalese Families: Ilangakon*, vol. 4 (Colombo: Times of Ceylon, n.d.)

Pieris, Ralph, *Sinhalese Social Organization: The Kandyan Period* (Colombo: Ceylon University Press Board, 1956).

Plessis, Jacques du, "Comparative Law and the Study of Mixed Legal Systems," in Mathias Reimann and Reinhard Zimmermann (eds) *The Oxford Handbook of Comparative Law* (Oxford: Oxford University Press, 2006).

Price, Pamela G., *Kingship and Political Practice in Colonial India* (Cambridge: Cambridge University Press, 1996).

Raben, Remco, "Batavia and Colombo: The Ethnic and Spatial Order of Two Colonial Cities 1600–1800," PhD Thesis, Leiden University, 1996.

Raben, Remco and Max De Bruijn (eds), *The World of Jan Brandes, 1743–1808: Drawings of a Dutch Traveller in Batavia, Ceylon and Southern Africa* (Zwolle, Amsterdam: Waanders Publishers, Rijkmuseum, 2004).

Raman, Bhavani, *Document Raj: Writing and Scribes in Early Colonial South India* (Chicago: University of Chicago Press, 2012).

Renton, A. Wood, "The Roman-Dutch Law in Ceylon under the British Regime," *South African Law Journal* 49 (1932), 161–82.

Risseeuw, Carla, *Gender Transformation, Power, and Resistance among Women in Sri Lanka: The Fish Don't Talk about the Water* (New Delhi: Manohar, 1991).

———, "Urban Middle-Class Elderly in Sri Lanka and the Netherlands: Everyday Sociality and Ways of Keeping Company," in Brigitte Röder, Willemijn de Jong and Kurt W. Alt (eds), *Alter(n) anders denken: Kulturelle und biologische Perspektiven* (Cologne: Bohlau Verlag, 2012).

Roberts, Michael, *Caste Conflict and Elite Formation: The Rise of a Karāva Elite in Sri Lanka, 1500–1931* (Cambridge: Cambridge University Press, 1982).

Roberts, Michael, Ismeth Raheem and Percy Colin-Thomé, *People Inbetween: The Burghers and the Middle Class in the Transformations within Sri Lanka, 1790s–1960* (Ratmalana: Sarvodaya Book Pub. Services, 1989).

Rogers, John D., *Crime, Justice, and Society in Colonial Sri Lanka* (London: Curzon Press, 1987).

———, "Early British Rule and Social Classification in Lanka," *Modern Asian Studies* 38, no. 03 (2004), 625–47.

Ross, Robert and Alicia Schrikker, "The VOC Official Elite," in Nigel Worden (ed), *Cape Town between East and West* (Johannesburg: Jacana, 2012).

Rupesinghe (writing as Seneviratne), Nadeera, "Strange Cooperation: Revenue Farmers in Eighteenth-century Sri Lanka," MPhil dissertation, Leiden University, 2010.

Rupesinghe, Nadeera, "Defining Land Rights in Dutch Sri Lanka," *Portuguese Journal of Social Science* 16, no. 2 (2017), 143–61.

———, "Navigating Pluralities Reluctantly: The Marriage Contract in Dutch Galle," *Itinerario* 42, no. 2, (2018), 220–37.

———, with Luc Bulten, Jan Kok and Dries Lyna, "Contested Conjugality? Sinhalese Marriage Practices in Eighteenth-century Dutch Colonial Sri Lanka," *Annales de Démographie Historique* no. 1 (2018), 51–80.

———, "Facing the Law in Eighteenth-century Galle," in Manon van den Heijden, Griet Vermeesch and Jaco Zuijderduin (eds), *Uses of Justice and Legal Pluralism: A Global Perspective 1600–1900* (Oxon: Routledge, 2019).

———, "Do You Know the Ninth Commandment: Tensions of the Oath in Dutch Colonial Sri Lanka," *Comparative Legal History* 7, (2019), 1–30.

Ryan, Bryce F., *Caste in Modern Ceylon: The Sinhalese System in Transition* (New Brunswick: Rutgers University Press, 1953).

Samaraweera, Vijaya, "An 'Act of Truth' in a Sinhala Court of Law: On Truth, Lies and Judicial Proof Among the Sinhala Buddhists," *Cardoza Journal of International and Comparative Law* 5 (1997), 133–63.

Santos, Boaventura de Sousa, *Toward a New Legal Common Sense: Law, Globalization, and Emancipation* (Cambridge University Press, 2002).

Schepper, H. de et al., "Prolegomena voor onderzoek van rechtspraak en bestuur in de oude Nederlanden," in J. Koster van Dijk and A. Wijffels (eds), *Miscellanea forensia historica: Ter gelegenheid van het afscheid van Prof. Mr. J. Th de Smidt* (Amsterdam: Werkgroep Grote Raad van Mechelen, 1988).

Schonthal, Benjamin, "The Legal Regulation of Buddhism in Contemporary Sri Lanka," in Rebecca Redwood French and Mark A. Nathan (eds) *Buddhism and Law* (Cambridge: Cambridge University Press, 2014).

Schrikker, Alicia, *Dutch and British Colonial Intervention in Sri Lanka, 1780–1815: Expansion and Reform* (Leiden: Brill, 2007).

———, "Conflict Resolution, Social Control and Law-Making in Eighteenth Century Dutch Sri Lanka," in Catia Antunes and Jos Gommans (eds), *Exploring the Dutch Empire: Agents Networks and Institutions, 1600-2000* (London: Bloomsbury, 2015).

———, "'Op de dijk gezet': Schuld, onrust en bestuurlijk onzekerheid in Jaffna in de achttiende eeuw," in Lodewijk Wagenaar (ed), *Aan de overkant: Ontmoetingen in dienst van de VOC en WIC (1600–1800)* (Leiden: Sidestone Press, 2015).

Schutte, G.J., "Een hutje in den wijngaard: Gereformeerd Ceylon," in G.J. Schutte (ed), *Het Indische Sion: De Gereformeerde kerk onder de Verenigde Oost-Indische Compagnie* (Hilversum: Verloren, 2002).

Scott, James C., *Seeing Like a State: How Certain Schemes to Improve the Human Condition Have Failed* (New Haven: Yale University Press, 1999).

Serrão, José Vicente, "The Portuguese Land Policies in Ceylon: On the Possibilities and Limits of a Process of Territorial Occupation," in Bárbara Direito et al. (eds), *Property Rights, Land and Territory in the European Overseas Empires* (Lisbon: CEHC-IUL, 2014).

Shapiro, Martin, *Courts: A Comparative and Political Analysis* (Chicago: University of Chicago Press, 1986).

Shukri, M.A.M. (ed), *Muslims of Sri Lanka: Avenues to Antiquity* (Beruwala: Jamiah Naleemia Institute, 1986).

Silva, Chandra Richard de, "The First Portuguese Revenue Register of the Kingdom of Kotte, 1599," *The Ceylon Journal of Historical and Social Studies* 5 (1975), 69–153.

Silva, Chandra Richard de, *The Portuguese in Ceylon 1617–1638* (Colombo: H.W. Cave, 1972).

Silva, K.M. de., *A History of Sri Lanka* (Delhi: Oxford University Press, 1981).

Silva, K.M. de, (ed), *University of Ceylon, History of Ceylon: From the Beginning of the 19th Century to 1948*, vol. 3 (Peradeniya: University of Ceylon Press Board, 1973).

———, (ed), *University of Peradeniya, History of Sri Lanka (From c. 1500 to c. 1800)*, vol. 2 (Peradeniya: University of Peradeniya, 1995).

Silva, Rajpal Kumar de and Willemina G.M. Beumer, *Illustrations and Views of Dutch Ceylon 1602–1796: A Comprehensive Work of Pictorial Reference with Selected Eye-Witness Accounts* (Leiden: Brill, 1988).

Silva, S.B.D. de, *The Political Economy of Underdevelopment* (London: Routledge & Kegan Paul, 1982; repr. 1984).

Singh, Anjana, *Fort Cochin in Kerala, 1750–1830: The Social Condition of a Dutch Community in an Indian Milieu* (Leiden: Brill, 2010).

Singha, Radhika, *A Despotism of Law: Crime and Justice in Early Colonial India* (Delhi: Oxford University Press, 1998).

Siriweera, W.I., *History of Sri Lanka: From the Earliest Times upto the Sixteenth Century* (Colombo: Dayawansa Jayakody & Co, 2002).

Sirks, B. and J. Hallebeek, "Uit het archief van de Raad van Justitie te Colombo: Rechtsbedeling in Ceylon in de 18de eeuw," *Libellus ad Thomasium: Essays in Roman Law, Roman-Dutch Law and Legal History in Honour of Philip J. Thomas (Fundamina)* 16, no. 1 (2010), 390–412.

Sivasundaram, Sujit, "Buddhist Kingship, British Archaeology and Historical Narratives in Sri Lanka c.1750–1850," *Past & Present* 197, no. 1 (2007), 111–42.

———, *Islanded: Britain, Sri Lanka, and the Bounds of an Indian Ocean Colony* (Chicago: University of Chicago Press, 2013).

Smail, Daniel Lord, *The Consumption of Justice: Emotions, Publicity, and Legal Culture in Marseille, 1264–1423* (Ithaca, NY: Cornell University Press, 2003).

Stern, Philip J., "'Bundles of Hyphens': Corporations as Legal Communities in the Early Modern British Empire," in Lauren Benton and Richard J. Ross (eds), *Legal Pluralism and Empires, 1500–1850*, Kindle edition (New York: NYU Press, 2013).

Strathern, Alan, *Kingship and Conversion in Sixteenth-Century Sri Lanka: Portuguese Imperialism in a Buddhist Land* (New Delhi & Colombo: Cambridge University Press & Vijitha Yapa, 2010).

———, "Sri Lanka in the Long Early Modern Period: Its Place in a Comparative Theory of Second Millennium Eurasian History," *Modern Asian Studies* 43, no. 4 (2009), 815–69.

Subrahmanyam, Sanjay, "Peasants before the Law: Recent Historiography on Colonial India," *Etudes Rurales*, no. 149–50 (1999), 199–209.

Tamanaha, Brian Z., "The Folly of the Social Scientific Concept of Legal Pluralism." *Journal of Law and Society* 20, no. 2 (1993), 192–217.

———, "Understanding Legal Pluralism: Past to Present, Local to Global," *Sydney Law Review*. 30 (2008), 375–411.

———, *Beyond the Formalist-Realist Divide: The Role of Politics in Judging* (Princeton: Princeton University Press, 2010).

Tambiah, S.J., *Polyandry in Ceylon, with Special Reference to the Laggala Region* (Colombo: Social Scientists' Association, 2011).

Taylor, Jean Gelman, *The Social World of Batavia: European and Eurasian in Dutch Asia* (Wisconsin & London: University of Wisconsin Press, 1983).

Twining, William, "Normative and Legal Pluralism: A Global Perspective," *Duke Journal of Comparative & International Law* 20 (2009), 473–517.

Villiers, Melius de., "Succession *Unde Vir Et Uxor*," *South African Law Journal* 33 (1916), 158–61.

Vismann, Cornelia, *Files: Law and Media Technology* (Stanford, CA: Stanford University Press, 2008).

Vos, F.H. de, "The Dutch Governors of Ceylon," *Journal of the Dutch Burger Union of Ceylon* 2, no. 3 (1909), 141–42.

Vroom, Wilhelmus Hermanus, "Jan Brandes, de Landraad Te Colombo in 1785," *Bulletin van Het Rijksmuseum* 37 (1989): 253–55

Wagenaar, Lodewijk, *Galle, VOC-vestiging in Ceylon: Beschrijving van een koloniale samenleving aan de vooravond van de Singalese opstand tegen het Nederlandse gezag, 1760* (Amsterdam: De Bataafsche Leeuw, 1994).

———, "The Cultural Dimension of the Dutch East India Company," in Thomas Da Costa Kaufmann and Michael North (eds), *Mediating Netherlandish Art and Material Culture in Asia* (Amsterdam: Amsterdam University Press, 2014).

Wamelen, Carla van, *Family life onder de VOC: Een handelscompagnie in huwelijks- en gezinszaken* (Hilversum: Uitgeverij Verloren, 2014).

Washbrook, David, "South India 1770–1840: The Colonial Transition," *Modern Asian Studies* 38, no. 03 (2004), 479–516.

———, "Sovereignty, Property, Land and Labour in Colonial South India," in Huri Islamoglu (ed), *Constituting Modernity: Private Property in the East and West* (London: I.B. Tauris, 2004).

Weerasooria, W.S., *Buddhist Ecclesiastical Law: A Treatise on Sri Lankan Statute Law and Judicial Decisions on Buddhist Temples and Temporalities* (Colombo: Postgraduate Institute of Management, 2011).

Wessels, J.W., *History of the Roman-Dutch Law* (Grahamstown, Cape Colony: African Book Co., 1908).

Wettasinghe, Saroja, "Digitisation of Land Records for Access and Preservation," in *Public Requirements and National Archives: Archives Week Souvenir* (Colombo: Sri Lanka National Archives, 2004).

Winchester, Ian, "What Every Historian Needs to Know About Record Linkage for the Microcomputer Era," *Historical Methods* 25, no. 4 (1992), 149–65.

Witte, John Jr., *The Sins of the Fathers: The Law and Theology of Illegitimacy Reconsidered* (Cambridge: Cambridge University Press, 2009).

Woolf, Leonard, *The Village in the Jungle* (Oxford, Chennai: Oxford University Press, 1913; repr. 1981).

Worden, Nigel (ed), *Cape Town: Between East and West, Social Identities in a Dutch Colonial Town* (Auckland Park & Hilversum: Jacana Media, 2012).

Yalman, Nur, *Under the Bo Tree: Studies in Caste, Kinship, and Marriage in the Interior of Ceylon* (Berkeley & Los Angeles: University of California Press, 1967).

Zwart, Pim de, "Population, Labour and Living Standards in Early Modern Ceylon: An Empirical Contribution to the Divergence Debate," *Indian Economic & Social History Review* 49, no. 3 (2012), 365–98.

Index

FSC
www.fsc.org
MIX
Papier | Fördert gute Waldnutzung
FSC® C083411

Kolibri 360 GmbH
Ferdinand-Jühlke-Straße 7
99095 Erfurt, Deutschland
produktsicherheit@kolibri360.de